Union Education in Britain
A TUC Activity

John Holford

Department of Adult Education
University of Nottingham
1994

ISBN (PB) 1 85041 073 9
      (HB) 1 85041 074 7

© John Holford, 1993

'education has become a TUC activity ... and you must understand that when we move into this field we must move in with TUC traditions and TUC characteristics'

George Woodcock, Speech to TUC
Blackpool 1964

'People learn by doing. In trade union education, this principle is applied through the idea of activities.'

Methods in Trade Union Education,
TUC 1983

'Purposeful trade union activity in the real world, in the union, at the workplace and in the community is the intended outcome of a successful course. ... Trade union education exists to help trade unionists become more effective.'

Aims and Methods in Trade Union Education,
TUC 1990.

For Hilary, who deserves them all

Contents

	page
List of Tables	*vii*
List of Figures	*viii*
Abbreviations	*ix*
Preface	*xi*

1 **The Trades Union Congress and the Politics of Workers' Education**   1

    Echoes of a Great Dispute
    Union Education and the State
    Education and Workers' Movements

2 **Trade Unions and Working Class Education before 1945**   15

    Labour, Capital and the State
    Ruskin College and Education for Trades Unionists
    The WEA and Education for Trades Unionists
    The Labour College Movement
    The TUC and Trade Union Education

3 **Educational Methods and Strategies between the Wars**   34

    Working Class Students and the Learning Environment
    Development Strategies and the Curriculum:
        the Labour Colleges
    Development Strategies and the Curriculum:
        the WEA and the WETUC
    Workers' Education and the Labour Movement
        between the Wars

4 **The Development of the TUC Education Scheme 1945-1968**   57

    Competition in Trade Union Education 1945-1964
    The Formation of the TUC Scheme, 1964
    Consolidation and Control 1964-1968
    Shop Stewards and the Political Economy of Full Employment
    The Origins of Public Funding

5 **Great Leap Forward: the TUC Scheme 1968-1979**   86

    A Climate for Growth
    Formulating Policy and Holding the Line, 1968-1969
    Defence and Development: Policy 1969-1974
    Turning Point: Policy and the State 1974-1975
    The Meaning of 1975

6 **Reaction and Retrenchment 1979-1987**   118
    Ideology, Depression, and Trade Unionism
    Government Industrial Relations Strategy
        and Trade Union Education
    The Ten-Day Programme 1979-1988
    The Institutional Framework
    Areas of Advance

7 **Post-war Methods and Philosophies: Tensions and Trends**   143
    Trade Union Education and the New Social Order
    Active Methods and Programmed Learning
    Liberal Education and the Politics of Content
    Union Education and Industrial Relations Research
    Educating for Change: TUC Course Content 1980-1987
    Schools, Youth and Members

8 **Late Thatcherism and After: the Educational Challenge**   188
    Change at the Top
    The 1987 Reviews
    Educational Strategies: Regional Courses
        for Workplace Representatives
    Educational Methods and the Quality Initiative
    Educational Services and the Future of the TUC

9 **State Challenge, Union Response**   215
    Defending in Adversity
    Organisation and Resources
    The Clouds Darken

10 **The TUC and Trade Union Education: Retrospect and Prospect**   239
    The Politics of Public Funding
    Curriculum: Changing Concepts of Relevance
    The TUC and Trade Union Education
    A Road Ahead

Appendices   258
    A.   Course Materials Issued by the TUC Education Service 1977-1992
    B.   Statistics of TUC Courses
    C.   Public Funds for Trade Union Education
    D.   TUC Tutor Briefings 1977-1992
    E.   TUC Campaign Workshops

Bibliography   282

Index   305

List of Tables

page

3.1	Courses Provided by the Edinburgh Labour College 1925, 1926 and 1938	45
4.1	NCLC and WETUC Course Provision 1962	70
4.2	TUC Training College: Course Provision 1963/64	71
4.3	TUC Training College: Course Provision 1968/69	71
4.4	TUC Regional and Postal Course Provision 1968/69	71

List of Figures

	page
2.1. Shoddy Goods	27
3.1. The Evolution of the Working-Class Movement	42
4.1. Education for Efficiency	67
5.1. Collective Bargaining	88
5.2. Rights to Time off Work for Union Training	101
5.3. Building on Legal Rights to Paid Release	109
6.1. Union Power and the Right to Manage	121
6.2. Conservative Strategy	126
6.3. The TUC Programme	130
6.4. Images of Women	139
7.1. Model Timetable	152
7.2. PIP Checklist	157
7.3. Activity	168
7.4. Discovery Exercise	169
7.5. Case Study	173
7.6. Guide to TUC Education	178-9
8.1. Facing up to the 1990s	193
8.2. A Trade Union Class	204
9.1. Offending Passages	220

Abbreviations

ACAS	Advisory, Conciliation and Arbitration Service
AEL	Assisted Educational Leave
AEU	Amalgamated Engineering Union
AIDS	Acquired Immune Deficiency Syndrome
ATAE	Association of Tutors in Adult Education
AUEW	Amalgamated Union of Engineering Workers
ASTMS	Association of Scientific, Technical and Managerial Staffs
BBC	British Broadcasting Corporation
BDC	Biennial Delegate Conference
BEC	British Employers' Confederation
CAPITB	Chemical and Allied Products ITB
CIR	Commission on Industrial Relations
CBI	Confederation of British Industries
CLC	Central Labour College
COHSE	Confederation of Health Service Employees
DE	Department of Employment
DEP	Department of Employment and Productivity
DES	Department of Education and Science
DFE	Department for Education
EC	Executive Committee
EETPU	Electrical, Electronic, Telecommunications and Plumbing Union
ESRC	Economic and Social Research Council
ETU	Electrical Trades Union
FDTITB	Food, Drink and Tobacco ITB
F&GPC	Finance and General Purposes Committee [of TUC]
FBI	Federation of British Industries
FEFC	Further Education Council
GC	General Council [of TUC]
GCHQ	Government Communications Headquarters
GLC	Greater London Council
GMB	General, Municipal and Boilermakers' Union
GMWU	General and Municipal Workers' Union
HMI	Her Majesty's Inspector(ate) [of Education]
HSC	Health and Safety Executive
ILO	International Labour Organisation
ILP	Independent Labour Party
IRSF	Inland Revenue Staffs Federation
ISTC	Iron and Steel Trades Confederation
ITB	Industrial Training Board
LCC	London County Council
LEA	Local Education Authority
LGIU	Local Government Information Unit
LSE	London School of Economics and Political Science

MSF	Manufacturing, Science, Finance
NALGO	National and Local Government Officers' Association
NATFHE	National Association of Teachers in Further and Higher Education
NATSOPA	National Society of Operative Printers and Assistants
NCLC	National Council of Labour Colleges
NEC	National Executive Committee; [TUC] National Education Centre
NEDC	National Economic Development Council
NUPE	National Union of Public Employees
NGA	National Graphical Association
NUR	National Union of Railwaymen
NUS	National Union of Seamen
NCVQ	National Council for Vocational Qualifications
NHS	National Health Service
NVQ	National Vocational Qualification
OECD	Organisation for Economic Co-operation and Development
OEEC	Organisation for European Economic Co-operation
PEL	Paid Educational Leave
POEU	Post Office Engineering Union
PPPITB	Paper and Paper Products ITB
PSI	Policy Studies Institute
REAC	Regional Education Advisory Committee (of TUC)
REO	Regional Education Officer
SCOTVEC	Scottish Vocational Education Council
SCPS	Society of Civil and Public Servants
SED	Scottish Education Department
SERTUC	South East Regional Council of the TUC
SIT	Society of Industrial Tutors
SSRC	Social Science Research Council
TASS	Technical, Administrative and Supervisory Section [of AUEW]
TGWU	Transport and General Workers' Union
TUC	Trades' Union Congress
TUDF	Trade Union Development Fund
TUEC	Trade Union Education Committee [of TUC]
USDAW	Union of Shop, Distributive and Allied Workers
WEA	Workers' Educational Association
WETUC	Workers' Educational Trade Union Committee

General Note: Organisations (unions etc.) are spelled with capital letters, to distinguish them from the categories of people who compose them. Thus 'Engineers' for Amalgamated Society of Engineers, Amalgamated Engineering Union, etc.; 'engineers' for the occupation. Unless otherwise indicated, references to 'Education Committee' and 'Education Department' are to the respective bodies of the TUC

Preface

This book is about trade union education in Great Britain. Its main focus, as the title implies, is on the role played by the Trades Union Congress. The TUC is largely responsible for the existence of trade union education as a distinct, and in many ways now dominant, form of workers' education. It masterminded, in the 1960s and 1970s, a massive expansion of educational opportunities for trade unionists. It formulated a clear strategy, which was implemented with little compromise. It shaped what was taught, and how. This study stems from my belief that the TUC's educational contribution — and the role this plays in labour relations and trade unionism — is neither sufficiently recognised nor properly understood.

I hold that the TUC's role in union education has been broadly positive. I know that, for some, this view will be controversial. Trade union education has been too little studied, but some believe strongly that the TUC has played a damaging part. While I sympathise with the desire for a wider workers' education, and see many grounds for wishing trade unions and the TUC were different, I disagree with this evaluation. I trust that my argument is convincing. In any case, I hope that this book will serve as a foundation for, and stimulus to, further discussion, analysis and research.

The TUC has not constructed British union education alone. I have not, however, tried to write a general history of the field. Unions, universities, and other organisations enter the story, but I have focussed on the TUC. This is partly because of its central role. But I also feel that the educational traditions of several individual unions deserve study in their own right. This book is long enough; I hope others will carry this task forward.

Education has a vital part to play in the regeneration of the trade union movement. As I write, however, the future of British union education hangs in the balance. It is clear that there will, at the least, be far-reaching change over the next few years. A shift to a competency-based system is mooted: this will mean major challenges to what people study, and how. The movement must make greater financial demands of its members if independent union education is to be preserved on any scale. I believe positive decisions can be made. I hope this book will mean they can now be made in the light of a fuller and more balanced assessment of how and why union education developed its present approaches, traditions and organisation.

In preparing this study, I have incurred many debts. I should like to thank Lord Carlisle of Bucklow, Mr Donald Gold, Lord Joseph, Lord Mulley, Lord Murray of Epping Forest, Sir Reg Prentice, and Lord Prior for their courteous and helpful replies to correspondence. Lord Tebbit was also kind enough to reply. I had two useful telephone discussions with Mr Digby Anderson. Two anonymous readers made valuable comments on an early draft of the text. I am grateful to the TUC for permission to quote from and reproduce various documents. At Congress House, Alan Grant and Stan Greaves in particular have been most generous with their time. Rosemary Stone guided me into some of the darker recesses of Congress records. I should also like to express my thanks to the staff of the TUC Library, who have helped on more than one occasion. In Hong Kong, Polly Kwok's assistance in preparing the statistical appendices has been invaluable.

For nearly a decade, I taught in British trade union education, working closely with the TUC. This was in various degrees challenging, exhilarating, and frustrating. I am deeply grateful to the trade union members, representatives and organisers who were my students and colleagues. I should also like to thank the South Eastern District of the Workers' Educational Association, which employed me and (despite the ravages of Thatcherism) maintained its commitment to independent trade union education through the 1980s. Many of my views were formed during those years: many colleagues and friends contributed, and I should like to thank in particular Ken Davenport, Harold Goodwin, David Gover, Stephen Grinter, Peter Jarvis, and Stirling Smith (who later read several chapters in Hong Kong). I worked so closely with, and learnt so much from, John Thirkell that I suspect some of my views may be his in origin: if so, they can only be more valid. Despite these debts, any failings in the book and the arguments it contains are mine alone.

Finally, I should also like to thank my father, who read the manuscript and made a number of very helpful comments; my daughters Naomi and Zillah; and Hilary, without whom neither daughters nor books would have come to fruition.

Hong Kong   JAKH
April 1993

Chapter 1

The TUC and the Politics of Workers' Education

In the public eye, the Trades Union Congress is linked with British politics and industrial relations. It is more. It is an important educational body: a major provider of adult education. Every year, some 30,000 students attend its courses. The TUC has shaped, and now dominates, British trade union education. Conversely, education is very much the largest single area of TUC activity, accounting for between one-quarter and one-third of what the TUC spends,[1] and for rather more of what it does.[2] Developing union education is arguably the TUC's greatest achievement of recent years. Yet the TUC is still seen mainly as a political and industrial relations organisation. Little has been written about its educational role.[3] The result is a very partial view of a major institution. In the 1960s and 1970s, when its political and industrial authority was greater, this was perhaps understandable. In the 1990s, silence about the largest area of its work can hardly be justified.

For the TUC's future is now questioned. 'In the industrial, just as much as in the political world,' thundered *The Times* in a leading article (5 September 1992), 'the TUC has ceased to answer any realistic need. Having no useful function to perform, it is time the old carthorse was put out to grass.' As affiliated unions lose members, Congress faces ever-more straitened finances. Especially after the 1992 general election, it has little foreseeable prospect of a renewed role in national political affairs. While no trade unionist would look to *The Times* for sympathetic comment on union affairs, the TUC *is* searching for a renewed mission. Education is clearly a vital ingredient in any TUC development — or survival — strategy.

TUC education also commands attention in its own right, as a major educational experiment. It involves several singular, even unique, features. The overwhelming bulk of TUC courses are designed for the voluntary, unpaid, workplace officials of its affiliated unions — men and women elected by their colleagues to be shop stewards and safety representatives.[4] They are taught not by TUC staff, but by tutors in colleges and other public educational institutions. The curriculum is, however, more or less uniform throughout the country. Students attend the courses during their working time, normally on day release from their employers: they enjoy legally-enforceable rights to paid time off work for education — rights unique in British law. Students pay no course fees: these fees have been met (since the mid-1970s) largely by a government grant. Since 1975, well over half a million adult students have attended TUC day-release classes.

These features are the product of a strategy evolved, and pursued with quiet resolution, since the 1960s (although its roots stretch back much further). Certain principles have been held to with little deviation. Union education should serve union aims. The most important stratum of students is the unions' workplace representatives. Trade unions and their members are entitled to the full benefits of publicly-funded education, and should have access to the skills of teachers employed by public-sector institutions. Nevertheless, the aims and content of courses should be controlled by unions, rather than by the state.

This book explores the development of this approach to trade union education, how the strategy was evolved, and how it has been carried through. We also examine the difficulties which the TUC faced: for the approach has been challenged on a number of occasions, by tutors, by educational organisations, by employers, and in particular by the state. The relationship between union education and the state is a recurring theme: partly because the TUC's decision to seek specific state funding broke with a central tradition of workers' education; partly because of the intricate relations between unions and the state in post-war Britain. The story takes us back to the early years of the century, to the origins of union involvement in workers' education. Most of the book is, however, devoted to the years since the second world war, and particularly to the last three decades.

The Trades Union Congress has stood at the centre of the twentieth-century British labour movement. An arcane institution, born of the era of Victorian ironmasters and labour aristocrats, initially no more than an annual forum for bowler-hatted trade unionists to debate their differences, the TUC by the 1960s was a force in the land. In the corridors of its headquarters — Congress House in the heart of London — the union 'barons' and their 'civil servants' debated and formulated policy not only for the trade unions, nor just for industrial relations, but for the economic and social welfare of the nation. They believed, and firmly, that national prosperity depended upon trade unions — through their leaders: men, and perhaps a few women, such as themselves —being close to the centre of national decision-making. A democratic and fair society could mean nothing less than trade unions being able to give an informed and knowledgeable voice to the working men and women who were their members.

In support of these views, the TUC in the 1960s had developed a number of functions. Most were concerned with ensuring the unity of the trade union movement, and providing it with an effective voice. Each year, Congress — the definite article was rarely used — met, normally in a famous seaside resort, to debate political and industrial issues. As the political voice of the trade union movement, consulted by governments of both parties, the TUC had departments devoted to research and development on economic, industrial relations, social welfare and educational policy. It regulated and played umpire in disputes between its member unions. Its international department oversaw the foreign policy of British trade unionism.

Closeted away beneath these great TUC 'departments of state'[5] there was, in the early 1960s, a small section devoted to educating trade unionists. This 'Training College' was part of the Education Department (which spent much of its time developing the TUC's policy on public education generally). Formed shortly after the war, and reorganised in 1956,[6] the College still employed just one full-time member of staff — a Director of Studies. Most of its teaching was done by 'members of the TUC staff who leave their other work to lecture' (Clegg and Adams 1959: 58). Apart from one or two summer schools — organised annually since the early 1930s — the TUC's entire educational provision was arranged in this way. Among 8.3 million union members, the programme (37 courses and 685 students in 1960/61: TUC 1961: 168) could have but a modest impact.[7]

This changed when, in 1963, the TUC took over the work of the two organisations which had dominated education for trade unionists over the previous fifty years: the National Council of Labour Colleges and the Workers' Educational Trade Union Committee. With this transfer came a commitment to develop a programme of education for the trade union movement throughout the country and (from the NCLC) a band of regional organisers. The TUC's Education Department took to its new role with a will. It developed, and implemented, its new strategy — brushing aside protests that the traditions of the NCLC were being discarded. Structures and policies were developed in the 1960s, and were defended under Edward Heath's Conservative government. During the years of the Labour government's 'Social Contract', TUC education cemented its central role. By the mid-1970s its primacy in the field was undisputed. The structures built in the 1970s were defended in a hostile world during the 1980s, but the defence became increasingly difficult. By the early 1990s the entire edifice so painstakingly constructed over a quarter of a century and more was at risk. This, in outline, is the process we shall examine. Against this background, we shall consider what education for trade unionists consisted of through the century: what was taught and learnt, and how; why these subjects and approaches became dominant, and what they implied. But union education in the 1960s, and since, has also borne the marks of history.

Echoes of a Great Dispute

In her classic study of *Workers' Education in England and the United States*, Margaret Hodgen (1925: 4) offered a definition of workers' education, distinguishing it from other forms of adult education or vocational training. 'As a man and a bread-winner,' she wrote, 'the worker seeks knowledge in order to enrich his leisure or improve his earning power.' This might be general cultural study, or training in vocational skills. Through such study, the worker-student 'may even plan to emerge from the constraints of working-class existence.' But these approaches were 'fundamentally different' from workers' education.

> *As a unit in a group effort for more complete participation in the common life, the working-man ... has been frankly sectarian. He has sought information as a member of a social class, a voter or a trade union official. ... [W]orking-men enrolled as students in the [workers' education] movement are committed to some programme of class action, for which special knowledge and a peculiar technique are necessary. In other words, Workers' Education ... is a discipline for a specific purpose. It concerns itself in teaching the social sciences to men and women who seek to use that knowledge for class, and possibly social, advancement. (Hodgen 1925: 4-5)*

Until the present century, the TUC played virtually no part in this movement. Its educational concerns were devoted to arguing the case for improved educational facilities for children, and for improved vocational training. As the new century began, it found itself — if not unwillingly, then certainly without enthusiasm — cast in a supporting role in the formation of Ruskin College. But this experience did nothing to inspire Congress. Rather, in the years before the Great War, and indeed through the inter-war period also, workers' education in Britain was left largely to two movements: the Workers' Educational Association, and its Marxist rival, the National Council of Labour Colleges.

Many have written about early twentieth-century workers' education. Much of their writing has, however, been highly institutional, devoted to recounting — in an heroic mould — the formation and struggles of the WEA, Ruskin College, and the various labour colleges. While the story is presented in broad outline in Chapters 2 and 3, we concentrate on making sense of the developments of the period, especially the emergence of approaches to the education of trade unionists, and to the evolution of a TUC role.

The disputes of the first quarter of the century left a profound mark on British workers' education. The WEA, Ruskin, the National Council of Labour Colleges were all well-entrenched, with their own traditions, by the

1930s. They had been shaped by the character of their formative years: they were the creations of labour strength, optimism and vitality in a politically and industrially turbulent period. Two traditions evolved. On the one hand stood the labour colleges, committed to a Marxist analysis of society, to a view that workers' education must be 'independent' of the capitalist state and linked to revolutionary political action. On the other, the WEA and Ruskin College, committed to a liberal notion of education, broadly reformist in politics, saw no difficulty of principle about accepting financial support from an increasingly democratic state — indeed, argued that the state had a positive duty to finance education for the working class.[8] For the labour colleges, the WEA's belief in objectivity and impartiality made it (at best) a dupe of the capitalists: as John Maclean (1978: 125) wrote during the industrial unrest of 1917, 'big attempts will be forthcoming to use the WEA to muddle the minds of the workers'. For the WEA, the labour collegers — blinded by dogma — could neither see the complexity of truth nor distinguish between education and propaganda.

The echoes of this bitter dispute pursued workers' education down the century. Many of the issues were real and vital. Should labour accept finance for education from the capitalist state? Was truth to be found through honest open inquiry, or was it determined by the class position of the inquirer? Was education to be valued of itself, or only so far as it served the aims of the workers' movement? But for workers' education, and for the labour movement, the bitterness with which the arguments were prosecuted was extremely damaging. Still more damaging, the dispute became institutionalised in the relations between the NCLC and the WEA. It in no way diminished (indeed, in some respects it became more virulent) when the political divisions on which it had been based eroded. (As Brian Simon (1990b: 63-4) notes, by the 1940s and 1950s Marxism was more often discussed in the WEA than in the NCLC — which had become 'the voice of the more extreme right-wing in the labour movement'.) For decades, it prevented the movement from establishing a coherent strategy for workers' education; when one did develop in the 1960s, it did so forty years late.

But for historians too the bitter dispute has been a fixating point of reference. When discussing it, few — even recently — have been able to separate their analysis from their loyalties, and this has deflected attention from three important considerations. First, the discussion of highly-charged political issues has obscured the deeper tension in workers' education between the need to serve the labour movement, and the commitment to educational purpose itself. When the two coincided, no difficulty arose. In the labour colleges and the WEA between about 1900 and 1925, for instance, a curriculum oriented to strengthening the political development of local leaders — studying economics, politics, history —

was seen as highly relevant to the needs of the movement. It was also in step with the educational outlooks of the of two organisations. But what education would best serve the labour movement was ultimately a matter for the decision-making processes of the movement itself. From the mid-1920s, the various organisations which made up the movement became more precise and narrow about their objectives and functions. Trade unions began to avoid political engagement save through Labour Party channels, and to define their success in terms of routinised industrial activities. In the Labour Party, now concentrating on electoral politics, routine organisational development was also at a premium. Both unions and Labour Party perceived an increasing need for education which would contribute quite directly to improving their efficiency in these regular activities. (This was most clearly articulated by the trade unions, as we shall see.) This tension between educational purpose and serving the movement has often been conflated with the question of whether the content of education was 'political' or 'industrial', and with arguments about whether courses were 'education' or 'training'. These tensions often overlaid, and became confused with, the fundamental tension — educational purpose or serving the movement — which sprang from the aims and structural position of workers' education itself.

Second, the labour colleges were justified in arguing that the WEA, in taking money from the state, had compromised its independence, as Roger Fieldhouse (1985a and 1990) has documented. However, in making these accusations, the labour colleges oversimplified in two vital respects. On the one hand, with a highly reductionist concept of state power, they were unable to conceive that engagement with the state might involve various levels of autonomy, and that some of these might provide acceptable areas of compromise — space in which worthwhile workers' education might occur. This was, of course, a dangerous area: engagement can be a slippery slope. As the century advanced, educators in the WEA and elsewhere — including the TUC — explored these areas of relative autonomy. There were major problems (many of which we shall discuss), but the experience was not wholly negative. The labour college critique of the WEA also ignored its own Achilles' heel: if the WEA was subject to pressure from the state, so the labour colleges had to listen to their own paymasters. Increasingly their paymasters were the trade unions, and from the 1920s this drew the colleges inexorably away from their revolutionary roots.

The third reality of twentieth century workers' education, obscured by the smoke of the WEA-NCLC fracas, was apparent to an acute observer in the mid-twenties. 'Whatever may be said ... in favour of one side of the controversy or the other', wrote Hodgen (1925: 151), 'is not of great importance. The future of Workers' Education belongs to the unions, and the unions are beginning to realize it.' From the 1920s, when the revolutionary fervour of the Great War and its immediate aftermath began to wane, only the trade union movement provided a basis for workers' education on a large scale. The issue, in short, was not whether workers' education would be oriented to the political or the industrial: that was historically settled (even if it was not universally apparent). Rather, the question had become: how would the centrality of trade unionism be institutionalised? What body could co-ordinate and sustain a programme of workers' education? The WEA and the NCLC tried: but they lacked both the resources and the legitimacy to establish any national hegemony. As we shall see, the TUC tried — but proved unable — to fulfil this role in the 1920s. It then largely abandoned the field for forty years. But Hodgen's observation was acute: in the absence of the TUC, no other body was able to take such a role.

This, at least in large part, reflected the fact that the British labour movement never evolved legitimate central decision-making structures, outside the TUC and the Labour Party. Those two bodies must of course share much of the responsibility for this: ever jealous of their positions, they discouraged the growth of potential rivals. But the allocation of responsibility should not obscure the fact: unless through the TUC or the Labour Party, no widely-accepted structure of decision-making on workers' education could emerge. The tragedy was that — no doubt partly as a result of the confusion generated by the great dispute itself — both the TUC and the Labour Party lacked the vision, the will, or the ability to initiate any national system of workers' education until the 1960s.

When the TUC did move back into providing education for trade unionists, it felt no more than a residual responsibility to workers' education in a broad sense; by the 1970s, a more or less distinct sub-field of 'trade union education' had evolved. The seeds of the trade union education approach are to be found in the thirties and even earlier, but its roots were not established until after the Second World War. At that time, the TUC — together with a number of unions — began to develop courses and institutions designed to provide education (or training) which would meet their perceived organisational needs. In the early 1950s, a WEA working party produced the first major statement of policy and method in the field (WEA 1953). During the 1950s a number of university extra-mural departments began to explore broadly similar approaches. By the end of that decade, it was widely accepted that education for trade unionists would centre on (though not necessarily be limited to) their organisational and bargaining functions at the workplace.

The development of this kind of trade union education was a complex process, and is a major theme of this book. It took place against the background of a tension (present in Britain's labour movement from its inception) between 'political' and 'industrial' activity. During the period around the Great War, the distinction these forms of behaviour became blurred: strikes and other forms of 'industrial' action were commonly seen as part of a political strategy. By the late 1920s, however, an electoral definition of political activity was quite firmly established within the movement, and trade unions' activity was quite closely tied to the workplace. Industrial action for political ends was shunned. Legal limitations on the political activity of trade unions, and on the methods they could legitimately use to achieve their industrial aims, were strengthened by legislation after the General Strike. The trade union movement, certainly the TUC, broadly accepted these definitions of political and industrial activity — and, in so doing, accepted that legitimate trade union action must be limited to the industrial sphere. Many of those involved in trade union education would have rejected these assumptions; some even saw in their work a mission to radicalise the outlook of trade unionists. But the evolution of a specifically 'trade union education' also owes much to narrow assumptions about what sorts of action were legitimate for trade unions.

Union Education and the State

In the 1920s, state concern about workers' education was fuelled mainly by fear of its links with revolutionary politics. By the late 1920s, fear of revolution had dissipated. Certain forms of workers' education (broadly those offered by the WEA) had been deemed acceptable, and were modestly supported by public funds. For the following three decades, the state took a background role: intervening only occasionally to 'police' the terms of grant-aid. But in the 1960s the state's relationship with workers' education took on a quite new dimension. After taking over the NCLC and the WETUC, the TUC began to offer courses in collaboration with public sector or grant-aided educational bodies: technical colleges, university extra-mural departments, the WEA. British education was then heavily subsidised from the public purse. The fees charged by colleges were by no means (in today's jargon) 'economic'. It was a short step from taking advantage of subsidised fees to directly accepting public funds, although a few issues of fundamental principle (largely ideological relics from the labour colleges) held Congress back for several years.

The public funding of union education was also retarded, and clouded, by the tribulations of the TUC's more general relations with the state. After the Second World War, with the Labour government reshaping the nation's economic and social institutions, the TUC expected — and secured — a special influence. This did not end when Labour fell from office. TUC leaders were consulted about policy; their views were not ignored. But this new relationship involved tensions: in particular, union leaders were increasingly expected, in return for this influence, to deliver a measure of industrial peace, and to restrain wage increases. The result, for the trade union movement, was recurrent internal tension, for in a context of 'full employment' and inflation it was very difficult to control their members' pursuit of better pay. For governments, the TUC often seemed ineffectual: expecting a say, but unable to deliver in return.

These tensions came to a head in the late 1960s and early 1970s. In turn, both Labour and Conservative governments attempted to control workplace trade union activity — the root, according to contemporary wisdom, of 'wage-drift' and inflation — by law. Their attempts were not, in the event, successful, but they cast a cloud over the unions' attitude to the state. By no means did the TUC repudiate its earlier stance: but it did develop a very guarded attitude to how its relations with the state should develop. If the TUC were to accept public funding for trade union education — as it wished to do — there must be measures to ensure some autonomy. It found two main approaches to achieving this. Funding for trade union education was to be located in the education apparatuses of the state: the Department of Education and Science, with links to the educational Inspectorate. This, it was hoped, would distance it from the industrial relations priorities of governments of the day — which would be to the fore if funding were to fall to the Department of Employment. Second, the grants would be made to the TUC, and would be subject to its control: the TUC would therefore, subject to the general terms of grant-aid, be able to set its own priorities, and to develop mechanisms (such as setting curricula and designing materials) which would further these.

The relationship between the TUC and the state has rightly been a central feature of the (albeit small) literature on the politics and history of trade union education in Britain. Regrettably, only one view has been effectively developed.[9] The case is that by the 1960s and 1970s the TUC was deeply integrated into a state-led — 'corporatist' — project of reshaping workplace trade unionism, and saw its courses for shop stewards as an important mechanism in achieving this. This was not education: shop stewards were to be trained in the skilful execution of their procedural functions, but should not raise wider questions about their role. On this view, state funding was a natural progression. It did, however, have important implications, as it enabled the TUC to take a more central and directive role in the field, to control the curriculum, and to stifle dissent.

While inspiring some illuminating research, this approach seems to me to over-simplify, and occasionally even to distort, the complexities of the TUC's relations with the state. It has also served to direct attention away from the substantive achievements of the TUC scheme, and from other important factors in the development of trade union education. The TUC had — shifting — views of priorities for industrial relations: these often overlapped with state priorities, but were not identical. Similarly, both TUC and governments had views about the future of trade union education (or shop steward training) — although on neither side did the major policy-makers see it as a matter of central importance. But these views varied over time, and they were influenced by their institutional framework. For example, the attitude of the Department of Employment and Productivity (as it then was) was significantly different from that of the Department of Education and Science—a difference which the TUC attempted, with some skill and no little success, to exploit.

The decision to accept public funding (together with the related legislation on paid educational leave) was a critical turning point in the development of trade union education. It enabled the TUC, by the late 1970s, to establish unprecedented — and sophisticated — national programme structures for union education. Colleges, polytechnics, WEA districts, and university extra-mural departments were brought into a national scheme which delivered essentially similar courses for union workplace representatives in every region of the country. A central curriculum development unit was set up, and a variety of course materials produced. Firm views were taken on teaching methods, with a commitment to active learning and participative teaching methods, a strong emphasis on group work, case studies and role playing, and the conviction that students came to courses with a wealth of information and knowledge. Recruitment to courses mushroomed. Trade union education was expanding and innovating, and the TUC was the central focus of development and initiative in the field.

But very soon, with the new Conservative government after 1979 rapidly distancing itself from any post-war consensus, advance slowed. Growth was no longer the order of the day: indeed, union education had again to be defended against incursion. The story of the 1980s and early 1990s is of dogged defence of structures and programmes gradually displacing initiative and vision, as optimism waned and the prospects of rebuilding a positive relationship with the state became ever more dim. Defence on adverse terrain against overwhelming odds is rarely crowned with success, but the TUC's struggle was not without achievement. If public funding of trade unions for education ends (as the government has mooted) in 1996, it will have survived for twenty-one years. For all but three of these, the funds will have been dispensed by a—fiercely anti-union — Conservative government largely on the trade unions' own terms.

This achievement should be acknowledged. It was based on a key decision (which, for the TUC, was really no decision at all). Major public debate with the government on union education was to be avoided. Defence would be based on maintaining low-key and courteous relationships with government departments, local authorities, the education services, and so forth. Arguments and allies would be deployed, but through essentially bureaucratic channels. There was a deep sense that if it came to public confrontation with government, the unions and their members would emerge the poorer. There would, therefore, be no 'national campaign' to defend trade union education.

Education and Workers' Movements

Labour movements have long been at the centre of social and political progress. Workers and their organisations have toppled governments, overthrown tyrannies, defeated colonialism, threatened capitalism, destroyed and built societies, new and old. They have not, of course, always acted alone, nor always with success — but labour's place in history seems secure. Its future now seems less clear. To paraphrase Marx and Engels, as industry restructures, workers seem to decline in number; they work in smaller groups, their strength declines, and they feel less confidence in what strength they have. Labour's progress has slowed, or halted. Some even doubt whether labour movements will survive. Newer social movements — the green and women's movements, for example — can seem to provide more hope for human progress. Indeed, the very notion of 'progress', the idea that rational men and women, acting together, can build a better society, is now widely questioned.

Labour movements are, in origin, social movements. Many social movements are unable to manage a transition to organisation. Starting as diffuse collections of individuals and small groups acting together on a more or less spontaneous basis, they cannot successfully change into more structured social institutions. It is therefore difficult, if not impossible, for them to sustain a long-term role. Most labour movements have achieved this transition. Permanent organisation, however, produces problems as well as strengths: permanence raises problems which the transient never have to face. Routines, for instance, are essential: without them, every situation is entirely new and unpredictable. But if routines embody what has been learnt, they also rigidify and exclude new learning. Hierarchy means groups can avoid constant struggles over who makes decisions: it also implies inequality, and stipulates that only certain forms of communication are acceptable. Motivation, no problem for transient social movements (without it, they would not exist), is a fundamental issue for institutions which seek a long-term role.

Workers' education is one mechanism by which labour movements can attempt to overcome these problems of permanence.[10] Education in this sense contributes, as it were, to their cognitive processes. It helps them to understand external stimuli, to develop responses, to maintain coherence, to overcome (or at least bypass) some of the rigidities of organisation. British trade union education has played this role. It has enabled central leaderships to alert local union organisation about important issues, and to develop strategies to deal with them. It has helped to motivate the lay representative, whose role is often thankless. Local union organisations, facing new problems, have often sought support from union educators in developing their thinking. Education provides alternative lines of communication, complementing the formal, and often rigid, structures of union democracy, and the hard-pressed full-time official.

Union education cannot, of course, be immune from the problems of its parent organisation. British union structures are often rigid, bound by procedures, by highly formal — and ironically, often hierarchical — democratic and accountability structures. The TUC is no exception: TUC education has always been subject to the authority of the General Council. Despite a good deal of decentralisation (particularly through collaboration with educational bodies), central control has been strong. The causes of this (from memories of the NCLC to concern to protect public funding) are understandable. It has, however, been a point of recurring tension, and is in some respects a weakness. The local initiative of union educators is a vital resource, which the trade union movement should nurture and encourage.

The British trade union movement, indeed British labour as a whole, now faces the need to reorient itself for new conditions. What these will be, none can say with precision. Union education can be a vital catalyst as the movement tries to come to terms with new realities, and to shape it in the interests of its members. It can strengthen the movement's ability to respond flexibly as circumstances change. There are many questions to be discussed about how the movement should adapt, and about what the organisation and methods of union education should be. The first priority, however, is to ensure that union education has a viable future as an enterprise which responds to union needs. If this book helps the movement to understand the importance of education to its development (both past and future), and provides a basis for more informed debate about the movement's educational aims and methods, it will have served some purpose.

The chapters which follow are organised broadly chronologically, but there is also some separation of themes. In Chapters 2 and 3 we explore the main issues in education for trade unionists before the Second World War:

Chapter 2 concentrates on politics and policies, while in Chapter 3 we examine educational methods and organisation. Chapter 4 examines how, in the 1950s and 1960s, the TUC began to assert an independent role. In Chapter 5 we turn to the growth and experience of 'mature' trade union education in the 1970s, including the implications of the decision to make public funds available to the TUC education scheme. Chapter 6 discusses the experience of the TUC scheme under the first two Thatcher governments. Chapter 7 covers the evolution of educational methods and philosophies in the post-war period. Chapters 8 and 9 examine TUC education's experiences, innovations and tribulations under the third Thatcher (and first Major) administrations. In Chapter 10, we draw some conclusions and some lessons, and speculate about the future.

1   TUC accounts are by no means easy to interpret. These estimates are based on the accounts for the 1991/92 financial year, as presented to the 1992 Congress. The wide margin of uncertainty results chiefly from whether government grant passed directly to affiliated trade unions for course provision (£766,506, or roughly 7 per cent of total TUC income) should be included as a TUC educational activity.

2   Another one-sixth of TUC spending, for instance, consists simply of affiliation fees to international trade union organisations, and can therefore for practical purposes be deducted from the total which the TUC devotes to its domestic activities. (Much of international trade union organisations' work is also educational.)

3   E.g., Dorfman (1983), Martin (1980) and Panitch (1976) do not mention TUC education. A number of general studies of trade unionism have touched on the TUC's educational activities, of course, but typically have said very little about it. Bell (1953) gives education for trade unionists two pages; the TUC's work in this field just a few lines. Roberts (1956) devotes eleven of his 570 pages to union education, but mentions the TUC only in passing. Clegg (1972 and 1976) provide three (identical) sentences. Coates and Topham (1980) devote a 40-page chapter to the TUC, but only two paragraphs to its educational activities. The most recent major study of trade unions' role (Marsh 1992) says nothing about education. Griggs (1983) is an exception, but necessarily concentrates on TUC policies on public education: in the period he considers, the TUC was not itself a provider of education.

4   The term 'shop steward' is in common use for the lay workplace union representative, but the proper term varies. Other common terms include Father or Mother of the Chapel (particularly in printing trade unions), and union or branch representative. In some unions, other branch or chapel officials are also in effect shop stewards. The safety representative is also a lay elected union workplace official, concerned with representing members on health and safety at work issues. Sometimes the safety

5. representative and shop steward roles can be held by the same person.
5. The 'departments and sub-departments' in the mid-1950s were: Finance, Organisation, International, Education, Research and Economic, Production, Social Insurance and Industrial Welfare, Publicity and Editorial. None of these was in reality large. They were typically staffed by two or three specialists. 'The total staff employed, including clerical assistants, numbers less than eighty, and the staff officers less than thirty, which might be regarded as a low for the central body of an organisation with eight million members.' (Roberts 1956: 444)
6. The opening of the new TUC headquarters building at Congress House, in Great Russell Street, enabled the Education Department (and its 'Training College') to vacate its former premises in Maritime House, Clapham, the National Union of Seamen's headquarters. The main TUC headquarters until 1956 were in Transport House, Smith Square, the headquarters of the Transport and General Workers' Union.
7. Education made up roughly 6 per cent of TUC expenditure in 1950, and only 9.5 per cent in 1962. (Calculated from TUC 1950, 1962.)
8. This case was argued forcefully in the 1919 Final Report of the Adult Education Committee of the Ministry of Reconstruction (Cmd 321 1919: 117-91): '... the high social value of adult education entitles it to special consideration [for state financial assistance]. ... The State should not, in our opinion, refuse financial support to institutions, colleges and classes, merely on the ground that they have a particular "atmosphere" or appeal specially to students of this type or that. All that it ought to ask is that they be concerned with serious study. It is said in criticism of this view that the work of sectarian bodies ought not to be subsidised out of public funds. We do not agree; in our judgment, whether the State ought to help with such education depends on the quality of the work and not upon the institution which conducts it. ... In our view, the only sound principle is that the State should be willing to help all serious educational work, including the educational work of institutions and organisations which are recruited predominantly from students with, say, a particular religious or political philosophy.'
9. Although this view is shared by several other authors, its most prolific and forceful advocate is John McIlroy. His argument is discussed at greater length later in this book.
10. This is not the only function which workers' education can perform, e.g., internationally, much workers' education is concerned with creating workers' organisations, rather than altering them.

Chapter 2

Trade Unions and Working Class Education before 1945

While our concern is with the twentieth century, the developments we discuss were by no means the first attempts to organise education for workers, or even for trade unionists, in Britain. With the industrial revolution, the urban working class grew. So too — for a variety of reasons — did middle class concern that the workers should be better educated. Typically priority was given to religious, scientific and technical education. The adult school movement spread rapidly during the early nineteenth century, gradually expanding from its initial concern with study of the scriptures to a broader liberal adult education (see, e.g., Pole 1816; Rowntree and Binns 1903: esp. 10-24). The mechanics' institutes, growing over much the same period, stressed scientific and technical rather than religious knowledge. As the latter failed to attract significant numbers of working people to genuine educational courses, the working men's colleges developed from the 1840s onward, aiming to provide social, political and economic, as well as practical, instruction. Also during the mid-Victorian years, the Co-operative movement began to support a number of educational classes for its members. From the 1870s, the university extension movement sought to promote extra-mural lectures for 'the whole nation'.

Meanwhile, the new working class developed its own political agenda. Improved education was a part of this: 'the want of knowledge and information in the general mass of the people has exposed them to numberless impositions and abuses,' declared the Sheffield Society for Constitutional Information in 1792. Its 'exertions' were therefore directed toward 'the acquirement of useful knowledge' — and they had derived 'more true knowledge' from Paine's *Rights of Man* than from any other source. (Quoted Harrison 1961: 102.) At this time the unions themselves undertook little educational activity — their members did not regard them as the appropriate vehicles. But there was a growing desire among union members for 'that knowledge which it has ever been the study of our tyrants to withhold from us, namely, a knowledge of our rights as men' (*Northern Star* 5 February 1842, quoted Harrison 1961: 102). From the 1840s a number of trade unions began to run schools or classes for their members, although these concentrated on technical, trade-related, subjects. (Fieldhouse 1977: 1-2.) In the 1870s and 1880s, a few unions were collaborating with the university extension movement in providing courses for their members, although many found that their rules did not specify education as a purpose for which funds could be spent (Harrison 1961: 241; Hodgen 1925: 119-21; Kadish 1987). In 1879, the TUC's Parliamentary Committee recommended a list of books which would help trade societies, trades councils and workmen's clubs 'to more fully understand and appreciate the work in which we are engaged' (quoted Griggs 1983: 177).

When, three decades after Chartism, a labour political movement independent of Liberalism re-emerged during the 1880s, however, education of these kinds formed no substantial part of its activities. Little initial attempt was made to develop classes or study groups. The Social Democratic Federation and the Socialist League, both essentially Marxist, and the broader and larger Independent Labour Party, set out to win the working classes to socialism. Their varying political outlooks mask strong similarities in approach. The common issue was making contact with the people: educating them, to be sure, but through propaganda, conducted largely by speakers at indoor and outdoor public meetings. A common problem was the gap between rhetorical flourish — hundreds, even thousands, would attend meetings, often a popular form of entertainment — and the commitment which political organisations require from a significant proportion of their supporters (Howell 1983: 337-41; Thompson 1977: 412-22). But in practice the education of the early labour leaders was accidental. In a world of long and enthusiastic meetings, there was room for new men and women to gain public-speaking experience. Committees, so often in need of any willing hands, 'trained' new members on-the-job. For the enthusiastic, temperance cafes and clubs provided a forum for informal discussions and debate. The early labour leaders were above all self-educated: learning through their enthusiasm and activity, and supplementing this by reading. (Levy 1987b: esp. 165-73.)

Labour, Capital and the State

Education which resembles 'trade union education' as we know it today, emerged during the first half of the current century. At the turn of the century British capital still exercised a dominant world role, though competition from rising economic powers — Germany, the United States of America, even France and Japan — placed its hegemony in some long-term doubt. Generalising, the economic story of the first half of the twentieth century is of finance capital which found profit more easy to come by in colonial and imperial ventures, and which indulged in relatively limited domestic investment. This was masked, of course, by the two world wars. The Great War, in particular — a conflict centred in France, and consisting largely of the mass slaughter of infantry by artillery — might have been custom-designed to fit the productive capacity of Britain's traditional industries. As international competition intensified, British industry responded defensively: by protection; by making agreements with foreign competitors, rather than by radical capital restructuring or investment; by intensifying the demands it made of its labour force; and by closure, short-time working, dismissals, unemployment.

Against this background the labour and trade union movement established itself at the centre of domestic politics. The Labour Party, founded only in 1900, and breaking with some difficulty from Liberalism, was participating in government by 1916, if on restricted terms. By 1924 there was a—minority and short-lived—Labour government; another followed in 1929-31. The trade union movement grew from strength to strength in the years to 1920. It then experienced a numerical decline, but it had established relationships with employers and the state which were bolstered by the growing presence of the Labour Party. Leading trade unionists (or former trade unionists) held cabinet posts in both the inter-war Labour governments (and, which is less often mentioned, during the early years of the National Government of 1931-35).

For governments of all persuasions the politics of labour, industrial relations and trades unions were matters of unceasing concern, at least after about 1910. From 1910 until 1913 British politics were rocked by a wave of trade union militancy — underpinned by political understandings grounded in Syndicalism, Industrial Unionism, and forms of Marxism — unparalleled during the previous half century. During the Great War and the early post-war years, this militancy, with its political overtones, was again to the fore, especially in major centres of heavy industrial production such as Clydeside, Sheffield and Coventry. At the same time, European governments were shaken by revolution: the spectre of Bolshevism haunted the British government for a number of years after the war. Gradually, a state strategy was evolved which — although worked out in somewhat varying forms — accepted that trade unions and the politics of the working class were legitimate, but sought to prescribe closely the bounds of legitimate trade union and labour political action. In essence, this meant defining trade unionism in terms of collective bargaining at the workplace, asserting the illegitimacy of any industrial action for political purposes, and defining the limits of acceptable political action in electoral and parliamentary terms. (Foster 1976; Middlemas 1979.)

This strategy was extremely effective. It was also highly flexible. It encouraged the development of a broad coalition within the labour movement including a wide range of trade union and political views. It underpinned this with institutions. Parliamentary-electoral politics provided routinised forms of activity and rewarded them with constant (if modest) success. They also protected trade unions from exposing their organisations to the dangers of industrial action for political purposes. (See Holford 1988a: esp. 193-241.) The definitions of what was legitimate were far from clear: as the industrial strength of labour ebbed with depression and the growth of unemployment, 'political' — and thus illegitimate — labels were attached to important forms of 'solidarity' action, above all the General Strike, despite their leaders' very clear denials of such intentions.

The strategy also underpinned government policy in adult education. The Workers' Educational Association (and its offspring, the Workers' Educational Trade Union Committee) were supported not least because of the greater political threat supposedly posed by the broadly Marxist labour college movement. As Lord Eustace Percy, the (Conservative) President of the Board of Education, explained to a colleague in 1925:

> *In adult education there is a continual struggle going on between the Universities and those bodies, like the Workers' Educational Association, who work with the Universities, on the one hand, and the Communist or semi-Communist Labour Colleges on the other. Hitherto the Workers' Educational Association and the University Extension people have been able to make headway against these undesirable propagandists because, largely owing to Government assistance, they can offer better facilities. On the whole, too, I think the education that they do offer is extremely useful. ... If we force the WEA and the Universities to cut down their work we shall not choke off the demand for local classes which is extraordinarily strong in all parts of the country, but we shall open a wide door to the Labour Colleges, and I believe the result will be deplorable. In fact my own view is that £100,000 spent annually on this kind of work, properly controlled, would be about the best police expenditure we could indulge in ... (Quoted Fieldhouse 1985a: 123.)*

Ruskin College and Education for Trades Unionists

Residential education for the working class, important in itself, was also fundamental to developments in all forms of education for trade unionists after 1900. This was for three main reasons. Before the Great War, and throughout the inter-war period, working class education was riven by the legacy of a dispute which arose at Ruskin College in Oxford in 1908-9. Second, Ruskin, and its Marxist competitor, the Central Labour College, were the major enduring centres of educational expertise 'within' the labour and trade union movement. Third, they provided between them the bulk of those within the movement with lasting interests in education for workers: the nature of the expertise which they fostered, and the matters in dispute between Ruskin and the CLC, coloured the educational understandings of such men and women. These included both those who made up the full- and part-time tutors of the local labour colleges (and to a lesser extent the

WEA), and those who formulated and executed policy on union education within the TUC and individual unions. We begin, therefore, by exploring the character of the two residential colleges.

The early histories of Ruskin College and the Central Labour College have been oft-told (Craik 1964 and Pollins 1984 are standard accounts). A number of themes emerge — control and independence, objectivity and commitment in the curriculum, the aims of workers' education, links with capital and the state. These recur in later periods. Ruskin was founded in 1899, on the intiative (and finances) of three American philanthropists. They assumed that the students would largely be trades unionists, and at the founding conference the bulk of those present were representatives of trade unions, trades councils and co-operative societies. Shortly after its formation, the TUC's Parliamentary Committee accepted an invitation to appoint three trustees (out of seven; one other was from the co-operative movement) — though on the strict understanding that no financial responsibility would be involved (Griggs 1983: 178). There was a fund of goodwill toward the project, which few initially doubted.

Gradually, however, problems emerged. The staff, though generally sympathetic to the project, had widely divergent conceptions of the function of a 'Labour College'. Their differences became clearer as the early years went by. Dennis Hird, for instance, Ruskin's first Principal, was a committed socialist, a member of the (Marxist) Social Democratic Federation, and held that Ruskin should provide teaching from a socialist viewpoint to enable its students to take leading roles in labour's struggle against capital. Vice-Principal H.B. Lees-Smith, on the other hand, stressed that a Labour College was not a Socialist College: 'All the teaching is carefully impartial, and all its tutors are not socialists' (quoted Griggs 1983: 179). The differences were not merely political: the staff's very values often did not meet. One criticised another for drinking with the students; two objected to students' expressing their political views in public; one honestly admitted he found working class students—especially socialists — difficult to deal with. One tutor (later to become Principal) recorded that when first appointed to the staff:

> *I was completely ignorant of Trade Unionism or of the Co-operative Movement. I had read Economics entirely from what is rather absurdly, though conveniently, called the 'orthodox' point of view. I had never read a line of Marx, I knew very little of the Socialist writers, and those I had read had made no impression on my mind. I had hardly ever spoken to a working man except gardeners, coachmen, and gamekeepers. (Quoted Millar 1979: 9.)*

Another member of Ruskin's staff described the working class as 'the tidal multitude and blind' (quoted Craik 1964: 57). Personal relationships among the lecturers were thus often strained.

Associated with these differences of politics and values were different attitudes to education. For the more 'traditionalist' staff, it was vital that Ruskin be respected by the academic establishment. Ruskin's physical presence in central Oxford no doubt strengthened this tendency. After Labour's advances at the 1906 General Election — perhaps cause and effect — Oxford University itself began to show more interest its young neighbour (Pollins 1984: 20-21). In due course, some Ruskin students were allowed to study for the University's Diploma in Economics or Political Science. Such advances were much welcomed by some Ruskin teachers. They were also vital if Ruskin was to secure funding from moneyed private donors. Its founding philanthropists had returned across the Atlantic in 1902, leaving the College in constant financial difficulty, and the trade union movement was unwilling, unable — or perhaps not sufficiently canvassed — to cover the shortfall.

As trade union students began to arrive in large numbers, their expectations of finding tutors in sympathy with labour aspirations were often disappointed; friction arose between students and several staff. In 1907 many students applied for exemption from the lectures of two non-socialist members of staff: in response, the lectures were made compulsory. New tests were introduced, backed by sanctions. Many of the students were militantly socialist, and maintained that as the working class controlled its own trade unions, political party, co-operative movement, so it should control its own education.

> We do not rely upon the politics of our employers for measures of progressive legislation. We established our own economic fortifications — we have our own political weapons — we control our own literary despatches. Why then should we not as independently manage our own educational affairs? (Plebs 1909: 27, quoted Millar 1979: 8.)

Oxford was the focus of the politics of workers' education at this time: the internal politics of Ruskin simmered in the cauldron of the University's forays into education for working people. The report *Oxford and Working-class Education*, in many ways an attempt by a number of dons to reform and extend the University's role, seemed to radical Ruskin students 'a barefaced attempt to seize control of the education of working men in the interests of the governing class' (Millar 1979: 6).

In the face of this general ferment over working class education, though also a product of the internal politics of Ruskin itself, many of the College's students established the Plebs League in 1908. In February 1909 the League began to publish its own magazine, *The Plebs*, 'to transform Ruskin College into a genuine *Labour* college run by workers for workers'

(Millar 1979: 7; emphasis in original), and

> *To make clear the real position of Ruskin College, to point out its present weaknesses, to outline its possibilities, to demonstrate its value to the Labour Movement, if definitely founded thereon, to stimulate active interest in working-class education ...* (Plebs *February 1909, quoted Craik 1964: 63).*

At just this time Ruskin's governing body called for the Hird's resignation. Fierce personal antagonisms among the staff of a small college, and their widely differing values, played a part in this call. Hird's managerial style (including a failure to maintain discipline) was also a factor. Others might perhaps have avoided an overt dispute (Pollins 1984: 22-3). But such matters only fanned the fire. Working class politics were already ablaze, and for Ruskin the fundamental issues were its relations with the University and the labour movement — its ideological character. Teachers' attitudes and approaches, the subject-matter of their lectures, the College's attitude to its (adult) students, were inevitably central questions of workers' education. The radical students supported Hird: they went on strike. In due course, they were outmanoeuvred, but ten withdrew from the College, resolving to establish an independent Labour College. The new Central Labour College opened in Oxford in August 1909.

What general lessons for the education of trade unionists can we draw from Ruskin's first decade? First, there is a deep tension within the very notion of working class education, at least for adults. (The tension also emerged within later forms of working class education, as our explorations of trade union education will show.) In the circumstances of 1909 this was bound to be posed sharply. At one pole is the view that education must serve the labour movement. One variant of this (held by the Ruskin strikers) was that since socialism is in the interests of the working class, and Marxism is the theory of the working class, Marxian socialism must be the content of working class education. But the view rests easily with other views of the purpose, aims, and ideology of the labour movement. At the other is a liberal view, according to which education is intrinsically good, and a matter of individual (rather than collective) development. In the early Ruskin situation, and often since, this view was expressed by many who also adhered to firm political views. Labour would not be helped by Marxist theorising (which was in any case intellectually unsound). Workers would benefit from progressive and peaceful reform, which those in power could be relied upon to ensure. The working class could be allowed to gain power only when it had accepted the basic presuppositions of civilised political behaviour.

Second — a closely related, but analytically distinct, issue — is the tension within adult education on the question of control. Who decides what is appropriate for adults to learn? What role should students have in this? Of course, this is not restricted to adult education, nor to workers' education, but it is stronger among adults (whose claim to equality with tutors is perhaps stronger than children's or adolescents'), and *de facto* it is stronger in a movement based upon (supposedly) democratic decision-making, and whose main objects include extending democracy to the mass of the people. It is perhaps significant that disputes turning on this matter have resurfaced on many occasions in residential working-class education: not least at the Central Labour College itself during 1912-13 (Atkins 1981: esp. 42-7), and more recently in a dispute at Fircroft College in 1975 (Houlton 1978).

Finally, at the centre of the Ruskin dispute was the issue of finance. The College could be set up only with the aid of capitalist philanthropists; its work depended on injections of income greater than the trade unions themselves were willing or able to make. Those staff who wished closer relationships with the University, for instance, were strengthened and (as they saw it) justified in their views by the strength which University approval would give to their approaches to potential benefactors. Finance has long been a stalking-horse for disputes over control in trade union education.

The WEA and Education for Trades Unionists

If the radical students of Ruskin were incensed by the 1908 report on *Oxford and Working-class Education*, others in the labour movement regarded the University's growing links with the working class more favourably. Indeed, at a conference on adult education held in the University's Examination Schools in 1907, John Mactavish, a leading Portsmouth trade unionist, that city's first Labour councillor and prospective Labour candidate for the parliamentary division, made an impassioned and celebrated speech — a powerful factor in the University's establishing a joint committee of academics and working-class representatives to prepare the report:

> *I am not here as a suppliant for my class. I decline to sit at the rich man's table praying for crumbs. I claim it as a right — wrongfully withheld — wrong not only to us but to Oxford. What is the true function of a University? Is it to obtain the nation's best men, or to sell its gifts to the rich? Instead of recruiting her students from the widest possible area, she has restricted her area of selection to the fortunate few. ... We want work people to come to Oxford [and] ... to come back as missionaries. ... We want her [Oxford] to inspire them not with the idea of getting on, but with the idea of social service. (Quoted Mooney 1979: 13-14.)*

It was men and women sharing Mactavish's outlook who built the early

Workers' Educational Association — as, in Albert Mansbridge's words, a 'partnership between labour and learning' (cp Jennings 1973: 12-14; Jennings 1976: esp 5-12; Stocks 1953: esp. 19-36).

Mansbridge, the greatest founding influence on the WEA, was a Co-operator rather than a strongly 'political' member of the labour movement. The WEA's early years — up to the end of the Great War — were marked by courteous but essentially formal relations with national trade unions and the TUC. The TUC's Parliamentary Committee, for instance, was represented on the WEA's Advisory Committee, but only in 1915 did the TUC agree to make a grant (of £50) to the Association (Grigg 1983: 184-5). Locally, it is true, some WEA branches were building warm relationships with the trade union movement. Reading WEA had a Trades' Council representative on its committee from its formation. Belfast WEA was established when the Trades' Council and the Co-operative jointly approached the Queen's University. Trades' councils initiated meetings to establish WEA branches in Leicester, Northampton, Derby, Blackpool, and Glasgow (Clinton 1977: 42). But in general the early WEA was more concerned to build its relations with the universities, taking its working class roots to some extent for granted. In her history of the WEA, Mary Stocks (1953: 60-61) summarised the position in 1914 thus: 'The trade-union movement is interested, indeed co-operative and responsive; but ... has so far shown little evidence of educational initiative.'

When in 1915 Mansbridge stepped down from the WEA's Secretaryship on health grounds, the Association settled on Mactavish. 'As a matter of general policy,' records Stocks (1953: 70), 'many people felt that as Mansbridge had tipped the balance of the Association on the side of the universities, it was now time to tip it on the side of the trade unions ...' Gradually, too, the Central Labour College was developing its programme of extension classes and winning union support. The first class started in 1909/10; within three years there were 24 such courses around the country (Atkins 1981: 70-71). Mactavish was seen as the man for this task — although he was apparently only a 'mildly interested' member of the WEA who attended the occasional meeting (Mooney 1979: 4). He set about strengthening and widening the Association's union links. The WEA published Mactavish's pamphlet, *What Labour Wants from Education* in 1916. He then began an energetic programme of lobbying both national and local union bodies.[1]

Apart from Mactavish, the centrepiece of the WEA's strategy to win trade union support for adult education was its formation, in October 1919, of the Workers' Educational Trade Union Committee (WETUC). This rested substantially on the support of the Iron and Steel Trades Confederation (ISTC) and its able General Secretary, Arthur Pugh. It was innovative in several ways. It was the first scheme designed to provide and encourage education not for members of the labour movement in general, but specifically for its member trade unions (Corfield 1969: 12). Pugh and Mactavish 'sold' the scheme to a number of unions, arguing that unions should take their share of what public funds were available for adult education: otherwise, a union education programme would impose 'an intolerable burden' (quoted Corfield 1969: 14). Indeed, Pugh held that the state had a positive duty to provide such funds, bearing in mind the 'additional functions and responsibilities' which it had placed on the trade union movement (quoted Corfield 1969: 15).

The scheme also succeeded in squaring some of the circles of control. It represented a concession by the WEA on control of the curriculum, in that the WETUC was a joint committee of the WEA and its affiliated unions, the latter being in a majority. 'By joining W.E.T.U.C. they [affiliated unions] could leave to professionals the problems of organising and providing an educational service, whilst retaining executive control over the general policy of the scheme, and determining the programme of courses for their members' (Corfield 1969: 14). This left untouched some of the thorny questions of student influence over the curriculum and course content, but it was a powerful concession — such as had been rejected in the earlier Ruskin dispute — to the legitimacy of labour views on labour education.

The statistics of the WETUC between the wars record modest success. It was constantly in competition, both ideological and promotional, with the labour college movement. But it secured the affiliation of a significant number of trade unions nationally, rising from five in 1923 to 13 in 1931 and 27 by the outbreak of the Second World War. Its provision of courses was also significant, if modest. In 1931, after ten years' work, there were 122 WETUC classes around the country; in addition, 3,738 students enrolled in 55 day schools, and 1,117 students in 33 week-end schools. (Corfield 1969: 16-17, 248-9.)

The WETUC was not, of course, the only form in which the WEA attempted to attract working class — or even trade union — students. Many, though not all, WEA branches throughout the country continued to have warm relationships with the labour movement — seeing themselves as, if not an arm of the labour movement, then certainly with fraternally linked hands. But the essential differences between the general WEA programme and that of WETUC were, first, the latter's concession of significant control to the unions themselves, and second, the strategy of targetting courses specifically at certain unions, rather than merely inviting union members to attend courses developed by a WEA committee.

The Labour College Movement

When the Ruskin strikers left to form the Central Labour College in 1909, they did so on the crest of a wave of political, as well as educational, ferment. The Labour Party had recently made real advances in elections. Trade unions were marching forward. The politics of the left were alive with competing political and industrial theories. Industrial unionists, syndicalists, Marxists of many hues: these were the people who made up the supporters of the new Labour College. Although the labour and trade union movement was at that stage more fluid ideologically than it later became, the Labour College supporters represented just one band of opinion within it: essentially, a somewhat revolutionary socialism, stretching from the more radical members of the Independent Labour Party leftwards. They carried with them views of the state heavily influenced by Marxism, syndicalism, and even anarchism. The state was a tool of the capitalist class. Labour's role was to undermine the capitalists, wrest hold of their power. The state would, on this view, become involved in an enterprise with representatives of the working class only to infiltrate, influence, buy off, control. (For a contemporary analysis of the state in this vein, see Paul 1920; see also Holton 1980.)

The infant Central Labour College relied upon the commitment of a band of supporters around the country. The Plebs League, to which they belonged, had not remained a narrow, Oxford-based, movement: as the Ruskin strikers returned home, they carried with them *The Plebs* and its message. The League and its members breathed the air of a socialism whose roots were strongest in certain areas and industrial groups: in the Miners' lodges of South Wales, Durham and Scotland, with their histories of militant socialism; among the engineering industries of the west of Scotland and the north-west of England; among railwaymen. (Macintyre 1980a: esp. 17-46; Millar 1979: 16-21; Holton 1976: esp. chs. 4-8.) During the later war years, and up until the early 1920s, this strand of socialist thought had wide currency. But from about 1920 onward, a political bloc was established around the centre-right of the labour movement, encompassing what Stuart Macintyre (1980a: 47-65) has called Labour Socialism, as well as trade union labourism (Holford 1988a: esp. 193-232). As a rule, this group — which grew stronger through the twenties — had little sympathy for the labour colleges' brand of education.

The energies of the pre-war Plebs League were largely dissipated in creating, winning support and students for, and financing, the Central Labour College — no mean achievement in the face of two evictions in Oxford. (The CLC finally moved to premises in Earl's Court, London.) However, a modest number of 'Extension Classes' were run before the war.

Some were taught by the Plebs League's ex-Ruskin students (Craik 1964: 92-3); others by such figures of the revolutionary left as John S. Clarke of the Socialist Labour Party (Holford 1988a: 150). The real growth in labour college provision took place, however, during the later years of the Great War, and during the industrial and political ferment of 1919-20. The position can be gauged from a local example. In Edinburgh, one of the labour colleges' stronger areas to be sure, the movement had just a single class in 1917. In the autumn of that year a Plebs League branch was started; the District Organiser began to attend union meetings to promote classes. But still the Leith class enrolled only 17 members, and as late as April 1918 the Edinburgh class could report an advance only 'in knowledge not numbers'. The real advance came in 1919 and 1920: in 1919/20 120 students were enrolled in four classes; in 1920/21 an initial October enrolment of 490 students rose over the succeeding months to 617, 654, and finally 'nearly 700' in 21 classes. Sales of *The Plebs* rose from eleven, to twenty and then thirty dozen monthly. (*Plebs* June 1917-June 1921; Roberts 1970: 57.) This pattern of growth seems to have been reflected elsewhere, especially in Scotland and the English north and north-west (Simon 1990b: esp. 28-9; Frow 1990).

The strength of the labour colleges was their grounding in a vital strain of labour and trade union activism. Rather more than the WEA — for they lacked the latter's academic pretensions — they were *of* the trade unions and the labour movement; 'making contact' with the working class was not an issue. At the same time, their roots were rather narrow, and when the economic, social and political base of Marxism began to be seriously eroded during the mid-1920s, the labour colleges suffered. The early twenties were years of continued growth, with institutional development. The National Council of Labour Colleges, a federation of the local colleges, was established in 1921, effectively superseding the individual-membership Plebs League. In 1923 it was organised into divisions. There was also numerical growth —the number of local labour colleges grew from 37 to 91 in fifteen months. By 1924/25 there were 139 local colleges and groups (Millar 1979: 51). But the trend soon altered. The NCLC's 529 classes enrolled nearly 12,000 students around the country in 1922/23. By 1925/26 there were 1,234 classes with over 30,000 students. Then decline set in: by 1937/38 the number of students was down to 13,274 in 728 classes (Millar 1979: 252).

The development of the labour college movement was very sensitive to the fate of the particular working class communities in which it grew its roots. There was local variation. In Scotland, for instance, there were 264 classes with 6,238 students in 1924/25 and roughly similar numbers in the two following years; but the number had more than halved to 111 classes

No education is of any use to the workers which does not aim at the emancipation of the workers. But your masters will do their best, here as elsewhere, to put you off with SHODDY GOODS

Fig.2.1: Shoddy Goods. The Plebs League expresses its contempt for capitalist education — and universities in particular.

and 3,061 students by 1931/32, falling again the following year. Thereafter the decline was slightly reversed, but during the later 1930s the Scottish Labour College's average annual provision was between a third and a half of what it had sustained twelve or fifteen years earlier. (Roberts 1970: Appendix A.) In South-east Lancashire, the early 1930s recovery was stronger, regaining the 1926 level of activity — though there was then a sharp decline (Cohen 1990a: 126-33). But despite this variation, the local evidence broadly reflects the national statistics. These figures represent, for the United Kingdom as a whole, a substantial provision through the inter-war years: smaller than the WEA, which had 3,978 classes in 1938/39 (Stocks 1953: 123), but — as the NCLC would vigorously have pointed out — all working class and members of the labour movement.

The contribution of the labour college movement to the development of education for trades unionists was major. For nearly two decades it sustained the Central Labour College, which became a staff college for a generation of working class educationalists (as well as activists). For rather longer it sustained a major programme of education for members of the trade union and labour movement. It generated and gave unceasing institutional, ideological and propagandistic backing to the notion of 'independent working-class education' — education independent of capital and the state. It gave similar backing to the view that workers' education must be committed, purposive, political — and probably Marxist. It argued that such education must be rooted in the working class and its political and trade union movements, rather than 'imported' from outside. The last three were a profound legacy to later generations in the education of trade unionists: for good and ill, they remained central and recurring themes.

The TUC and Trade Union Education

The TUC between the wars was not the substantial organisation it later became. Until 1918 it had just a single full-time employee. Only from 1921 was its organisation overhauled to provide a General Council and administrative support on a 'civil service of the trade union movement' model. But even in 1924 its paid staff numbered just three (Allen 1960: 24-6, 30-35). There was a widespread view after the Great War that it should become a 'general staff' of the trade union movement, and following the reorganisation some of its permanent officials, notably Walter Citrine, tried to build its role, influence and authority within the trade union movement. At this time, it gave some attention to educating trade unionists. But its initiatives came to naught, with the result that the TUC played no significant part in the provision of union education until after 1945. Nevertheless, the TUC's interventions in the 1920s were an important formative influence in the later development of its educational work.

We have seen that the TUC enjoyed courteous and friendly, but hardly close, relations with the WEA before the Great War (see also Griggs 1983: 184-5). It was somewhat closer to Ruskin College — though this was complicated by the bitterness felt by some TUC delegates and unions over the 1909 strike and the formation of the Central Labour College. After the war, as the competition between the WEA and the NCLC developed, unions became entwined in internecine struggle. The Steelworkers, Railway Clerks, Engineering and Shipbuilding Draughtsmen, and Printers' Assistants (NATSOPA) joined up with the new WETUC; the Building Trade Workers and Engineers with the NCLC. With major unions involved, the TUC could hardly remain unaffected: congresses became amphitheatres for recurring set-piece debates. (Griggs 1983: 186.)

Then, in early 1921, Arthur Pugh of the ISTC and the WETUC established the Trade Unions' Educational Inquiry Committee. Sponsored by sixteen unions (Corfield 1969: 42), this was in part a promotional device for the newly-established WETUC. But — what may be the same thing — it was intended to help the WETUC become 'the framework for a completely co-ordinated system of trade union education ... before there was any nation-wide rival in the field' (Corfield 1969: 42). In this objective it was already too late, but the Inquiry was the first major attempt by the trade union movement to plan its educational provision. The Inquiry report (reprinted in Corfield 1969: 209-28) made several important recommendations. Many of these will be covered in Chapter 3: many did not come to fruition. But the Inquiry was an important catalyst, encouraging trade unionists and the TUC to think about the educational needs of the movement and how they could be met.

At the 1921 TUC a resolution was agreed instructing

> *the General Council to co-operate with the Trade Union Education Inquiry Committee as to the best means of giving affect to the aims and objects of the inquiry, including the taking over and running of existing Trade Union Colleges, including the Central Labour College and Ruskin College (quoted Griggs 1983: 187).*

As a result, the General Council established an Education Committee comprising representatives of its own Education Sub-Committee (responsible for links with Ruskin, WETUC, and the labour colleges), and of the Trade Union Inquiry Committee. After interviewing representatives of all the educational bodies concerned, the committee produced a report which bore a strong family resemblance to the previous year's Trade Union Inquiry. This report, like the Inquiry's, suggested that the existing provision of education for trade union members was overly restricted. It suggested that there should be a wider spread of levels of provision, and that subjects should include study 'not only of economics and industrial history, but also of the general and social history of their own and other people, of literature, and the arts and sciences' (TUC *Annual Report* 1922: 188, quoted Griggs 1983: 190). It also gave prominence to the importance of education in the practical tasks of trade union representatives:

> *The extent to which Labour will win control over local and national affairs will for some time to come be determined by the extent to which the average wage-earner thinks it is more capable of managing every-day affairs than those who oppose it (TUC Annual Report 1922: 198-90 quoted Griggs 1983: 190).*

But such 'deeper' questions of educational strategy and method (dealt with in Chapter 3) were elbowed aside by the dominant influence of the existing institutions, particularly the residential colleges. The 1921 Congress resolution specified precisely only that any scheme should include 'the taking over and running of existing trade union colleges, including the Central Labour College and Ruskin College'. As the financial difficulties of the colleges became more acute, this consideration became more and more the central issue. At the same time, whilst both the WETUC and NCLC were formally committed to accepting TUC control of workers' education, each was jealous of the nature of whatever joint scheme might emerge. Mark Starr of the NCLC accused the WEA of being 'in that stage of working class education, which, in the political sphere, is known as the Lib Lab, ... this Mr. Facing Both Ways' (quoted Griggs 1983: 193), whilst the WEA and WETUC representatives were anxious that the scheme should not jeopardise their educational integrity and their relationships with the Board of Education.

After far from easy negotiations, a TUC Education Scheme was agreed by representatives of the WEA, the NCLC, Ruskin and the Central Labour College, and the General Council (see Fieldhouse 1981: 46-8). It was approved by Congress in 1925 (for the text of the agreement, see Fieldhouse 1981: 61-3). It came to grief, however, on a number of rocks. The intensifying economic and industrial crisis, and recurrent major industrial disputes, gave the TUC leaders many other more pressing matters to deal with. The rapid erosion of membership after 1920 brought financial crisis for many unions (and for the educational schemes they might otherwise have supported). The intense and uncompromising commitment of the NCLC to the twin principles of financial independence and socialist education made the negotiations long and acrimonious, and led to personal friction with WEA representatives (their prospective collaborators) and the WEA's and WETUC's trade union supporters.

The scheme's main aim, if grudgingly, had eventually been accepted by the WEA representatives:

> *To provide working class education in order to enable the workers to develop their capacities and to equip them for the Trade Union, Labour and Co-operative activities generally, in the work of securing social and industrial emancipation (quoted Millar 1979: 67).*

Millar and the NCLC leaders suspected the WEA's commitment to this clause was only skin-deep. In a campaign which, if not designed to embarrass the WEA leaders, undoubtedly meant that every nuance and ambiguity of the agreement was subjected to merciless scrutiny, Millar argued that '"Mr Cole and representatives of the WEA"... had only been with great difficulty ... induced to accept the objects clause because they all realised "social and industrial emancipation" of the working-class meant *ending capitalism*' (Fieldhouse 1981: 49; emphasis in original). Millar's campaign extended beyond the labour press, including an extended correspondence in *Education* (25 September to 13 November 1925: Fieldhouse 1981: 49).

This embarrassed prominent members of the WEA, such as its Vice-President, A.D. Lindsay, Master of Balliol College, Oxford, and G.D.H. Cole, who denied that they had committed the Association to education explicitly aimed at raising class-consciousness or bringing down capitalism. The WEA was under strong pressure not to accede to any notion of political aims or trade union control of the scheme. Pressure was internal — most prominently, the Edinburgh branch disaffiliated on the ground that the the TUC agreement deprived the WEA of its independence (Roberts 1970: 83-4). It came also from the educational establishment — the Board of Education, the Association of Education Committees, and a number of universities and education authorities. In particular, the Board of Education sought to introduce more restrictive terms for the allocation of grant-aid to WEA classes, which would have precluded any question of tutors having trade union membership or commitment (which the scheme agreed with the TUC would have required). Some local education authorities and universities acted independently to introduce such requirements. (Fieldhouse 1981: esp. 53-61.)

The new scheme did specifically envisage that the TUC would take over both Ruskin and the CLC. Trade unions' financial anxieties were, however, mounting, especially after the General Strike. The TUC was offered an apparent solution to an impending crisis when a wealthy socialist socialite, the Countess of Warwick, offered to donate her country house in Essex, Easton Lodge. The detail of the nefarious dealings which led to the collapse of this initiative need not concern us greatly (for contending views, see Griggs 1983: 197-203; Craik 1964: 140-4; Corfield 1969: 53-5; Millar 1979: 73-6). The overall upshot was that the TUC failed to take over Ruskin and the CLC (which closed in 1929 when the Miners' unions withdrew support).[2] It also failed to integrate the WEA, NCLC and WETUC in a TUC education scheme. It had, in short, severely burnt its fingers. As an American observer (Senturia 1930: 681) commented at the end of the decade, and with some justice, the TUC had a 'definite commitment ... to educational work':

> *Resolution after resolution has been adopted on the desirability and necessity of working-class education. But the struggle between the contending groups over a Congress convinced of the value of education has deadlocked that Congress, and prevented it from supporting either of the class-work organizations.*

The TUC's chief negotiator in the educational disputes of the mid-twenties, Walter Citrine, was to be its General Secretary for the remaining inter-war years. It is hardly surprising, therefore, that the TUC showed little enthusiasm to involve itself with educational issues again for well over a decade — and to the modest extent that it did so, it avoided collaboration with the educational bodies. In 1929 it introduced a new summer school programme which was

> *in the nature of a trade union technical school dealing with matters immediate and of practical interest and importance to those actually involved in the day-to-day work of the trade union movement (TUC Annual Report 1929: 148, quoted McIlroy 1985c, 35).*

This technicist approach to education avoided renewed controversy and the charge of trying to compete with the NCLC or WEA. It no doubt also appealed to Citrine, who had little enthusiasm for the political visions of the labour colleges or even of such WEA stalwarts as G.D.H. Cole: his main concern was that unions should function efficiently as organisations pursuing a legitimate range of aims, and that their officials should, as far as possible, be committed to these. To broadly these ends, too, a study course was developed in the 1930s (TUC 1936a), covering trade union history, structure, functions and policy. Again, this was an independent production, in which the TUC stood apart from the educational bodies.

But if there were pragmatic reasons for standing apart from the WEA-labour college dispute, the tone of the dispute also jarred with the TUC's increasingly firm commitment to a 'responsible' social role. As we shall see in the next chapter, both educational bodies were capable of offering curricula strongly relevant to routine union activities and organisational development. But the language of their disagreement was the language of socialism and Marxism, reform versus revolution, independence and the capitalist state, class loyalty and betrayal. These were concerns for which Citrine had no time — an attitude shared by a majority of the General Council. In this setting, the difficulties confronting any attempt to establish common ground were marked: and the TUC had neither the necessary authority, nor the enthusiasm.

1   In late 1918, for instance, Mactavish met the executive committee of the Edinburgh Trades Council to discover their attitude to the WEA and win support for its classes. (The impression he made was not profound: after the meeting, the Trades Council's Secretary thought he was the WEA's *local* organiser! (Edinburgh Trades Council Minutes: 15 October 1918.))

2   Craik has suggested that the demise of the CLC in 1929 owed not a little to its having buried its energies for two years into these negotiations, rather than in campaigning for continued support at this most difficult time. The CLC, of course, relied heavily on financial support from the Miners' unions, which were under intense pressure during and after 1926. But staff-student tensions were also a factor: continuous through the 1920s, there was a period of fierce factional in-fighting among students and staff after 1926. Seven students were expelled in 1928 for refusing to take part in Dietzgen centenary celebrations — they sang in a Communist choir elsewhere. (Macintyre 1980a: 84-5 provides the best summary judgement of the last years of the CLC; cp Craik: esp. 137-44; Millar 1979: 97-104.)

Chapter 3

Educational Methods and Strategies between the Wars

Before the Great War, trade unionists would not have recognised the expression 'trade union education'. They debated questions of working class education, of course, and they were concerned about the education of trade unionists. But though these debates included questions of independence and control ('independent working class education'), of education for socialism or for its own sake ('education for emancipation' or, as Mansbridge had it, 'education is emancipation'), and about residential courses and tutorial classes, the notion of education for trade unionists as such grew up only during the inter-war years. This idea developed alongside shifting conceptions of the labour and trade union movement: we begin, therefore, by outlining the political culture of the inter-war labour movement.

Working Class Students and the Learning Environment

Victorian Britain, the workshop of the world, required enormous numbers of workers. Much of the labour industry needed, relatively skilled and in relatively short supply, was able to command relatively high wages. Men with these skills (and they were chiefly men) were able to enjoy a measure of security with their families, and — the term itself entered the language — an artisan's standard of housing. They had modest leisure, modest wealth, sufficient at least to distinguish themselves from their fellow-men, and were able to aspire to greater. They established for themselves networks of social institutions — clubs, co-operative societies, pubs, trade unions; and they built up ethics, of respectability and self-improvement, which took a firm grip on the working class movement. (For a critical survey of this process, and of theories of the 'labour aristocracy', see Gray 1981.)

Of course, as the trade union movement grew, it embraced wider and more diverse social groups. But it retained many of the morals and attitudes of the Victorian 'labour aristocracy'. In particular, it retained a sense of the virtues of self-improvement. These built on education's longer-standing roots in the radical tradition. 'A passion for education had been a distinctive feature of the radical movements in the first half of the nineteenth century, variously manifested in coffee-house reading rooms, Owenite Halls of Science and the flourishing popular press ...' (Macintyre 1980a: 70). This culture of self-improvement permeated the Victorian and Edwardian trade union and labour movement. It meant, to be sure, the self-improvement of the journeyman establishing himself in self-employment or building a small firm. It meant the self-improvement of mechanics' institutes and Samuel Smiles' *Self Help*. It also meant — for some — reading and studying the labour press, attending public meetings, reading political works: the culture, for instance, which built a mass readership for *The Clarion*, and made Robert Blatchford's works, especially *Merrie England*, into bestsellers.

Stuart Macintyre (1980a: esp. 94-105) makes much of a tradition of 'autodidacts' who 'read in search of understanding':

> *This was an essentially individual pilgrimage. The autodidact might share his interests with fellow workers, and in some workplaces the atmosphere could be extremely conducive to intellectual discussion. ... Nevertheless ... the search for knowledge rested perforce on books, which are a primarily individual medium of education. (Macintyre 1980a: 94-5.)*

Autodidacts in this tradition were an important foundation of the achievement of the labour colleges and the WEA in the years before and just after the Great War.

The political culture of the labour movement after the Great War was recognisably a child of the late Victorian and Edwardian movement. The Independent Labour Party and the Co-operative movement, above all, did much to preserve a Labour sub-culture. This was a world of cradle-to-grave Socialism, of Socialist Sunday Schools, the Woodcraft Folk, the Independent Labour Party's Guild of Youth, cycling clubs: buoyed up — in the ILP — by unceasing propaganda. (See Reid 1966; Prynn 1983; Attfield 1981: esp. 38-59.) And propaganda was educational: it developed skills (of public speaking, constructing a case, and so forth) among the propagandists. It spread fact and opinion about social and political issues. It generated a climate of political debate and exchange which encouraged reading and study. 'Six years' membership of the ILP,' one local trade union activist remarked in 1926, 'had left him woefully lacking in Socialism, but it had imbued in him a taste for literature. ILP literature was second to none ...' (*Labour Standard* 9 October 1926, quoted Holford 1983: 357.)

But while a 'snapshot' of the inter-war labour movement would show such an image of continuity, much was in flux. With mass unemployment and economic depression, with shifting patterns of wage rates, incomes, job security, skill, and so forth, no pre-war aristocracy of labour could return in a recognisable form. As the intensity of the depression grew after 1920, leisure was scarce even for skilled workers to indulge in reading and learning — except, of course, for those cast entirely out of work. Though rapidly eroded after 1920, much of the wartime growth in union membership remained: the movement had many new members from previously non-union workplaces and industries. The ILP's role was eroded in the 1920s by the growing Labour Party: by the thirties, no longer the premier membership organisation on the political side of the labour movement, it was ejected from the Labour Party. Marxism was effectively marginalised by Labour Socialism.

An illuminating example of this flux may be found in the Co-operative movement, which advanced by leaps and bounds between the wars. Membership of the Royal Arsenal Co-operative, for instance, in south-east London and north-west Kent, grew from 69,000 in 1919 to 382,000 twenty years later, by extending 'from its traditional strongholds in the engineering districts of Woolwich, Charlton and Erith, affected after 1918 by trade depression', into inner London (Deptford, Peckham, Lambeth, Bermondsey, and so on, and 'the new LCC estates to the south and west' (Attfield 1981: 39-40). Although accompanied by a massive growth in Co-operative education, the most significant features were the erosion of the 'traditional' base of the labour movement, and the social change involved in large-scale movement of families to new, council estates. Apart from fighting to assert their various political views, the men and women of the inter-war labour movement had to grapple with major shifts in the social base of their potential and actual constituencies.

With these social changes, the educational culture of the labour movement also changed. To begin with, the expansion of secondary education and the educational opportunities it created for the gifted working class child eroded the 'autodidact' stratum. Between 1894 and 1934, an English elementary schoolchild's chances of winning a scholarship to secondary school improved beyond recognition (from 271:1 to 11:1). The odds were still against them, but able and ambitious working-class students were increasingly able to advance to secondary school and thence to non-manual occupations. The blocked ambitions on which the 'autodidact' tradition had fed were now increasingly satisfied within the established educational system. (Macintyre 1980a: 98-9.)

There were also other — more obviously political — changes: the shifting character of Marxism as the Communist Party 'bolshevised' itself and became more sectarian from the mid-twenties; the growing bureaucracy (albeit writ small) of the labour and trade union movement, creating a new route to a form of 'education' in attending committees; the mushrooming network of minor public offices to which trade unionists could now be nominated; the real possibility of election to public office at municipal level. Before 1914, certainly before 1900, these avenues hardly existed. They were not, of course, educational in the sense that reading and discussing Darwin, Marx or Dietzgen were educational; neither, for many, were they the true work of labour to which education should be directed.

But they did offer an avenue for advance in the movement and in the community, for the exercise of some power — and for learning — which had not existed ten or twenty years earlier.

Development Strategies and the Curriculum: the Labour Colleges

During the period of labour advance which lasted from about 1910, through the Great War until 1920 or so, and during the years of union militancy which followed — until, that is, about 1926 — the growth of the labour colleges was organic to the growth and militancy itself. As men and women in their hundreds of thousands joined the labour and trade union movement, and with war, revolution and lightning political change, learning was at a premium. New experiences had to be digested, comprehended, understood.

The development of the labour colleges in these circumstances was a matter of local initiative, energy and enthusiasm, rather than deep thought and planning. There was little central control. Indeed such — limited — opposition as there was to the formation of the National Council of Labour Colleges in 1921 was largely due to a fear that national organisation would reduce local colleges' autonomy (Millar 1979: 32-3). Local colleges worked, and with no little success, to provide their own brand of education to their local labour and trade union movement, but they did so by essentially by following well-established methods of the then labour movement.

The major change came with the formation of the NCLC, and the vision of its Honorary Secretary (from 1923) and General Secretary (from the following year), J.P.M. Millar. Millar has had a poor press, the butt of anger from both the WEA and universities (which he attacked mercilessly in true labour college style) on the one hand, and the Marxist and Communist left on the other. Millar was a young Scot (just 30 in 1923), who saw the labour colleges' future as the educational arm of the trade union movement. He set about ensuring that the new NCLC had the organisational efficiency and consistency to attract union support. For him, this implied a degree of central control. Millar pressed for (and won) a divisional structure, strengthening the national executive committee. He implemented national policies against opposition from many local activists and organisers, and fought to exclude Communists from positions of power in the NCLC (Cohen 1990a; Macintyre 1980a: 79; Miles 1984: esp 104-5; Millar 1979: 51-3, 80-2, 107-8).

Gaining trade union support meant winning support from national trade unions: and as we saw in Chapter 2, Millar had some success. The plan was simple. When national unions affiliated (at a *per capita* rate) to the NCLC, their members were entitled to join classes without charge, or at a reduced fee, in local labour colleges. Local college activists would encourage members of those unions in their area to join classes. They would also seek the local affiliation of union branches, whose members would secure similar rights. A local college organiser explained in 1927:

> *The financial basis of these local classes is provided by funds solely contributed by working class bodies ... The affiliation fee is twopence per member per year. This fee entitles all the members to attend all the classes arranged for the winter session. (Gibbons 1927.)*

The shift in strategy implied changes in the curriculum. In the early years, the labour college curriculum had been 'confined ... largely to economics and history, especially to industrial history, Marxian economics and the materialist conception of history. ... [T]he emphasis was unequivocally placed upon socio-political issues.' (Millar 1979: 208.) A flavour of this early approach may be found in a 1923 book, *What to Read: A Guide for Worker Students*, compiled by the Plebs Text Book Committee. The introduction explains its purpose:

> *to advance that kind of working-class education which is of use to the workers in achieving their own freedom. In this book will be found guides to reading only in subjects which can be of use in this way. (Plebs League 1923: v.)*

The contents pages set down these subjects in order: Economics, History, Geography, 'Modern Problems' (including Russia, Imperialism, and Industrial and Trade Union Problems), Psychology, Biology, 'A Course of Reading in Exact Science', Philosophy, English, and Esperanto. The largest single section by far is that on History (17 pages out of 61), followed by Philosophy and Modern Problems (10 each), and Economics (7). The section on English, which covers the mechanics of grammar and writing, runs to just two-thirds of a single page. Similar outlooks on content may be found in other works of the period, such as James Clunie's *First Principles of Working-Class Education* (1920) (see also Casey 1979).

Certainly, the labour colleges' early post-war courses seem to have been pitched at a relatively high level, appealing perhaps to autodidacts' desire to advance from an already quite sophisticated level of knowledge. Fred Douglas, then a young Communist militant, recalled a class in Edinburgh in 1919 or 1920:

> *Our instructor sat facing us with deeply-knit brows during the reading, obviously cracking the shell of each problem by sheer cerebral compression. After a few paragraphs [of Marx's* Capital*] he stopped the reader with the tap of his pencil on the water-bottle and proceeded to*

> *expose the kernels, or at any rate give his interpretation of the difficulties Marx had promised us.*
>
> *He allowed us to question him on his interpretation or on any difficulties he had missed. This opened the ring for two or three rival interpretations. Then followed a free discussion without time limit, in which the war of the rival interpretations raged without restraint. (Douglas 10 August 1955.)*

Such approaches, whatever their appeal to more scholarly autodidacts, were not to the taste of the younger militants who flocked to the socialist cause after the war. Douglas calculated, at the end of the winter's classes, that they might complete their study of *Capital* in another fifteen years. But in fact the plan was to 'start the ascent of *Das Kapital* all over again, from the beginning'! Douglas, by his own admission 'a young man in a hurry', found a life of practical politics — demonstrations, organising the unemployed, Communist congresses — more worthwhile. The class returned to its studies without him.

Plainly, as more men and women joined the movement, the labour colleges had to change their educational approach. Possible responses included lowering the level of the course content, making classes more relevant to the concerns of student activists, and altering teaching methods. But large-scale provision by the labour colleges began only toward the end of the Great War: this was an educational movement in its infancy. A number of tutors began to raise questions about method, content and relevance, though at a rudimentary level. Fred Casey (1979: 116) posed the question in 1920: 'Educate, educate, educate! Um — yes, but how? Just precisely how?' He gave an account of the typical class of his experience:

> *The promoters advertise a course of, say, 24 weekly lectures on Economics, starting in October — twenty enthusiastic students turn up — lecture starts on time — students studiously attentive — lively questions — slight shrinking in numbers as Christmas approaches — after Christmas, slump in attendance — students coming late — occasional good question and some poor ones — attention not really bad (in between yawns) but indefinable dullness pervading atmosphere — teacher tries to rouse things by questions of his own — after that, a few have urgent appointments elsewhere at question time, excuse themselves graciously and go out on tiptoe — very few studying at all after first couple of months and hardly one with a view to teaching. During one course I have in mind we started with twenty students and finished with three.*

Casey felt 'the majority of working class students are not students either by nature or training': as they could not 'cover a long line of detailed argument ... why weary them and waste time when the conclusions are all they they will get when we are finished?' He therefore advocated a short course (about six lectures) which he could repeat several times in a session. He was also moving toward some more interesting conclusions.

> *I would avoid the technical phrases, ... and if they wanted to know any more about it, let them ask. ... [It] could come out in questions ... The idea was to keep within the limit of what interested them, and to tell them only as much as would excite further interest and make them want more. From such students I would select a very few individuals, force them to guarantee time for study or otherwise have nothing to do with them; these I would take on another evening, give them the best detail study I could, and then let them go to the Trade Unions in the district with the same summary as the general class was having. (Casey 1979: 117.)*

Leaving aside a somewhat vigorous language — Casey seems to have had a somewhat abrasive personality (see Macintyre 1980a: 134-8; cp Cohen 1990a: 125) — we see a genuine concern to see working class education as not mere lecture, delivery, but also as development on the part of the students. At the same time, Casey shows something approaching contempt for the ability of the majority of students — linked, perhaps, to a desire to allocate scarce teaching resources most effectively. An elite could benefit from intensive study, but most should make do with 'the conclusions'.

Clunie's *First Principles* is also an attempt to grapple with this problem — and a more sustained, sophisticated and original one, not least because he attempts to draw an educational method from his conception of Marxism. 'The professional academic method of presentation is not appreciably grasped by the worker', Clunie maintained (1920: x):

> *such method does not belong to his actual life. Spheres of industry are natural conditions, implements of production are natural conditions, human labour is a natural condition; hence the most natural condition for the teaching of working class education is the workshop.*

Clunie's solution was a 'method of objective presentation', which rested on 'the Marxian-Dietzgen dialectic'. 'Method is the key to the secret of understanding. The objective method is the constructive form embodied and manifested in the Dietzgen System of Philosophy and the theoretical systems of Karl Marx.' (Clunie 1920: x.) The method was the key: with this method — the kernel, as it were, of Marxism — the mysteries of the social world could be unlocked. Thus

> *History records the life process of the past to the present, providing the material upon which the wage-labourer student must build ... by a profound method of general observance, aided by the ability to divide and sub-divide by means of an analytical classification. An intelligent analytical classification of historical data involves a method whereby the student is able to work out his objective and so arrange his matter that the human understanding may be served at a glance and the purpose*

thoroughly grasped. (Clunie 1920: 1.)

So Clunie maintained that Marxist theory was educationally important because it gave working class students a profound method of understanding social phenomena. Once they had grasped the method, understanding became intuitive, rather than a matter of prolonged intellectual enquiry. But Marxism's being in this way a science also had vital pedagogical implications.

> *Marx was a master of method. By means of an analytical division, sub-division, and classification of the Capitalist structure he wrote 'Das Capital' [sic] in such a form that it is capable of being reproduced in objective diagrams. (Clunie 1920: xi.)*

As a result, Clunie's book is peppered with 'self-explanatory diagrams [often of bewildering complexity] which may be reproduced in full size on paper, on the blackboard or, better than all, on the screen. By this method popularity impels realism and raises the dismal science to a position of profound interest' (1920: xi).

So from its very early days, labour college tutors up and down the country were developing approaches to the problems of educating working class students whose average levels of knowledge (and perhaps ability) became more basic as the number of classes grew. At the same time came pressure from the centre. Through the twenties and thirties, labour achieved ever stronger representation in local and central government, and in various quasi-governmental bodies. Unions grew, and their organisation matured; collective bargaining became more institutionalised. The demand for education in — as it were — more practically useful issues strengthened, and Millar was determined to meet the demand:

> *The Labour Colleges had originally confined their attention largely to economics and history, especially to industrial history, Marxian economics and the materialist conception of history. ... But as the labour movement began rapidly to enlarge its membership, and as some of its members attained positions of responsibility, the curriculum had to be widened so as to embrace not only new subjects but also functionally useful subjects. (Millar 1979: 209.)*

The centrepiece of Millar's strategy from 1923 or 1924 onward was to tailor educational programmes increasingly to the needs of the labour movement. But the labour movement which was emerging, and which became more and more entrenched from the mid-1920s, was no longer dominated by the revolutionary socialists. Rather than the revolutionary overthrow of capitalism, the transition to socialism would be based on a progressive achievement of power in the institutions of a state seen as open to democratic influence.

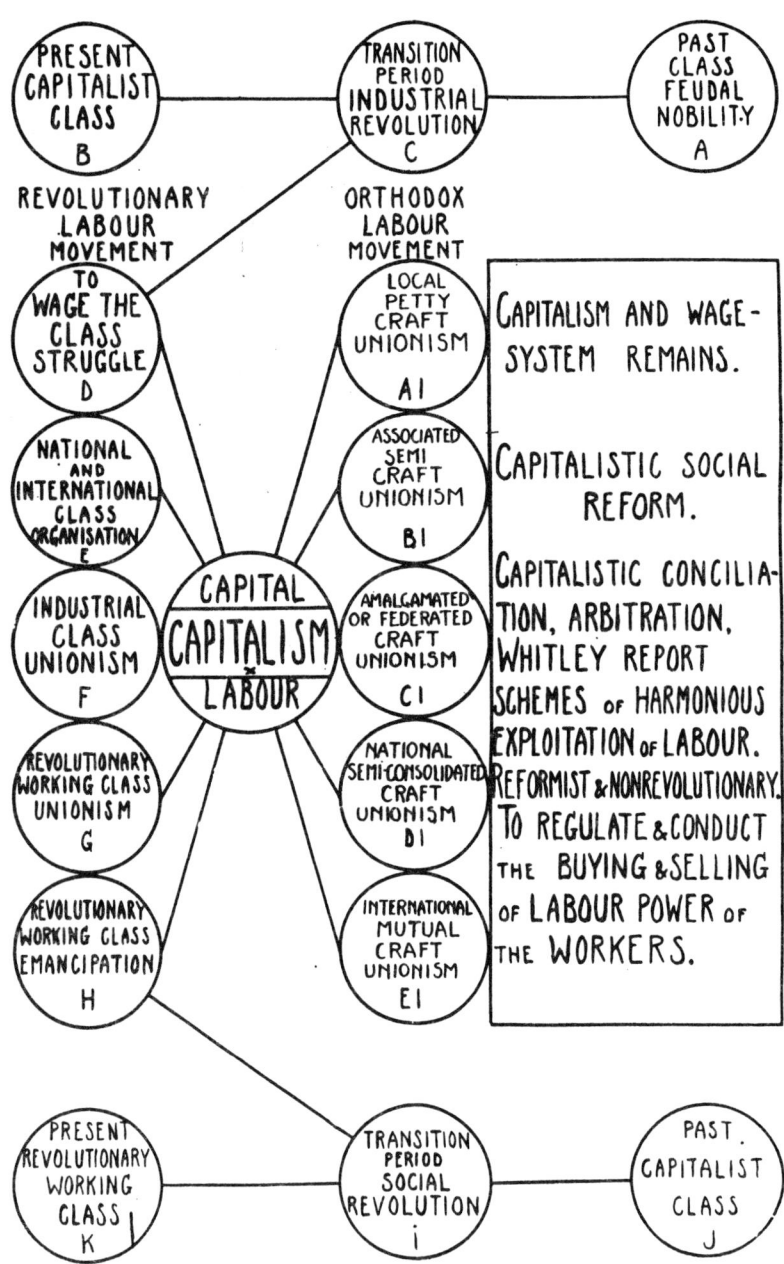

Fig.3.1: The Evolution of the Working-Class Movement. One of James Clunie's 'self-explanatory diagrams'. Primarily a teaching aid, it was accompanied by a 'reading order of the diagram' and an extended commentary.

The Millar strategy, if we may so label it,[1] was helped by a number of factors which need not long detain us. The Communist Party — which had become the repository of the great bulk of the revolutionary traditions on which the early labour college movement drew — consciously distanced itself from the colleges during the mid-twenties. For five or six years from 1928 it was consciously distancing itself from the entire labour movement. This may have strengthened the Party's own educational coherence and level (probably it did not): but it undoubtedly left the field to the Millar line within the labour colleges.[2] The Marxism of both labour colleges and Communist Party was ill-adjusted to addressing the problems of depression. A trade union's involvement in the colleges was often a matter of controversy. Decisions to affiliate could be reversed, and the colleges felt a need to provide a curriculum which would appear relevant to the national union officers — especially in view of the developing competition from the WETUC.

A problem in delivering uniformity in the curriculum was the quality of the labour colleges' tutors. Central to the colleges' approach, of course, was their rejection of state control and state funding. This meant, as a rule, that their officers and tutors were unpaid. (There were a few salaried organisers.) On a WEA view, of course, they were also unqualified: WEA tutors were normally expected to have degrees, but few NCLC tutors did. However, this is not to say that they were untrained, nor that the labour colleges ignored the quality of their teaching. Some tutors had been students of the CLC (in 1923 one-quarter of CLC graduates were NCLC tutors), but even this was not a sufficient source. In 1924 some tutors were 'inadequately qualified': a test and training were recommended. When the CLC closed, the educational quality of the local colleges was severely undermined (Senturia 1930: 682). Although the NCLC executive committee recognised the need for regular tutor training facilities, money was too short to allow a coherent or sustained response. Some NCLC divisions contributed to a national fund for this purpose, but 'the majority pleaded poverty' (Millar 1979: 114). Some divisions organised their own programmes. Fred Casey, for example, was the central figure in a 50-week tutor training course in South East Lancashire, which emphasised his own approach to 'method in thinking' (Cohen 1990a: 122-4). Many tutors had, of course, been local labour college students, and many were students and teachers in different classes simultaneously (Millar 1979: 184). Training and support were provided when postal courses were introduced, and made available free to tutors. Tutor quality, and the absence of coherent training, were nevertheless recurring problems — never satisfactorily resolved — which made the implementation of Millar's new strategy more difficult.

What did the shift to the Millar strategy mean in practice? It implied, first, an increasing emphasis in the colleges' promotional activities on the notion of 'independent working class education', rather than socialist or Marxist education. The term 'working class' referred more and more to who was being educated rather than to the nature of the education itself. For James Clunie or John Maclean, for instance, 'working class education' would have been virtually synonymous with Marxist or socialist education: Millar and his supporters were shifting to a more institutional or descriptive interpretation. It meant, second, a shift toward more practically useful topics such as 'Britain's Economic Problems, Local Government, Secretaryship, Economic and Political Geography' (Millar 1979: 209). It meant, third (and reflecting the kind of thinking Casey had outlined), a programme of shorter rather than longer courses. Twelve weekly meetings became the preferred format. In longer courses, it was felt that

> the level of attendance tended to fall off during the second half, that in order to keep interest alive it was desirable to cover more than one major theme in a given year, and that the more separate courses there were, the greater the number of people who could attend. Moreover, twelve-lesson courses were less strain on the tutors. (Millar 1979: 196.)

The programmes offered by the NCLC in one city, Edinburgh, between the wars show some of this strategic shift (see Table 3.1). We see here the introduction of 'practical' classes even by the mid-1920s. But it is clear too that there was continued provision of highly 'political' courses. Provision elsewhere seems to have followed a broadly similar pattern (Cohen 1990: esp. 120-22, 129-30; Jones 1984: esp. 95-9).

Millar's new strategy also saw the introduction of what was to prove one of the NCLC's most profound contributions: distance learning or, as they were then known, postal courses. Millar was to become a firm advocate of this method, which made NCLC education available to isolated workers as far afield as the Shetlands and, later, Commonwealth countries. He rejected the suggestion that correspondence learning 'can never be anything more than second best'. Correspondence courses could be better than face-to-face tuition. The 'average lecturer or teacher is ... usually second class, and sometimes third class, because first class people are comparatively rare', and in any case, many teachers had no training as teachers. When a 'properly run postal courses institution' such as the NCLC prepared a course, on the other hand,

> it does not go to a third class or a second class lecturer. It goes to a first class man. Not content with getting a draft from him, that draft may be gone over by several other experts .... Moreover, the course itself is edited by an expert not only in editing but in knowing the kind of people for whom the course is intended.

Table 3.1: Courses Provided by the Labour College in Edinburgh 1925, 1926, and 1938

1925 (Oct/Dec)	Economic Geography; Elementary Marxian Economics; Evolution of Capitalism; Esperanto; Chairmanship of Meetings, Public Speaking, Debating; Evolution of Man; Imperialism; Evolution of Capitalism; Early Social Development
1926 (Jan/Mar)	History of European Working Class; Economics (Marxian); Esperanto; Literature during Capitalism; Trade Union Law; Business Meeting Routine; Crises in History; Evolution in Capitalism; Social Development
1938/39	Social Development; Economic History; History of the Labour Movement; Modern Social Problems; Marxian Economics; Imperialism and Economic Geography; Psychology for Workers; General Evolution and Evolution of Man; Chairmanship and Public Speaking; Business Meeting Routine; Electioneering; Debating; Scientific Way of Thinking

Sources: *Labour Standard* 26 September 1925, 9 January 1926; Edinburgh Trades and Labour Council 1938/39: 33.

The postal course lessons also provided a 'specially written book' which could be referred to later. The postal student received individual feedback from the tutor, as well as a model answer, and overall 'more training in putting his ideas in writing'. (Millar 1965: 285.) In contrast to most NCLC classes, the postal course also provided a 'reliable means of certification' (Millar 1979: 215).

Commencing in 1923, within three years the NCLC was offering twelve courses with 2,373 postal students: by the later thirties there were over 10,000 postal students annually, while during the 1950s and early 1960s the number varied between 15,000 and 22,000 (Millar 1979: 54, 252; see also 214-27). Apart from the educational arguments, the postal strategy provided Millar with a sector of work over which the NCLC central office had virtually total control, and with which it could respond to the needs of the nationally affiliated unions. (Millar's wife, Christine Millar, a former teacher, was co-ordinator of the postal courses department.) For many local labour college activists, however, these 'costly correspondence courses ... starved the local colleges of funds' (Cohen 1990a: 118), 'discouraged local initiative and stultified the movement' (Cohen 1990a: 133). Cohen estimates (though on what seem questionable assumptions) that in 1936

> *nearly two-thirds of the NCLC's income was spent on only 7,000 correspondence students and central administration whereas the one-third allocated to local colleges provided a service for 15,000 class students. ... [As a result] many able voluntary tutors decided they could serve the labour movement more effectively in other ways ... (Cohen 1990a: 133.)*

The shift in the labour colleges' strategy—touching language, curriculum, development strategy — was, however, no more than a shift. The colleges remained socialist and Marxian in ethos. For many years they were the only significant source of Marxism in Britain outside the Communist Party. But as the Communist Party 'bolshevised' the mainstream of British Marxism, the labour colleges took a different track. They were ideologically more rooted in the pre-1914 world: class struggle was vital to their understanding of society and social change, but so too was a Darwinian view of evolution. This notion of society as evolving organism was shared by many on the centre and right of the labour movement, such as Ramsay MacDonald — a trend characterised by Macintyre (1980a: 47-65) as 'Labour Socialism'. The Darwinian Marxism of the labour colleges was always susceptible to influence from the right; many labour college figures were seen by the Communists as cloaking right-wing theories in Marxist language. As Tsuzuki (1983: 199) has argued, labour college Marxism between the wars was 'the Marxism of the Second International in the sense that it was revisionist at heart', happier accommodating itself to British utilitarianism and evolutionism than making a radical — Leninist — break with these traditions. But this contradictory position — reformism speaking the language of revolution — meant the labour colleges were a relatively congenial home for a wide range of views: perhaps an appropriate attitude for an educational body.

In 1927, a local labour college organiser — a veteran of the pre-war Central Labour College and a former South Wales miner — summed up the object of his college's classes:

> *1. To turn out reliable members of the industrial, political, and co-operative departments of the Labour Movement, by giving them a grounding in economic and political science; and,*
>
> *2. Making these members useful practically by teaching them the elements of Public Speaking, the Routine of Business Meetings, Trade Union Law, Trade Union Accounts, and Business Methods, also Esperanto (Gibbons 1927).*

This succinctly described the aims of the labour college movement between the wars. But the notion of reliability was a contested one — reliable to whom? Although temporarily it might mask the tension between serving the movement and the colleges' own educational aims, it was in reality a recognition that 'independent working class education' was ultimately education to meet the ends of the labour movement itself.

Development Strategies and the Curriculum: the WEA and the WETUC

The cornerstone of the WEA's inter-war strategy for developing educational work with trade unions was the WETUC. The strategy was based on the approach outlined in the 1921 Trade Unions' Educational Inquiry Committee Report (reprinted in Corfield 1969: 209-28.) The crux of the Report was its proposal that trade unions (and the TUC) should develop their own educational programmes. Apart from the Iron and Steel Trades Confederation,

> *no trade union has yet devised a way by which interest in education may be stimulated amongst its members and a demand — varying from single lectures to full-time courses of study — provided for and an educational enthusiasm and tradition developed within the trade union movement generally under conditions adequately controlled by the trade unions themselves. (Corfield 1969: 209.)*

It proceeded to argue, of course, for the ISTC-WETUC scheme, whilst extending some concessions to the supporters of independent working-class education in the interests of unity. But the Report was original in more than its mere proposal that unions should establish their own schemes.

It made, first of all, the case for education for trade unionists as such. It did not argue for working-class education, nor for education for the labour movement, but for the education of trade unionists. Of course, this was no doubt in part a matter of opportunism: of making a case in the terms most likely to be accepted. But the significant point is that these *were* the terms in which no mean collection of union officials felt their recommendations were likely to be best received. The authors argued that the pace of social and industrial change 'gives education a new meaning to trade unionists' (Corfield 1969: 211).

But second, the Report argued primarily for the education of trade union representatives and officers, rather than of members in general. (It did not oppose the latter: indeed, it made a number of specific proposals to advance the education of various union members. But the emphasis was unmistakeably on the official and representative.) The case was that

47

> *so far as possible, trade unionists, but more especially those holding positions of responsibility in executive, district, and branch organisations, should be men and women having a wide range of knowledge germane to economic and political problems, and such trained capacity as will enable them not only to understand the immediate results of decisions and actions but also to foresee possible ultimate results (Corfield 1969: 211).*

This argument was grounded above all in some of the then recent changes in how trade unions functioned, in the nature of industrial relations, and in the relationship between trade unions and the state. 'Trade union government,' the Report (Corfield 1969: 211) maintained, 'involves an ever-increasing responsibility. The administration of trade union rules and regulations has become more intricate and difficult, and each new amalgamation and federation increases these complexities.'

This case had implications for the content — as well as the target groups — of union education. As the quotation above shows, the Report envisaged these people 'holding positions of responsibility' as being educated in a 'wide range of knowledge'. But they also required more specific skills. 'Branch records require[d] to be kept with greater accuracy'; friendly and unemployment benefit had to be 'administered' in compliance not only with union rules but 'with the regulations governing ... the National Health Insurance and Unemployment Acts' (Corfield 1969: 211-12). In negotiations with employers and 'before the arbitration court', 'mental alertness and trained minds are more and more essential' if unions were 'to hold their own', especially in view of the resources available to employers. And

> *Vital questions of policy and principle tend to shift more and more from national executives to branch and district committees, and executive officers require to rely to an increasing extent on branch and district officers for such interpretation of their decisions as will maintain harmony and unity within the union (Corfield 1969: 212).*

However, if we examine the 'wide range of subjects now being studied by trade union students', we find not just 'the whole field of social science' but 'many other subjects which are not usually included in this category, such as literature, music and art' (Corfield 1969: 212). Such subjects were in no sense the product of a narrow view of organisational requirement. The implicit view was that 'intelligent loyalty' and 'tact and trained judgement' should be developed in the general membership. 'The power, prestige, and influence of trade unionism rests on the mental calibre of its membership.' (Corfield 1969: 212.)

This seems, in part, to have been a conflation of the authors' case for education for union office-holders with its general but little-argued desire for more general education of trade unionists. But an important assumption was spelled out, which parallels comments by some more recent writers on adult learning.

> *The majority of working men and women leave school before they have acquired the reading, much less the study, habit. On leaving school new interests enter into their lives that take up all their spare time for periods from six to twenty or more years. Usually it is only when confronted with the more serious problems of life, or through interests in the aims and objects of their respective organisations, that the desire for study is awakened. (Corfield 1969: 213-14.)*

In short, motivation was central to education, and would take place better when related to developments in an individual's life. For trade unionists, this would often be when some new role was taken on. There was, to be sure, a need to support and encourage the individual. 'For many reasons (one of the most important being their doubt as to their capacity to undertake study),' many trade unionists 'do not seek opportunities' (Corfield 1969: 214). But the fundamental inspiration would come from the development of individuals' careers within the trade union movement.

This was based on firm assumptions about the permanence and stability of trade unionism within the body politic — of a labour culture. It reflects, no doubt, the mood born of the state's wartime wooing of labour; and to that extent it proved ill-founded. But the essential realisation — that education follows and extends, rather than initiates, individual or group development — was an important principle, which has remained at the root of a central strand in trade union education.

Of course, the 1921 Inquiry Report's recommendations were never carried through in the fullness desired by its authors. The WETUC became and remained very much the creature of the WEA; the bridge with the NCLC was never built. But it is worth exploring two issues. How far were the aims and methods of the Report realised in terms of educational practice? And what, in practice, were the similarities and divergences between WETUC and the labour colleges? Let us look at the subject matter of courses offered; at their length and shape; at the depth of study and the teaching methods employed.

Just as the early WETUC was the child of the WEA, so its classes were remarkably similar to the WEA's own provision (and to that of the university extra-mural departments) — where, indeed, its provision was separate, as often it was not. In Kent, for instance, its early activities were restricted: 'it remits class fees and provides scholarships to Summer and Week-end schools' (Baker 1931: 42). But even where the WETUC employed its own tutor-organisers, there was little difference to be seen in the early years. Classes on 'Industrial History' and the 'Social Movement in the

Nineteenth Century' were provided in South Wales in 1921/22; 'Social Economics', 'Political Science' and 'Historical Economics' were reported from Scotland. As the 1920s progressed, however, and particularly into the 1930s, there was some movement. In 1924/25, workers' control was a central theme of five of the twenty-one subjects dealt with in the WETUC's weekend schools; while seven dealt with trade unionism generally, three with nationalisation, two with trade unionism and the law, and one with housing. Corfield (1969:61) comments that these seem 'a little remote from the immediate problems of the day', pointing out that no school dealt directly with economic policy or collective bargaining, while only one tackled wages. This smacks of hindsight: in the early 1920s, collective bargaining was by no means a universal trade union function, and even in 1925, many saw nationalisation and workers' control as offering realistic solutions to trade union issues.[3] The more interesting shift is from the academic, discipline-oriented classes of 1921/22, to a stronger issue-orientation three years later.

Gradually, the WETUC began to provide courses of more immediate practical value to trade unions. By the 1930s, a correspondence course on English composition and grammar dealt with 'the rudiments of expression' (Corfield 1969: 68). Special branch officials' courses, dealing with the technical aspects of their duties, were organised for NATSOPA, for the Post Office Workers, for the Civil Service Clerical Association, and for the Post Office Engineers. Weekend schools were organised for young Post Office Workers Union members. The balance of provision, in terms of length and pattern, also shifted. The early predominance of the tutorial class was eroded — in proportional rather than absolute terms — by the advance of the day and weekend school, which became something of a hallmark of the WETUC, and the correspondence course. While the number of tutorial classes had risen from 46 in 1930 to 74 eight years later (and the total number of (evening) classes from 101 to 171), the correspondence courses, which were only initiated in 1932, had 568 students by 1938. The weekend and day school provision was established in the early twenties: during the thirties something over eighty such schools were promoted in virtually every year, enrolling between 3,000 and 6,000 students. (For detailed statistics see Corfield 1969: 248-9.)

What, then, of the teaching methods employed, and the depth of study which resulted? At a formal level, the WETUC at this stage regarded standards as being assured by association with Ruskin College and the university extra-mural departments: hence the emphasis on the tutorial class as the flagship of provision. When launching the correspondence programme, care was taken ensure a link with Ruskin. More informally, much weight was attached to the involvement in the WEA of such intellectual and academic 'heavyweights' as R.H. Tawney, G.D.H. Cole, Harold Laski, Barbara Wootton, and Hugh Dalton: who also typically valued highly their involvement with the trade union provision of the WEA.

The extent to which respected and worthy institutions and individuals, some at the frontiers of their disciplines, sought involvement in the WEA and WETUC is impressive, and historically significant. Yet we cannot infer from this that the educational experiences of trade union or working class students in WETUC and WEA classes were uniformly (indeed, ever) of a high standard. In contrast to the NCLC, the WEA and WETUC approach was to employ and pay academically qualified tutors. The assumption was that tutors would explain all (or both: the choice of terminology can be revealing) sides of an issue; students would then be able to make up their own minds. Of course, this was an ideal: apart from the question of how far tutors were knowledgeable enough to put both sides, there was a tendency to base presentations on what were currently considered the acceptable bounds of debate in academic circles — with the not uncommon result that 'all sides' excluded the Marxist! (The strength of the labour colleges does seem to have been a corrective to this: despite the vicious polemic of their ideologues, there was a strong degree of cross-fertilisation at the grass roots, with students attending classes in both organisations (Macintyre 1980a: 74-5, 88-9).)

Moreover, as Brown (1980: 116) suggests, when the WEA's Socratic approach was 'handled badly' it could have unintended and adverse results. Students who came to classes looking for solutions might instead find themselves more confused and uncertain about where the truth lay. As Barbara Wootton (1937: quoted Brown 1980: 117), a committed and able WEA tutor, had it, the danger was that with excessive scepticism 'the [student's] original practical and constructive approach gets forgotten, the vital drive is lost, and the only tangible and lasting gift that the expert leaves his student is inoculation with the Socratic tradition'. She proposed that at the end of a class's process of inquiry, students should commit themselves to conclusions. 'I do quarrel with a sceptical tradition which is sceptical and nothing else,' she wrote. Other WEA tutors disagreed. J.L. Stocks, for example, complained in 1936 that many of his students were 'too much interested in the conclusion of the argument, too little interested in the methods and consisderations by which the conclusion is reached' (quoted Brown 1980: 118).

Typically, the WEA or WETUC class seems to have consisted of a lecture, lasting perhaps an hour, followed by discussion. An early study of adult education in Kent (Baker 1931: 68) remarked on the introduction into a class in 1922/23 of 'a new method, of opening up points for discussion throughout the two hours'. This probably remained the exception: most tutors seem to have delivered a lecture of some length (during which note-taking might be encouraged). Such lectures themselves could, of course, be moving. Brown (1980: 118) quotes a student — a greaser in a cotton mill — who attended Stocks' Rochdale class:

> *I absorbed all that I could from my tutor, and as I sat listening to his wise and so charmingly delivered talks, I earnestly hoped that the day might come when I should be as cultured, as wise, and as gentle as he.*

After the lecture came discussion. Very often class discussions were 'combative occasions' (Brown 1980: 118), where students — frequently associated with some political or trade union organisation or trend — would argue with their tutor and with other students. The first Secretary of the WEA in Wales actually feared that the influence of students in classroom discussions was making some WEA classes 'a disseminating ground for Marxian teachings to be discussed, if not actually spread' (quoted Brown 1980: 119-20). Whether combative discussions, clearly often resembling political debates, were the best way of developing habits of intellectual inquiry among students is a moot point. We may also wonder at the nature of the political skills which they encouraged, and their impact on the nature of British socialism.

There were more innovative developments, however. G.D.H. Cole organised one of his classes in the early 1920s as a role play of a joint council for the railway industry. Cole, Laski, and others produced annotated bibliographies in the social sciences for tutors' and students' use. Leading figures, at least, in the WEA, WETUC and extra-mural world were aware of the need to provide extra support and counselling for working class and trade union learners. 'It has been necessary to build up slowly, and it requires several years of ordinary Tutorial Class work before the conditions necessary for advanced work can be secured' (Peers 1926: 17). Cole wrote a guide to reading and writing, which sold in thousands in the forties and fifties: probably it expressed methods and approaches he had been using earlier (Corfield 1969: 104-05). And certainly when the WETUC began to provide correspondence courses in the 1930s, Ernest Green (the WEA's Assistant General Secretary) soon remarked that they were 'one of the most expensive and, unless properly controlled, one of the least effective methods of education' (quoted Corfield 1969: 67).

If we compare the WEA and WETUC with the labour colleges, what conclusions can we draw? The WEA and WETUC started from a clearer statement of policy and strategy in the early 1920s. Their policy and strategy were rather more closely associated with trade union — as distinguished from working class or labour movement — education; but this was a distinction of degree rather than of kind. In both traditions provision in the area of organisational skills tended to increase during the later twenties and thirties. On balance, though, this trend was probably more pronounced in the labour colleges, with their greater reliance on union funds, and with the increasingly abstract nature of their Marxist commitment. Both traditions had to cope with the unpalatable fact that the labour advance of 1919 and 1920 did not last. Opportunities for growth did not arrive in the areas where they had been thought most likely. Probably the WEA was more creative and innovative in teaching methods, at least to modern eyes: but we should not underestimate the labour colleges' achievement in providing a vast programme using voluntary tutors without formal qualifications. The degree of commitment among labour college tutors and students was remarkable. The labour colleges in particular, but also the WETUC, made advances in distance learning (which they, more modestly, referred to as postal or correspondence courses). Both were successful in recruiting very substantial numbers of trade unionists into adult education. Both made strenuous attempts to make the education relevant to their students demands. Both were — within their lights — democratic.

We began this section by remarking that, for the WEA, education for trades unionists was always a missionary question: of 'going out to', rather than of self-education. How far did the WETUC enable the WEA to become (or, not to prejudge the issue, to remain) an organisation of trade unionists? In fact, we can only give an approximate answer to this question — but nonetheless a helpful one. To a large extent the trade union movement was, for the WEA, a surrogate for the working class in general: a mechanism for reaching those people education did not otherwise reach. (But only to an extent: the trade unions were also seen as important in themselves, as vehicles by which the people in a newly democratic state would generate and train their own leaders.) In a study of *Adult Education in the East Midlands*, Peers (1926: 42) found that 46 per cent of extra-mural students were 'manual workers', whilst another 21 per cent were 'non-manual workers (clerks, municipal employees, etc.)', and a further 13 per cent were 'women engaged in domestic duties'. An occupational analysis of all WEA students in England and Wales in 1931/32 suggests that 33 per cent were 'manual workers', 23 per cent 'clerical, shop and postal workers, etc.', and 23 per cent were engaged in 'domestic and home duties'. Even if the manual working class figure did not decline during the 1930s, it had fallen to 22 per cent by 1946/47. (Fieldhouse 1977: 29.) While not strictly comparable, it seems likely that the work of WETUC — at best — merely reduced a general trend for the working class student to represent a smaller proportion of total WEA provision. (The total number of working class students, of course, no doubt grew broadly in line with the overall scale of WEA activities.)

Workers' Education and the Labour Movement between the Wars

When such pioneers of workers' education as J.P.M. Millar were asked to assess their achievement between the wars, they typically referred to the role played by former workers' education students in building the post-war labour movement. The number of former labour college and WEA tutors and students in Attlee's government is a commonplace. 'Scores of NCLCers are among the MPs elected to the House of Commons,' Millar reported to his executive committee in 1945. Three were original Ruskin strikers; four were members of the Cabinet; five were parliamentary secretaries. (Millar 1979: 131-2.) The WEA was if anything better represented. Less frequently pointed out is how far the leadership of post-war trade unionism (not merely at general secretary and presidential, but at national and regional officer level) — and through to the 1960s and 1970s — was moulded in the inter-war labour college movement and WEA.[4] And while the educational bodies lost no time in claiming credit by association with the achievement of Labour in 1945, they have as yet largely escaped criticism as the post-war Labour record has been re-evaluated.

Labour educational organisations can legitimately claim credit when they have proved responsible for educating a substantial section of the labour leadership. But what was the legacy of workers' education between the wars for the post-war education of trade unionists? Four main features stand out.

First, workers' education between the wars was education for activists. The men and women who attended WEA and labour college classes were, in the main, people who organised trade unions, Labour Party branches, trades councils, and so forth. This was often not by design: but it was a reality. To this extent, workers' education was (to use a term introduced a quarter century later) 'role education': education related to specific social roles played by the students.[5] This was, of course, quite explicit in the case of the NCLC and the WETUC — not to mention Ruskin and the CLC. Their organisers would have scoffed at the notion that workers' education could be separated from the political and trade union activities of their students. The labour colleges, the WETUC, were part of the labour movement; they shared its aims (though often disagreeing about what these were!)[6] This tradition, that education of labour is education for labour movement purposes stemmed naturally from the political climate of the period. It was carried forward into the post-war years, as we shall see. But the notion of the 'labour movement' was changing. In the early 1920s the idea of a clear division between the political and industrial dimensions of the labour movement would have been unthinkable for many. During the later 1920s and 1930s legal and political developments made it rather more marked. After 1945 Labour governments often found themselves in conflict with the trade union movement. The notion of a single labour movement — albeit encompassing political and industrial wings — weakened. The nature of the movement to which workers' education related therefore shifted, and in ways not always fully comprehended at the time. This has had a profound impact: education related to a labour movement has different requirements, and is subject to different pressures, from education concerned with trade unions alone.

Workers' education before 1939 was also beset by a tension between being the servant of a movement, and the views of labour college (and to a lesser extent WEA) activists that workers' education should be an agent for social change. On one influential — indeed, predominant — view, the role of education as servant of the movement implied serving the aims and objectives specified by those duly elected and appointed to positions of leadership. It also meant providing education or training for the trade union and Labour Party official — whether lay or full-time — in the skills required to execute his or her role. For others, in contrast, the aims of workers' education were established not by the leaders or democratic processes of the labour movement, but rather by the political or revolutionary aims of the movement itself. These views could, of course, co-exist: but there was a tension. The tension was carried forward into the post-war world, where it was complicated by the belief of some that the social changes which the movement had fought for were largely achieved.

Third, there was a recurring tension between the view that education should relate to the specific organisational role of the student, and the view that education should have an important 'wider' dimension. This wider dimension was social, economic, political, historical and so forth: for the labour colleges, from a socialist or Marxist perspective; for the WEA from a more liberal perspective. This tension was related to, and somewhat confused by — though in principle is distinct from — the common view that education in wider issues should be related to the practical tasks of the worker. This tension remained a central theme in post-war debates on workers' and trade union education.

Finally, from its inter-war experiences the TUC had learnt a strong and abiding scepticism of collaboration with the educational bodies: the WEA and the NCLC. It regarded both as often irresponsible, always unpredictable. In the post-war world its approach was to proceed in the educational field, as far as possible, alone. The great practical difference was that where between the wars the TUC was unable to assert effective authority over well-entrenched educational bodies, after 1945 its position was very much enhanced. And while in the thirties it could offer little beyond a modest summer school programme,[7] by the 1960s it had established a measure of educational expertise and self-confidence.

1   Others shared this approach, but Miller's singleminded commitment to it, and his domination of the organisation, justify the personified label.

2   Communist-labour college relations have been much discussed: see esp. Phillips and Putnam 1980: esp. 31-8; Macintyre 1980a: esp. 81-3; Miles 1984; Ree 1984: esp. 46-55; Simon 1990b: 58-63.

3   It is also worth noting that 'industrial democracy' formed an element of the TUC's curriculum in the 1970s and 1980s.

4   This assertion is based on impressions gathered from wide reading of labour and trade union histories and biographies, rather than hard evidence: but cp Brown 1977: esp. 51-4; Craik 172-6; Jones 1984; Millar 1979: 193-4; Stocks 1953: 143.

5   On role education, see Chapter 7 below.

6   For the WEA, of course, it was not so unambiguously clear that workers' education had to be linked to labour movement aims and activities: but the importance of 'role education' is demonstrated by the decision to establish the WETUC.

7   The TUC's summer schools of the 1930s had some lasting impact. Partly because of the prominence of the NCLC and WETUC (and their unhappy relations), these schools proceeded in non-contentious ('industrial' rather than 'political') curriculum areas. To the extent that the TUC established an educational tradition and expertise between the wars, therefore, it was of this character: and this coloured its post-war educational thinking.

Chapter 4

The Development of the TUC Education Scheme 1945–1968

There are many studies of the early years of British workers' education. The long feud between the Workers' Educational Association and the National Council of Labour Colleges has been a recurring theme. There has been less interest in studying the development of workers' education after 1945. Although Labour set the parameters of politics in the post-war years, paradoxically the language of 'working class' became taboo. The term 'workers' education' itself became less popular, subsumed within a spectrum of less contentious terms: adult education, community education, education for the disadvantaged — and trade union education.

If there is a direct line of institutional descent from the Workers' Educational Trade Union Committee and the NCLC to modern trade union education, it lies in the education scheme built up by the Trades Union Congress since 1945, and especially since 1964. Yet this — and the entire area of trade union education — has been the subject of remarkably little sustained study. No full-length study has been published since well before the critical year (1964) when the NCLC and WETUC ceased to be, and only two before that (WEA 1953; Clegg and Adams 1959). This applies alike to studies from the perspectives of education, adult education or industrial relations. Official reports have been few, and while some have been politically significant, none has been based on deep research.[1]

Yet during recent years, there has been a burgeoning of minor studies of aspects of the TUC scheme in adult education journals (there is still very little coverage of trade union education within industrial relations literature). Most have been written by the staff of British university extra-mural departments (Campbell and McIlroy 1986; McIlroy 1985b, 1985c, 1988a, 1988b, 1990a, 1990b, 1990c; McIlroy and Spencer 1989; Mackie 1986; Vulliamy 1985). Most are highly critical of the TUC's education scheme. The burden of their critique — or at least that of McIlroy, the most prolific — is an uneasy blend of a leftist political critique of corporatism, conspiracy theory, mainstream educational liberalism in the university extra-mural tradition, and Marxist or Socialist education in the labour college mould. The post-war TUC, he argues (1985c), increasingly close to government and concerned above all with controlling its ever more errant lay workplace representatives, saw trade union education as a method of instilling basic practical skills, knowledge of procedure, and so forth. Shop stewards were to be trained in the proper execution of their function, rather than to question what that function might be. In pursuit of this aim, the TUC and its Education Department established and maintained firm central control over the content and methods of trade union courses.

Post-war trade union education, and particularly the TUC's activities in the field, have naturally reflected the outlooks of the TUC. The TUC developed in the 1950s and 1960s what has been termed a 'corporatist' view of its role in society and the national economy (Panitch 1976; Winkler 1976); its development during the 1960s and 1970s was in a close — if changing — relationship with the state.[2] But to view the TUC education scheme primarily as a control strategy, designed to suppress or channel dissent, conceals — or distracts attention from — its substantive and substantial achievements.

This chapter surveys the organisational development of the TUC education scheme from the end of the second world war to the later 1960s, and the main factors which account for this. By the late 1960s the first of two major shifts in post-war trade union education had occurred, and the scene was set for the second. The TUC had supplanted the NCLC and WETUC, and had moved on to develop the central planks of its own educational structure and approach (the latter being spelled out in its 1968 Report, *Training Shop Stewards*). In this chapter we are concerned primarily with structures and policies: issues of course content and method are covered in Chapter 7.

Competition in Trade Union Education 1945–1964

As we have seen, trade union education between the wars had been dominated by the NCLC and WETUC. The TUC succeeded in the far from easy task of co-operating simultaneously with two organisations which frequently treated one another as anathema. With the formation of the Labour Government in 1945, some unions began to lobby for a more planned and coherent approach. A resolution, moved by the Mineworkers at the 1945 TUC, urged

> *that steps should be taken to inaugurate a comprehensive scheme of education in all phases, with special emphasis upon those subjects calculated to be of the greatest assistance to trade unionists, and members of the working class movement in general. ... Congress calls upon the General Council to investigate the possibility of arranging a co-ordinated scheme of education run under centralised control to secure this end. (Quoted Atkins 1979: 5.)*

There was, however, little enthusiasm for this move within the TUC itself. The TUC's Education Advisory Committee responded very slowly, making no report until the 1948 Congress. Based on a survey of the views of NCLC, WEA, WETUC and Ruskin College, this proposed three possible schemes, each of which it rejected as impracticable (Atkins 1979: 5).

At the same time — and this is the key to the General Council's, and the Education Advisory Committee's, lack of enthusiasm for the 1946 resolution — the TUC had begun to establish itself as an educational provider in its own right. In 1944 it began to co-operate with the London School of Economics in providing a one-year 'advanced course' (quoted Atkins 1979: 12) 'primarily intended for persons engaged in or proposing to take up responsible work in the Trade Union Movement' (TUC 1946a: 29). It was, in effect, a staff course for actual and aspiring full-time officers.

More fundamentally, from 1946 the TUC was itself offering a programme of three- and four-week courses. 'The aim of the TUC is to fill a gap which they believe to exist ... [to] provide facilities for training those who are to serve as officers and active members of the Movement' (quoted Atkins 1979: 12). A Director of Studies[3] was appointed in 1946 'generally to take charge of these courses'.

> *The subjects covered ... will be the following: Industrial and Trade Union History; Trade Union Structure (including T.U.C.); Trade Union Organisation; Trade Union Administration and Accountancy; Industrial Relations and Negotiations (including Personnel Management); Industrial and Social Legislation (Legal Status of Trade Unions, Factories Act, Young Persons, Shops Acts, Social Insurance, National Health and Rehabilitation Services); Lectures on Work of each Department of T.U.C. by Officers in Charge (TUC 1946a: 27).*

Despite appearances, these courses were, according to the 1946 General Council report 'essentially practical in character'. But they had a shaky start, and were never a real success. The 'teaching and lecturing' was 'mainly undertaken by members of the Congress staff' whose 'departmental duties ... related to the subjects of the Courses' (TUC 1951: 161). Only eight courses were held in the first eighteen months (April 1947-September 1948), attracting 83 students; by 1951 only 25 courses had been held since 1947. Recruitment of students was a problem. The courses 'depended too much on the regular support of a very few unions'. (TUC 1951: 162.)

By the early 1950s, the TUC was aware that the mixture was not working. Matters improved, however, following the introduction of more topic- or problem-oriented courses from 1951. The initial impetus came from the TUC's Production Committee, which suggested 'one-week courses in production and management subjects for workshop representatives'.

> *[T]here was an urgent need for courses under trade union control designed to assist workshop representatives and others who represent the interests of unions in negotiations or joint consultation to acquire knowledge of the terminology, the principles and the elementary*

> *techniques of management, which would increase their effectiveness as representatives (TUC 1951: 162).*

The subjects covered reflected these concerns: 'factors in industrial productivity; works management; organisation of production; motion study; time study; systems of wage payments; job evaluation; merit rating; costing; financial accounts; trade unions and scientific management'. Most of the students were 'concerned in joint negotiations or consultations with management as shop stewards or branch officers'. Short courses also began on 'Industrial Negotiations', designed for 'younger trade union officers'. (TUC 1951: 163.)

Despite this new approach, the General Council — which rarely *admits* to error — initially reaffirmed its commitment to the four-week 'General Training Course' as the 'central feature' of TUC direct provision was maintained (TUC 1951: 163). But demand for places improved significantly, and it was soon clear that the new formula was a distinct improvement. Not only were the courses in production and management subjects maintained: the general training course was altered in their image. Following a review conference of union general secretaries and education officers in February 1953, general training course students 'of broadly similar experience' were to be recruited by the TUC itself (rather than through union nomination), and admission was to be limited to 'voluntary officers and workshop representatives' (TUC 1953: 164-5). The general training course was also shortened from four weeks to two; content was widened to include the International Labour Organisation, law, the international trade union movement, and trade unions and the control of industry (TUC 1954: 162-3).

Major early problems included shortage of adequate course accommodation. Until 1957, courses were held at Maritime House in Clapham, the headquarters of the National Union of Seamen. As long planned (TUC 1946a: 27), Congress House — the new TUC headquarters — incorporated a Training College. The two-week General Training Course was offered in two versions, designed for 'voluntary officers, members of committees and workshop representatives' and for full-time officers respectively. One-week courses were offered in Production and Management (at two levels, 'Stage 1' and 'Stage 2'); Collective Bargaining for 'newly elected or younger full-time officers'; Industrial Relations in the Workplace 'for voluntary officers and workshop representatives'; Social Security and Industrial Welfare; and Industrial Finance for those who represented 'their organisations in industrial negotiations' (TUC 1957: 164-5). During its first full year of operation 37 courses took place, with 680 students enrolled (Atkins 1979: 15), and provision remained at roughly this level — 657 students attended 35 courses in 1963/64 (TUC 1964: 190).

But it was not just the TUC which threatened the NCLC-WETUC monopoly of education for trades unionists after the war. Individual unions began to develop their own provision. Between 1948 and 1952, unions' expenditure on education doubled to £100,000 (Roberts 1956: 336). From 1949 the General and Municipal Workers began to organise courses in conjunction with technical colleges around the country, covering 'works study, ... industrial relations, methods of payment, factory organisation and production control' (WEA 1953: 95-101). In 1954 a full-time Education Officer was appointed (Clegg and Adams 1959: 61-2). The Transport and General Workers increased its expenditure on education from £4,000 in 1946 to £25,000 in 1951: a summer school was started, which grew from 51 students in its first year (1950) to 445 in 1957; syllabuses were developed to match. Although affiliated to the NCLC, the Amalgamated Engineering Union instituted a modest programme of one-week courses on management techniques for shop stewards, together with a summer school. (Clegg and Adams 1959: 59-61.)

The Mineworkers, with its highly decentralised structure, developed a wide variety of courses in conjunction with both the NCLC and WETUC; but several of its areas moved beyond these ties. Yorkshire, Derbyshire, and Nottingham built up strong links with Sheffield, Leeds, and Nottingham university extra-mural departments, running long (one to three year) day-release courses covering economics, politics, and industrial relations (Clegg and Adams 1959: 48-50; Croucher and Halstead 1990; Williams 1954). South Wales instituted a full-time training course of six to twelve months with Coleg Harlech in the late 1940s, and then from the mid-1950s, a day-release course run by its own Education Officer of 15 weeks' duration. 'The subjects are chosen so as to be related to the experience of the students, but far enough removed from their immediate interests to enable discussion to get away from the "pit-bottom"' (Clegg and Adams 1959: 63). The Scottish area developed an annual summer school covering mining issues, and 'current industrial political and economic affairs' (Clegg and Adams 1959: 63). From the late 1930s, Durham had 'a most unusual tutorial class ... conducted by its general secretary each winter' (Clegg and Adams 1959: 64), from which many of the area's leaders graduated.

The Railwaymen, despite being affiliated to the NCLC, experimented with three one-week residential schools of its own covering a wide range of topics: from 1957 the number of their schools was raised to five (each with 24 places), and the course content reduced to branch administration, industrial law and collective bargaining (Clegg and Adams 1959: 64; see also Moxley 1963: 693-5). The Shopworkers, affiliated both to the NCLC and WETUC, ran its own one week summer school (with 84 places) from 1950. In addition, 50 to 60 one-day or week-end schools were held around the country.

These developments should be kept in perspective. Throughout the period 1945-60 the NCLC organised annually between 700 and 900 classes (with between 10,000 and 15,000 students); between 200 and 400 day and weekend schools (with between 8,000 and 14,000 students); and over 2,000 branch lectures (50,000 to 90,000 attenders); 9-11 summer schools (400-700 students). It also enrolled between 15,000 and 20,000 postal course students. (These figures are rounded from Millar 1979: 267.) Although WETUC one day schools declined from a peak of 10,681 students in 1952 to 5,140 in 1962, their week-end schools grew in number, from 32 in 1945 to 229 in 1962, with an average attendance of 28 or 29 (Corfield 1969: 95-6). But the growth in TUC and individual unions' separate provision suggests some doubts over how far the educational bodies' provision was appropriate to the needs of a trade union movement in an economy of (relatively) full employment. It also suggests a desire to use education as a method of organisation-building. To some extent, the WETUC and the NCLC reflected a belief in the centrality of the — labour or trade union — movement, rather than in the particular organisations of which it was composed. To this extent, the declining status of the educational bodies was an aspect of the erosion of the ideology of 'the Movement' in the post-war world.

The post-war developments did not pass the educational bodies by unnoticed. The WEA promoted two enquiries. In 1951 it established what was almost a mini Royal Commission, chaired by the former Labour MP and Colonial Secretary, Arthur Creech Jones.[4] It included a number of trade union and academic luminaries, including Harry Douglass, General Secretary of the Iron and Steel Trades Confederation, and Professor S.G. Raybould, Director of Extra-mural Studies at Leeds University. Its Report, reflecting the then dominant TUC view, disclaimed 'any intention of elaborate system building' (WEA 1953: 84): in effect, the WEA and WETUC declined to take a major initiative. Its practical proposals were largely limited to what the WEA and WETUC themselves should do. One was potentially of major import, and could have established a leading role for the WEA in the field: the establishment of a Trade Union Education Bureau for 'the development of subject scope, teaching methods, tutor recruitment and training, and educational material' (WEA 1953: 86). A second recommended a limited number of pilot schemes. On the question of subject matter, the report acknowledged that the 'greatest present need' was in aspects of union activists' roles, but still stressed 'the value to the trade union movement of high standard education of a liberal type' (WEA 1953: 84).

In the WEA, good ideas always coincide with crises. The Creech Jones Report arrived at a difficult time. The Ashby Report (Ministry of Education 1954) lent support to serious criticism of the WEA, arguing (in effect) that the Association was ineffectual and should raise a greater proportion of its income from non-governmental sources. Only with great difficulty were funds won from the Ministry to undertake Creech Jones' proposal for pilot schemes. The proposal for a central bureau was shelved.

A few years later, Hugh Clegg was asked to review these pilot schemes (though in the event he and his collaborator, Rex Adams, widened their brief somewhat). The schemes had met with mixed success. Developing a Creech Jones proposal, Clegg and Adams (1959: 82-5; 91) suggested a 'college of trade union education which would combine the tasks of research and of preparing material with the training of tutors and certain other functions'. They also recommended that, if the WEA were to make a serious commitment to trade union education, it should appoint a member of staff of Assistant District Secretary rank to handle the trade union programme in each WEA district, reorganise districts to fit more logically with trade union regions, accept that trade union provision must be the work of full-time staff rather than (voluntary) branches, and reorganise its accounting methods.[5] Again, the WEA was unable effectively to confront the Clegg-Adams recommendations; and in due course these were overtaken by the reorganisation of the TUC scheme.

The Formation of the TUC Scheme, 1964

If it was true in the early fifties that the 'British trade union movement possesses no comprehensive and centralised scheme of education to meet the needs of its members' (WEA 1953: 14), it was more true a decade later, after the growth in union schemes. But this growth meant that the writing was on the wall for the educational bodies. The General Secretary of the NCLC, J.P.M. Millar, 'was acutely aware of the implications for the NCLC's future of the introduction of independent trade union educational schemes' (Millar 1979: 145). As he wrote in 1961 to the Durham Miners' General Secretary,

> *The competition for trade union funds for educational purposes has increased very greatly in recent years. This is because a passion has developed for unions doing some educational work of their own. Even some small unions now flatter themselves that they are doing educational work by running one week-end school that costs £200 a year for a handful of students. (Quoted Millar 1979: 145-6.)*

In 1958 USDAW, one of the NCLC's two founder unions — but one which had recently developed its own independent programmes — disaffiliated.

In these circumstances (and knowing also that Millar must soon retire after nearly forty years) the NCLC revived the notion of 'rationalising' trade union education. It sponsored a motion to the 1957 TUC which argued that 'much of the existing overlapping of educational facilities should be eliminated' and instructed the General Council 'to try to bring about a co-ordinated educational policy with affiliated unions and other educational bodies, thus making better use of the total amount of money and facilities available' (TUC 1957: 389). The motion was remitted, and initial indications from the General Council speaker — the matter was 'fraught with difficulties' (TUC 1957: 393) — were not auspicious. Behind the scenes, however, much was afoot.

The General Council had in fact decided early in 1957 to look at 'the provision of trade union facilities', but felt that 'they should take account of the results of the training college scheme which they were then planning to launch after the 1957 Congress' (TUC 1959: 383). In this review process, the development of trade union schemes, and the role of the new stratum of union education officers, was decisive.

> *The union education officers made a habit of meeting informally at the T.U.C. and frequently discussed the advantages and disadvantages of centralising education. On balance they came down firmly on the side of making a change. Many of them were impressed with the importance of strengthening the unity of the trade unions, and looked towards the development of an educational service within the T.U.C. as one of the major means of helping to achieve this. The unions' education officers felt that this was an opportunity not to be missed. (Corfield 1969: 151.)*

With the growth of this new group of education officers, the locus of influence and power in the politics of union education had shifted decisively against the NCLC and WETUC. The educational bodies could hardly influence the course of development which the NCLC had initiated. When the report emerged, it showed that unions were spending 'nearly twice as much' on their own schemes as on schemes with the NCLC and WETUC 'put together' (TUC 1959: 383). The main finding was summarised thus:

> *It is difficult, if not impossible, to escape the conclusion that the weaknesses and defects in the present provision of trade union educational facilities arise essentially from the existence of separate and rival educational organisations. Any overlapping of facilities, competition for trade union support, discouragement of unions from embarking upon educational schemes because of the prospect of rival claims, wastage of educational funds upon the maintenance of duplicate country-wide propaganda organisations, obstacles to introducing any planning into the provision of facilities and to meeting certain important current*

educational needs, seem to arise fundamentally from this basic situation. (TUC 1959: 179.)

A 'more radical change' was called for. In discussions with the TUC, the NCLC had made proposals which 'imply a readiness to sink its identity and merge its organisation in a wider structure' (TUC 1959: 179). The WETUC was far more an institution of administrative convenience; few would miss it. The two could be replaced by a single body.

The General Council then embarked on an extended period of consultation with affiliated unions, and behind-the-scenes policy formation. Two years later, at the 1961 Congress, the General Council proposed 'a national trade union educational body representative of the Movement as a whole' (TUC 1961: 179). There would be a Joint Trade Union Education Committee made up primarily of General Council members, but including representatives of the WEA and Ruskin College. This would 'arrange (in co-operation as appropriate with the Workers' Educational Association) the provision of educational facilities' intended:

(a) to provide opportunities for trade union members to undertake systematic social, economic and political studies relevant to their trade union interests;

(b) to supplement the direct provision by trade union organisations of facilities for trade union training;

(c) to provide some opportunities for trade union members to remedy deficiencies of general education which might handicap them in their trade union work; and

(d) to provide, both directly and indirectly, opportunities for trade union students to acquire some knowledge and experience of the techniques of study. (TUC 1961: 179-80.)

The recommendation was for a scheme in which all affiliated unions would be obliged to partake, financed by a grant from the General Council amounting to 2d or 3d per member. The scheme was to be inaugurated in January 1963.

In the event, it was well into 1964 before the affairs of the NCLC and WETUC were fully wound up. The delay seems to have been the result of two factors. First, the administrative, legal and financial aspects of the transfer of responsibilities proved formidable, particularly as the 'educational bodies' — particularly the NCLC — were democratic organisations. All organisations have internal politics: the NCLC had more than most, and personal tensions were overlaid by differences of political principle. Second, the NCLC showed increasing anxiety about the organisation which would succeed it. Millar had pressed that 'in addition to a national committee and regional committees the proposed new organisation should hold an annual conference, which would provide a forum for the discussion of ... trade union educational problems' (Millar 1979: 157). The General Council's 1961 plan was rather less than this, but by 1962 even the Joint Trade Union Education Committee had disappeared. A delegate expressed the fear — 'that they wish to control the whole scheme through the Education Committee of the General Council' (TUC 1962: 344). This was to prove an accurate prediction.

The TUC's desire for full control over the new education service had its roots, no doubt, in its experience since the 1920s of democracy in workers' education. But it seems to have been George Woodcock's firm resolve which ensured the exclusion of any central representative body, even of an advisory nature. Following the 1962 Congress, the Head of the Education Department, Dennis Winnard, wrote a paper for the Education Committee on 'Trade Union Educational Facilities', devoted to the new arrangements. He forwarded a draft to the General Secretary (Winnard to Woodcock: TUC inter-departmental correspondence, 2 November 1962: TUC file 817.2) with a covering memorandum requesting 'instructions concerning any amendment of the draft note'. Winnard asked in particular whether the paper should cover staffing, which was 'not normally a matter for committees'. Woodcock returned the memorandum endorsed 'OK for circulation as amended'. Following Winnard's suggestion, he had deleted the section on staffing, but — without prompting — he had made one further alteration to Winnard's draft. At the end of a paragraph on the development of 'tutorial courses', which argued that 'the co-ordination and development of this work would need to be based upon a more detailed examination of current facilities than has so far been undertaken', he deleted a single sentence. The sentence read: 'A small Advisory Panel might also be formed to assist the [Education] Committee in formulating proposals for developments in this field.'[6]

Woodcock's central role in cementing a hostile TUC attitude to the NCLC is argued (and documented from personal experience) by Millar (1979: esp. 157-69). At about the same time as Woodcock deleted any reference to an Advisory Panel, he controversially appointed Ellen McCullough — Women's Officer of the Transport and General Workers' Union and a prominent figure in the WEA — to the Education Department 'to assist in the reorganisation and development of proposed educational facilities' (General Council minutes 28 November 1962; see also Millar 162-3). But it seems clear that, as negotiations with the NCLC proceeded, others in the TUC found their patience wearing thin. There was a profound difference of perception. For the NCLC leaders, the TUC was taking responsibility for a proud and valuable heritage; the TUC's role was, with its far greater resources, to advance this tradition. The TUC, to the contrary, regarded the

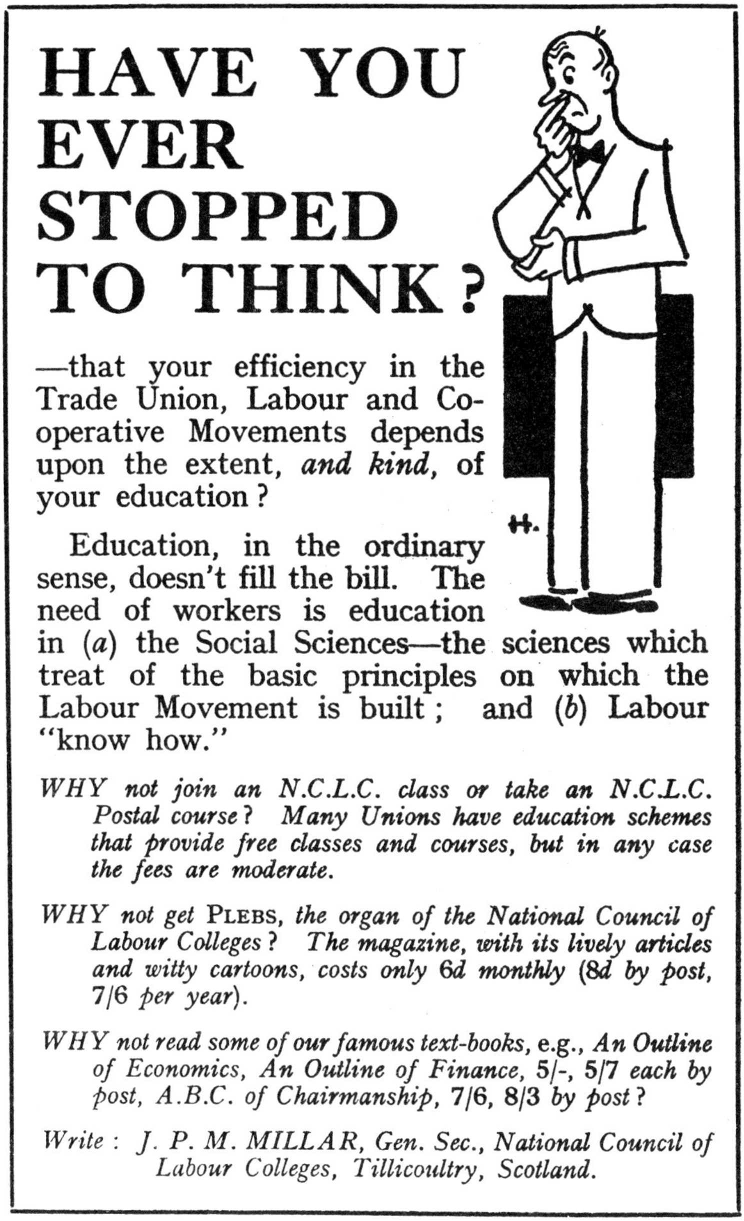

HAVE YOU EVER STOPPED TO THINK?

—that your efficiency in the Trade Union, Labour and Cooperative Movements depends upon the extent, *and kind*, of your education?

Education, in the ordinary sense, doesn't fill the bill. The need of workers is education in (*a*) the Social Sciences—the sciences which treat of the basic principles on which the Labour Movement is built; and (*b*) Labour "know how."

WHY not join an N.C.L.C. class or take an N.C.L.C. Postal course? Many Unions have education schemes that provide free classes and courses, but in any case the fees are moderate.

WHY not get PLEBS, *the organ of the National Council of Labour Colleges? The magazine, with its lively articles and witty cartoons, costs only 6d monthly (8d by post, 7/6 per year).*

WHY not read some of our famous text-books, e.g., *An Outline of Economics, An Outline of Finance*, 5/-, 5/7 each by post, *A.B.C. of Chairmanship*, 7/6, 8/3 by post?

Write: *J. P. M. MILLAR, Gen. Sec., National Council of Labour Colleges, Tillicoultry, Scotland.*

Fig. 4.1: Education for Efficiency. An early 1960s NCLC view of workers' educational needs.

labour college tradition as largely spent: the construction of a TUC education service was a mechanism for ensuring modern, co-ordinated 'educational facilities' relevant to the needs of the movement in the 1960s. They might respect the NCLC's historical role: but they did not wish to be encumbered by outdated democratic and administrative impedimenta.

For the TUC leaders, the labour college leaders appeared unable to cope with the fact that their role in history was at an end. Not only did they ask the TUC to take over their work; they wished to determine what the TUC would do when it had done so. This was unacceptable. In March 1963, Woodcock wrote to Millar about the NCLC's 'apparent reluctance ... to accept the inevitability of changes in the educational work when it came to be conducted under TUC auspices' (quoted Millar 1979: 164). In a paper submitted by Winnard to his General Secretary ('Dissolution of NCLC and WETUC', 16 August 1963: TUC file 817.2), irritation with the labour colleges is unmistakable:

> *Dissolution of the NCLC and the WETUC at a relatively early stage is essential if the General Council are to secure undivided responsibility and reasonable freedom of action in developing the educational work. ... The magazine 'Plebs' should be discontinued. ... When a firm date has been determined for the dissolution of the NCLC the WEA should be requested to dissolve the WETUC from that date or as soon thereafter as may be practicable.*

In the months leading up to the 1963 Congress, Winnard and his colleagues in the Education Department planned a role for the new TUC education service. They prescribed radical change to introduce a centrally-planned and administered regional education service. The proposals were outlined in Winnard's paper to Woodcock on the 'Dissolution of NCLC and WETUC' (16 August 1963: TUC file 817.2): 'An effective education service cannot be based upon the haphazard pattern of facilities which results from regional or local initiatives; nor upon the indiscriminate local recruitment of students by educational organisers.' The chief cost taken over by the TUC from the educational bodies was the NCLC divisional organisation, which with its eighteen divisional organisers cost not less than 'about £20,000 a year'. This NCLC regional organisation was, however, not regarded as cost-effective:

> *The Divisional Organisers secure some local publicity for the educational services, assist in the recruitment of students for the services organised centrally (postal courses and summer schools), and promote some evening classes of moderate quality. But much of the[ir] work ... takes the form of single lectures, day schools or other very short courses, mainly on subjects of topical trade union and political interest. Their services are made available to local Labour Parties, local Co-operative*

Societies and other local bodies as well as trade union organisations. The expenditure of so substantial a sum on such very short term work is not justified either educationally or financially.

The NCLC divisional organisation (along with the far less substantial WETUC) should therefore be 'dissolved'.

The TUC's 'central planning of the educational service' would require 'some information and advice about circumstances in the regions'; and there might be some continuing need for 'very short-term facilities' (Winnard's quaint term for short courses and single lectures) locally. These functions would fall to the TUC's regional advisory councils, which would be encouraged to establish educational advisory committees including trades council and WEA representation. 'In some regions as an experiment an officer (who might be one of the present NCLC organisers) might be attached to a Regional Advisory Committee to assist it in the performance of its educational role.'[7]

The TUC education scheme which came into being on the 1 January 1964 was organised by the TUC Education Department, which was responsible to the General Council through its Education Committee. Regional organisation was more substantial than Winnard's 1963 paper implied: regional education officers (initially former NCLC staff) were appointed, and regional education advisory committees, on which the WEA would be represented, were established (TUC 1964: 200-02). But the emphasis was on retaining, rather than dispersing, control. The REACs were explicitly advisory. Apart from the WEA, no providing bodies were represented as such. (In practice, however, a common Congress House gripe was that REACs were dominated by tutors, often co-opted in their 'personal capacities'; certainly it often proved difficult to persuade union full-time officials to serve.) At the centre, there was no outside representation, even in an advisory capacity. Instead of the semi-autonomous trade union educational body envisaged by the NCLC in 1957, the NCLC and WETUC had dissolved themselves in favour of a department of the TUC.

Consolidation and Control 1964–1968

How successful was the new TUC scheme? Even in the most straightforward — quantitative — terms, this is not easy to gauge. The categories of provision varied, and although there are plenty of statistics, their meaning is by no means clear. During 1962, the penultimate year of their operation, provision by the NCLC and the WETUC was as shown in Table 4.1. The TUC Training College was also in operation in the early 1960s: its provision during the Congress year just preceding the 'takeover' of the NCLC and the WETUC (1963/64) is summarised in Table 4.2. By the end of the decade,

Table 4.1: NCLC and WETUC Course Provision 1962

	Number	Students
NCLC		
Classes	766	12,257
Day and weekend schools	298	9,306
Branch lectures	1,964	56,493
Summer schools	11 [a]	572 [a]
Postal courses		17,751
WETUC		
Classes	368	n.a.
Day and weekend schools	463	9,851 [b]
Summer schools	34	n.a.
Individual unions for which one-week courses arranged	5	743
Correspondence courses		2,279

Notes: [a] 1961 figures. [b] Excludes students on 63 of these courses.
Sources: Millar (1979): 267; Corfield (1969): 249.

the character of provision at the Training College had altered a little, but its quantity had — if anything — marginally declined, as Table 4.3 shows. The main indicators of success — in quantity terms — for the TUC programme, however, were its new regional education and postal course programmes. The figures for these are shown in Table 4.4.

Comparing Tables 4.1 and 4.4, a number of points stand out. Clearly, by 1969 the NCLC programme of lectures for union branches had gone. The programme of 'classes' — essentially, evening classes of serious study on general political, economic or social subjects — had contracted sharply, from a total of over 1,000 classes to just 120. Postal course enrolments were also down, to around one-third of the joint WETUC-NCLC total. The number of day and weekend schools had fallen from a joint figure of 761 to 448; enrolments were correspondingly down. In short, provision in the main 'traditional' areas of the WETUC and NCLC had been drastically or substantially reduced. But the TUC had developed new areas, largely unknown in the days of the old educational bodies. These were the linked

Table 4.2: TUC Training College Course Provision 1963/64

	Number	Students
Two-week courses	18	357
One-week courses	17	300
Totals	35	657

Source: TUC 1964: 190.

Table 4.3: TUC Training College Course Provision 1968/69

	Number	Students
Nine-week courses	3	9
Three-week courses	3	49
Two-week courses	15	329
One-week courses	11	162
Totals	32	549

Source: TUC 1969: 283-4.

Table 4.4: TUC Regional and Postal Course Provision 1968/69

	Courses	Students
Linked weekend schools	93	1,964
Weekend schools	251	5,330
Day schools	197	4,357
Classes	120	1,458
Summer schools	5	324
Day release classes	236	3,438
Postal course students		7,203

Source: TUC 1969: 287-9.

weekend schools, and above all day release courses.

A number of factors contributed to these innovations. The structure of control instituted by the TUC was clearly designed to — or at least had the effect of — minimising the influence of union educationalists of the old school. At TUC Congresses in the mid-1960s, the NCLC's apostles and former students could be heard lamenting developments, and vainly pressing for change. Their central educational complaint was that the new scheme was excessively narrow, excising the critical, the political, the socialist, the committed, tradition of the NCLC. Thus C. Smith, a Post Office Engineering Union speaker at the 1966 Congress:

> *I think there is a fairly widespread feeling among those who are particularly interested in this matter that ... the stated aim of providing opportunities for trade union members to undertake systematic social, economic and political studies related to their trade union interests (and that was the stated aim) has been rather narrowly interpreted.*

The claim was, of course, not just that such education was important for its own sake, but that it was vital for the effective operation of the trade union and labour movement. Jock Shanley of the National Union of Furniture Trades Operatives applied it to a big issue of the day, automation:

> *Let us look at the programme of the TUC training college. You could go through the lot, you could attend every course, you could be excellent on industrial relations, you could become an expert on management techniques, you could know about collective bargaining: but you could take all those courses and you would not have a clue what to do about automation. (TUC 1964: 483.)*

But in making this argument, Shanley and his labour college allies had effectively conceded the case. He did not assert the need for socialist, or even working class education as such: his appeal was to the needs of union representatives. This was common ground.

The former NCLCers' campaign eventually focussed on the demand for some kind of central advisory committee or conference on trade union education. An annual conference had been a central part of NCLC life, and in 1961 the General Council itself had recommended a Joint Trade Union Education Committee with external representation. But George Woodcock was now unshakable on the issue: and the Council was adamant in its opposition. Woodcock put their case bluntly to the 1964 Congress (TUC 1964: 483-4):

> *I want all those who have spoken today to understand that this [education] has now become part of the T.U.C. activity. Just as we deal with economic affairs, international affairs, social insurance affairs, we now deal with this, it is now within the T.U.C. There will obviously be changes. What they will be I do not know. We are taking over and we shall*

> *do the best we can and we shall be as flexible as we can ...*
>
> *Take this question of conferences. We do not have annual conferences on economic affairs or international affairs; we deal with those subjects at this Congress. If education has become a T.U.C. activity then the T.U.C. must be absolutely in control of it. The General Council answer to this Congress and to nobody else ...*
>
> *We have not put the N.C.L.C. out of business, we have simply moved into a field of activity and you must understand that when we move into this field we must move in with T.U.C. traditions and T.U.C. characteristics.*

Although former labour college supporters were vocal in arguing the case at Congresses, unease about the TUC's new role was quite widespread among trade union educators. As early as 1964 the Association of Tutors in Adult Education — representing chiefly extra-mural and WEA tutors — arranged a meeting (10 July) with McCullough. It was the 'formulation of syllabuses centrally' which caused the ATAE 'particular anxiety' (L. Speak, Hon. Sec., ATAE to E. McCullough, 17 October 1964: TUC file 817.2). Concern grew especially strong in the university sector. Initially, it centred on the new regional education advisory committees, on which the extra-mural departments were given no formal representation. (In contrast, WEA districts were directly represented, reflecting their former role in the WETUC.) Tom Kelly, Director of Extra-mural Studies at Liverpool University, wrote to Winnard (12 January 1965: TUC file 817.2) expressing the Universities Council for Adult Education's concern that the committees made 'no provision for the collaboration of extra-mural departments'; but the core of the opposition was the Sheffield Department of Extra-mural Studies. Its Director, Maurice Bruce, wrote to *The Times* (11 January 1965: TUC file 817.2).[8] An extensive correspondence ensued. There was also an exchange between the Bristol Extra-mural Department and the Regional Education Officer (G. Cunliffe to B.K. Preuss, 30 March 1965 and ensuing correspondence: TUC file 817.2), and other extra-mural departments were also apparently concerned (T. Kelly to Winnard, 15 February 1965: TUC file 817.2).

The TUC 'certainly hope[d] to have the co-operation and help of Extra-Mural Departments ... but naturally in such forms and under such arrangements as we consider appropriate to trade union educational needs and interests' (Winnard to Boyden, 15 January 1965: TUC file 817.2). In a letter to Bruce (10 February 1965: TUC file 817.2) Winnard explained the TUC's position on the REACs in some detail. His key point was that the committees were

> *responsible to our General Council (through the Council's Education Committee) for advising upon the conduct of a TUC service for which*

> the General Council will be held accountable to the affiliated unions in the Congress. The committees must therefore be predominantly trade union bodies representing trade union interests and performing a trade union function. At the same time they must be small enough to work effectively ... without a proliferation of sub-committees. They consist, therefore, of a majority of members of the established TUC Regional Advisory Committees, a number of additional trade union members to provide a wider representation of affiliated unions, ... representatives of Trades Council Federations, and some WEA representatives. The last provision replaces the machinery of WEA District Trade Union Advisory Committees which has been discontinued at our request.

There was, of course, room to co-opt a ('limited') number of other members, and in some cases these would include staff of extra-mural departments (albeit in their personal capacities). And there was 'no obstacle to consultation at any time' between the new regional education officers and the extra-mural departments. (Winnard to Bruce, 10 February 1965: TUC file 817.2.) In retrospect, it seems clear that the extra-mural departments were mistaken in detecting a bias against them as such in the new TUC scheme: but there is no question that the TUC was determined to control the scheme of education which emerged. Consultation was welcome: but while the expertise of extra-mural staff might be especially welcome, they and their departments would advise on and provide — rather than make central decisions about — the curriculum. As Winnard wrote,

> the educational purposes which the schools and courses are to serve, and related questions such as the ... scale, nature and standard of the facilities most suited to these purposes, of the categories of students for whom facilities should be provided in order to promote those purposes, of how those students might best be recruited ... must ... be decided by the trade union Movement itself ... (Winnard to Bruce, 18 February 1965: TUC file 817.2).

With this resolute approach to establishing union control over the educational programmes, friction recurred from time to time, especially with those extra-mural departments which had established substantial industrial and trade union studies programmes and traditions. Shortly after Bruce's complaint about representation on the REACs, seven Sheffield tutors wrote raising some administrative points about specific union courses, and expressing general concern that 'certain limitations' might in future be 'imposed on the type of syllabus employed in trade union classes': for example, would classes in Literature and History, Philosophy and Politics still be 'allowed'? (Royden Harrison et al. to Winnard, 10 May 1965: TUC file 817.2.) Through the rest of the decade, tutors from Sheffield and elsewhere continued to cross swords with the TUC (McIlroy 1988a: 65-8).[9]

In 1966, supporters of a more traditional — or wider — view of union education succeeded in winning the TUC Congress to call for greater regional co-operation with educational bodies, and for 'the establishment of a National Advisory Council on Trade Union Education and the greater involvement of lay members at local level in the planning of programmes' (TUC 1966: 518). It is indicative of the authority of the General Council (and no doubt of the General Secretary) that the point was still not conceded. The Education Department did establish a 'TUC Education Service Consultative Group', which met for the first time in January 1967. Its members were 'invited to serve in an individual capacity by reason of their personal interest in and experience of the educational work, but with the knowledge and approval of their unions'. But the Group seems to have been in large part a regularisation of the informal meetings of union education officers, with a slightly broader membership (minutes 18 January 1967: TUC file 817.211; TUC 1967: 210-11; cp Corfield 1969: 151). One motive for this formalisation was to 'go some way to meeting the terms of the resolution' advocating a National Advisory Council.

Overall, however, there is little sign that the General Council was worried about being overruled. Other consultations (with the Scottish TUC and Irish Confederation of Trade Unions) were discontinued (TUC 1967: 215). The General Council held that 'the case for an advisory body in relation to educational work was no more valid than in relation to the General Council's work in other fields' (TUC 1967: 214). This point was hardly a logically strong one, as the mover of the 1966 resolution commented: 'Since the General Council have an advisory committee for local government, and for Commonwealth affairs, I for one am unable to see the force of that point' (TUC 1967: 591). But logical strength and consistency mattered little. The central issue was control: the General Council's responsibility was of a 'direct nature'; there was a 'necessity to develop the educational work as a national service to affiliated unions'; 'financial considerations [were] involved' (TUC 1967: 215). The General Council therefore emphatically 'reaffirmed' its view that TUC education should 'give a service to affiliated organisations as such rather than to *ad hoc* local groups' of union members (TUC 1967: 214).[10]

The General Council in the mid-1960s was single-minded in asserting central control over union education. It was determined, in taking over the NCLC, to establish a scheme which served — in the General Council's view — the interests of the movement. There was no question of its administering a *de facto* continuation of labour college programmes, which it regarded as ill-directed, haphazard and inefficient. Any proposal which threatened to dilute the TUC's future freedom of action was unacceptable. The protests of labour college supporters and former WETUC tutors alike were brushed aside. The former could only move resolutions. The latter, tutors in WEA and extra-mural departments, remained a force in the field; the mistrust bred during these years continued to blight the development of trade union education during the decades which followed.

Shop Stewards and the Political Economy of Full Employment

The new scheme was formed in the political, as well as the educational, context of its time. With the post-war commitment to (more or less) full employment, the bargaining strength of unions at workplace level increased, and with this, the strength and vitality of shop steward organisation. From the late 1940s governments became concerned at the impact of wage increases on price inflation. The blame was widely placed on shop stewards, whose negotiating power at local level allowed increases in pay to be achieved without equivalent increases in production. A number of disputes from the later 1950s, and inquiries into them, raised the profile of shop stewards — often seen as being under Communist influence. The popular press, and films such as the Boultings' *I'm All Right Jack*, generated and reinforced a negative — and highly tendentious — image of the shop steward. (For contemporary popular accounts in this vein, see Jacobson and Connor 1956; Wigham 1961: esp. 91ff.) The TUC responded with an inquiry of its own. Reporting to the 1960 Congress, this suggested certain types of steward organisation were an attempt 'to usurp the policy making functions of unions' and 'a challenge to existing union arrangements' (TUC 1960: 129). The report suggested that union leaders should 'increase their information services' to develop 'a greater awareness among stewards of the policy they should be supporting' (TUC 1960: 130). Gradually, union education began to be seen as one means of helping to overcome problems of disorder within the union movement.

At the same time, the political parties were moving into the world of incomes policy. The Conservative government after 1959, seeking a more permanent solution to balance of payments problems than 'stop-go', examined the merits of incomes policy. This trend was strengthened by the publication of the Organisation for European Economic Co-operation's *The Problem of Rising Prices* in early 1961 (Fellner et al. 1964). The government introduced, between July 1961 and June 1962, a pay pause, a 'guiding light' pay norm, and a National Incomes Commission. The last was associated with a commitment to indicative economic planning, and the establishment of the tripartite National Economic Development Council. At the 1963 Labour Party Conference, every affiliated union supported a resolution (passed overwhelmingly) calling for an incomes policy 'to include salaries, wages, dividends and profits' (quoted Panitch 1975: 52).

Trade union leaders, and especially George Woodcock, valued the TUC's increasing role in economic planning. 'We left Trafalgar Square a long time ago,' the General Secretary told the 1963 TUC: 'we have to deal with the affairs of the moment in committee rooms with people who have power ... The whole work of the TUC in my time has been centred on developing this process.' The TUC envisaged working closely with a Labour government which would adopt broadly similar policies.[11] This approach presumed that the essential contours of political and economic power had been sufficiently equalised for the TUC to be able enter into joint and rational planning processes with employers and a Conservative government. The politics of mobilisation, of ideology, were at a discount. And indeed, for some union leaders a major problem was the different — and irresponsible — approach of many 'unofficial' groups of members. As Woodcock was to complain, when TUC leaders decided to 'pull the lever', nothing happened (Dorfman 1983: 41). He feared existing trade union structures were unable to exploit the opportunities created by unions' new political role. On this view, union education should help in training active trade unionists to make the most of their responsible (if minor) role in managing a well-ordered economy.

Whether or not it was a national political problem, the increasing number of shop stewards (and their equivalents) did pose a problem for the trade union movement. Shop stewards were not new, of course. They had existed in various forms — particularly in engineering — since the turn of the century. But during and after the Second World War they became more numerous. Marsh and Coker (1963) estimated that the number of AEU shop stewards increased by 50 per cent between 1947 and 1961. Shop stewards spread into industries where they had been previously rare or unknown, and they began to get involved in more spheres of activity. (For a survey of the origin and development of shop stewards, see Goodman and Whittingham 1973: 26-44.) Although early estimates of their number were highly speculative, figures of 90,000 (Clegg, Killick and Adams 1961: 153), 100,000-120,000 (Marsh and Coker 1963), 175,000 (McCarthy and Parker 1968: 15) and 200,000 (TUC 1960) were common currency in the sixties. In terms of TUC policy-making, the last mentioned — its own estimate, and the earliest — is probably most significant.

A number of studies in the fifties and sixties, as well as officials' own observations, suggested that union branches were far less vibrant than they had been between the wars (Goldstein 1952). This was often seen as 'one of the fundamental problems of trade union democracy' (Bell 1954: 165).

Some (including many in the NCLC) argued that branch attendance could be improved by making branches more central to unions' educational activities (Bell 1954: 166). But if the focus of union activity was shifting from branch and community to workplace, there was also a strong case that union education should concentrate on union officials active in the workplace, rather than on the traditional participants in union courses — the quasi-political labour movement activist. Through the sixties the TUC was moving rapidly toward the view that day release courses for shop stewards were the way forward. This was underpinned by the views of the group of union education officers.

Day release as such was, of course, far from new. Day release courses for trade unionists had been developing in the universities through the 1950s. But in the early 1960s extra-mural departments and WEA districts developed courses 'increasingly focused on skills and techniques of industrial relations, and increasingly aimed at the shop steward' (McIlroy 1990b: 224-5). From 1961 Jack Jones, then the Transport and General Workers' Union's Midland Secretary, argued that if managers were concerned about the state of industrial relations in the motor industry, they should grant paid release to shop stewards for training — as they did for supervisors. Courses developed with Birmingham University Extra-mural Department, with the WEA, and with Lanchester College of Technology. The experiment was commended by the Ministry of Labour. Other universities and WEA districts developed day release courses, mostly for mixed groups of workers and managers. London Extra-mural Department worked with the TGWU at Fords, Dagenham, from 1963 (Stuttard 1980, 1987, 1991). Oxford developed courses at the British Motor Corporation (McIlroy 1990c: 252-4; Marsh 1991). Technical colleges began to develop courses for shop stewards (Corfield 1969: 134-5).

The first major policy-statement on this trend was issued after discussions between the TUC and the British Employers' Confederation (a forerunner of the Confederation of British Industry) in 1963. The discussions followed 'initial discussion in the National Joint Advisory Council to the Ministry of Labour' (TUC 1963: 190). The statement was very much from the 'good industrial relations' stable. It was 'generally agreed' that there was 'a need to increase the amount of training so that more stewards can obtain a broader understanding of their functions and responsibilities' (TUC 1963: 190). The statement continued:

> The first consideration on which realistic training of shop stewards or their equivalent must be based is the fact that an employee acting as a steward is a union officer. Consequently the aim of training must be to assist stewards to carry out their functions as responsible officers of their unions. ... It is in the interests of employers that stewards should

represent their unions and the members of those unions effectively.
This was, of course, a significant statement for an employers' association to make. The BEC also recommended its members 'to consider the possibility of extending the co-operation between employers, unions and educational organisations or institutions with the object of providing more courses of an appropriate nature, for attendance at which stewards might be released with pay' (TUC 1963: 192).

For the TUC, the 1963 agreement was a negotiated document, in which concessions were made in pursuit of the major aim. In a highly critical article, McIlroy (1985c: 39) has suggested that the TUC's aim in the 1963 statement was 'the re-creation of the shop steward'; training was 'an instrumental means of civilising and incorporating lay officials to further a joint interest conception of employment relations. ... To this end, the content of courses should be agreed with the employer.' This goes too far. The TUC ethos then leant towards tripartism and 'good industrial relations'; agreeing course content with an employer may not have seemed so large a concession then as later. But there is no sign that the TUC sought or desired employer influence over course content. The statement indeed conveys a firm union concern to retain as much control over course content as possible. Five categories of training were described in outline: Induction, Basic, Practical, Specialised, and General. For the first three, the statement (TUC 1963: 191) emphasised, 'Responsibility ... must rest primarily with trade unions themselves'. There was a desire to expand steward training. It was 'recognised' that this could be achieved 'more rapidly ... if training could be provided to a greater extent in working hours', and it was 'accepted that where day release with pay is granted for this purpose the syllabuses of courses should be agreed with the employers' (TUC 1963: 190-1). Overall, it gives the impression of a document reached after negotiation.

The statement was attacked at the 1963 TUC Congress by shop stewards' representatives who asserted the importance of independence in union education. In reply, the General Council speaker (George Lowthian) provided an explanation which (in contrast to some General Council speeches on the NCLC and the control of the TUC scheme) has the ring of truth.

> *There are a considerable number of misconceptions in relation to this paragraph. ... We emphasise that it [shop steward training] is the task of trade unions. Employers will not be allowed in any circumstances to determine the syllabuses that different trade unions, in accordance with their own constitutions and agreements, devise. ... The shop stewards are mainly responsible for adequate consultations in industry and therefore we believe that the employers have a responsibility to enable these*

> *stewards to function, not for the employers but for the members represented by shop stewards. It is in order that they should be given some opportunity during working hours of getting trade union education that this is put forward. We will not surrender to any group of employers. (TUC 1963: 432.)*

The 1963 statement was, in short, the work of a TUC concerned about the shop steward question. Through training it sought to secure more orderly and 'responsible' approaches to industrial relations on their part. It sought above all to develop a programme which would be available to the enormous and growing number of lay workplace representatives. This desire to expand day release courses was not a priority of the union corporatist right-wing alone. Thus we find Jack Dunn, Communist Secretary of the Kent Miners, arguing for their rapid development: 'I believe that day release courses are among the most practical and efficient educational media for our shop stewards and work-place representatives' (TUC 1967: 591). To permit this expansion, the TUC made concessions — concessions which, a few years later, it might have shunned. But the 1963 statement was neither a simple subordination of union interests to employers', nor a step in a sophisticated corporatist strategy. It was a deal, made by union leaders to whom negotiation was an everyday and inescapable part of trade union activity.

During the years of the Labour Government, the TUC become more closely involved in state policy-making. The relationship between shop stewards and union hierarchies was subject to continual stress as a result of incomes policy. The pressure to develop shop steward training continued. The years from 1965 were also marked by the work of the Royal Commission on Trade Unions and Employers' Associations (chaired by Lord Donovan). Woodcock, serving on the Commission, was highly conscious of the developing pressure for statutory control of union activity, and of the Commission's developing analysis of 'two systems' — formal and informal — of industrial relations (Panitch 1976: 153). It was in this climate that the TUC developed its major policy statement, *Training Shop Stewards* (1968a).

Training Shop Stewards remains probably the most educational policy document ever issued at a high level by the TUC, in the sense that it was concerned with educational methods, with how teaching should take place, with the educational needs of shop stewards. It also covered administrative questions, but was silent (for instance) on such vexed questions as employer endorsement of syllabuses (save in reprinting the 1963 TUC/BEC statement as an appendix). The report of a working party of union education officers,[12] it contained survey and analysis, as well as policy recommendation. It surveyed the number of shop stewards (unions comprising 78.94 per cent of TUC membership reported 148,563 stewards). It reported the typical activities of shop stewards. It surveyed the then attendance at various types of union educational event (under six per cent of workplace representatives in each case). It surveyed the teaching methods then in use in union courses (lectures predominated, but discussion and role play were also common).

But the main purpose of *Training Shop Stewards* was missionary. It argued the importance of training, against those (and they were many) who thought experience the only way to knowledge and skill. It argued that not only unions, but also management and government, had a common interest in the proper training of workplace representatives:

> *all the parties have a common interest in getting a union workplace representative who knows his job. Although success in protecting his members could conflict with management's interest, employers are nevertheless concerned that he should act within the constitutional procedures of his union and industry, and observe agreements reached. Training cannot guarantee this, but it does give the opportunity for the purpose and nature of these agreements to be examined. (TUC 1968a: 11-12.)*

And it accepted that the motives of each party might differ — even when the language was the same. In an important qualification to the dominant unitary view of 'good industrial relations', the document stated:

> *For example, from better industrial relations one person might hope for greater efficiency, another for improved quality in human relations in industry, another for the more equitable distribution of any surplus profit. To ignore these differences would threaten the basis of continuing co-operation between unions and other parties concerned. (TUC 1968a: 11.)*

The Origins of Public Funding

A central theme of *Training Shop Stewards* was the importance of developing a system of union training which was thoroughly professional in its approach. Day release was seen as the key to this; funding from the public sector would overcome many of the financial difficulties. 'Training has in the past been so much a matter for voluntary spare-time effort on the part of both its organisers and the representatives, that it is not surprising that much of it still tends to be haphazard' (TUC 1968a: 21). The developing view, which was to underpin the educational policy of the TUC through the following two decades, was that the trade union movement should construct a coherent and properly-resourced system of union education which could compete with the facilities on offer to management and in other fields of industrial training.

In order to achieve this, TUC leaders were now clear that they should seek — and, if the terms were right, accept — public funds. The argument was framed in terms of securing for union purposes a share of the resources which the Labour Government was directing at industrial training.

> *If society accepts that it is in the public interest to assist companies pursuing private profit to improve their managerial efficiency by using public educational and training facilities at less than the full costs, trade unions should not be denied the use of public educational resources which they themselves are applying to this purpose (TUC 1968a: 16).*

Contrasted with the principled rejection of state funding which had characterised the labour colleges until the end, such a shift might seem remarkable: but the TUC scheme was, of course, a child not only of the labour colleges. Trade unions in the 1960s had been working more and more with public-sector colleges; the WEA and extra-mural departments had become established providers of union education. Union leaders seldom now saw the state as a threat to union interests, in even the residual Marxist terms of the NCLC. Within the TUC, the shift to seeking better public funding seems to have been uncontroversial.

TUC leaders did, however, see a divergence of interest between trade unions and employers in the educational field, and it was over this issue that such discussion of public funding as did occur was articulated during the later 1960s. The primary source of funding for work-related courses in colleges at that time was the industrial training boards, established under the Industrial Training Act 1964. The TUC was interested in securing funding from this source, but there were three obstacles. Two were of the TUC's making — attempts to tackle the question of control. The first was the technical question of whether ITB funds could be dispensed for courses which, though work-related, were not vocational in the normal sense. The second was that ITBs were essentially joint bodies of employers and trade unions, and to establish them as the major channel of funding for trade union education would be to accept a strong measure of employer control. The third issue was the sheer dispersal of control. ITBs were established by industry. To encourage them to fund union education would lead to a highly variegated system, differing not only by industry but also (given the ITBs' approach of often funding training schemes proposed and organised by individual employers) by workplace. TUC thinking — as represented in its whole approach since 1964 — favoured a standardised approach, and indeed in January 1967 the Education Department established a working party to consider the 'development of standardised regional courses' (TUC Education Service Consultative Group minutes 18 January 1967: TUC file 817.211M).

In early 1967 the TUC agreed a joint statement with the CBI on industrial training boards and shop steward training. This established that the ITBs should be seen as a possible source of funding for course provision; but despite this prospect, the TUC was less than enthusiastic. It appears that at least some voices within the TUC were resisting any ITB role, and used the issue of the ITBs' proper aims and role in striking a hard bargain. The 1967 joint statement (TUC 1967: 215-16) is notable for what the CBI conceded about the desirability of union control over shop steward education.

> *The TUC and CBI, while recognising the need for a considerable expansion in the training of shop stewards and the contribution to be made by training courses based upon release from work with pay, believed that ... the primary responsibility for trade union education and training must remain with the trade union Movement itself (TUC 1967: 215-16).*

The statement also commented on the specific problem — for trade unions — of employer provision of shop steward training. ITBs should support courses organised by employers only when they were 'appropriate in form and content and efficiently conducted by qualified persons'. And 'before approving particular courses for grant purposes', they should 'obtain the agreement of the employers' organisations and trade unions or appropriate joint bodies in the industries concerned'. (TUC 1967: 216.)

The TUC educationalists' reading of this joint statement was backed up by a Note on 'Industrial Training Boards: Training of Shop Stewards' prepared by the Education Department and considered by the Education Committee along with the joint statement (Education Committee document 6/6, 1967; Education Committee minutes 14 March 1967). This Note was emphatic:

> *The provision of satisfactory courses requires that unions should have a predominant voice in the formulation of syllabuses, the choice of tutors, the teaching methods employed and the selection of students. ... The functions of Industrial Training Boards must be primarily related to vocational training, and the Boards cannot assume a responsibility for trade union education and training, which must remain the responsibility of the trade union Movement itself.*

The TUC's educational stance in the later 1960s should, then, be seen as the product of a number of factors. The TUC's increasing involvement in national economic management with a — supposedly broadly benign — state formed the background. Within this framework, the TUC's educationalists faced the problem, after 1964, of developing and managing an education service for the movement. No time was wasted over the desirability of a centralised and co-ordinated system: this was assumed. The new system must have a viable aim: the central role of the lay workplace representative — the shop steward — provided this. Finance was a problem. The subsidised public education sector offered the prospect of good quality programmes relatively cheaply, but the cost of a national service would still be high. Control was a major issue. TUC education functioned in a highly diverse environment where different trade unions and educational institutions competed and collaborated, and where employers were not only major operators, but generally the best-resourced. The way TUC educational policy and provision developed during the late 1960s and early 1970s reflected these factors. But it also suffered as a result of trade unions' increasingly fractious relationship with government during the six years from 1968.

1   The main government reports touching on trade union education are: Cmnd. 3623 (the Donovan Commission); Commission on Industrial Relations 1972a; Department of Education and Science 1972 (the Gold report) and 1973b (the Russell Committee).

2   This is not to assert that the TUC achieved a full corporatist role in society: indeed, the experience of the 1980s reflects the fragility and limitations of the role which it did attain. However, this image of the TUC's role and importance was held by most senior TUC figures in the 1950s, 1960s and 1970s.

3   Alan Winterbottom. 'Mr Winterbottom, who holds degrees of LL.M. and B.Com., has always had close contacts with the Trade Union Movement and has had wide experience of research into industrial problems. He is the author (with R.Y. Hedges) of the standard text book: *The Legal History of Trade Unionism.*' (TUC 1946a: 27.)

4   Creech Jones (1891-1964) was MP for Shipley (1935-50) and for Wakefield (1954-64). Elected Secretary of Camberwell Trades Council, he was a Conscientious Objector during the Great War, National Secretary for clerical and administrative workers, TGWU (1919-29), and Organising Secretary, Workers' Travel Association (1929-35). (*The Times*, 24 October 1964.)

5   Clegg and Adams also made important recommendations anent the relationship between trade union education and liberal education; see Chapter 7 below.

6   It is impossible to be certain that the deletion was made by Woodcock; however both deletions appear to have been done in the same (ball-point) pen as the initialled phrase 'OK for circulation as amended'; Winnard seems normally to have written (and signed the memorandum in question) with a fountain pen. (It should be noted that a reference in the same paper to a 'small Advisory Panel' in relation to revising and planning postal courses, and consisting of educational experts 'including, for

example, union education officers', was not deleted.)

7   This paper was accompanied by a memorandum to Woodcock ('Re-organisation of Educational Facilities') in which Winnard stated that the accompanying paper summarised 'the conclusions we have reached and the recommendations we should like to make as to how we should proceed in this matter'. It is unclear whether 'we' refers to Winnard and Woodcock, or to Winnard and his colleagues in the Education Department (it is unlikely that it refers to the Education Committee). The memorandum is endorsed (apparently by Winnard, perhaps following a discussion with Woodcock), 'Ideas in general OK. Get on as quickly as possible'.

8   Bruce copied the letter to Jim Boyden, Parliamentary Under-Secretary at the Department of Education and Science, who forwarded it to Winnard for comment.

9   Relations between the TUC and the extra-mural departments during this period are discussed in some detail, though somewhat tendentiously, by McIlroy (1988a and 1990c).

10 This question of control was clearly an issue of some concern. At the first meeting of the Consultative Group, the Chairman (Les Cannon of the ETU, a member of the General Council), stressed that 'the functions of the Group must be of an advisory nature, and that responsibility for policy decisions must rest with the Education Committee, the General Council and, ultimately, the Congress'. In addition, the 'Education Committee itself accepted that questions regarding the staffing of TUC Departments, and related matters, were primarily matters for the TUC General Secretary'. (Minutes 18 January 1967: TUC file 817.211.)

11 This account draws on Panitch 1976: 47ff.

12 According to *Training Shop Stewards*, the Working Party was 'acting under the auspices of the consultative group of trade union officers which advises the TUC Education Committee on the development of the TUC Education Service' (TUC 1968a: 1). The full truth is a little more complex. The Consultative Group was established in early 1967 (partly in response to the call from the 1966 Congress to establish a National Advisory Council on trade union education). At its first meeting, Dennis Winnard reported 'that a working party had been formed some time previously ... to advise upon the provision of courses intended to assist in the training of workplace representatives' (TUC Education Service: Consultative Group minutes 18 January 1967: TUC file 817.211M). Thereafter the Working Party appears to have reported to and through the Consultative Group.

Chapter 5

Great Leap Forward: the TUC Scheme 1968–1979

By 1968 the TUC had evolved the kernel of a substantial education (or training) scheme. At its heart lay the 1968 Report, *Training Shop Stewards*. But this only set down the central features of a strategy which came to fruition in the political and economic climate of the times. Within a decade, the TUC education scheme had expanded almost out of recognition. The eighties, in contrast, were years of quantitative decline — at best of retrenchment — with constant fears that the entire provision might be swept aside, jetsam of an unebbing anti-trade union tide. This Chapter examines the period before the election of the Conservative government in 1979; the Conservative years are considered in Chapters 6, 8 and 9.

A Climate for Growth

The 1970s saw, for the trade union movement, both the years of its greatest political influence, and a period when trade unionism itself was widely seen as Britain's major social and economic problem. These periods coincided to a large degree. When the Conservative government was elected in 1970, the role of trade unions was already inescapably a matter of 'public debate' — as the report of the Donovan Commission in 1968, closely followed by the Wilson government's debacle over Barbara Castle's ill-fated white paper, *In Place of Strife*, ensured. The incoming Conservative government addressed the perceived problem in two main ways.

On the one hand, it introduced an industrial and economic policy designed to re-invigorate industry by exposing it to market disciplines and breaking what was regarded as the dead hand of state interference. As John Davies, Secretary of State for Trade and Industry, put it in a renowned speech to the House of Commons (4 November 1970), the vast majority 'lives and thrives in a bracing climate, and not in a soft, sodden morass of subsidised incompetence'. The need was to gear policies 'to the great majority of the people, who are not lame ducks, who do not need a hand, who are quite capable of looking after their own interests and only demand to be allowed to do so.' The result of 'treating us all, the whole country, as though we were lame ducks,' he continued, would be 'national decadence.'

The second element in the new government's strategy was a plan for legal regulation of industrial relations — and in particular of trade union activity — based largely on Donovan and *In Place of Strife*. The Industrial

Relations Act 1971 established a National Industrial Relations Court and introduced binding collective agreements. It also established a statutory basis and powers for the Commission on Industrial Relations, which had been set up by Royal Warrant in 1969. Although of more modest importance in the overall pattern of events, the CIR — charged with initiating reforms in collective bargaining — came in due course to see shop steward training as one method of achieving this, and thus plays a modest role in our story.

Of course, this took place at a time of — and was stimulated by — very substantial trade union strength at shop floor level in British industry. This strength was founded on the commitment of post-war governments of both parties to maintaining full employment. The circle to be squared thus became how to reduce trade unions' (as it was perceived) negative impact on corporate profitability, national wage rates, inflation and so forth, whilst maintaining the fundamental basis of their strength in the workplace — full employment. The Heath government's strategy fell apart when the social cost — in terms of unemployment — rose to what was regarded, in those enlightened days, as an unacceptable level (about one million), and in the face of the Miners' strike in the winter of 1973-1974. But the TUC had been able to sustain a substantial campaign against the Industrial Relations Act — a campaign of non-recognition. And at workplace level, shop stewards' strength had led to widespread collusion between them and employers to circumvent key aspects of the legislation.

The Labour governments of 1974 to 1979 started from similar fundamental beliefs about the role of trade unions in achieving national economic prosperity. They also carried other political baggage. On a practical level, the Heath government having fallen in its contest with the Miners, Labour had a firm sense that union strength was a reality no government — at least, no Labour government — could alter. Perhaps there was also a subliminal sense of debt. A buoyant left-wing in the Parliamentary Labour Party enjoyed close links with the Labour Party outside Parliament (and with a radical shop stewards' movement — though this was not representative of all shop stewards). The left was represented in key Cabinet positions during the early years of the government (1974-1976) — above all by Tony Benn as Secretary of State for Industry, and by Michael Foot as Secretary of State for Employment.

The core of Labour's political strategy was the 'Social Contract': the agreement by which trade union leaders were to deliver restraint in wage increases in return for substantial influence on economic and social policy. In particular, they sought advances on the welfare front, and on trade union rights and facilities. While this is not the place to review the history of the Social Contract, several features are relevant. The years of Labour

Union Education in Britain: A TUC Activity

Terms and Conditions

Improving your collective agreements

One of the essential requirements for improving your collective agreements is the use of your trade union strength. Unions have been trying to build up their bargaining strength over many years, but even now there are many parts of the British workforce which don't have unions at all.

The following diagrams illustrate the process which unions have gone through and are going through in order to improve the wages and conditions of their members.

Unions not recognised — no collective bargaining

In this diagram you can see that management has control over all aspects of work and the running of the company. Management does not recognise unions and there is no collective bargaining.

Unions begin to get organised — bargaining starts

In this diagram you can see that the union has been recognised by the employer and is powerful enough to get management to negotiate about wages, holidays and hours.

Unions become well organised — collective bargaining is extended

TUC Copyright

Fig. 5.1: Collective Bargaining. A page from the 'Red Pack' conveys the optimism of the late 1970s.

government coincided with a major crisis of the western economic order, as the major oil-exporting nations of the 'Third World' demanded (from 1973) a larger share of the fruits of their natural resources. As usual, the economic crisis was particularly intense in Britain, and the government was compelled to negotiate an agreement with the International Monetary Fund in 1976. Second, while Labour achieved an absolute majority in the House of Commons at the October 1974 election, having governed without a majority since February, its overall majority of a mere five was rapidly whittled away by by-election defeats and desertions. After 1976, the government's majority was assured only by a pact with the Liberal Party — which intensified the internal strains of the Labour Party and the trade unions within Parliament and outside. From 1976 also — a not unassociated event — the role of the left in government was substantially reduced, as the new Prime Minister, James Callaghan, replacing Harold Wilson, shifted Benn and Foot from ministries with a central role in industrial and labour relations policy (they became Secretary of State for Energy and Lord President respectively).

Third, through the 1970s the decline of manufacturing industry's share of the labour market — known by the early 1980s as 'deindustrialisation' — continued. This meant, over time, that the unions of public sector employees grew in number and importance within the trade union movement. A major feature of the Social Contract period was leaders of public sector workers asserting their new power against the traditional authority and status of the major manufacturing unions. At the same time, the leaders of general unions found their public sector members growing more numerous in relation to their private sector members. So while the 1970s provided a climate for growth in union education, the decade was a turbulent one for trade unionism in general. Trade union education could not escape this. The following sections examine how the growth occurred, and how the political, social and economic environment influenced the pattern of union education which emerged.

Formulating Policy and Holding the Line, 1968-1969

With the takeover of the NCLC and the WETUC, the TUC in the 1960s had to confront some tricky issues of educational policy-making. As we have seen, it had shifted away from the liberal and socialistic assumptions of the WETUC and the labour colleges. Shop stewards had been identified as the primary target of training. Its relationships with the public-sector education service were broadly good. In 1970, however, it was still feeling its way toward a sustainable position. Its attempts to achieve a consensus with the state and employers had been subject to severe strain, even under the

Labour government. When the Conservatives were returned, the tensions became more marked.

The groundwork for the TUC's educational policy had been set down in *Training Shop Stewards*' 1968 claim for unions' right to public funding. The claim for public funds was to prove an important departure. But it was a modest claim, modestly if clearly made, and it was by no means the centrepiece of the document. Hostility remained within the movement, and perhaps especially among union educators, to accepting state funds for union purposes. These undercurrents were brought into the foreground by Donovan and *In Place of Strife*. The Royal Commission Report was presented to Parliament in June 1968. Woodcock, and presumably other key figures in the TUC, knew its recommendations rather earlier. Five of the twelve commissioners had argued for legislation to control the power of shop stewards and the unions (Cmnd 3623: 282-302; see also Panitch 1976: 168-9). Within weeks of the Report's publication, the Department of Employment and (as it was then rather quaintly named) Productivity forwarded a consultative document to the TUC and the CBI, indicating that a White Paper would be published before the end of the year. In November Barbara Castle, the Secretary of State, made her intentions known to a select private conference: although the CBI Director General and the Chairman of the Prices and Incomes Board were present, only two relatively junior trade unionists were among the company. Legal restrictions on union action were now on the agenda: a 'cooling-off' period in unofficial disputes, compulsory strike ballots, and restrictions on 'inter-union' disputes. (Panitch 1976: 170; Ponting 1989: 352-3.) The White Paper was in fact delayed until late January 1969: when Castle put her proposals to a special TUC General Council in December, they had a frosty reception. Opposition also developed in the Cabinet itself.

During 1968 and 1969, therefore, the TUC was rapidly reassessing its relationship with the state. New limits to the corporatist strategy — the move from 'Trafalgar Square' to 'the corridors of power' — had emerged; and under a Labour government. The General Council by no means rejected the strategy. It was committed to maintaining the TUC at the centre of power and influence. This meant a permanent accommodation with government. But in such a relationship the TUC must be an independent party. Legal constraint on union activity was a price it would not pay: on this, there was to be no compromise. (Dorfman 1983: 38-53; Panitch 1976: 176-7.) The General Council also expressed itself as 'by no means enthusiastic' about a suggestion to introduce state financial aid for trade union development (TUC 1969: 206).

Training Shop Stewards, published in June 1968 (TUC 1968: 232) but completed seven months earlier (Education Committee minutes 14 November 1967), was therefore considered amid a major political debate on the future of industrial relations, in which shop stewards' role was central. The evolution of TUC thinking on shop steward education in the months which followed should be viewed in this light. In June 1968 the General Council accepted all the recommendations of *Training Shop Stewards* with some enthusiasm. It went further, deciding

> *that representations should be made to the Secretary of State for Education and Science to the effect that additional public funds should be made available to permit the employment by the educational bodies of a larger number of full-time tutors qualified to teach in courses of trade union education and training (TUC 1968: 232).*

By December, when it considered the Donovan Commission's recommendations on the training of union representatives and full-time officials, the General Council's tone had changed: 'the trade union Movement itself would not wish to become the recipient of public funds for any purpose' (TUC 1969: 292). This was a shift of emphasis, rather than of substance. Co-operation with publicly-supported educational bodies could still be 'mutually satisfactory'; support from employers and industrial training boards for paid release was still sought. But while *Training Shop Stewards* emphasised practical and educational questions, the stress in the General Council's response to Donovan was on who controlled and conducted the education.

The training appropriate to unions, as voluntary organisations, differed in kind from that required by companies, the TUC argued. It should be provided in a distinct way. In particular, the 'inevitable difficulties of communication and cohesion within large-scale voluntary organisations require that the training of officers should reinforce their identification with their unions, and that no aspect of training arrangements should weaken or diminish that relationship' (TUC 1969: 291). Training should be conducted by or in close association with the movement itself: unions must have 'a decisive voice in regard to the content and methods of training, and in regard to the selection both of those who are to conduct training and of those who are to be trained'. Tutors and institutions associated with trade union education should be 'prepared at least for this purpose to identify themselves with the aspirations of trade unions'. (TUC 1969: 292.)[1]

Vigorous defence against *In Place of Strife*, and the repudiation of direct union receipt of public funds, was tempered by signals about what developments in public policy would be positive for union education. Involvement with publicly-supported educational bodies should be strengthened by ensuring that appropriate teaching resources were supplied, at reasonable fee levels. Employers should be encouraged to pay wages to union representatives attending union courses. The Industrial Training

Boards' role should be regularised — while ITBs should compensate employers for wages paid to shop stewards attending union-approved courses, their resources 'should not be wasted in support of training which is ineffective and possibly counter-productive, as any training of union workplace representatives must be if not provided in association with trade unions or the T.U.C.' (TUC 1969: 293). In short, while the TUC would under no circumstances accept public funds, they should be liberally dispensed to ensure the provision of relatively cheap courses at institutions where staff were committed to trade union aims and objectives; and they should ensure that trade unionists attending courses did not lose pay.

The vigorous repudiation of direct state funding appears, in hindsight, as a departure from longer-standing TUC traditions of engagement with the state. TUC education in the 1960s was already alive to the question of control. It had asserted its authority, for instance, in relation to the university extra-mural departments. It was seeking ways of introducing forms of 'standardisation' into a very diverse pattern of provision.[2] But Donovan and *In Place of Strife* closed options (as Woodcock's involvement in the formation of the TUC education scheme had done). The Education Department could no longer seek accommodations with educational institutions as a relatively free agent: it was now constrained by a political environment in which the TUC's relationship with the state was pivotal.

Defence and Development: Policy 1969-1974

During the late 1960s, the TUC's educational thinking was formed amid frequent contact with the state and public educational bodies. The latter stretched far beyond its partners of twenty years earlier — the WEA, extra-mural departments, the labour colleges — to include 65 technical colleges (DES 1972: 4). In addition to high-level policy debate, and internal consideration of 'standardisation' and similar issues, the TUC in the late 1960s was engaging in operational discussions on the development of union education in the public sector. A joint TUC-CBI statement on Donovan in October 1968 had mentioned 'the training of managers, union officials and shops stewards in the light of their greater responsibilities' as one measure which would 'strengthen the negotiating capacity of both management and unions at company and factory level' (TUC 1969: 204). Early in 1969, the government initiated discussions on the National Advisory Board in Supervisory Studies which led to the establishment of a Working Party 'to review the national pattern and organisation of Shop Stewards' Courses'. Perhaps because shop stewards' courses could hardly be seen as supervisory studies, perhaps to encourage TUC involvement, the Working

Party was in the event set up under the auspices of the Department of Education and Science.³

The TUC was represented on the Working Party by two functionaries, the Head of the Education Department and a member of his staff. The Gold Committee was concerned with questions of implementation, rather than formulating high policy. The TUC officials were joined by a couple of HMIs, representatives of the Department of Employment and the CBI, three departmental heads from technical colleges teaching trade union courses, and Arthur Marsh, an industrial relations academic from Oxford University. Only the WEA was represented at a high level, by its General Secretary. The terms of reference were modest too:

> *to review the national provision of Shop Stewards' Courses as run by the Technical Colleges, Trades Union Congress, the Workers' Educational Association and the Extra Mural Departments of the Universities. Particular reference would be made to the current and future development of the work done in the Technical Colleges as a principal sector in which management education and Trade Union Studies were developing. (DES 1972: 3.)*

The Working Party carried out an important information-gathering role. It surveyed trade union provision in all colleges known to be running industrial relations courses. Returns were received from 77 colleges: all were teaching courses for shop stewards with employers' support; some 65 were running courses with TUC support. (DES 1972: 4 and 15-26.) Its report, completed in 1970 but issued in mid-1972,⁴ also made recommendations. These covered many of the prosaic issues vital to the development of a successful programme: centres, approval machinery, course content, relations between basic and advanced courses, the training of tutors, teaching materials, and administration. The TUC was successful in establishing the centrality of unions in the process. The TUC had 'an essential part to play in planning and developing these Courses', and the Working Party 'hope[d] that in the future all courses will be run in close consultation with the trade union movement acting with the continued support of industry' (DES 1972: 6).

> *It is clear [the Report continued] that the training of shop stewards can be effectively conducted only in close association with the trade union movement and the employers. Consequently, continuing competence in this field of any educational body or institution depends upon close liaison being maintained, and upon the recognition that the TUC and its affiliated unions have a responsibility to advise and assist the Technical Colleges and other bodies undertaking this work. (DES 1972: 8.)*

The trade union campaign against *In Place of Strife* was remarkably successful. In the summer of 1969 the White Paper proposals were withdrawn in favour of a 'solemn and binding' — but weak — undertaking by the TUC.[5] But the victory was short-lived. The Conservative Government under Edward Heath, returned in 1970, was committed to a major programme of industrial relations and trade union reform based on a rightist interpretation of Donovan. According to Andrew Shonfield, the Royal Commissioner whose 'Note of Reservation' was now embodied in the new Industrial Relations Act, there was 'nothing much wrong with British industrial relations which a few effective unions exercising more authority over their members could not remedy' (*The Times* 6 October 1970, quoted Panitch 1976: 222). The core of the strategy was to codify the responsibilities of unions to employers and the state, and back them with legal sanctions. In particular, union leaders were compelled to discipline unofficial strikes. The strategy failed. The TUC's response was 'non-cooperation': unions were 'strongly advised' neither to register nor to cooperate with any state agency administering the legislation. Backed by widespread and well-organised unofficial militancy, this policy rendered the Act inoperable within three months of its full implementation in February 1972.

The rigid tactic of eschewing contact with all institutions created under the Industrial Relations Act had implications for trade union education. In 1970 the Employment Secretary referred 'the facilities for training in industrial relations available to the members and staff of employers' associations and trade unions and to employees generally, including those engaged in management' to the Commission on Industrial Relations, 'for inquiry and report' (CIR 1972a: viii). The CIR, however, was boycotted. Unions were therefore ill-represented in the preparation of the CIR report on *Industrial Relations Training*.[6]

Potentially, this was a major hazard. The CIR's (informal) brief was to complement the Industrial Relations Act by detailing the institutions of the new industrial relations order. *Industrial Relations Training* proposed a significant shift from the approach which the TUC favoured (and which was reflected in the Gold Report). While the TUC, especially in the early 1960s, was prepared even to agree syllabuses with employers in pursuit of paid release for students, it had long stressed that 'Responsibility for ... training must rest primarily with trade unions themselves' (TUC 1963: 191-2). This view was strengthened in 1968 by *Training Shop Stewards* and the response to Donovan which emphasised that 'the training of union officers can be effectively conducted only by the trade union Movement itself ...' (TUC 1969: 292).

The formula adopted by the CIR was simple yet powerful. If the TUC and trade unions wished to control trade union education, so be it. However, trade unions were not just voluntary organisations: they functioned in employers' workplaces, and had an impact on the operation of the enterprise. As a result, 'employers and unions have a joint interest in the effective operation of the institutions and procedures of industrial relations'. Training related to these was defined as 'industrial relations training' and was 'the common concern of all sides' (CIR 1972a: 2) — including, naturally, employers. This statement of principle was accompanied by strong recommendations for action. These included the development of company or workplace level industrial relations training, arranged by training committees comprising both management and trade union representatives. These committees would draw up 'workplace-based training programmes' for shop stewards. The TUC and trade unions were advised to separate trade union from industrial relations training. Perhaps most ominous for the TUC, *Industrial Relations Training* envisaged an enhanced and interventionist role for the ITBs. They should develop 'comprehensive industrial relations training recommendations for their industry'. Each should employ at least one industrial relations training advisor, together with trained regional advisors and assessors. 'We hope that to the maximum extent possible boards will use their future grant policies as well as their advisory functions to encourage establishments to adopt the approach to industrial relations recommended in this report.' (CIR 1972a: 60.)

The CIR Report posed a strong challenge to the TUC's educational position: public funds would be used to develop and sustain a sector outside trade union control. The government was 'overtly encouraging' employers to develop joint industrial relations training, and was 'expecting the Industrial Training Boards to put up the money in grant support' (TUC 1973: 497). Even during the height of struggle against *In Place of Strife* and the Industrial Relations Bill, the TUC had sought and found ways (the Gold Working Party, for example) to advance union education in co-operation with government and the public sector. Now the TUC was obliged to rethink its position: to formulate a position which would not merely justify its rejection of the CIR view, but also rally a campaign.

The TUC based its response on the inseparability of the shop steward's functions, and the importance of identifying with trade union aspirations. The CIR had taken too narrow a view. Training shop stewards was not merely a matter of maximising the efficiency of industrial enterprises: it was also a matter of education for wider purposes, including both education in the aims and aspirations of trade unionism, and for individual benefit. (TUC 1973: 147-8.) This case was argued in a meeting at the DES with Norman St. John Stevas in May 1973: the Minister of State was 'left ... in no doubt as to the TUC's forceful opposition to the CIR report' (Education Committee document 7/3: 12 June 1973). Similar views were expressed in a short debate at the 1973 Congress. W.J. Bailey of the Journalists argued: 'you cannot make sense out of industrial relations techniques until you have had a sound grounding in trade union education, because you have to relate them to things like social justice ...' For Con Russell of ASTMS, trade union members yearned for 'a knowledge of our society'. Questions had to be posed:

> *why is it that the anarchy of private enterprise must cease - and here we have got to draw attention to the dangerous inadequacy of Enoch Powell's laissez faire theories. Why is it that the only answer is socialist nationalisation, with the development of true political and economic democracy?*
>
> *I believe that these courses and discussions are necessary in order to raise the understanding and consciousness of our members as to the role of the working people of this country to bring about fundamental changes in our society ... (TUC 1973: 497-8.)*

No voice was raised against such views. 'For trade unions industrial relations training is ... synonymous with trade union education', a TUC spokesman told Norman St. John Stevas. He spoke the truth. But in using the term 'trade union education' he was referring to the pattern of union education developed 'under TUC auspices ... by the ready co-operation of educational bodies'. (Education Committee document 7/3, 12 June 1973.) The venting of opinions on the floor of Congress implied no reversion at Congress House toward liberal adult education in the sense beloved of the WEA and the extra-mural departments.

The TUC's tactic with the DES was to shift debate back to the recommendations of the Gold Report, which were 'in general accord with the TUC's views'. Discussion at the meeting covered many of the administrative and resourcing questions with which Gold had been concerned. (Education Committee document 7/3, 12 June 1973.) The aim was unchanged: to explore the development of a relationship with the state under which union education could expand on an independent footing. Under the Heath government, and in the climate of the times, such an approach was not crowned with success. But the issue was kept alive; as and when the government's relations with the TUC returned to a more positive footing, such soundings might bear fruit.

If maintaining a dialogue with the Conservative government was one arm of the TUC's educational development strategy, the other was to ensure that union education was on the agenda in discussions with the Labour Party on social policy for the next Labour government. The TUC/Labour Party Liaison Committee had been established in 1971 to develop a 'constructive alternative' to the Industrial Relations Bill (as it then was)

(F&GPC document 11/4, 21 June 1971). Over the next two years it developed both a detailed framework for the employment legislation of the mid-1970s, and the social policy agenda later known as the 'Social Contract'. Union education was not a high priority for TUC representatives in these discussions, but there is some suggestion that the possibility of funding may have been mentioned,[7] and certainly the question of paid release for training was raised — though only through an intervention at a relatively advanced stage by the Head of TUC Education (Winnard to K. Graham, 24 November 1972: TUC file 40.2).

Turning Point: Policy and the State 1974-1975

The debate on union education at the 1973 Trades Union Congress centred on a motion (TUC 1973: 496) in which Congress called upon the General Council

> *to allocate additional funds to trade union education to assist members of affiliated unions to equip themselves better to act as representatives of the whole trade union movement at local, district and national level. It believes that the TUC must face up to its responsibilities in this field and the field of industrial relations training to ensure that the task of training workpeoples' representatives is not left solely to employers.*

The motion was carried. Within six months the Heath government had been swept from office.

The General Council — more accurately, the Education Department — was already facing up to its responsibilities. As the Education Committee pointed out, the TUC's expenditure on its educational service already amounted to 'approximately one-fifth of their income'.[8] After a hiatus in the early 1970s, the number of courses and classes provided, and the number of students attending them, began to increase again from 1973/74 onward (Smith 1984: 78, 81). In the context of the Social Contract with the Labour government, new opportunities appeared. Apart from allocating extra funds, the General Council instituted a major review of trade union education services in January 1975. Although the results of this were formally reported to Congress in September 1975, a number of the principal recommendations were executed rather earlier.

The 1975 Review was conducted in the framework of the educational approaches which the TUC had already developed. The stated aim was to

> *plan the future development of the different TUC education facilities as an integrated whole which would provide a more effective service to unions and would also contribute towards the co-ordination of TUC services with the work of individuals in this field (TUC 1975: 188).*

The basis of the Review was, in effect, a cost-effectiveness survey of existing provision. Unions were asked a number of questions about their membership and educational services. The returns (from 46 unions with membership totalling 7,240,037 or 72.2 per cent of TUC affiliated membership) provided substantial information about union educational structures and provision.

The survey (when multiplied up for the movement as a whole) produced figures of 291,000 shop stewards, 2,800 full-time officials, and 37,500 branches. It was assumed that each branch, on average, would have three officers. The total number of voluntary union officers would thus be 'just over 400,000' (TUC 1975: 189). This implied, assuming 20 per cent annual turnover, 'a basic training need for 80,000 voluntary officers' annually. Yet the TUC and affiliated unions combined 'would have provided [in 1973/74] only half a day for each union voluntary office holder during that year' — a total of 234,050 student days. And provision was not evenly spread: the 'actual number receiving any form of education or training was probably as low as 30,000' (TUC 1975: 189-90). The survey also found major divergences between unions' provision of education. There was 'a preponderance of membership in unions with low levels of educational activity' — less than, say, one student day per 100 members per annum (TUC 1973: 190). At the same time, the survey found that 'unions representing virtually a third of the total trade union membership spent less than 5p a member on education' during 1973/74 (TUC 1975: 191).

The Review also reported some simple but revealing figures about the TUC regional education scheme itself. The figures could hardly have been more telling. On average, a linked week-end course cost the TUC 87.3 pence per student hour: a day release course cost just 9.7 pence.[9] The case for day release now ceased to be merely educational or strategic: it became financial. At a time of rapid inflation the 'noticeably low cost per student hour' of day release courses made them still more attractive. The Review also established where the TUC's own strengths lay. Taking TUC and affiliated unions' provision together, the TUC provided just 22 per cent of weekend courses, 12.7 per cent of day schools, and 18 per cent of week-long courses. But it provided 78 per cent of in-plant and day-release courses. (Calculated from figures in TUC 1975: 189.) In the circumstances the General Council's decision was hardly surprising: after 'careful examination of all the educational and cost factors involved ... after March 1975 the regional programmes of weekend schools should be withdrawn'(TUC 1975: 192).[10] A target annual provision of 1,000 TUC day release courses by 1977 was established (TUC 1975: 192).[11]

The decision to concentrate resources on the provision of day release courses was one of two key developments for which the 1975 Review argued, and which its acceptance endorsed. The second key decision, however, was to approach the government for additional funding for trade union education. The Review set the scene for this by briefly surveying trade union education in seven countries — 'often state-aided' (TUC 1975: 195). Given the TUC's firm view, reiterated over a number of years, that it would — on principle — 'not wish to become the recipient of public funds for any purpose' (TUC 1969: 292), there was a certain amount of special pleading in the 1975 document. The fees charged for trade union courses by colleges 'were often well above fees charged for other day release programmes'. There was 'extensive provision from public funds for management education' (TUC 1975: 197). Even if the proposal were accepted, the TUC would not really receive public funds: it would merely 'make an annual claim to the DES for a refund of all fees paid by the TUC and individual unions' to public educational bodies (TUC 1975: 206). The distinction, if such it were, was nice indeed!

In reality, however, the Review was merely asserting a rationale for a decision reached some time earlier: perhaps even before the Labour government was returned. Reg Prentice (1992) suggests that the matter was mentioned in the pre-election talks between the TUC and the Labour Party which led to the Social Contract. He specifically recalls that

> The initial meeting to start this programme took place in my office at the DES some time in 1974 [when he was Secretary of State], probably fairly soon after we had taken office. Len Murray was there with the Education Officer of the TUC.

Having been a union official, and lectured at union summer schools and union courses in further education colleges, Prentice was 'personally keen'. But the matter had already been settled in principle. Prentice recalls that, at the time he met Len Murray, there was already 'some prior Treasury approval providing the cost was not too vast', and that although the meeting was held at his invitation, the TUC was expecting it and would probably have asked for it in any case. According to Prentice (1992), the 'preparatory stages' — detailed talks between the TUC Education Officer and Prentice's special adviser, Maurice Peston, followed by processing through the DES and Treasury machinery — took 'some time'. Part of this was no doubt the problem of winning union support for accepting public funds, which involved careful argumentation. Formally, it was only in July 1975 that the TUC General Council submitted a Memorandum to the Department of Education and Science, arguing that public funds should be allocated to trade union education.

This has rightly been seen as a most significant departure, and the TUC's

Memorandum deserves study. It had five key features. First, there was a general assertion that if trade unionists were to play a responsible and constructive role in the economy and society, they should be educated, and the state should contribute to this. This was argued in two main ways. On the one hand was a simple economic argument about 'the importance of trade union education and training to the efficient conduct of industrial relations and to the wellbeing of the nation as a whole' (TUC 1975: 197). This was backed up by an assertion that employers had 'recognised the importance of having competent union workplace representatives by facilitating their release with pay to attend union courses in working hours' (TUC 1975: 197). On the other hand, changes in social legislation 'raise[d] issues of fundamental importance' for trade unions: 'These measures which are intended to strengthen our democracy at a time when rapid industrial changes are necessary, are ... dependent upon the capacity of trade union representatives to deal with them effectively.' (TUC 1975: 198.) The measures in question were government legislation and proposed legislation on health and safety at work, industry, employment protection, sex discrimination, and pensions — in short, the stuff of which the Social Contract was made.

Second, the Memorandum argued both for 'training shop stewards' and for 'membership education'. There was a certain amount of fudging or ambivalence in this area. For many shop stewards, union training courses,

> *because of their direct relevance to their trade union needs, are probably the most meaningful educational experience they will have participated in. Highly motivated by their trade union interests such courses assist in providing the essential foundation on which to develop a critical appreciation not only of trade union affairs but of industrial life in general. ... [T]he debate between the 'trainers' on the one hand and the liberal educationalists on the other is [therefore] necessarily sterile and misleading. (TUC 1975: 199.)*

At the same time, shop stewards and 'other trade union activists' should be offered 'educational facilities that go beyond assisting them in effectively discharging the duties demanded by their immediate office' (TUC 1975: 199). The scope of union concerns, and unions' extensive involvement in 'industrial and public affairs', meant that the range of subject matter appropriate to 'trade union studies' was 'extensive indeed' (TUC 1975: 199).

Third, and in relation to this last assertion, the Memorandum included a statement of the movement's aims which asserted trade union entitlement to a substantial social and political role:

> *trade union objectives seek not only to improve the terms of employment*

3 Time off for Union Activities

For some time, shop stewards in well organised workplaces have had the right to time off for union work. Often the right has simply been built up through custom and practice.

So the recent provisions on time off introduce nothing new for many trade unionists. But you may find that management refers to the law in negotiations, or you may want to know if the law can be of any help to the union side as a negotiating tool. So it is worth while being familiar with the law.

What the Law says

The main rights here are:

- a right to reasonable time off with pay for shop stewards undertaking industrial relations duties, and union training related to these duties
- a right to reasonable time off for union members and shop stewards taking part in union (as opposed to 'industrial relations') activities. The law says nothing about pay in this respect.

> *These rights are now to be found in the* **Employment Protection (Consolidation) Act, 1978, s 27-28.**

The relevant sections are reproduced below. (There is an exercise on p. 10 of the **Skills** section which will help you to make sense of what they say.)

Section 27 deals with time off for 'industrial relations duties', and s 28 deals with time off for 'union activities'.

Time off work

27.—(1) An employer shall permit an employee of his who is an official of an independent trade union recognised by him to take time off, subject to and in accordance with subsection (2), during the employee's working hours for the purpose of enabling him—

(a) to carry out those duties of his as such an official which are concerned with industrial relations between his employer and any associated employer, and their employees; or

(b) to undergo training in aspects of industrial relations which is—

(i) relevant to the carrying out of those duties; and
(ii) approved by the Trades Union Congress or by the independent trade union of which he is an official.

Turn over

Fig.5.2: Rights to Time off Work for Union Training. A page from the 'Rights at Work' pack introduces a discussion of legal rights to paid release and quotes the law first introduced in 1975.

> of working people but also to create for them a safer working environment, to secure and maintain full employment, to provide for security of employment and income, to improve social welfare through education, housing and other public services, to establish fair shares in national income and wealth, to establish industrial democracy and to strengthen workers' trade union participation in Government (TUC 1975: 199).

Trade unionists needed constantly to assess 'policy priorities based on sound economic, political and social judgments, and to establish strategies for the achievement of policies involving the interaction of collective bargaining, with influencing Government ...' (TUC 1975: 200).

Fourth, the Memorandum made number of practical or procedural points. It argued implicitly for a distinct area of 'trade union studies'. Trade union studies tutors needed to be 'well-versed in teaching methods appropriate to adult students', capable of taking an 'inter-disciplinary approach', and 'widely informed about union affairs' (TUC 1975: 203). They also needed time and resources to update their knowledge continually, especially in industrial relations, and to apply 'considerable research' to the particular circumstances of their trade union students. The development of 'centres of trade union studies' at further education colleges should therefore be encouraged. In these centres some staff would be engaged 'almost full-time on trade union studies', and 'senior appointments' could ensure resources and time were available for 'local course development', which was 'essential' if courses were to be 'relevant to the needs of the students' (TUC 1975: 203). In addition, the Memorandum argued that the TUC had 'developed a special competence' in developing curricula and materials, having piloted new courses in its Training College (TUC 1975: 202). TUC syllabuses were increasingly being adapted for local courses. The Training College also provided training for full-time officials who might make contributions to education, and conferences for tutors.

Fifth, the Memorandum stood its ground in relation to positions developed by the TUC over previous years. There was an extensive rebuttal of the CIR view. Industrial relations training and trade union education and training were intimately related. 'The nature and function of union representatives is, in any case, a matter solely for the unions to decide as are their training and education needs.' To have encouraged 'separate training arrangements for stewards' which were not 'part of a total scheme ... properly reflecting the students' trade union and educational study needs' would have been 'wholly inconsistent with sound educational practice'. And education and training should be conducted 'in an educational setting free from the influence of management and supported by specialist tuition and appropriate teaching aids'. (TUC 1975: 201.) There was, furthermore, a strong assertion of the terms on which public funds would be acceptable. 'The British trade union Movement values its independence and would not favour any form of public funding that would enable decisions about trade union educational priorities and purposes to be subject to outside control' (TUC 1975: 205).

The 1975 Memorandum was, then, no craven capitulation to the interests of the state, let alone to state control. Reg Prentice (1992) recalled the initial meeting with Len Murray in 1974: 'the TUC expected to have a powerful voice on the curriculum'.[12] The Memorandum asserted the importance of educational values and methods. It asserted that education for trade unionists should be broad, and not narrowly attached to industrial relations functions. It asserted that education should be available to active trade unionists, and not merely to representatives. It asserted the legitimacy of trade union aims, defined these broadly, and argued for public funds on this basis. It asserted that trade union education should be independent of the state — although a financial partnership was possible on the basis of a number of common aims and through collaboration with educational institutions.

But while trade union education was educational, it was to be *trade union* education. The TUC by 1975 was clear about its distinctive educational approach. On this approach, evolved through the 1960s and early 1970s, union education must reflect union aims and philosophy. The approach crucially also stressed union control. Courses should be organised by trade unions rather than by employers. To this end, involvement by non-union agencies, such as the ITBs, was to be discouraged. Educational bodies should be encouraged to develop staff and units which identified with union aims and approaches; conversely, educational institutions must be discouraged from organising union education other than through proper trade union channels. Finally, trade union education in the late twentieth century must be systematic. The movement had suffered for decades from an educational provision (by the WETUC and the labour colleges) which lacked 'any close acquaintance with union educational needs', and which operated by 'reacting to casual, haphazard and unrelated local demands' (Education Committee document 5/2, 6 April 1971). Modern trade union education would provide a 'co-ordinated' system, which would be marked by relatively uniform standards and curricula across the country, progression between levels of programme, consistency as between provision by various providers, and by a targetting of resources toward centrally-identified objectives.

Although the initiatives of 1975 were consistent with the trend of TUC educational policy over the previous decade, the experience of the Heath government had left its mark in several ways. First, the role of education in the campaign against the Industrial Relations Bill and Act had a profound impact in convincing 'union sceptics about the utility value of education' (Taylor 1975). For the first time, the Education Department had been brought into the mainstream — asked to deliver immediately relevant objectives of vital importance to major policy issues. In the 1960s, the debates over union education had been arcane, of interest only to a small coterie of educational activists. Now it was seen to perform a clear role, and one whose importance was readily perceived by the leaders of the movement at every level, from national officials to shop stewards.

The strategy adopted was vital, for it provided a blueprint for TUC education over the following decade and more. A package of materials was written centrally,[13] 'for use by officers at half-day or full-day schools'. The materials were 'tested for effectiveness' in pilot courses. Four or five industrial relations tutors would be selected in each TUC region: they would be 'closely associated with the TUC Education Service and fully committed to the aims of trade unionism'. After attending a one-day 'briefing conference' at the TUC Training College (in which 'the use of the prepared teaching materials will be explained and demonstrated'), these tutors would themselves train full-time officers in the use of the materials. The full-time officers would, in turn, 'convene meetings and arrange schools for their own shop stewards and members from mid-January [1971] onwards to explain, with the help of the teaching materials provided by the TUC, the full implications of the proposed legislation'. (Education Committee document 2/5, 10 November 1970.) The Donovan Commission (Cmnd. 3623 1967: 26) estimated there was a total of about 3,000 full-time union officials: in the early months of 1971, 1,750 went through this 'intensive short course' (Education Committee document 8/4, 13 July 1971).[14] Apart from its formal aims, it was a profoundly important public relations exercise for TUC education.

The Heath years also embedded within the TUC an abiding suspicion of management-provided shop steward training, and of any role for the Department of Employment[15] in the development of trade union education. Doubts about a role for management were not new: but in the 1960s the TUC had been prepared to accept some such involvement as a *quid pro quo* for funding and release, either by employers or indirectly through ITBs. Just before the defeat of the Wilson government in 1970, for instance, the TUC Education Committee (minutes 13 January 1970) debated what attitude it should take to the proposed referral of industrial relations training to the CIR: there was opposition, but also a measure of support.

Under Heath, the CIR became anathema, of course: but TUC educators saw the Department of Employment as the fountainhead of CIR thinking on shop steward training. It had 'long sought to establish "Training Within

Industry" courses for stewards and following the publication of the C.I.R. Report ... prompted the Training Boards to review the contribution they could make to such training' (Education Committee document 5/2B, 11 February 1975). This led to problems. In particular several ITBs encouraged employer involvement through 'sponsoring and promoting ... [shop steward] courses by Boards or by employers' (Education Committee minutes 13 February 1973). The Local Government Training Board, for instance, issued a recommendation which

> *related the purpose of shop steward training to the efficiency of local authority services, not to the furtherance of trade union objectives; separated training in subjects of mutual interest to management and union from training in union subjects; and emphasised a joint responsibility of management and unions for the training of shop stewards.*

This recommendation (incorporated into collective agreements) led to some local authorities questioning release of shop stewards to attend TUC courses 'which had previously been developed in consultation with the authorities and unions concerned'. (Education Committee minutes 23 May 1973.) Concern at developments by the Paper and Paper Products Industry Training Board led the TUC to arrange discussions with its officials and trade union members to ensure that its actions 'should not conflict with the policies' of the TUC, and 'to avoid the placing of courses with educational bodies known to be unsatisfactory' (Education Committee minutes 10 July 1973).[16]

Under the Conservatives, an important TUC tactic was to draw the DES into debate about shop steward education. But even after the change of government in 1974, the TUC remained suspicious of the Department of Employment. Following the submission of the July 1975 Memorandum on public funds, Len Murray and Roy Jackson (TUC General Secretary and Head of the Education Department respectively) met the Secretary of State for Education. The 'first major issue' they raised was 'the TUC's reluctance to seek financial help for trade union education other than from the DES'. Despite pressure from the DES, they continued to emphasise 'that the TUC did indeed hold strong views' on Department of Employment involvement in trade union education (Education Committee document 1/1, 14 October 1975). The DE was never wholly excluded, but for many years the TUC was successful in minimising its influence, and dealt primarily with the DES.

Two other matters discussed with government at this time also had a major influence on the pattern of trade union education. First, and most profound, during 1974 the TUC pursued its argument for the inclusion in the Employment Protection Bill of a statutory right to paid educational leave for trade union representatives to enable them to attend union courses. First aired in the Liaison Committee, Len Murray renewed this case in a letter to Michael Foot, the Employment Secretary, shortly after the government was returned (14 May 1974: TUC file 40.2). For the government, a right to paid educational leave was uncontentious. But there was a protracted dispute between the TUC and the Department of Employment (which was responsible for drafting the legislation, and ensuring its safe passage through Parliament) over whether the right should apply to any training for shop stewards, or only to that approved by the TUC or a recognised trade union.

The TUC early came to the view—entirely consistent with its longstanding views about independence in union education—that the 'only criteria that the [Employment Protection] Act should specify in relation to trade union training was that the course should be approved by an independent union or the TUC' (F&GPC minutes 21 October 1974). Officials at the DE were clearly unhappy with this. The Bill was a highly contentious piece of legislation, which the government had to steer through on a wafer-thin majority in the House of Commons (and a minority in the Lords). But TUC officials may have come to suspect more sinister motives behind civil servants' desire 'not to give emphasis to certain detailed items in the main body of the Bill' (Education Committee document 7/6, 8 April 1975). The legislation would represent little advance, from a trade union viewpoint, if employers could refuse release to shop stewards on the ground that adequate training was already offered 'by employers directly or in co-operation with management consultants or agencies such as the Industrial Society' (Education Committee minutes 8 April 1975). This was a complex problem, which TUC officials pursued over the following months with ACAS as well as the DE. The CBI was lobbying too: for employers to have a right to approve which courses were suitable for shop stewards they employed (Education Committee minutes 10 June 1975). In July, the TUC stepped up the pressure, with correspondence between Len Murray and Michael Foot (2 and 22 July 1975: TUC file 40.2) and, when that proved ineffective, a delegation of senior General Council members (31 July 1974: notes in TUC file 40.2). Finally, the General Secretary wrote a very strong letter (21 August: TUC file 40.2). This point was a 'matter of fundamental trade union principle. ... The Bill ... breaches this principle ....' Under such pressure, Foot appears to have decided against the earlier view of his officials: the requirement for union or TUC approval was included.

However, the right to release as enacted (Employment Protection Act 1975: s.57),[17] was by no means absolute. It required only that an employer should permit employees who were officials of an independent trade union recognised by the employer, to take 'reasonable' paid time off work during working hours in order to 'undergo training' concerned with 'aspects of industrial relations'. The training should be 'relevant' to carrying out industrial relations duties with their own or an associated employer. Ample space remained for judicial interpretation. The point about union control of training was an important victory, but it did not give union representatives a general right to attend training: workers still had to apply to their employer in the first instance, and the legal mechanisms for enforcement were far from straightforward.

Second, the Health and Safety at Work Act 1974, a direct descendant of legislation drafted under the Heath government, envisaged (in Section 2(4)) the appointment of Safety Representatives by employees. This legislation had been under consideration for some years (preliminary discussions about the educational implications had been held between TUC departments as early as 1970 (Education Committee document 5/5, 10 February 1970). During 1973 pilot courses on health and safety at work were developed by the TUC Education Department for workplace representatives of the AUEW (Foundry Section). The TUC was concerned that Safety Representatives should be appointed only by trades unions, and that they should have specific trade union functions. This was vigorously opposed by the employers. Changes introduced to the Health and Safety at Work Act (by the Employment Protection Act 1975) however, and regulations subsequently introduced, largely met the TUC concerns. As a result, safety representatives enjoyed similar rights to paid time off for training as shop stewards. Again, the TUC was emphatic that courses should be under trade union control, and the right to paid time off work was limited to courses approved by the TUC or an independent trade union.[18]

The Meaning of 1975

The Labour government's response to TUC lobbying was to make a grant of £400,000 for the year 1976/77. The era of public funding for union education had commenced. The significance of this decision can best be judged in the light of the TUC scheme's subsequent development. But it is important to recall the political climate of the mid-1970s. The TUC sought and accepted state funding at the height of the Social Contract. The Conservative government had posed major problems for the trade union movement. Heath's fall had been, frankly, fortuitous, and Labour's slim majority produced little confidence that the government would see out a full term. Under Heath the state and employers had been generating a strategy for trade union education. As a speaker remarked at the 1973 TUC,

> *It is no secret that the Department of Employment, through the Training Services Agency, is overtly encouraging employers at this time to include in their training plans courses in industrial relations, and they are*

> *expecting the Industrial Training Boards to put up the money in grant support for them. While that may sound fine, that the boss in fact pays for the training, he will also be expecting, because he is putting up the cash, to call the tune on what is in the course, how it is run, and how it is angled.*

The political environment might revert at almost any time; such approaches would again be in vogue. (Even without government encouragement, many employers continued to initiate training for shop stewards.) For the trade union movement, and for TUC, the imperative was to use public funds to establish a structure and system of trade union education which would be secure against foreseeable political vicissitudes.

The strategy identified during the Heath years was to continue: union education would be developed within the public education sector, building up a network of working relationships with educational institutions. At the top there would be funding by the DES,[19] and working relationships with DES officials and the HMI. There would be provision through colleges of further education (and a few polytechnics), and relationships with the local education authorities which governed and financed them. There would be continuing provision through the Responsible Bodies: the university extra-mural departments and WEA districts. This approach would have dual virtues. It would provide an institutional structure capable of delivering a large programme across the country. It would also enmesh union education with a range of institutions in a decentralised educational system.

The TUC's approach had the advantage of being in harmony with thinking in the educational establishment. We have discussed at some length the influence of industrial relations and economic policy on union education, especially through Donovan, *In Place of Strife*, and the CIR Report. But following TUC initiatives in the 1960s, the expansion of educational opportunities for trade unionists was a matter of wider consideration in government. Trade union education was increasingly of concern to educational policy-makers. The Gold Report (DES 1972: 14) asserted the 'urgent need to ensure that all shop stewards receive some basic training and education'. These needs should be brought to employers' attention 'in the interests of the community as a whole'. The entire Report is concerned with how to provide the mechanisms to develop such work. Gold's committee was 'a group of specialists' (DES 1972: covering circular): also significant was the coverage of union education in the Russell (DES 1973b: esp. 89-92) and Alexander (SED 1975: esp. 66-8) reports.

Russell (DES 1973b: 90-91) blessed the 'partnership' between trade unions and adult education as 'fruitful'; it 'ensured that genuine educational values and an objective approach are fostered'. Trade unions, 'like other voluntary bodies,' could not be expected to pay the full cost of

Your Job as a Shop Steward

Extract from a TUC publication:

MODEL AGREEMENT

PAID RELEASE FOR TRAINING OF UNION REPRESENTATIVES

1. In order to carry out their duties effectively union representatives shall receive appropriate training as approved by the TUC and/or their unions.
2. Union representatives shall be entitled to undertake such training in working hours without loss of any earnings (including bonus, overtime and all enhancements) which they would normally have earned had they been at work for the days at which they attend the course.
3. Where a union representative works on a shift or rota system, payment will be granted for one full shift per day of the course (including shift premium).
4. The employer will reimburse expenses and the cost of lunch and refreshments for attendance at day release courses.
5. This agreement will apply to the following types of training:—
   (a) *Induction Courses*
      Day/Block release courses involving a minimum of fifteen study hours. Release facilities will normally be made available within three months of the representative taking office, and as soon as possible for representatives who are already in office. Courses provided by unions will be suitable to meet this need.
   (b) *Basic Introductory Courses*
      TUC or appropriate union courses normally of 10-12 days. Release will be made available within twelve months of appointment for newly appointed representatives, and as soon as possible for representatives who are already in office.
   (c) *Further Training Courses*
      TUC or union courses normally of 10-12 days. These are intended for:—
      (i) Representatives with special responsibilities (eg senior representatives, safety representatives, pension fund representatives)
      (ii) Updating courses for all representatives, dealing with new developments. Each representative will normally attend three such courses in any three-year period.
   (d) *Advanced Courses*
      For key representatives such as convenors and union representatives serving on company boards. These will be longer courses, normally provided on a residential basis.
6. For the purpose of meeting these training needs TUC and union courses shall be deemed appropriate. The unions will notify management of any other courses which meet with their approval.
7. The union agrees to:
   (a) Provide management with appropriate syllabuses of training courses where requested.
   (b) Normally give a few weeks' notice of nominations for appropriate training.
   (c) Take due account of the operational requirements of the employer.
8. The union and management shall endeavour to reach agreement on any problems arising from the operation of this agreement, and shall refer any differences to the normal procedure for dealing with disputes and grievances.
9. Notwithstanding any time limits in the normal procedure, the management appreciate that a decision will be required as quickly as possible, and in any event a reasonable time before the commencement of the course.

TUC Copyright

Fig.5.3: Building on Legal Rights to Paid Release. Model agreements, common in TUC course materials in the late 1970s, conveyed union policy and the importance of collective agreements. Paragraph 5 of this example (from the 'Red Pack') outlines policy on the types of course representatives should attend.

courses themselves. The Committee proposed that the TUC, the CBI, and government should ensure that adequate paid release was available for 'appropriate courses'. In the Department of Education shop steward training was viewed as 'a useful growth area, as a counterpart to increased provision of management industrial relations training in further education' (Vulliamy 1985: 15). In Scotland, the Alexander Report (SED 1975: 66-7) argued for extended facilities for shop steward training, and for 'the fullest possible co-operation between universities, colleges of further education and other teaching institutions' and trade unions. Unions also had 'much of importance to contribute' to community education. In short, there was a momentum for the development of union education from the educational sector as well as from trade unions themselves. To this extent, union educators in 1974 and 1975 were pushing at an opening door. But there was also some danger that — in the absence of initiative from the TUC — an institutional (and perhaps even a legislative) structure of education for union representatives might evolve over which the trade unions had no real influence.

With public funds 'in the bag', the TUC's task became one of development. The general lines of policy had been sketched in the TUC's various statements — from *Training Shop Stewards* to the 1975 Memorandum — but much detail still had to be worked out. The first priority established was for the day release programme: to achieve an annual provision of 1,000 ten-day courses by 1977 (TUC 1975: 192). This represented a substantial increase — about 50 per cent over the 1973/74 figure. But not only was this figure reached: the plan was over-fulfilled, and the growth continued. By the end of the decade, provision within the TUC scheme was roughly four times larger than it had been in the year before the decision to seek public funds. This was prodigious growth, which deserves to be recognised as the major achievement it was. Larger numbers of classes implied no significant fall-away in the number of students on each course: indeed, the mean student number per course in 1978/79 (14.14) was actually larger than it had been in 1973/74 (13.56). (For statistics on TUC day release programmes, see Appendix B.) And the growth achieved by 1978/79 appears still more remarkable when compared with the TUC's provision a decade earlier: in 1967/68 the TUC sponsored just 155 day-release courses, enrolling some 2,263 students.

This formidable growth is a key to understanding many of the developments of the 1970s. To achieve it, vast resources were needed. Public funds were an essential prerequisite; but they were hardly sufficient. It is instructive to look at some of the findings of the Gold Report, which reviewed (*inter alia*)

Great Leap Forward: 1968-1979

> *problems of coverage over the country, the possibility of furthering the degree of co-operation between the bodies offering Shop Steward Courses, problems of staffing and the supply and training of teachers, together with the related question of teaching material and the pooling of resources (DES 1972: 3).*

It conducted a detailed analysis of institutions. Several of its findings echoed the views expressed in *Training Shop Stewards*. First of all, Gold found 'an overall shortage of teachers of industrial relations'. An extra 200-300 teachers would be required to meet demands expected in 'the next three to five years' (DES 1972: 11). (The Report was written in 1970, well before public funds became available.) In most colleges providing trade union courses (and only 80 of 230 colleges providing management and industrial relations courses surveyed claimed to do so (DES 1972: 10)), 'there are only one or two industrial relations teachers', so that the departure of just one member of staff might have a major effect on the quality — or even the possibility — of courses.

> *If demand is to be met, there must be an increase in the number of teachers capable of meeting it, and strong centres must have at least at least three or four members of staff of this kind. Indeed, effective teaching cannot develop if the trade unions and firms consider that the quality and quantity of staff is insufficient to guarantee successful courses. (DES 1972: 11)*

The WEA alone estimated that it would require a further fifty tutors to meet increasing demands for shop steward education.

Second, if new tutors and lecturers were to be supplied, they had to be trained. Gold (DES 1972: 11) suggested three categories should be considered. There were qualified teachers who needed 'greater knowledge of Industrial Relations, particularly of trade unionism and the function of shop stewards', and who would 'require short courses, with secondment to a trade union and/or industry for a period if possible'. There were teachers experienced in industrial relations who would need 'help in the teaching methods ... applicable to Shop Steward Courses', and some 'topping-up' material. And there were those 'interested in the subject but who would require comprehensive training'. The Report (DES 1972: 12-13) noted that there were 'no full-time courses specifically arranged to meet this need' for trade union studies tutors, although short courses were offered by the Oxford University Extra-mural Delegacy ('topping-up' for fairly advanced lecturers), and jointly by Ruskin College, the TUC Education Department, and the WEA (an eight-week course for industrial relations lecturers likely to become involved in shop steward courses). Gold proposed that in-service training courses should be provided by 'two or more of the more experienced Technical Colleges', that the DES itself should provide extended short courses in the area, and that the TUC's offer of adding to the training of a number of tutors through their secondment to the TUC Education Department should be accepted.

Third, a need had been 'expressed by teachers' for 'organised teaching material and documentation, and for making material widely available to them' (DES 1972: 13). However, Gold suggested that 'existing services' in this area — Ruskin, the Nottingham, Oxford and Sheffield Extra-mural Departments, the WEA Service Centre for Social Studies, and the TUC Education Department itself could be 'expanded to meet the demand as it grows'.

Gold's concerns were no less significant to the TUC. But the TUC also had an agenda of its own. There were two main prongs to its thinking at this time. It was concerned to see 'the development of a distinct sector of trade union education within adult and further education' (TUC 1975: 203). This was not a new line of thought: it reflected the TUC's evidence to the Russell Committee (DES 1973b: 90), and was a logical development of the assertive approach of *Training Shop Stewards*. At the same time, the TUC remained highly sensitive about who controlled shop steward education. Public funds must cement for the TUC a central, hegemonic, role in union education.

The first problem, of course, when public funds became available, was to spend the money and provide the courses. Action had to be taken in short order — quite apart from whatever the long-term agenda might be. Resources had to be shifted toward trade union courses throughout the country. This was not just a matter of how to spend money. There was enormous pressure for growth from the grass roots: from union full-time officers and shop stewards. The legal changes of the mid-1970s (especially the Employment Protection and Health and Safety at Work Acts) demanded more of all union workplace representatives, apart from creating a whole new stratum of safety representatives.

This rapid growth raised the issue of quality control in several ways. There was an educational methods dimension. In colleges, courses often had to fit into an existing timetable: as a result they were often multi-tutored by a variety of lecturers. In some colleges and extra-mural departments, lecturers apparently lectured. The TUC Education Department saw this as inappropriate to the needs of shop stewards, whose educational backgrounds required not so much programmed inputs as careful and individual nurturing and counselling through a course. There was an expertise dimension: as the programme mushroomed, some tutors were being drafted in with little or no knowledge of the subjects or issues involved. As new topics and subject-matter were introduced (in particular, the legal changes of the 1970s), there was also a real need even for existing staff to be retrained or up-dated.

There was also an ideological or political dimension. College lecturers, especially in those colleges with little history of providing trade union courses, were allegedly often — and certainly sometimes — unsympathetic to trade union aims and objectives (having been recruited with backgrounds in management to teach management studies). The WEA may have been seen as having 'too many left-wing maverick tutors' (Vulliamy 1985: 15): it had certainly been too keen 'to include some element of "liberal" workers' education in the schools and courses provided by the TUC' (Education Committee document 5/2, 6 April 1971). But on the whole its tutors were regarded as reliable allies committed to trade union objectives. A number of university extra-mural staff were also regarded as allies, and trusted by the TUC's regional education officers. But since the early 1960s there had been 'prevailing misunderstandings and frictions' between the TUC and 'all but a relatively few' extra-mural departments. These reflected (in Dennis Winnard's view) the latter's 'arrogance' and their 'assumption ... that they know better than the TUC what the interests of the trade union Movement demand in the way of educational provision' (Winnard to F. Pickstock, 22 March 1974: TUC file 817).[20]

These issues reflected the categories of concern raised by Gold; but they did so from a particular angle. And while the TUC tackled them vigorously, and in the light of its established broad strategy, the short-term was paramount. First, in the matter of tutor training, rather than seeking to establish the kind of tutor-training structures suggested by Gold — involving liaison with Ruskin, the WEA, extra-mural departments, and so on — it decided to 'go it alone'. It built up a course development unit at Congress House — the number of staff in the Education Department at Congress House grew four-fold during the 1970s (McIlroy 1985c: 46). This did not make it a large organisation: until 1972 the Training College (the section of the Education Department concerned with developing and teaching courses, rather than with programme administration and servicing committees) had only two staff. But employing educational staff allowed the TUC to train tutors. A programme of short (one-week) tutor-training courses was introduced; all TUC tutors were expected to attend.

Second, the TUC decided to establish a common curriculum — and again, rather than liaising with institutions already working in the area to produce jointly-agreed (or even a range of) course materials, it committed itself to providing course materials from its own resources for the entire range of courses. Until about 1978, materials were largely duplicated. The syllabus was standardised, but the content was subject to a large degree of local variation. In developing materials, the TUC drew heavily, especially in the early years, on contributions from experienced tutors in the WEA, extra-mural departments, and colleges up and down the country. But it generally dealt with them individually as 'TUC tutors', rather than with their institutions: there was to be no external 'control' over the shape of the curriculum or the materials produced. These materials also served a major quality control function, establishing minimum standards for courses. They enabled less well-trained tutors to 'learn on the job' without causing serious problems over course quality. They ensured that the TUC's view of union aims and methods were represented in the classrooms.[21] They meant that tutors could not, as Stan Greaves (1992) put it, 'body-swerve' elements of the course, or offer 'the memoirs of a not very good convenor'.

The decision to introduce a 'national curriculum' in TUC education had another — promotional — aspect. It had been the practice of the best trade union tutors to involve themselves in 'local course development, an activity which is essential if courses are to be made relevant to the needs of students' (TUC 1975: 203). Commonly, this had involved tutors meeting with union full-time officers and senior shop stewards to plan courses and their content. Often, such senior union personnel might contribute to teaching on the courses. But with a limited programme these contacts had needed only to be modest. The expansion of the programme required that far more full-time officers should be convinced of the importance and value of union education. Full-time officers and senior stewards were central to the process of student recruitment. Many still adhered to the notion, vigorously rebutted in *Training Shop Stewards*, that 'the job of representing members' interests can be learned only by doing it' (TUC 1968a: 10). Some feared that courses might be threaten their positions. Others were far from convinced that the TUC's rejection of joint training (with management) was necessary or worthwhile. The common teaching materials enabled the TUC education service to show union officials precisely what the content of courses was: soon printed, they also looked very impressive.

The achievement of TUC education in the 1970s was remarkable. In the single decade ending in 1978/79, the TUC's provision of day release courses increased by 1,300 per cent.[22] During the same period, a major assault from a hostile government with its own agenda for industrial relations training was overcome. Funding was negotiated from the Labour government, largely on the TUC's own terms. Legislation was won which provided unprecedented rights to paid educational leave. A network of relationships with public sector educational institutions was created. The course development unit ensured that more or less uniform curricula, and a more or less uniform quality of provision, were maintained across the country. A cadre of committed trade union studies tutors was developed.

It is difficult to 'measure' the impact of these developments. In a number of instances the education service provided 'crash' programmes which played a major role in making TUC policy successful. The earliest, and probably most telling, example was the campaign against the Industrial Relations Bill. But the mid-1970s were also marked by important legislation developments from which workers stood to benefit — if their union organisations could develop effective strategies at workplace level. The outstanding case was health and safety at work. Nearly 70,000 students attended the TUC's day release health and safety courses between 1975 and 1980.[23] Along with the 'crash' programme of one and two-day workshops on the legislation (and many courses arranged by individual unions but based on TUC materials), the day release courses established the framework by which the new laws were interpreted and operated at workplace level. Managers in the late 1970s and early 1980s could be heard to complain that safety representatives often knew more about the subject than they did themselves. More important, perhaps, than knowledge were attitudes and approach: TUC courses were profoundly important in establishing the principle that health and safety was a matter for bargaining and negotiation, rather than of joint interest.

1   *Training Shop Stewards* had also 'strongly emphasised' that union representatives themselves 'are, and must be, an integral part of their union's total structure'. Their training therefore 'cannot be isolated from the total pattern of trade union education designed to equip officers and members for the multiplicity of tasks and duties involved in trade union work'. (TUC 1968a: 1.) This 'strong emphasis' was, however, considerably weaker than the stance taken by the General Council six months later.

2   But although, for instance, the TUC Education Service Consultative Group (largely union education officers) had been meeting throughout 1967 and early 1968 to consider the development of standardised regional courses, the discussion hardly touched on questions of control (in the sense of considering the relationship between the TUC, educational institutions, and the state). They appear to have been conducted largely in the language of standards. The nearest to an explicit comment on control issues comes in the note of a discussion on a working paper: in relation to 'Other educational Bodies' — universities, colleges, the WEA, etc. — 'one would expect that there would be a need for guidance but without actual control' (report of meeting, 15 March 1968: TUC file 817.211B).

3   Chaired by Mr D.J. Gold, HMI, it subsequently become known as the Gold Committee, and its report (Department of Education and Science 1972) is generally referred to as the Gold Report. Mr Gold recalls (letter, 27 February 1992) that 'the initiative for the setting up of the Working Party came from the DES, which had been asked by the government to do so'.

4. Mr Gold (1992b) recalls that 'the report was complete in mid 1970'; the TUC Education Committee was informed (minutes 13 February 1973) that the report was completed 'at the end of 1970'.
5. An incidental casualty of the campaign was *In Place of Strife*'s proposal for a state-financed Trade Union Development Fund administered by the CIR; one function of the TUDF would have been the provision of funds for trade union education.
6. The reference was originally made under the Labour government on 29 May 1970, three weeks before the general election. The study was chiefly conducted in the first half of 1971. Limited consultation with the TUC and various unions was possible before the TUC withdrew co-operation. (CIR 1972a: viii, 6-7.)
7. Reg Prentice (1992) 'believe[d] that the proposals were mentioned in these talks 'in 1973 or thereabouts', but was 'not absolutely sure on this point'. I found no paper or minute about this. Any question of state funding for trade unions would have been controversial, of course, and the discussions may have been very informal and exploratory. Prentice may have confused public funding with the issue of paid release for (*inter alia*) union training, which was discussed.
8. The Education Committee (minutes 9 October 1973) rejected 'the implication ... that the TUC was failing to meet its responsibilities' in trade union education as 'unjustified and unacceptable', although it welcomed the 'general intention of the resolution to encourage the provision of facilities by the trade union Movement itself was to be welcomed'.
9. Costs were worked out for other categories of course also, and provided (TUC 1975: 191) for two years (1971/72 and 1973/74). The figures (in pence per student hour) were as follows:

	1971/72	1973/1974
Linked Weekend Courses	66.5	87.3
Single Weekend Courses	60.6	83.3
Single Day Schools	21.7	23.8
Evening Classes	13.6	11.5
Day Release Courses	8.9	9.7

10. The TUC's review did not, of course, prevent individual affiliated unions continuing to promote their own courses as they saw fit.
11. Parallel developments in membership education are dealt with later.
12. The tenor of discussions within the TUC during the early 1970s confirms that this was perceived as of central importance.
13. The materials were written by Roy Jackson, then Director of Studies at the TUC Training College (1958-74), but Head of the Education Department 1974-86. (He then became Assistant General Secretary).
14. When the Bill became law, a similar exercise was undertaken to 'meet the needs of trade union officers' in working under the new legal regime (Education Committee document 8/4, 13 July 1971).

15 At that time, still formally the Department of Employment and Productivity.
16 In addition to the ITBs, there was concern about the work of the Industrial Society 'and other bodies' (e.g., productivity associations). For example, the Education Committee (minutes 13 February 1973) felt that 'while some of the work of the Industrial Society was of some value to unions, the Society's involvement in the provision of education and training for shop stewards was more dubious. The courses were provided mainly for individual companies and were designed with minimal consultation with the unions, with the result that the teaching was biased towards management interests and based upon a view of shop stewards, not as union officials, but as liaison officers for the company.'
17 In 1978 the right to paid time off was backed up by an Advisory, Conciliation and Arbitration Service (ACAS) Code of Practice (see ACAS 1978), which had legal standing, and was transferred into the Employment Protection (Consolidation) Act (ss. 27-8).
18 These came into force under paragraph 4(2) of the Safety Representatives and Safety Committees Regulations 1977 (SI 1977 No 500); they were backed up by a Health and Safety Commission Code of Practice.
19 In Scotland, by the Scottish Education Department.
20 A rather different, and less sympathetic, perspective on the TUC's relations with the university extra-mural departments during this period is provided by McIlroy (1988); see also Campbell and McIlroy (1986).21 Questions of the curriculum, and teaching and development methods, are dealt with in more detail in Chapter 7 below. They have been the subject of substantial debate, in relation to how far the TUC exercised control over course content and method, what the dimensions of the 'acceptable' were, how far tutors were encouraged or permitted to make positive contributions to course content, and how effective 'TUC methods' actually were.
21 Questions of the curriculum, and teaching and development methods, are dealt with in more detail in Chapter 7 below. They have been the subject of substantial debate, in relation to how far the TUC exercised control over course content and method, what the dimensions of the 'acceptable' were, how far tutors were encouraged or permitted to make positive contributions to course content, and how effective 'TUC methods' actually were.
22 In terms both of numbers of courses provided, and of number of students.
23 This figure should be seen in the light of the Education Committee's estimate (9 March 1975) that the extension of safety legislation implied 'meeting the training needs of upwards of 100,000 safety representatives in a very short time'.

Chapter 6

Reaction and Retrenchment
1979–1987

By 1979 the TUC's Education Department had largely cemented the essential structure of its regional education service. In a talk to trade union studies tutors at the TUC's summer school that July — for several years a number of tutor briefings were held together in Sheffield as a residential summer school — Stan Greaves (1979), the Department's Assistant Secretary, reflected on the achievement. The TUC was now working with 181 public educational bodies, providing 3,100 courses for some 44,000 students annually. There were now about nine designated 'trade union studies centres', with four more 'in the pipeline'. Roughly 230 tutors were working full-time on trade union studies ('sometimes at the cost of their own careers'); a further 100 or so were devoting 70 per cent of their time to trade union courses. The TUC was 'quite a big buyer' in the public education sector, purchasing about 2.6 million student hours per annum, and enjoyed 'generally good relations with colleges'. The TUC's regional education officers were often 'in with LEAs, principals, and heads of department'.

Yet he was speaking two months after the election of the Conservative government under Margaret Thatcher — a government committed to radical reform of the economy, of industrial relations and trade unionism, of the public sector. The eighties were to be years of major challenge — and threat — to trade union education; and perhaps particularly to state-funded trade union education. Greaves made some reference to this in his talk: there was, he asserted, no question of 'shabby compromises' on finance or content: if public money ceased to be available, the necessary funds would be found 'somewhere'. But there was, understandably, no real appreciation of how deep the challenge to trade unionism would be, or how long it would continue.

In fact, the 1980s saw a marked decline in the provision of trade union education: just as they saw a marked decline in trade union membership. But throughout the decade the government continued to finance trade union education in public sector educational bodies through a grant provided to the TUC — that is, by essentially the same mechanism as was established in 1975/76. There were, it is true, a few attempts to influence the content of courses: but these were not sustained. Their effect was probably to restrain the TUC from certain more radical or controversial moves it might have taken, rather than to alter an existing provision. At the same time the

TUC scheme adapted in various ways to the new and more hostile climate, and made a number of innovations.

The present chapter examines the political and economic climate of the 1980s, and in particular its relationship to industrial relations and workplace trade unionism, and then turns to the main developments which occurred in trade union education. Coverage of developments in curriculum and methods is broadly held over until Chapter 7.

Ideology, Depression, and Trade Unionism

The Thatcher government came to power in May 1979 with decided views on trade unions and industrial relations. It held that the balance of power in industry had been tipped away from 'responsible management' and toward trade unions. This balance had to be redressed: the approach adopted was to introduce legal changes which would limit trade unions' or employees' rights in areas such as industrial action (introducing a notion of, and proscribing, 'secondary action'), picketing, the closed shop, how trade union ballots were carried out, trade union recognition, and unfair dismissal. Second, along with this went support for firm management: a repudiation of the notion that government had any role in settling or arbitrating in industrial disputes (apart, a cynic might add, from ensuring that management always had the upper hand). Third, there was a firm belief that public spending was too high, and should urgently be reduced as a share of the national income. This, of course, had profound implications for the public sector, particularly — to begin with — the nationalised industries, where the profitability of the enterprise (as a prelude to disposal to the private sector) rapidly became an over-riding objective. 'We need to ensure, so far as possible,' said Sir Geoffrey Howe (Treasury 1979) in his first Budget speech in 1979, 'that those who take part in collective bargaining understand the consequences of their actions.' One important method, with highly effective demonstrative effects, was to ensure that management in the public manufacturing sector defeated the unions in key disputes.

The government had a profound faith in the efficacy of the market and the moral virtues of market disciplines. The market was seen as a real, natural, unavoidable feature of human society: only through it could human beings appreciate and exercise their real individual responsibilities. Any attempt to fetter the market deprived individuals of their need to choose between genuine alternatives, and thus removed their responsibility — indeed, tended to make them irresponsible. This meant that, as time passed and elections were won, practices which tended to protect areas of employment, enterprise, or service from the rigours of the marketplace were gradually removed: or, where this was all but impossible, surrogates for competition were sought — mechanisms which would introduce important aspects of market disciplines. For instance — one major example — throughout the public sector a procedure for limiting expenditure by cash rather than volume limits was introduced in 1981.

In addition, and of great importance for our discussion, the government's approach — especially during the early eighties — reflected a deep sense of guilt and failure about the experience of 1970-1974. The Heath government had not had the courage of its convictions, and had done a 'U-turn' when its policies led to unpalatably high levels of unemployment. (The unacceptable level, in those much-reviled days, was in the region of a million.) The Thatcher government had been given backbone by the dominance of the extreme free-market right in Conservative intellectual circles during the 1970s, and was not prepared to change course just because unemployment rose to high levels. In any case, government was not responsible for levels of employment in the economy; these were determined by individuals' willingness to accept work at market rates. There can be no doubt that the inordinately high levels of unemployment which resulted from the Thatcher governments' economic policies had an important effect in weakening trade unionism.

Although this is not the place for an economic or political history of the Thatcher years, we should sketch some essential features of the 1980s which relate to industrial relations. Unemployment rose steeply in the early years: from an annual average of 1.3 millions in 1979 to 1.6 millions in 1980, 2.5 millions in 1981, and 2.8 millions in 1983. The following year it reached 3.0 millions; it remained somewhat over this figure for the following four years despite a series of measures designed to exclude various categories of unemployed people from the figures. The index of industrial production declined from 113 in 1979, to 105 in 1980, 100 in 1981, and 92 in 1982, before edging upward to 94 the following year. Although the 'recovery' continued fitfully, only in 1987 did the index again reach the figure of 1979. The index of Gross Domestic Product fell from 103 in 1979 to 100 in 1980 and 98 in 1981; it then began to recover, reaching 100 again in 1982, 106 in 1984, and 114 in 1986. (Calculated from Treasury *Economic Progress Reports*.) In short, the years from 1980 to 1983 were a period of profound and deep economic depression. (For a succinct economic account of this period, see Donaldson and Farquhar 1988: 125-31.)

The depression was deepest in manufacturing industry. This was the bedrock of trade unionism. It had traditionally accounted for the great bulk of trade union membership. In addition, union organisation in major areas of manufacturing (particularly engineering) had traditionally been very

To sum up, the way the conflict of interest between management and unions is resolved looks like this:

Where does trade union power come from?

Your trade union power is based on the effectiveness of your trade union organisation. In the last analysis the strength of your union depends on its ability to hurt the employer. This can be achieved by collectively stopping or restricting the employer in conducting his business. There are many forms of industrial action which can be used to achieve this.

We looked at the key points for effective trade union organisation in the last section. Effective trade union organisation is the foundation on which all workers' rights are built. Without strong trade union organisation you will be unable to make improvements in the wages and conditions of your members.

The ability to take industrial action is crucial to trade unions, whether it's a go-slow, a work to rule, an overtime ban, a sit-in, a strike, or the threat of a strike. In the last analysis unless you can mobilise your membership to action there is no need for your employer to take you seriously. On the other hand using your industrial strength when it's not necessary may damage your union's credibility and involve your members in unnecessary sacrifices. Using just the threat of industrial action may be enough if you are well organised. We have seen attempts by some governments to limit your trade union ability to take industrial action. If that happens then trade union power will be undermined. The ability to take industrial action is central to trade union power.

Fig.6.1: Union Power and the Right to Manage. The 'Red Pack' resolves conflicts in industry and explains the foundations of union power.

strong, and bargaining in these areas had set the pace for other sectors of the economy. Closures and dismissals ('redundancies') in this sector thus cut away fiercely at trade union membership and power. Further, when growth eventually returned, it was often on the basis of more advanced production technology: the demand for labour remained lower. Job losses were initially concentrated disproportionately in manufacturing. However, with cash limits on the public sector, and steadily reducing allocations of expenditure in real terms, employment in central and local government and the health service also began to suffer. Along with this went a number of measures designed to import private enterprise into the public sector, especially in the areas traditionally staffed by 'unskilled' manual workers — for example, hospital cleaning and laundries.

With burgeoning levels of unemployment, trade union bargaining strength was inevitably sapped. This was emphasised, and reinforced — trade union strength is inescapably a matter of how much workers feel their strength, or weakness — by a succession of high-profile union defeats: the national steel strike, the National Graphical Association's action at Warrington, the coal strike of 1984-1985, the printing unions' dispute with News International, and so forth. These setbacks reflected trade unionists' general reluctance to take action — which itself reflected the deep inroads made by the state on the legal status of trade unionism.

Yet when all this is said, several studies suggest that the story was not so straightforward. The economic indicators and the high-profile defeats were only one aspect of reality. Workplace trade union organisation in fact remained relatively widespread and — taking into account the general economic and political climate — effective. The Workplace Industrial Relations Survey found that in 1984 'there had been a slight increase in the number of lay representatives' in the economy as a whole, compared with the first such Survey four years earlier (Millward and Stevens 1986: 304). This apparent paradox can be explained in several ways. The increases in the number of representatives occurred in the public sector and in the non-manual areas of the private sector (especially the service industries). There was a sharp drop in the number of shop stewards in manufacturing industry — the traditional stronghold of trade unionism. Similarly, while manual full-time 'convenors' or senior stewards became far less numerous, among non-manual workers they became more common. (Millward and Stevens 1986: 304-05.) The essential point is that, in the depths of the early 1980s recession, where union-organised enterprises survived so did union organisation (Millward and Stevens 1986: 17n1; Batstone 1984: 214).

Batstone's review of the evidence on change in workplace trade union strength during the 1980s (1988: esp. 210-17) concluded that government policies (other than through their impact on unemployment — no minor caveat), had far less impact than was commonly supposed. Union density declined, although 'not as dramatically as one might expect'. Closed shops probably became less widespread. The range of issues on which collective bargaining occured appears to have narrowed (although it remained 'higher than it was at the time of Donovan'). Strikes became less common. But, during the 1980s, 'on most counts the role of trade unions within the workplace does not appear to have changed significantly'. Although union power declined from its high point of the late 1970s, it remained 'greater than at the high point of the Donovan debate when trade union power was meant to be such a major problem'. It must be said that this picture conflicts with the commonsense of the day. Many shop stewards and trade union educators were at the time conscious above all of their declining ability to organise and negotiate effectively. This more commonsense view is supported by Marsh (1992: 191-237), though his discussion focuses on a rather longer period (1979-91) than we do in this Chapter.

Government Industrial Relations Strategy and Trade Union Education

During the 1960s and the early 1970s, a view emerged within government circles that training shop stewards was a mechanism by which the state could influence trade union activity at workplace level. While governments grappled with the contradictions of maintaining full employment, high corporate profitability, and low inflation, controlling 'wage drift' — the product of shop stewards' bargaining power at workplace level — was at a premium. With proper training about collective agreements and adherence to procedures, shop stewards' approaches to collective bargaining might become more orderly. Some scholars (e.g., McIlroy 1985c and 1988; Vulliamy 1985) suggest that this view had a significant impact on state policy in union education and training. In order

> *to control workers' behaviour through moulding trade union activities the state has ... specifically supported the integration of lay representatives, perceived as a stumbling block to state strategies ... [and] in certain crucial periods, seen union education as a means of civilising union representatives (McIlroy 1985c: 38-9).*

This belief underpins many studies of the growth of trade union education in the period. It clearly represents one dimension of state policy — though it attributes rather more importance to education and training than official prescriptions for industrial relations reform did at the time. (Shop steward training occupies, for example, only one of the Donovan Report's 278 pages.)

Whatever views were held in government at the time of *In Place of*

Strife and the Industrial Relations Act, during the 1970s the centre of political gravity shifted. Across the political spectrum, the idea that inflation could effectively be controlled by incomes policy was undermined. (So, incidentally, was commitment to full employment as a economic or social goal.) On the right, it became increasingly clear that controlling workplace trade unionism within a tight labour market was remarkably difficult. There was also a better way:

> *Every organisation (including those in the public sector) should be put into a position in which workers and management are obliged to face together the inescapable choice between realistic pay levels and job security, or excessive earnings and a doubtful future (Conservative Central Office 1976: 38).*

For Labour, radical industrial relations 'reform' had ceased to be an option with *In Place of Strife*. The Social Contract was a more positive attempt to work with (and integrate) trade unionism into a negotiated view of the national interest. Ultimately it failed, partly because union leaders — who were increasingly 'educated' — proved unable to convince their members. However, the weaknesses of the Social Contract should not blind us to reality: it did represent a negotiation, at a high level, between labour and the state. Concessions were won by the trade unions, and it is in this framework that we should view the shifts in policy on trade union education.

By the mid-1970s, there was no sign that training shop stewards had achieved what its advocates (within the CIR or Donovan approaches) would have hoped. Of course, it was unfairly early to make a judgement. Shop steward education on any scale was still in its infancy. But if *Industrial Relations Training* was representative of this approach, by the end of the 1970s a number of the central tenets of their prescription had been circumvented. The CIR had argued (1972a: 52-3) that employers and unions had 'a joint interest' in industrial relations training, and (in consequence) that senior managers, union officers and senior shop stewards should initiate industrial relations training. The TUC's arrangement with the Labour government paid lip service to the joint interest argument, but denied the implication: industrial relations training could not be carried through apart from trade union education, and the latter was exclusively and inevitably a trade union preserve. The CIR had argued for the separation of trade union from industrial relations training (1972a: 59): the TUC's rejection of this had been endorsed by government. The CIR had pressed (1972a: 59-61) for courses to be 'so far as possible, ... organised for stewards from the same industry or union'; general courses were 'of most value when used to supplement these tailored courses and provide more advanced training'. The TUC, in contrast, was committed to general courses as its core provision — 'sector' courses were the exception — and to stressing the aspects and issues common to different unions and industries. The CIR called for a new joint TUC and CBI statement on shop steward training: none was agreed.

The 'failure' of shop steward education to deliver industrial relations reform may account for a fundamental contrast between the 1960s and 1970s on the one hand, and the years since 1979 on the other. Whereas in the earlier period shop steward training was clearly an aspect — if a minor one — of government industrial relations strategy, in the 1980s it was not. Partly this was due to the changed focus of industrial relations policy itself. With full employment abandoned as an aim, politicians no longer tried to control inflation through reforming industrial relations. Industrial relations policy instead sought to shift the balance of workplace power away from trade unions and toward management. The 1974-79 government's labour legislation had, according to the 1979 Conservative Manifesto, 'tilted the balance of power in bargaining throughout industry away from responsible management and towards unions, and sometimes towards unofficial groups of workers acting in defiance of their official union leadership' (quoted Disney et al. 1982: 24).

In pursuit of their general aim successive governments in the 1980s brought forward a series of legal changes which altered the legal status of trade unions.[1] Trade unions could now be directly liable to civil action in a much wider range of cases. A legal notion of 'secondary' action was introduced, and deemed unlawful. Secret ballots were required before industrial action was begun. Direct election of voting members of unions' governing bodies was required. Union members were now to vote at least every ten years if their union was to retain a political fund. The 'closed shop' or union membership agreement was severely weakened. People lawfully dismissed between 1974 and 1980 as a result of infringing closed shop agreements were compensated. Together with economic trends, these steps seriously weakened trade unions. Whilst in workplaces which survived, unions were generally able to maintain some bargaining role, the extent of organisation and the ability to mobilise diminished, and so did the movement's political and moral force. There were no significant attempts to enlist unions' support in economic or industrial relations policies. That the government has made no real attempt to use union education to achieve any of its aims is thus little surprise.

More perplexing, indeed — certainly among trade union educators — was that a Conservative government, deeply hostile to trade unionism, continued to provide public funds for union education through the TUC. The TUC scheme, after all, was a product of the 'worst' years of trade union power: under TUC control, it explicitly denied a role for employers. We

Union Education in Britain: A TUC Activity

Putting back the clock...

the whole picture

These changes to employment law are part of an overall government strategy. The message for working people is a grim one — rising unemployment, rising prices, cuts in services, slashing of social security benefits. Attacking the legal rights of working people and their unions is all part of the strategy.

The Conservative approach to employment law reflects their overall economic principles. These say that the 'law of the market' — not collective organisation — should decide wages and conditions at work. Conservative policies aim to make sure that the law of the market favours employers, not workers.

One arm of their strategy is rising unemployment. Employers are naturally in a stronger position when many workers are looking for jobs. They can use the threat of the dole queue to make workers accept lower wages.

Slashing legal standards on wages and conditions, and trying to outlaw solidarity action, are all part of the same strategy.

The TUC campaign against employment law changes is part of its broader campaign for a positive alternative to Conservative policies.

As well as running workshops on the Employment Act, the TUC is also running workshops on unemployment.

The campaign book **Unemployment: the fight for TUC alternatives**, is a companion to this book.

the union response

The changes to employment law add up to an attack on union rights as bad as the bitterly-fought Industrial Relations Act. But unions refused to be beaten by the Industrial Relations Act. They stuck to trade union principles — and won.

With the Employment Act, the government hopes to divide and fragment workers and their unions. Workers will read in the newspapers, or hear from management, that certain activities are 'illegal' — and this may intimidate them from taking action. In the same way employers and government ministers are always warning workers about 'pricing themselves out of jobs'.

Morning Star, 16 May 1979

This book will help you work out ways of fighting this intimidation — and winning.

TUC policy

The 1980 Trades Union Congress passed this resolution on the Employment Act:

Congress deplores the policies of the Government in the field of industrial relations and expresses complete and outright rejection of the provisions of the 1980 Employment Act which remove traditional trade union rights, weaken the rights of individual workers and attack the employment conditions of working women.

In the view of Congress these provisions are intended to weaken trade unions in order to facilitate the implementation of callous economic policies which have as their basis large scale unemployment and the reduction in the living standards of an overwhelming majority of our population.

Congress deplores the singling out of journalists or other groups of workers for special restriction by the Government in the Code of Practice drawn up under the Employment Act.

Congress calls on the General Council to mount a sustained and vigorous campaign of non-cooperation with the Government including, if necessary, industrial action; calls upon all affiliated unions to unite and actively oppose this unfair and dangerous legislation; and demands strenuous and total opposition by the TUC to any further restrictions on either individual rights or the collective rights of trade unionists.

Congress demands the repeal of this law by the next Labour Government in full without delay and for it to introduce new employment legislation which provides at least the protection which was available for trade unions and their members prior to the election of the Tory Government.

Congress calls upon the General Council to seek an assurance from the Labour Party that, upon return to office, it will introduce legislation to provide adequate paid maternity leave which reflects the best European practice, and the right of a woman to return to her original job; and to make illegal the practice of employers operating a blacklist of trade union activists, which for some groups of workers is aggravated by systems of short term contracts.

This book will help union activists put this policy into action.

Fig.6.2: Conservative Strategy. Campaign workshops contributed to union opposition to government policies. This analysis was developed for one of the earliest programmes, against the Employment Act 1980.

know that it was an issue in government. The question of whether the grant to the TUC should continue 'did come up as a separate item during the first year of the Conservative Government', according to the then Secretary of State for Education (Carlisle 1992; see also Harper 1980). Sir Keith Joseph, Mark Carlisle's successor as Secretary of State, took a rather less sympathetic attitude: he recalled (1992) 'the problem of trying either to end education for trade unionists on its then basis or adapting it ...', although he admitted making little progress.

In the first year of the Conservative government, however, both departments involved (Education and Employment) agreed that the grant should continue. Indeed, a 14 per cent increase was approved (Harper 1980). Various factors lay behind the decision at that stage. There was the large amount of new labour legislation which had emerged during the 1970s: training made sense in this context (Harper 1980). 'The amount of the grant', according to the then Secretary of State for Employment, Jim Prior (1992), 'was considered small'. In addition,

> We always worried about the narrowness of Trades Union leaders and their lack of experience of the business climate. I felt that money spent on training would be beneficial. I recollect talking to Mr Murray ... and feeling that this small expenditure was worth while.

It is also likely that civil servants, at least early in the Conservatives' years of office, were protective of what was still a relatively new development.

There were also important political considerations, not directly related to education. 'As we were embarking on difficult negotiations with the Trades Unions', Prior (1992) recalled, 'it was not considered worthwhile to have an additional row with them.' One area of these negotiations may have been particularly important. The 1980 Employment Act gave unions a right to claim financial assistance from the government for expenses incurred when conducting certain membership ballots. Many trades unionists saw this as introducing state control of internal union affairs. The TUC adopted a policy of not accepting such funds: this was a touchstone of opposition to the legislation. (The analogy with the campaign against the Industrial Relations Act was clear.) Several unions, particularly those to the right of the movement, and those which in any case organised large and expensive internal elections, opposed this.

Through the early 1980s, declining membership brought financial pressure to seek funds from whatever source. When the 1984 Trade Union Act introduced legal requirements that unions' executive committees should be elected at intervals of not more than five years by ballot, together with the political fund balloting requirement, a fierce dispute broke out — fought at the 1985 Trades Union Congress in Blackpool. 'Many unions ... will cripple themselves financially if they cannot avail themselves of the public money that is available,' said John Lyons of the Engineers and Managers' Association, seconding a motion calling for a review of TUC policy (TUC 1985: 441). The case for non-acceptance was put by Ron Todd, General Secretary of the Transport and General Workers' Union. The centrepiece of his case (for our purposes) was the belief that accepting government money threatened union independence. It was the start of a slippery slope:

> *We said at Wembley [the TUC's special Congress in 1982 which agreed the policy] in our non-co-operation stand that we should not, and would not, seek to do the Tory Government's job for them by putting the legal frighteners on our members as we pursued the everyday processes of collective bargaining. And from this essential principle flowed the position that we could not allow ourselves to take money from our enemies in order to carry out their work for them. Certainly we could not entertain becoming economically dependent on a hostile government's cash, or sacrifice our basic independence for the equivalent of a penny a week on members' subs. That is what lies at the heart of the debate. (TUC 1985: 437.)*

An important argument used by those seeking to overturn the TUC's existing policy was the state funding of trade union education. 'Yes, it is true that there is a danger that future Governments will attach strings to public money which is not available without strings,' admitted John Lyons (TUC 1985: 441), 'but let us deal with that situation if and when it arises.' He continued:

> *Up to now nobody has worried about this in this Congress. We all quite happily accept £1.7 million of Government money a year for our union education, some part of which nearly every union here happily holds out its palm for year after year.*

Of course, this argument was repudiated by supporters of the non-acceptance position. 'Taking money for education, as agreed by the TUC and controlled by the TUC, is not the same as taking money which the TUC has unanimously regarded as bribe money', announced J.J. Carr of AUEW(TASS) (TUC 1985: 449). But the difference was a nice one, arguable — and argued — both ways. It was an embarrassment to the radical camp, and it seems highly likely that the government's decisions to continue making educational grants to the TUC took this into account.[2]

The Ten-Day Programme 1979–1988

The flagship of the TUC's educational provision from the mid-1970s was its provision of ten-day, day-release courses. In line with economic and political trends, the number of courses provided declined during the 1980s from the peak attained during 1979 and 1980. The decline (by 55 per cent in numbers of courses, and by 60 per cent in numbers of students, between 1978/79 and 1986/87) was of fundamental importance to union education, and had major implications for the structure so painstakingly constructed during the 1970s.[3]

Of course, a number of comments can be made on the statistics. First, the decline is far more marked in Health and Safety courses than in courses for shop stewards. The number of shop stewards courses (excluding follow-on courses) declined by 37 per cent between 1979/80 (their peak year) and 1986/87, and the number of students enrolled on them fell by 39 per cent. The number of Health and Safety courses, however, fell by 68 per cent, while the number of Health and Safety course students fell by 75 per cent, between 1978/79 (their peak year) and 1986/87. On the other hand, the bulk of the decline in Health and Safety courses occurred in the first three years after 1978/79: their number had fallen 59 per cent, and the number of their students 67 per cent, by 1981/82. The decline of shop stewards courses, on the other hand, has been considerably more gentle.

A decline in Health and Safety courses had been anticipated. The Health and Safety programme had mushroomed in the late 1970s with the introduction of the Safety Representatives and Safety Committees Regulations 1977, and the creation of an entire new stratum of workplace representatives with unprecedented functions. In 1977 the TUC passed a resolution on Health and Safety, stressing the need for extension of educational provision in this area (TUC 1978: 202-3). For several years it became the 'main emphasis' (TUC 1979: 189) of TUC education. The 1979 General Council report remarked that although courses for shop stewards had been 'consolidated', the numbers of safety representatives attending TUC Health and Safety courses had 'increased almost threefold from just over 10,000 in 1977/78 to more than 27,000 in 1978/79' (TUC 1979: 189). The following year, however, with the 'large majority' of safety representatives already trained, and 'the decline in demand for places on these courses last year', the growth was not expected to continue. It was decided therefore 'to divert some resources to expand the provision of education and training for shop stewards and staff representatives'. (TUC 1980: 158).[4] The sheer achievement of the late 1970s in safety representative training was a major factor in the rapidity of its decline during the early 1980s.

Second, the decline varied not merely by type of course, but by geographical region. The decline was more marked in some regions than in others; neither were the differences obviously linked to geographical variations in social, economic or industrial character. Thus the most successful region, without question, was the North-West, which (for instance) provided only 10 per cent fewer workplace representative courses in 1986/87 than in 1979/80. In contrast, provision of such courses in

Union Education in Britain: A TUC Activity

TUC Courses

for all union reps

Introductory Stage 1

This course will help you to develop the skills and knowledge you need to represent your members. You will learn about:

- building a strong union organisation
- handling grievances and disputes
- participating in meetings and making reports
- collective bargaining and agreements.

Introductory Stage 2

The essential course for all union representatives who have completed a basic stewards course:

- collective bargaining aims and techniques
- improving union organisation
- finding and using information
- developing skills for union work.

Health and Safety: Stage 1

This course is for all union reps involved in health and safety. It looks at:

- how to identify the main hazards and problems in your workplace
- how to find and use further information about safety standards for your workplace
- how to build union organisation on the question of safety, and how to develop effective procedures for taking up problems with management.

Health and Safety: Stage 2

For union representatives who have completed the Introductory Health and Safety course and who have had further practical experience since then.

Women trade unionists

These short courses are for women members who want to get more involved in the union and for women reps who may prefer to do a course with other women before going on to Stage 1. The course covers:

- problems facing women at work and in the union
- improving union organisation at your workplace
- the job of the union rep.

TUC short courses

The TUC is also offering a programme of short courses designed to suit your specific needs including instruction on a range of topics related to changes in practices at your workplace. For example, the introduction of new technology, changes in incentive payment systems and other changes in normal working practices.

Details of these and other TUC courses can be obtained from your REO whose name and address appear on this leaflet.

follow-on courses

Applicants must have completed Introductory Stage 1 course.

Work-study, productivity and pay

This course aims to help students develop a trade union approach to management techniques.

Bargaining information

This course looks in detail at the information you need in negotiations, how you can find this information and how you can make use of it.

New technology and collective bargaining

This course will examine the range of applications of New Technology and the problems posed for trade unionists.

Fig. 6.3: The TUC Programme. This extract from a 1987 TUC Education brochure explains the main TUC courses available and the order in which representatives should take them. Compared with ten years earlier (see Fig. 5.3), Stage 1 and Stage 2 courses are distinguished from Follow-on, and short courses and courses for women are emphasised.

Scotland fell 66 per cent over the same period, while in the South East it fell by 46 per cent. Of course, such comparisons beg important methodological issues (particularly the relative state of development in the base year chosen). But the contrasts are nevertheless marked. A major factor was probably the relative effectiveness of TUC educational organisation in the region concerned.

Third, it is instructive to compare the decline with the contemporaneous (and associated) decline in union membership itself. Between 1979 and 1985 the membership of unions affiliated to the TUC fell from 12,128,078 to 9,855,204 — a fall of 18.7 per cent (TUC 1985: 733). This is not, as Kelly (1987: 10) rightly points out, the first fall in union membership since the war, but previous losses had been 'small, sporadic, and quickly made up'. This percentage decline in membership was, of course, substantially smaller than the overall decline in number of TUC ten-day courses and students. But when the Health and Safety factor is set aside, the educational decline is far less marked. Indeed, over the same period (1978/79 to 1984/85) the decline in the number of TUC 'basic' courses was 16.7 per cent, while the decline in students on these courses was just 15.6 per cent. In short, the decline in educational provision for workplace representatives over these years proceeded more or less in parallel with the decline in union membership.

While analytically helpful to exclude the decline in Health and Safety provision, however, the reality which confronted trade union educators and educational organisers was the overall contraction in provision. Inevitably the 1980s were years of managing decline, and this decline had an impact in particular on the institutional structures built up during the 1970s.

The Institutional Framework

The erosion of the TUC programme caused some difficulties for the structure of provision. But, remarkably, most of the major stresses and strains — at least, those which led to public conflicts — which marked trade union education's institutional relationships preceded the years of decline. Moreover, such — relatively minor — incidents as occurred in these relationships during the 1980s took place in areas where the stresses had already become clear during the previous decade.

There are several reasons for this. By the 1980s, the TUC relied on further education for the delivery of the major share of its programme. This minimised the ideological element — the element of principle — in disputes over resources. Further education was used to delivering courses to outside specifications: the fact that the TUC set out the terms of its requirements produced few concerns.[5] Further education was also a large world, encompassing many other areas of industrial relations teaching. These could absorb the attentions of tutors for whom union courses were no longer available. As a result, when TUC provision declined, few colleges were left with insurmountable personnel problems.

In addition, the institutional stresses were minimised by the very fact that the decline followed so rapidly on the growth. Many institutions simply had not had time to take on substantial full-time staffing. There had been a shortage of suitably-qualified candidates: a shortage well-signposted in the reports and enquiries of the 1970s. As a result, many of the staff who made the expansion of the later 1970s possible were employed on part-time and very short-term contracts: generally, for the teaching of each particular ten-day course. They were easily dispensed with when the times got tough. (See Atkins and Stageman 1981: 12-13.)[6]

The problems faced by the Workers' Educational Association provide a case study of the institutional impact of decline. The WEA was not entirely typical, of course. Although the largest single contributor to the TUC scheme, its contribution was dispersed widely across the country. All of the districts were small — in terms of numbers of full-time staff employed — when compared with further education college; some were very small indeed, with only three or four tutor-organisers. The provision of TUC courses was, for some, a major part (in some cases approaching one-half)[7] of the district's work. However, its experience was not geographically specific. Its democracy has also required periodic public investigation of these issues; issues which elsewhere might be dealt with behind closed doors have received a wider airing.

Despite its long tradition of trade union education, and while generally supportive of the TUC scheme, the WEA had not increased its full-time staff substantially as the scheme expanded. Its provision had grown largely through employing part-time tutors.[8] In the early 1980s the number of WEA courses provided for the TUC plummeted: from 723 in 1978/79 to 603 the following year, 441 in 1980/81 and 422 in 1981/82 (WEA 1983: 13); by 1986/87 the figure had fallen to 317. Early in 1981 the WEA's Trade Union Studies Advisory Committee, confronted with a 30 per cent fall in provision over a year, surveyed eleven 'Districts experiencing a particularly sharp fall in provision' (WEA 1981: 1). It concluded that there was a number of general factors:

> *the worsening economic situation has had a major impact on student recruitment. Besides the absolute loss of potential students through unemployment, it is agreed that the recession understandably has concentrated trade union activists' minds on matters other than education. There is also some evidence to suggest that the recession has encouraged employer resistance to release. Districts identify a levelling*

off of demand for health and safety courses (which has occurred independently of economic influences) as a further contributory factor influencing the overall level of demand. (WEA TUSAC 1981: 1.)

But, besides these overall factors, some illuminating comments were made by various district secretaries (WEA TUSAC 1981: appendix). While these appeared at the time as largely specific, in retrospect they seem symptomatic of institutional responses to decline. There was the problem of competition: 'Within the Greater Manchester Connurbation there are no fewer than eight institutions doing TUC day-release courses. ... [Next term] there will be some 37 courses spread among 8 providers.' This had an impact on confidence and planning: 'the numbers of full-time Trade Union tutor organisers have been reduced because of the District Committee's reluctance to make new appointments when the financial position looks bad.' A small district with a large TUC programme could 'no longer rely upon the effectiveness of TUC ... recruitment,' it was 'necessary to aim for much greater diversification of Tutor-Organisers teaching and organising programmes if we are to justify these appointments'.

A few districts were clearly unenthusiastic about trade union courses and the TUC in any case. 'The Council of this District some years ago decided that none of the teaching costs of Day Release and other courses provided for the TUC should fall upon the voluntary members of the branches', recorded one district secretary: the fees offered by the TUC were insufficient for this purpose, and industrial tutor organisers who resigned were unlikely to be replaced. Several districts suggested that, if courses were scarce, the TUC would bolster institutions where full-time staff were employed. According to one secretary:

As these centres provided by colleges usually have a number of full time staff engaged mainly on T.U.C. work there may be a natural desire by the T.U.C. Regional Education Officer to channel work to that sector. Over the years he has encouraged College Authorities to develop these centres and hence feels some responsibility for ensuring that they have enough courses to justify their continued existence.

Some districts were less philosophical. They suspected darker motives behind TUC resource allocation. One secretary thought that the TUC had assigned his district a 'stop-gap' role 'until a local F.E. College can take over the work'. Another was concerned at the TUC Regional Education Officer's 'apparent determination to promote the interests of a few individuals who are unacceptable to the District'.[9]

Cycles of suspicion and mistrust are, of course, frequent fellow-travellers with decline and resource scarcity. Providing bodies faced the typical problems of institutional competition in a declining market: elimination of marginal providers, concentration on centres of strength, planning amid uncertainty, internal reallocation of resources, the search for alternative markets (or areas of work), the elimination of surplus labour, and so forth. In these circumstances it is perhaps surprising that the TUC managed the decline of the 1980s as smoothly as in fact it did. If we examine, for instance, the mean number of students attending TUC courses, the stability of the figure is remarkable, and the decline from the heady days of the late 1970s is modest (see Appendix B). Neither is there a significant variation in the mean attendance at specific types of course (with the exception of follow-on courses; and even here the discontinuity of 1983-85 may well be associated with changes in the categorisation of courses).[10]

To allocate resources is, of course, to exercise power. The TUC's decisions about the allocation of relatively scarce resources had implications for the work of individual tutors, college and university departments, and WEA districts. In this process the TUC's regional education officers had a pivotal role, negotiating with college authorities (as well as seeking to support able and committed teaching staff and encourage better recruitment of students). Their work was relatively closely supervised by more senior staff in the Education Department at Congress House. The TUC's power, of course, stemmed from its being 'quite a big buyer': it could purchase substantial numbers of courses at not uncompetitive rates. While the TUC maintained that it would do this in any case, it could hardly have been a 'buyer' on any comparable scale without public funds.[11]

Areas of Advance

Although the ten-day programme was the major focus of its educational work in the 1980s, TUC education was not simply a matter of coping with decline. A number of significant innovations were made, based largely on two of the educational strengths which built up in the 1970s. The course development unit in the training college at Congress House meant that a substantial force of educationalists (rather than simply educational administrators) was now at work. The unit's task was to write the (core) materials used in the TUC's courses up and down the country. Initially, the materials were printed 'packs' used in ten-day courses: gradually, however, they turned their hands to a variety of materials for a wide range of courses. These materials were a great resource, enabling a relatively small band of tutors in the field — many of them part-time — to offer a rapidly-changing range of short courses at short notice to a wide variety of union groups.

Second, the tutors who worked at the course development unit formed an essential core of tutors able to offer 'briefings' for the tutors who actually taught TUC courses in colleges, polytechnics, WEA and universities. The scale of provision of these briefings was impressive, especially in the light of the overall number of trade union studies tutors teaching (perhaps 500-600 at its largest).[12] The briefings were of two main types. There was a regular provision of initial briefings, either for tutors entirely new to trade union studies (within the TUC scheme) or for those beginning for the first time to teach a certain sort of course. Thus it was the rule that all tutors new to the TUC scheme would attend an introductory briefing on educational methods, concentrating on the 'Introductory' (later the 'Stage 1') union representatives course. Generally regional education officers also required tutors beginning to teach another course — say the 'Health and Safety Stage 1' course, or a 'Stage 2' course, or a course on 'Work Study, Productivity and Pay' or 'Bargaining Information', — also to attend a briefing, usually of five days' duration, concerned with that course alone.

A number of briefings, however, aimed to provide support and guidance for established tutors who had to cope with new developments in the mainstream materials or new types of course. Thus where the TUC was promoting a programme of short courses on some issue — for example, on the implications for union organisation of the compulsory competitive tendering and contract compliance clauses of the Local Government Act 1988 — a series of briefings would be organised around the country for tutors likely to be involved. In addition, therefore, to their quality control function, the tutor briefings contributed to the TUC's ability to respond flexibly and — in many ways — imaginatively to the pressures and demands of the 1980s.

Of the major innovations of the 1980s, several stand out (aspects of them are discussed further in Chapter 7). First, there was a great advance in the number of short courses and workshops. With the advent of the Conservative government, the TUC Education Service began to mount a programme of short courses (or 'workshops'), usually of one day's duration, designed to build union commitment to TUC policies on crucial issues. The notion of the workshop for this purpose stemmed partly from the developing emphasis throughout TUC education on organisation as the overriding aim, yet partly also from the experience of the campaign against the 1971 Industrial Relations Act when 3,000 full-time officers attended courses on that issue. (The parallels between the 1971 and the 1980 Acts were widely felt at the time — not entirely accurately — to be very close.)

Gradually, the 'campaign workshop' became a more and more central aspect of the TUC's educational armoury, called upon in modest campaigns as well as major.[13] Their success is difficult to gauge. The programmes of workshops in opposition to successive bouts of industrial relations legislation (1980, 1982, 1984) were — contrary to their early intention — clearly unsuccessful in overturning the legislation: but probably it was unrealistic to expect that they would. The 'campaign for economic and social advance' was, frankly if sadly, based on an idea of economic and social policy whose time had gone. Yet the unions' campaign to persuade their members to vote for the continuance (or, in one or two cases, establishment) of union political funds — a requirement introduced by the 1984 Trade Union Act — was entirely successful, very much contrary to early expectation. It is only fair to acknowledge the role of the campaign workshops in this process.[14]

Two observations may be made about the campaign workshops. Like the early 1970s campaigns on industrial relations legislation, they played a part in establishing for the mass of union officers, and particularly for senior national officers, that union education was contributing organisationally and strategically to vital and immediate issues confronting the movement. At the same time, a key feature of the campaign workshop was its clear rejection of neutrality. The workshops existed for specific — frequently highly political — reasons, in support of campaigns being promoted by trade unions. Often these were in direct opposition to policies of the government. In view of its concern to maintain public funding for general programmes of trade union education, the TUC was scrupulous to the point of obsession in ensuring that campaign workshops were financed from TUC — and not from public — funds.[15]

There was also a major advance in the provision of short courses of other kinds. This originated in a small shift in the TUC's educational stance during the early 1980s, but a fundamental factor was the government's agreement in 1984 to making funds available to the TUC for courses of between one and five days in length. Previously, the TUC had received funds for union short courses, but only — so to say — as an agent for individual unions. The logic for this arose from the fiction — or the aspiration — that TUC ten day courses would soon fit into a neat structure of union training, in which the representative's own union would provide a short induction course (of at least 15 study hours) immediately after his or her appointment; the TUC 10-day course would follow within a year of so; and there would then be further courses either within the TUC scheme or through the member's union.[16] In practice, the structure never worked very effectively: a number of unions certainly provided short courses for their representatives, but relatively few were scrupulous about linking their induction courses to the ten-day programme. Union courses of five days or so were often, in reality, competing for students with the ten day programme. So there was a strong case for providing at least some induction courses on a multi-union basis.

There were other reasons. With the decline in demand for ten-day courses, and the TUC's increasing need to protect its resources in the public education sector, it made little sense to restrict short course provision to individual unions. (Few unions organised courses in conjunction with public educational bodies.) Here was an area of work which the public sector could develop, and which would provide its tutors with work: why prevent it from doing so? If provided by institutions which also taught the mainstream programme, induction courses might be more successful in drawing students into further union education. At the same time, the TUC had recently opened its National Education Centre at Hornsey in North London: clearly it did not wish to be unnecessarily hampered in the types of courses it could promote there.

Nor was it only induction courses which were in question: in the light of the campaign workshops, short courses were increasingly seen as a way of responding to trade union representatives' educational demands and meeting their educational needs by providing issue-related up-dating and development. From 1984, therefore, the TUC promoted a growing programme of short courses.[17] Their subject matter varied widely. In addition to induction courses, there were various courses designed specifically for women and black workers: 'bridging' courses designed to give women the confidence and skills to play a fuller part in the ten-day courses; courses on specific issues, such as women's health, equal pay, tackling racism. There were courses on various health and safety topics: particular hazards, particular industries, or recent legal or technical developments. And there was a wide variety of courses on various union topics: pensions, privatisation, local government finance, financial management in the civil service, and so forth.

A second innovation of the 1980s will be covered in Chapter 7, but is related to short course developments. Courses were now increasingly aimed at specific curriculum areas and target groups. The bulk of provision continued to be on a ten-day, general, basis: but this was now complemented by more highly targeted courses. Relevance could no longer be achieved simply by providing general courses related to workplace bargaining issues. Workplace issues, indeed the union membership, were more and more seen as highly diversified.

A major third innovation was the establishment of the TUC's National Education Centre (NEC). Originally suggested in the mid-1970s, this took some time to reach fruition. During 1977 the TUC made approaches to the Labour government; the following year there had been 'little positive response' (TUC 1978: 200). A year later the TUC reached outline agreement with the government on the legal form of the National Centre. Indeed, although it was made clear that no public funds would be available during 1979/80 'other than through underspending' in the DES budget, 'a joint feasibility study was entered into with the Milton Keynes Development Corporation to consider the possible conversation of a site in Stoney Stratford' (TUC 1979: 188). Although the incoming Conservative government would not provide help with the capital costs involved, by 1980 the General Council had clarified its ideas about aims and function of the Centre:

> *Its key functions would be to expand courses for full-time officers, senior union representatives and trade union studies tutors, to promote a wide range of course development work, and to offer facilities for unions seeking to provide residential courses (TUC 1980: 156).*

In consequence, the TUC set about raising funds from within the trade union movement: by July 1980 the target figure (£1 million) had been reached.

A site was eventually found at the former Hornsey College of Art in north London. Formally opened by the TUC's Chairman on 22 August 1984, the first courses began the following month (TUC 1984: 174). The role of the Centre was defined now in terms of the pressures of the 1980s:

> *Apart from expanding the TUC education programme for full-time officers, executive committee members and representatives, it has also been necessary to develop new courses and new materials to meet the ever-changing issues and problems facing the Movement over this period. This itself has required special tutor training facilities and increased demands for educational help and advice from certain sectors and industries. In addition there has been a remarkable growth in trade union education in developing countries. (TUC 1984: 174-5.)*

The Centre's 'first class facilities' were also made 'available to affiliated unions for their own education programmes' through the allocation of half the residential places to union bookings. But the Centre was not seen as merely a residential college servicing union demands: it was to have a more strategic role in trade union education also.

> *The General Council hope that, with the establishment of all the TUC's course development functions at Hornsey, affiliated unions will see the Centre as an important resource in trade union education beyond its basic role as a residential college. Affiliated unions have been, and will continue to be, invited to discuss their education programmes with the TUC and to see for themselves the outstanding facilities which the Centre offers. (TUC 1984: 175)*

During its first year's work, the National Education Centre was the venue for 40 courses run by thirteen affiliated unions and enrolling over 600 students (TUC 1985: 200). In addition, a number of TUC and Commonwealth TUC courses were held there. In the second year a total of over 2,400 students attended courses at the Centre: of these, 1,100 attended 56 courses organised by fourteen affiliated unions. The programme of international courses continued. (TUC 1986: 240.) Enrolment grew again 1986/87: almost 2,500 students attended courses at the Centre, of whom 1,500 attended 77 courses organised by 22 unions (TUC 1987: 103). The Centre

32 / Images of Women

'That Goes on Here All the Time'

WOMEN HAVE NO SENSE OF HUMOUR.

'**What are you doing now**?', asked the young girl shampooing my hair when I went to the hairdressers recently.

'I'm writing a book about sexual harassment at work', I replied.

'**What's that**?', she asked.

I explained:

'Sexual harassment is any verbal or physical approach, including jokes and innuendos, right up to actual assault, that's unwanted, that makes a woman feel uncomfortable, is continual and affects her work'.

'**Oh that**', replied the girl. '**That goes on here all the time**'.

Sue Reed, author of Hamlyn Paperback '**Sexual Harassment at work**', *quoted in* Cosmopolitan

SEXUAL harassment is not new. What is new is that women are beginning to say 'Why should we have to put up with it'. And unions are beginning to see it as a trade union issue.

❦ I never really understood what sexual harassment was until I heard people talking about it recently. At first I thought 'I haven't come across that'. Then I thought, 'Yes I have come across it, but I can cope with it'. But then I thought 'Why the hell should I have to cope with it'. ❦

Jo, TASS

In 1981 NALGO published a leaflet called *Sexual Harassment is a Trade Union Issue*. The 1982 TUC Womens' Conference carried a resolution stating that 'sexual harassment is a form of discrimination that can damage women's trade unionists' morale, job security and prospects at work'. The TUC has drawn up guidelines for unions on tackling the problem.

What Is It?

❦ Sexual harassment can take many forms, from leering, ridicule, embarassing remarks or jokes, deliberate abuse, the offensive use of pin-ups, repeated and/or unwanted physical contact, demands for sexual favours, or physical assault on workers. ❦

Sexual Harassment at Work: Guidelines for Unions, TUC

Fig. 6.4: Images of Women. Short courses provide a way of tackling important or topical union issues. Courses for women have been a priority, but this 1983 discussion was also designed for use by 'all trade unionists'.

also worked to develop broader educational links with affiliated unions in line with the objectives spelt out in 1984: 'assisting [them] with the development of their own educational programmes' (TUC 1987: 103). However, whether these developments proceeded faster — or, indeed, the reverse — as a result of the existence of the National Centre, is a matter of judgement: they were also a feature of the course development unit prior to 1984.

The National Education Centre was no unmixed blessing. By 1986/87, its finances were causing real concern. For the first time a small element of qualification appeared in the General Council's report on the Centre. 'In 1986 the cost of operating the Centre's residential facilities had exceeded fee income from unions by £88,000' (TUC 1987: 97). Quarterly financial reviews not only continued, but were remarked upon. To 'ensure the Centre's cost-effectiveness ... certain measures, including a new fee structure for 1988' had been implemented (TUC 1987: 104).

A fourth area of innovation, in the eyes of the TUC, lay in membership education. The TUC Open School was first discussed at a high level in the TUC during 1984. 'A working party of union education officers has been examining the possibilities for developing both union and TUC distance learning schemes', the General Council reported (TUC 1985: 202). Their report proposed 'large scale schemes of membership education through distance learning'. A TUC distance learning scheme 'should build on ... existing organisation'. Course material should be 'dual purpose ... suitable for both individual and group study'. Provision should be made 'as economically as possible', and should complement union schemes. The General Council endorsed these views, and agreed that the TUC should provide support in drafting materials, training 'lay education activists and discussion leaders', and should examine the relationship between such a venture and the long-established TUC postal course service. 'Overall, the General Council are concerned to review the way distance learning relates to general membership education.' (TUC 1985: 202.)

We examine the concepts and strategy which underlay the 'Open School' in Chapter 7. For the present two observations will suffice. First, the TUC consistently — from 1945 — placed its major resources into the education and training of union officers, lay and full-time, chiefly in relation to their representational roles. After the TUC took over the NCLC and the WETUC in 1964, however (soon running down their diverse — 'haphazard' — programmes of political education) there has been a recurring concern about an ill-defined 'membership education'. The mushrooming of the workplace representatives' courses in the 1970s was associated with the ill-fated 'multi-media' TUC/WEA/BBC Trade Union Studies Project. A decade later the same concern resurfaced in the Open

School. Both schemes were clearly influenced by fashion in educational method. But more important, both were products of the TUC's desire to develop a system which would have an impact on the membership, but within realistic cost and resource bounds — and accepting that priority was given to educating workplace representatives. Second, and of antiquarian rather than historical interest, the Open School project was in part financed by the closing of the TUC's postal courses office at Tillicoultry in Scotland: the former headquarters of the NCLC. The services were moved to Congress House in 1986 — a final institutional break with the days of the NCLC.

1. Primarily, the Employment Acts, 1980 and 1982, and the Trade Union Act 1984. These are covered by McIlroy (1991); see also the discussion in Marsh (1992: 54-110).
2. Another factor in the Conservatives' maintaining the grant for trade union education may have been the fact that Britain's ratification of ILO Convention 140 on Paid Education Leave rested entirely on the rights to paid release for trade union education. However, given the government's cavalier attitude to ILO conventions on issues which it considered of major significance (e.g., in relation to union membership rights at GCHQ Cheltenham), this can have been of no more than marginal significance.
3. For national and regional statistics on day release course provision, see Appendix B.
4. With the 'worsening economic and industrial climate', the transfer of resources was not in the event 'fully realised' (TUC 1981: 236).
5. This is not to suggest that staff teaching trade union education in further education lacked ideology or principle: see, for example, Whyte (1980: 59-72), as well as countless contributions to *Trade Union Studies Journal* and *The Industrial Tutor*. But further education lacked the ideologically encumbring institutional traditions of the WEA and the extra-mural departments.
6. Of course, in an important sense this meant the problems were merely displaced, becoming personal rather than institutional.
7. For instance, in 1983/84 'industrial and trade union' work (in most cases overwhelmingly TUC courses) made up 48.4 per cent of the West Midlands District's total class provision; and 33.33 per cent of West Lancashire and Cheshire District's. In another six districts it made up between 18 and 22 per cent. (WEA 1985: 20.)
8. The WEA did apply to the DES in 1978 for funding for additional staffing (tutor/organiser posts). Various internal stresses meant that even when its application was accepted in April 1979, the Association then dithered until after the general election on 3 May; the new Conservative government promptly withdrew the offer (TUC 1980: 161).
9. Some details of university extra-mural departments' experiences during the decline of the TUC provision are to be found in Campbell and McIlroy

1986, esp. 220-28, 232-4.
10 The management (or, according to one's view, mismanagement) of decline forms the backdrop to one major, as well as a few minor, disputes between the TUC and providing bodies and tutors. The major dispute was that involving the TUC, the Manchester University extra-mural studies department, and to a lesser extent the WEA. (This dispute cast its shadow on the 1980s debates on control and the trade union curriculum discussed in Chapter 7.) In the context of resource reallocation within a TUC region (the North-Western) whose record in effectiveness of course delivery in the recession was unmatched within the TUC — but also in the context of his very public criticism of the TUC's educational approach — TUC courses were shifted away from a university staff tutor, John McIlroy. The dispute which ensued rumbled for some time in local and national press, as well as in negotiations between McIlroy's union, the TUC, and the University. (See, e.g., Campbell 1985; Richards 1985.)
11 For details of public funds, see Appendix C.
12 See Appendix D.
13 For a note on TUC campaign workshops, see Appendix E.
14 Marsh (1992: 154-5) acknowledges that the political fund campaign was 'a total success' because the unions 'chose the right strategy and pursued it effectively'. Regrettably, he makes no mention of the role of union education, other than to say that the campaign 'relied very heavily on proselytising in the workplace rather than glossy media campaigns; the emphasis was upon the unions communicating with their members, quite a novel idea in the history of British unions.' It was not, of course, novel in union education.
15 The TUC thus rightly took exception to the unsubstantiated assertion by the authors of *The Impossible Dream* (SIT 1988: 6) that 'some [of the grant from public funds] is used for ... "campaign workshops" in the regions'.
16 This structure is set out in the TUC's model agreement on paid release for union training issued in February 1978 (TUC 1978: 198); it was also reprinted in the TUC's *Introductory Course for Union Representatives* (1979) — the 'Red Pack': see Fig. 5.3.
17 For statistics on short course provision, see Appendix B.

Chapter 7

Post-war Methods and Philosophies: Tensions and Trends

The twentieth-century British labour movement, according a common metaphor, has had both industrial and political 'wings' — the trade unions and Labour Party respectively. This has long been the commonsense of the movement, and its self-image. It is paralleled by the distinction — now firmly entrenched in common and statute law — between legitimate industrial action (that taken 'in contemplation or furtherance of a trade dispute') and the illegitimate (that taken for other motives).[1] The Webbs (1911: 173-221, 246-78) classically distinguished between unions' methods of 'collective bargaining' and 'legal enactment' — both seen as proper union functions. The imagery is also similar to the view, to be found in Lenin (1970: 141-97) but common also in the industrial sociology of the 1960s and 1970s (see, e.g., Beynon 1974), that the working class on its own can develop only 'trade union consciousness'. The development of 'class consciousness', on this view, requires in some way the intervention of a 'conscious element' (a political party).

If the movement has political and industrial wings, however, there has also been continual tension between them. Trade unions have industrial aims and objectives — better wages and conditions, a safe and healthy working environment, and so forth. They must organise, bargain, take action, in the workplace in pursuit of these. But they function within a legal, social and economic framework which they must, broadly speaking, influence politically if they are to do so at all. Politics, in short, are a legitimate concern of a trade union. In addition, however, the trade union movement makes assumptions about human and social values — solidarity, fraternity, collectivism, and so forth — which are close to the politics of socialism. These values may, very often, be the language of the committed minority, rather than of all the members: but they are no less important for that. They condition the character, the ethos, of the movement; they influence the issues around which it will attempt to mobilise.

This tension has been a constant theme of trade union education. Broadly speaking, Britain's active trades unionists — and perhaps even more, trade union educators — have seen the movement in a political perspective. They have believed that an essential function of union education is to strengthen the political commitment of union members to the ideals, ethos and methods of the movement. Not infrequently, they have also felt the movement would be stronger if its commitment to socialist values and politics were deeper and more widespread. At the same time, the inescapable imperative of union organisation has been that expenditure of time, energy and money on education (or training) should serve the immediate interests of the movement — for stronger workplace organisation and through it, improved pay and conditions for the members. The broad range of political views held, especially among trade union leaders, has also made it difficult to orientate union education around any single political position.

Trade union education has therefore been beset with a series of dilemmas: political education or practical union skills; liberal education or industrial relations training; education or propaganda. These dilemmas have been reflected in what has been taught (and what is learnt), and in how the teaching and learning has taken place — in both content and methods. This Chapter explores some of the more important issues, debates and disputes over method and content which emerged in post-war union education.

Trade Union Education and the New Social Order

When, after the war, the TUC began to develop its own training college, it made no real attempt at elaborate system-building or theorising. Rather, it attempted (see Chapter 4 above) to fill a modest gap in the spectrum of a provision dominated by the Workers' Educational Association, the Workers' Educational Trade Union Committee, and the National Council of Labour Colleges. There was certainly no TUC move to exploit — in the union educational field — the opportunity presented by the return of a Labour government. However, many in the educational organisations appreciated that as the world had changed, their role must change. The Edinburgh and District Labour College, for instance, noted in 1947 that a shift in its approach was called for:

> *From being principally concerned with fostering an anti-capitalist viewpoint, independent working-class education had had to concern itself with the more difficult task of engendering a constructive socialist outlook and providing a training necessary to the intelligent grappling of the vast and complex problems confronting this country and the world. ... We must close our ranks in preparation for the coming struggle — a struggle which will determine the future of socialism in this country and perhaps the world. (Quoted Millar 1979: 132.)*

But the major attempt to grapple intellectually or theoretically with the implications for trade union education of the new order came from the WEA.

Not that the WEA moved with great alacrity. Indeed, there is more than a little irony in the timing. On the weekend of 27 and 28 October 1951, the

WEA's Annual Conference voted to establish a committee to examine how to advance the WEA's work in trade union education (WEA 1953: 7). The previous day — Friday 26 October — Winston Churchill had been appointed Prime Minister following Labour's defeat in the general election on the Thursday. In short, the major attempt to grapple with what Labour's elevation to power meant for union education came just as its most creative period of power came to an end — to be followed, as we now know, by thirteen years of Conservative government.

Nevertheless, the WEA had assembled a working party of men and women of substance and experience, which in due time — a Report was published in 1953 — made a number of substantial recommendations. The working party's chairman was Arthur Creech Jones — a sign, if nothing else, of the calibre of person the WEA could then involve in its work. Creech Jones, a Labour MP since 1935 and a National Secretary of the Transport and General Workers' Union through the 1920s, had been Parliamentary Private Secretary to Ernest Bevin as Minister of Labour during the war, became Parliamentary Under-Secretary at the Colonial Office in 1945, and was then Secretary of State for the Colonies from the autumn of 1946. During Creech Jones' tenure, there was (according to Morgan 1984: 205) 'a vitality and dynamism about the Colonial Office ... not known for over a generation'. One arm of this was the emergence of adult and community education as a central mechanism for achieving economic and social progress in the colonial empire (Holford 1988b). Creech Jones himself had a longstanding association with adult education, as a governor of Ruskin College since 1923, a member of Oxford University's Tutorial Classes committee, and a vice-chairman of the British Institute of Adult Education; he was also a vice-president of the WEA. (*Who's Who* 1949: 1480; Fieldhouse 1985: 64.)[2]

Creech Jones' background is also a pointer to the working party's thinking. Its members faced a number of difficulties. First of all, it was a commonplace that 'the level of demand for trade union education was very difficult to stimulate, and this was widely felt to be the fundamental obstacle to expansion' (WEA 1953: 35). At the same time, in relation to their primary constituency (the WEA), they remarked:

> *A notable feature of the discussions [with WEA district trade union education advisory committees] was the expressed fear that our enquiry implied that the W.E.A. was likely to be sidetracked into a utilitarian type of T.U. education. This, it is clear, would be generally regretted. (WEA 1953: 29.)*

And yet in reality the WEA's problem was its continuing, and perhaps escalating, inability to persuade trade union members to enrol in its classes in any substantial numbers. (Substantial, that is, in relation to the total number of trade unionists.)

The working party's response to these difficulties reflected thinking in the important, and then recently-developed, area of community education and community development. In this they could draw on Creech Jones' experience as a member of the Colonial Office's Advisory Committee on Education from the mid-1930s, and as a leading and founder member — former Chairman — of the Fabian Colonial Bureau, a major source of progressive thinking in this area. The essence of colonial community development was that education should be related to concrete and relevant tasks which improved the quality of community life; in the process, a range of practical skills and knowledge would be developed. But in addition, and fundamentally, the processes of task selection, planning and execution involved real education in the business of democratic policy- and decision-making. Colonial community development was, in short, education in self-government. (Holford 1988b.)

The working party's Report reflected this thinking. It sought to cut through the concerns about utilitarian versus liberal education for trade unionists by placing the entire enterprise on a new philosophical basis. The basis was, in effect, the reality of the new social order, in which trade unions were to be active participants in economic and industrial decision-making.

> *The development of nationalisation, a renewed interest in what is loosely called 'workers' control', the growth of joint consultation and joint production committees, have led to an increasing interest in management studies and the administration of industry. The relation of claims for higher living standards to obstinate national and international economic issues, and the propaganda for greater production through increased efficiency, raise a wide range of issues in which the trade unionist is involved. Factory re-organisation, modern production techniques, incentive wage systems, the less tangible but no less important matters that are now embraced in 'human relations in industry', all these have to be dealt with by trade union representatives and later their actions must be reported and justified to the rank and file. There are also problems of adjustment of labour supply as between industries, the re-adjustment of wage levels and differentials under conditions of full employment, and the maintainance of full employment through national and international action. These factors are giving a new direction and scope to trade union education. (WEA 1953: 24.)*

Let us overstate in pursuit of clarity: in the new world, union education must equip trade unionists to play a fuller role in society — rather than, as formerly, in the political and social movement of labour. The movement (through the Labour government) had constructed a wholly new network of political and industrial institutions open to working-class influence. The

Post-war Methods and Philosophies

task of trade union representatives was to make their mark within these.

This was, of course, chiefly a matter of emphasis. The Creech Jones committee was far from denying that unions were part of a purposive movement, that they were organisations with their own structural needs. The Report quoted the views of a WEA district trade union advisory committee:

> *One of the major weaknesses is the general apathy reflected in poor attendance at branch meetings, etc. This is probably due to the fact that the trade unionist regards his union as a means to a specific and narrow end and does not see it on the background of the wider and more significant social and political issues that are involved. (WEA 1953: 29-30.)*

But the committee sought to address the problem of how, given this fact, the mass of trade union representatives (and members and full-time officials) could be aroused from their apathy.

In part, the working party was redefining the problem. In the past, it implicitly held, trade union education in the liberal mould had been responsible for developing and educating a leading elite of the labour movement. (An elite not in the sense of those holding high office only, but leaders at every level.) In the post-war world, with the growth of educational opportunity for able children of the working class, there would no longer be the fund of intellectually able leaders 'trapped' within the labour movement, and ripe for the tutorial class. These latter had been the natural leaders of the working class: now the movement had to find — or cultivate — a new stratum of leaders. The Report quoted a WEA district secretary:

> *Herein, I think, lies a new challenge to the W.E.A. We have to be concerned with a new minority — the minority within the mass of the non-grammar school minded — who could be its natural leaders constituting that stable, responsible, and progressive element which the tutorial class student constituted in the past. (WEA 1953: 42.)*

The implication, for Creech Jones and his colleagues, was that new methods and approaches had to be found. The same district secretary continued:

> *We want an educational instrument and an educational technique for the non-academically minded, as effective and successful as the tutorial class was for the potentially grammar school minded. If we could devise new techniques, new methods, and make a new wing of our movement we should have a job of social significance set in the direction of democratic progress. (WEA 1953: 42.)*

In short, then, Creech Jones and his colleagues proposed on the one hand that the new order required new types of activity — and thus new types of skill, knowledge and ability — on the part of the trade union representative. On the other hand, they argued that union educators must accept that their students would be less intellectually or academically outstanding than formerly.³ 'The real question is whether methods which have worked well in the past in adult education are applicable to students who are not of the university tutorial class type' (WEA 1953: 57). The answer was unambiguous. In trade union education it was

> *particularly important ... to build on the immediate interests and experience of the students ... It is essential to move from the particular to the general by starting from common experience and in mutual discussion gradually to lay bare the conflicts of motive and principle and the obstinate material factors which are involved in a problem (WEA 1953: 58).*

Of course, there would still be a role for advanced courses: 'groups of trade union students dealing with trade union studies at the tutorial class level can achieve high standards ... [and] first-class results are possible.' But 'only a part of trade union education will be at this level': in consequence, different approaches would be required and — in a telling phrase for a WEA report — 'experience outside liberal adult education must be taken fully into account' (WEA 1953: 58-9). These areas of experience from which trade union education could learn included industrial training, particularly the training of supervisors. The Report assumed the existence of a new order:

> *In the 'human relations' branch of supervisory training there is strong emphasis on discussion and role playing because it is personal attitudes and social skills that have to be dealt with, and the methods of democratic leadership that have now to replace authority in industry (WEA 1953: 63).*

Each member of a group had to be given 'a sense of active participation'; the group had to 'find its own way, in good measure'. 'Frank expression of opinion and mutual and constructive discussion is found to ease the way to an adjustment of attitude.' (WEA 1953: 63.)

It was also possible to learn from technical colleges' experience with 'a type of teaching which seeks to equip the student with a prescribed body of knowledge and, for this purpose, pays a good deal of attention to systematic note-taking, to means of measuring student receptivity, and places a strong emphasis on the text-book' (WEA 1953: 60). The working party argued that techniques of study needed to be learnt. They quoted from a report of courses at Birmingham College of Technology: 'We found that most of the students felt note-taking at lectures a formidable task and the preparation of a record of a series of lectures an almost frightening experience' (WEA 1953: 40). Greater use might also be made — in the constant refrain of reports on educating adults — of advanced technology: 'wire sound recorders, and films and film strips' (WEA 1953: 63-4).

In sum, therefore, the report penned by Creech Jones and his companions set out a philosophy for trade union education which would move it beyond liberalism. Liberalism was — as they saw it — obsolete and inappropriate to the needs of most trade unionists in a socialist or quasi-socialist economy, marked by full employment, nationalisation, joint consultation in industry, and the like. This meant, of course, commitment to a view that education was not simply an individual matter: it was profoundly collective, and should be judged in large part by its role in developing a democratic organisation and culture for industry and unions. This is not to say that personal development was seen as unimportant: far from it. But education did not occur solely, or even mainly, in the classroom; union education could not helpfully be separated from union activity. This view was, of course, at one level a continuation of the traditional outlook of 'working-class education': that education must serve the movement and the struggle for socialism. But at the same time Creech Jones was not merely importing the Millarian approaches of the post-war NCLC. The working party assumed that the nature of trade union tasks had shifted irrevocably: union democracy, industrial democracy, and social democracy were all linked, and were all vital to the educational enterprise. By the same token, education was central to building democracy in all these dimensions. It was, in short, a far broader and fuller conception of education and its role than that of the post-war labour colleges.

The overall record of post-war British adult education is of a failure to analyse, and to adapt creatively to, a world in which the nature of progress, and of the social movement in which adult education was rooted, could no longer be taken for granted. In this light, the Creech Jones Report stands out as an early attempt to grapple with how an aspect of adult education should adapt to 'the welfare state'. It is, in retrospect, easy to find fault with its thinking: others, in time, took up the theme, and on occasion more profoundly (see esp. Harrison 1955). The Creech Jones vision was let down above all by the overwhelming modesty of its organisational proposals (see Chapter 4). These went little beyond suggestions for the WEA: to establish some pilot schemes, to carry out some further inquiries, and to set up a central trade union education bureau (WEA 1953: 79-82). But its philosophical importance should not be understated. It struck at the heart of the traditional — liberal — WEA and university view of adult education. This, it argued, was all but irrelevant to trade unionists. It set up an alternative intellectual framework which had roots in community education and community development, but which also drew from the teaching techniques of other sectors of formal education. It provided a basis for later developments in union educational approach. But above all it was a pioneering attempt to engage with the fundamental dilemmas and tensions of post-war union education: reconciling relevance with politics, the particular with the general, organisational with individual needs.

Active Methods and Programmed Learning

One tension latent in the Creech Jones Report was the contrast between an administrative, or political, desire for union education to be a mass activity, involving very large numbers of trade unionists, and an educational commitment to the learning and development of individuals or small groups. In Creech Jones, the enthusiasm for educational technology and the methods of industrial training rests uneasily beside the expressed desire that they 'should be used mainly as a means of reinforcing or making more relevant the mental discipline essential to effective education' or to encourage the 'serious study of facts, ideas and principles characteristic of liberal education' (WEA 1953: 63).[4]

This tension continued to bedevil trade union education in the years after Creech Jones reported in 1953. In pursuit of mass provision, union administrators have been recurrently struck by the possibilities of the frontiers of technology of the day: from wireless to tape-slide to television to video. A constant theme too has been the prospect of enhanced efficiency from centralising the production of teaching and learning resources. For Creech Jones (WEA 1953: 66-72) the WEA should establish a

> *trade union education bureau ... to collect and disseminate information about activities and experiments in the field of trade union education, to make available books, pamphlets and other educational material found to be needed, and generally to stimulate and to guide interest in trade union education ... and to provide assistance to individuals and groups engaged in it (WEA 1953: 71-2).*

For Clegg and Adams, reviewing the WEA's progress in trade union education six years later (the WEA had been unable, chiefly for financial reasons, to act on this particular Creech Jones recommendation), the need was for a 'college ... for research and teaching':

> *There is a need for the production of books, pamphlets and other material which will start from the interests of groups of active trade unionists in their own union and their own industry, help to give them knowledge useful to them in their work as trade unionists, and also lead them on to a wider interest in economics, industrial relations, government or some other liberal discipline. Besides that, there is need for the training of tutors in the use of this material, in its adaptation to fit the requirements of the particular parts of the country in which they teach, in the best methods of using other material for trade unionists, and in the kind of approach which will get the best out of a trade union class. (Clegg and Adams 1959: 82.)*

A large part of the problem was that 'at any one time several tutors in different parts of the country may be struggling to put much the same sort of material together'; the college 'could lead to a great improvement in efficiency' (Clegg and Adams 1959: 83). Again, the WEA never was able to find the resources necessary to make such a college a reality; nor did it initiate the development of such an institution by any other body (Clegg and Adams suggested Ruskin might be a possibility).

Later, of course, it was the TUC itself which took on — part of — the role spelled out for the WEA by the Creech Jones and Clegg-Adams reports. In 1968 *Training Shop Stewards*, noting the WEA's inability to establish 'a service for preparing teaching materials for use by tutors', set down a list of 'the types of prepared material that would be of most help to union tutors prevented from preparing their own material through other pressing commitments' (TUC 1968a: 34). These included:

> *first ... an outline or check sheet to enable them to organise their experience so that it can be presented in a way suited to the union representatives. Second come background information papers and source-lists .... Third are materials such as case studies and questionnaires that assist tutors in using teaching methods which involve the active participation of students — with accompanying notes suggesting how and when to introduce them. Fourth are simple visual aids such as charts on union and TUC organisation. And fifth come documents containing information for the student as a background or supplement to the course teaching. (TUC 1968a: 34.)*

In addition, there was 'a need for model teaching materials to be prepared on subjects that are widely taught' (TUC 1968a: 34-5).

Training Shop Stewards also showed a marked interest in 'programmed instruction' — 'a method of training through which *specified trainees* are led by tested steps to achieve a *prescribed performance*' — for subjects likely to be studied by 'very large numbers of students' (TUC 1968: 37; emphasis in original). During the later 1960s, the TUC's consultative group of union education officers was pushing the Education Department toward 'standardisation' of courses (a route the Department's leaders were by no means unhappy to take). This was partly necessary: the TUC was now a provider on a large scale, and clearly felt responsible to 'the Movement' for its work. The mechanisms through which this accountability was to operate reflected a particular image of 'efficiency' in educational provision — an image in which effectiveness can be judged only in relation to clearly-specified objectives. 'Only by defining the purpose clearly in advance will it be possible to assess the effectiveness of the course. Lack of definition in this respect can only frustrate tutors, students and unions supporting their attendance.' The consultative group interpreted 'standardisation' of courses

TUC TRAINING COLLEGE

MODEL TIMETABLE FOR 10-DAY COURSE 1.31

GENERAL MANUFACTURING

	SESSION 1	SESSION 2	SESSION 3	SESSION 4
WEEK 1	INTRODUCTION — THE T U ROLE OF SAFETY REPRESENTATIVES	IDENTIFYING THE PROBLEMS OF HEALTH AND SAFETY AT WORK THROUGH THE ANALYSIS OF PRELIMINARY SURVEY RESULTS		
WEEK 2	ESTABLISHING STANDARDS (1)			
	HEALTH & SAFETY LEGISLATION	THE HEALTH & SAFETY AT WORK ACT 1974: GENERAL DUTIES		EXERCISE AND CHECKLIST ON GENERAL DUTIES
WEEK 3	ESTABLISHING STANDARDS (2)			
	EXERCISE ON THE FACTORIES ACT 1961			ANALYSIS OF FACTORIES ACTS EXERCISE
WEEK 4	ESTABLISHING STANDARDS (3)			
	THE REGULATIONS	THE USE OF CHECKLISTS ON OTHER STANDARDS: CODES OF PRACTICE: JSC REPORTS: TDN's ETC		
WEEK 5	HAZARDS OF WORK (1)			
	SAFETY AND WELFARE – CASE STUDIES			
WEEK 6	HAZARDS OF WORK (2)			
	HEALTH HAZARDS – CASE STUDIES			
WEEK 7	HAZARDS OF WORK (3)			
	EXERCISES AND CASE STUDIES ON HAZARD PROCEDURES			
WEEK 8	WORKPLACE ORGANISATION (1)			
	THE HEALTH & SAFETY AT WORK ACT – IMPLICATIONS FOR T U ORGANISATION		ROLE OF THE H.S.I. & E.M.A.S.	SAFETY POLICIES
WEEK 9	WORKPLACE ORGANISATION (2)			
	EXERCISE ON ROLE OF SAFETY REPRESENTATIVE		EXERCISE ON ROLE OF SAFETY COMMITTEE	EXERCISE ON SAFETY POLICIES
WEEK 10	WORKPLACE ORGANISATION (3)			
	ACCIDENT PROCEDURE	SOURCES AND USE OF INFORMATION	COURSE REVIEW AND DISCUSSION	

Fig. 7.1: Model Timetable. A guide for tutor and student, these also give full-time officials and employers an image of what union representatives study. A valuable aid for tutors, for some they have epitomised excessive centralisation. This Health and Safety timetable dates from 1978, shortly before printed materials were issued.

broadly: 'to gain the maximum benefit, some degree of standardisation needs to be introduced *throughout* the TUC education service'. Whilst the paper left open the question 'How much less than *complete* standardisation will be acceptable for TUC purposes', its own preferences were apparent. (TUC Education Service Consultative Group: paper for meeting 21 February 1968: TUC file 817.211A.)

The trend to 'standardisation' continued in the early 1970s. After the allocation of public funds in the mid-seventies, and the decision to provide courses through public educational bodies, the case appeared inescapable. Quality control, as we have seen, was central. In 1977 the first set of printed core materials (the *Introductory Course for Shop Stewards*) was made available: 'For the first time shop stewards attending TUC introductory courses were able to work from a printed course book' (TUC 1978: 203). This, to become known in the trade as the 'Red Pack', was divided into daily sections; a model timetable suggested daily timings. Over the next two years, the course was a little revised (under the slightly but significantly different title *Introductory Course for Union Representatives*). Special versions were also produced for courses for union representatives in Local Government (the 'Green Pack') and the National Health Service (the 'Blue Pack').

Course materials were initially circulated in duplicated form for other courses, including 'Health and Safety at Work' and 'Rights at Work'. Printed materials for both were issued in 1979. A discussion paper on 'The Future of the TUC Teaching Materials for 10-Day Health and Safety Courses', issued by the TUC Education Service in 1978, reveals much of the thinking behind the move to make printed course packs available for classroom use by each student. It had 'never been the practice' to issue a complete 'pack' of materials for 10-day Safety courses. A 'range of materials' had been circulated, but these were often neither 'specifically designed for students' nor 'available in student quantities'. Their coverage was 'somewhat fragmentary', and they involved 'relying entirely on tutors to deal with those parts of the syllabus which have not been covered by TUC materials'. The paper noted certain 'advantages' of this approach:

> *it does provide the necessary flexibility to enable tutors to tailor courses to meet the needs of particular students and groups. Experienced tutors have been able to develop their own materials and approach, and have contributed greatly to advances in this work, and to the development of sector courses.*

But there were also several 'drawbacks', and these were clearly regarded as of overwhelming weight:

> *— new tutors are faced with a fragmented set of teaching notes which*

> does not provide complete or coherent guidance as to how different parts of the course should be run. Often this prevents new tutors from acting as 'course tutor' for all parts of the course, and leads to an over-reliance on visiting speakers
>
> — it has been very difficult to ensure that documents are printed in sufficient numbers to provide students with copies. As a result the development of effective learning techniques based on student activity has been inhibited. Tutor centred and 'visiting speaker' centred approaches have sometimes been over-used as substitute for good quality materials
>
> — there have been no reliable ways in which developments in methods and materials generated by some tutors could be made available to others. As a result the approach and quality of the TUC courses has varied quite widely
>
> — many safety representatives have not left the courses with information and resources which can readily be referred to later on. (TUC 1978d: 2.)

As well as standardising content, the new course development unit at Congress House sought to ensure some kind of uniformity in educational method. The methods used in TUC courses were to be 'active'. The 'TUC Day Release Course Outlines' described the methods used on the Introductory Course for Union Representatives:

> Small group work is the central method of the course. Students are encouraged to learn through activity, and during a typical day would be asked to work on three or four tasks in small groups. These tasks would be question-based and closely related to the experience of the shop stewards. In this sense the course is concerned with encouraging shop stewards to develop their own knowledge rather than have knowledge 'transmitted' to them.
>
> 'Discovery' exercises are used to help relate the issues in the course to workplace experience.
>
> Case studies are used to encourage the development of skills. Role plays may take the form of running a shop stewards' meeting, interviewing a member, or negotiating with management. Shop stewards are able to develop the skills of preparing and presenting a case to put to members, union meetings and management. (TUC 1979a: 13.)

Broadly similar methods were employed in other TUC courses.

While the authors of *Training Shop Stewards* made a strong case for the importance of union education, their comments on teaching method went little further than the coy observation that 'the unbroken lecture is often not the most suitable teaching technique' (TUC 1968a: 27). By the mid-1970s, however, the TUC Education Department was wholeheartedly converted to active methods. This was partly the mood of the time: as the course development unit expanded, it recruited a number of young educators imbued with radical educational ideas; active, co-operative approaches to learning were popular. But such methods also provided solutions to practical problems. If tutors were not to lecture, their need for technical expertise was that much less: the tutor-supply problems would be much reduced. This was a consideration the TUC was perhaps too diplomatic to acknowledge. With the rapid expansion of trade union courses, in both range and numbers, many tutors did lack the knowledge or skills to conduct extended lectures. Gee, who worked in Congress House on the development of health and safety courses in the 1970s, suggests (1982: 8) that one reason for adopting student-centred methods in his field was just that most 'tutors ... knew very little about safety ... [and] couldn't have lectured for ten minutes on technical or legal issues to begin with, let alone ten days'. The same could be said (though with somewhat less truth) of some other courses, such as Rights at Work.

The initial evaluation of the methods was positive. 'Evaluation conferences of trade union studies tutors' were held in 'most TUC regions' and an 'evaluation form was completed by all shop stewards attending introductory courses during the September-December 1977 session.' Apparently 'many of the aims originally set by the TUC Education Service for the new course' were being achieved. 'Shop stewards have reacted favourably to the learning methods adopted and the use of the course book.' (TUC 1978: 203.) In a smaller-scale survey, based on 175 replies from students on TUC courses in early 1977, Westbrook and Whitehouse (1978b: esp. 16-21) reached broadly similar conclusions. The course and course materials were regarded, almost without exception, as satisfactory; whilst in evaluation of the methods used, the approved TUC methods — discussion, role plays, small group discussion, and so forth — emerged toward the top of the order. (One contradictory feature emerged, however: lectures by the tutor came out second in the order — a matter which Westbrook and Whitehouse (1978b: 18-19) found it necessary to explain away on sociological and methodological grounds.)

In an important and much-debated article, Doug Gowan (then the TUC Assistant Secretary in charge of the course development unit) discussed how its thinking on educational methods had developed by the early 1980s. It was, he said, helpful to examine

> *succeeding editions of tutors' notes for the various courses introduced since 1976, starting with the Introductory course tutors' notes, then the Health and Safety notes, the revised guidance on the Introductory course, the new Stage 1 tutor notes, and the various editions of the Stage 2 course notes including the Health and Safety Stage 2. ... We have the conscious*

> view in the TUC Education Service that each course should not only cover a 'subject', but explore or consolidate certain ideas about educational method or policy. (Gowan 1982: 4.)

He proceeded to give examples:

> The old introductory course ... stressed the use of small groups, 'discovery exercises', and building skills development into all the course work. ... The safety course stressed the idea of adopting a systematic approach (later to re-emerge as PIP [Problem: Investigation: Plan] in Stage 1), the development of information-finding and analysing skills, and strengthened the idea of problem-based or case-study approaches. The New Technology and collective bargaining course reinforced the idea of strong central themes, with course work being assembled into a 'project'. The new Stage 1 course picked up the idea of a systematic approach from the safety courses, but carried it forward to form the basis for handling most of the course work. The course also put new emphasis on contact between reps and membership. (Gowan 1982: 4-5.)

There was, perhaps, an element of *post-hoc* rationalisation in this account: the course development unit in the 1970s was highly innovative, and each innovation had to be disseminated. But there is little doubt that course development in the 1970s was, for the Education Department, partly a matter of tutor development.

The early 1980s saw a subtle but significant shift in the TUC's approach to course methods. To a large extent, active methods and the use of centrally-developed learning materials had been advocated in the 1970s as practical responses to overcome the problems created by a relatively inexperienced and inexpert body of tutors. From about 1980 onward, a current of opinion developed in the course development unit — supported by many tutors around the country — which made a positive virtue of tutors' not being experts. A key advocate of this approach was Doug Gowan, who (under Roy Jackson, the head of the department) enjoyed a strong measure of autonomy in leading the course development unit. This shift in approach was introduced through tutor briefings, and the tutors' notes produced by the course development unit for each course. (Though the climate of opinion about method changed, many individual tutors of course continued to teach more or less as they had always done.)

The key elements of the new approach were the idea of shifting the 'balance of control' in the class from tutor to student, and increasing the 'student-centredness' of the course. Gowan (1982: 6) explained the chief mechanisms by which these were to be achieved: by introducing a 'course meeting', and by changing physical layout to move away from 'classrooms' toward a 'union office/workroom atmosphere'. He also explicitly asserted (1982: 4) that in 'the TUC Education Service we have tended to concentrate

22   Representing members

involving members

The members are the union. You speak on their behalf when you meet management. When you take up a member's problem they may go to the meeting with you. You should always keep them in touch with what's happening by:

- holding regular meetings
- listening to members' views
- giving advice about next steps.

You rely on your members to bring you their problems and to back you up. They need you to represent them. Where members' problems are handled promptly it gives them confidence in the union and in your ability to represent their interests effectively.

CHECKLIST

---

handling members' problems

Problem

- Are the facts known?
- Have you interviewed those concerned?
- Is it a genuine problem?
- Does it involve an individual or is it collective?
- Are other workers affected?

Information

- Look through your agreements:
  — local ones
  — any national agreements which exist
- What about custom and practice?
- Has it happened before?
- Is the problem covered by the law?
- What is union policy?
- Should you take advice?

Plan

- What should the union aim to achieve?
- How strong is the union position?
- How should the union approach it?
- How can you involve members?

Fig. 7.2: PIP Checklist. The three-stage strategic approach to handling issues has been central in TUC Education. In the 1970s, checklists were considered vital in helping representatives make sense of documentary standards, such as laws. By the 1990s, as in this Stage 1 course, the checklist had a more symbolic role.

on changes in approach and methods rather than in defining a particular "right" way of "teaching"': the approach he outlined nevertheless caused a good deal of anxiety among many tutors. Certainly his article was occasionally intemperate in tone. He was particularly critical of what he saw as an important but 'diseducational' strand of tutoring, which fostered the 'idea of a tutor as somebody "clever" who shows off'. A course taught by such a tutor

> *may have had a number of outward signs of being student-centred (tasks set for small groups and so on); but the reality was ... that the course was tutor-controlled and run in the interests of the tutor's ego. There is even a name for this kind of approach, as it represents a common deviation: it's called the 'prima donna' style. (Gowan 1982: 7.)*

And indeed the TUC education service was, in reality, attempting, if not to define a 'right' way of teaching, at least to draw more narrowly the parameters of acceptable tutorial practice.

In November 1983 a paper was issued entitled 'Methods in Trade Union Education' (TUC 1983a). Aimed at trade union tutors, it contained a great deal of uncontentious and practically helpful advice and suggestion: but it also made assertions which further delimited the range of acceptable educational approach. The major area of contention centred on what the paper termed '"Classroom" layout', but was also about the role of the tutor. The aim was to move 'away from a "classroom" with a "front" reserved for a "teacher", and towards a room based on activities for the students and a more democratic atmosphere.' In order to make this approach work, tutors were exhorted (*inter alia*) to 'rearrange the furniture so there is no "front" to the room'. A clear statement was made: 'do not keep a special place for yourself as course tutor — you are a course member like everyone else'. (TUC 1983a: 10.) Elsewhere, it was suggested that tutors could use

> *course meetings ... to allow the participants to have a say in the running of the course and the part they are expected to play. ...you can put 'group make up' on the agenda for the meeting, once more emphasising that the course participants must take more responsibility for their own learning. (TUC 1983a: 6.)*

It was around these developments that the most heated debates among trade union educators developed. The language of 'deviation' and 'prima donnas' in Gowan's 1982 article was undoubtedly provocative, serving to obfuscate rather than clarify important issues. In a series of articles (see esp. Brown et al. 1983 and 1984; Edwards et al. 1983; McIlroy and Spencer 1984), several tutors (mainly from the north-west of England) attacked Gowan's approach. The atmosphere became more intemperate. For in fact more was at issue than questions of method: the role of the tutor, student responsibility, and so forth. The debate also involved questions of content.

One accusation made against the TUC's preferred methods was that they implied an 'abdication' (Edwards et al. 1983: 51) by tutors (and the TUC) of their responsibility to ensure that the course content was appropriate. We return to this issue in the following section. It should be said, however, at this stage that the dispute was essentially between caricatures. The best advocates of the course committee,[5] for instance, used it as an opportunity for education, rather than simply leaving its outcomes to mayhap. Few advocates of the importance of 'content' were inveterate lecturers.

For the TUC, some kind of systematic, or 'standardised', approach to educational programming was a central objective from the mid-1960s. From much the same time, there was a recognition of the importance of active learning. This recognition grew through the 1970s so that, by the early 1980s, student-centred activity approaches were something of a fetish. The case for them was, of course, a strong one. Trade union students were not as a rule well-equipped to benefit from highly academic teaching methods. There was too a view that as democratic decision-making should be central to effective trade unionism, so union education should be schools of democracy — students should make decisions about what and how they learn.[6] But there was an inevitable tension: the TUC held fast to the view that it should be responsible for its educational programme, and it explicitly sought a standardised structure of progression through various levels of course. This meant that the extent of variation from the essential aims and syllabus of a course was highly circumscribed, and to this extent many of the claims made about the democratic nature of student-centredness were wide of the mark.

The innovative period in trade union education — in terms of method — was concentrated in the years of growth. By the mid-1980s it had passed. The debates had subsided; efforts and attentions had transferred to more prosaic matters (sustaining the programme, in the main). The printed materials for the major courses were periodically revised and updated. The Introductory course was substantially revised, and renamed 'Stage 1', in 1981; the 'Red Pack' disappeared, superseded by three, rather more flexible — if in the views of some, 'depoliticised' (Edwards et al. 1983: 52) — workbooks entitled *Organisation*, *Bargaining*, and *Skills*. Slightly amended versions of each were issued at roughly biennial intervals. The Health and Safety at Work course materials, first available in printed form in 1979, were revised in 1980; an entirely new edition — again encouraging a rather more flexible approach — was issued in 1985, and updated in 1987. With these new materials the 1970s approach — parodied, but not unfairly, as an entirely centrally programmed structure, in which daily timetables were followed rigidly by tutors around the country — was finally set to rest. Tutors were typically now more experienced: the great inrush of new tutors occurred in the later 1970s. The short course programme — encouraging tutors to develop courses to meet the needs of individual union organisations — required the stimulation of local initiative and resourcefulness. And most important, by the later 1980s the TUC seemed more trusting of its tutors.

Liberal Education and the Politics of Content

For Creech Jones, the question of liberal education and the proper and relevant content of trade union education was a live one. His committee's solution was, in essence, to cut the Gordian knot: to move beyond the education/training, liberal/utilitarian, dichotomies by asserting that the new order required a far broader rationale and focus for union education. It was no longer a matter of relevance *versus* disinterested education. Economic and social change meant that a much wider spectrum of subject-matter had become relevant to the tasks of trade unionism in the new world: 'trade union studies courses which, while retaining the character of liberal education, have focused attention on the special problems of the trade union movement in the post-war social order' (WEA 1953: 46).

By the later 1950s, however, it was becoming clear that some of the optimistic assumptions which permeated the Creech Jones approach had not been substantiated. Clegg and Adams, at the end of the decade, were rather more modest in their claims. The education/training dichotomy remained very much alive in the minds of practitioners. Surveying the pilot schemes run by the WEA in response to the Creech Jones recommendations, they noted that

> *although there are active trade unionists who are able and willing to profit from such [liberal] studies taken at a serious level ..., they are relatively few, and bringing them together is an onerous and expensive task. It can perhaps be justified, but it is not, by itself, a very large contribution to the trade union movement. (Clegg and Adams 1959: 76.)*

The WEA could make a larger contribution in the areas of public expression, work study, and collective bargaining, if it trained tutors and provided teaching materials and equipment. But, philosophically, all Clegg and Adams were able to offer was:

> *The narrowness of such courses ... is sometimes exaggerated. Work study or collective bargaining may be taught as purely practical skills in a technical college, but no W.E.A. tutor worth his salt would neglect their social implications, or fail to interest his class in them. (Clegg and Adams 1959: 76.)*

Although the 'education-or-training' dichotomy was a problem chiefly for the 'Responsible Bodies' (the WEA and the university extra-mural departments), the longstanding links between unions and the WEA and WETUC meant that the TUC could not entirely avoid the issue. This was reinforced when the TUC took over the WETUC in 1964. With the erosion of the quasi-socialist assumptions of the Creech Jones Report, two main approaches developed during the 1960s and early 1970s. They provided philosophical underpinning for the involvement of liberal educational institutions in activities which seemed significantly narrower than those in which they had traditionally engaged. They evolved, however, from educational practice.

The first was 'Role Education': the key institution in this was the Oxford University Delegacy for Extra-mural Studies, which developed a large and influential input into industrial relations during the 1950s and 1960s. It was closely linked to the developing 'Oxford school' of industrial relations (Clegg 1990; Marsh 1958: 128-9; Marsh 1991; Pickstock 1963: 58). The approach was marked by a strong emphasis on research projects on specific industries, and on critical study of relevant documents and analysis which emerged:

> *effective teaching must begin with the actual experience of the student himself ... [which] must be linked with the wider information provided by the tutor, analysed in critical discussion and generalised upon ... For example, in the engineering study, the first stage of which is defined as a study of 'The System of Industrial Relations in Engineering', the basic documents are the constitutions of the unions and the employers' associations, procedural and substantive agreements, national and local, together with the interpretative analysis contained in the research study itself. (Pickstock 1963: 57-8.)*

The notion of Role Education was defined and legitimised in the 1970 Report of the University's Committee on Extra-mural Studies as 'education providing a broad background of knowledge relevant to the performing of specific roles'. The roles might be those of shop stewards (whose activities the committee rather quaintly considered to be 'paid work') or magistrates or local government or armed forces officers. (University of Oxford 1970: 30.)

> *The distinction between providing a broad background of knowledge relevant to specific roles, and technical instruction, which is not the aim of the courses in Role Education, may best be illustrated by examples. ... [S]hop stewards attending the day-release course arranged for them would not learn the rate for specific jobs, but would learn about job evaluation, collective bargaining, productivity bargaining, and how rates are fixed. (University of Oxford 1970: 31.)*

Clearly the Oxford Committee's knowledge of union education was limited; and there were some who would have needed more convincing that collective bargaining, for instance, could be taught otherwise than by technical instruction. But the Committee had accepted that there was an appropriate function for the University's extra-mural department in this area. It had also accepted that it was legitimate, in a university context, to judge union education other than by liberal adult education criteria: and potentially this was of the greatest importance.

The second approach may be called Industrial Studies. This emerged from the practical work of tutors in the Responsible Bodies during the 1950s and 1960s, as they grappled to engage, from institutions rooted in the liberal tradition, with the needs of the labour and trade union movement. The approach grew from the work of Nottingham University College extra-mural staff between the wars (on which see Mee 1984: 3-16; Peers 1926: esp. 29-31), and from courses developed at Sheffield, London, and other university extra-mural departments, and within the WEA, in the 1950s and 1960s (see Williams 1954; Fyrth 1980: 150-51; McIlroy 1988a: 62-5; Croucher and Halstead 1990). The major theoretical statement of the Industrial Studies approach was in the Society of Industrial Tutors' substantial series of that name (see esp. Coker and Stuttard 1976, 1980; Stuttard 1988).

In an important article in one of these volumes, Fyrth (1980: 154) provided perhaps the clearest statement of the key principles of the Industrial Studies approach. 'Industrial Studies,' he wrote:

> *Begin from a study of the immediate problems faced by trade union activists, especially at the workplace, using their experience as the starting point so as to help them to tackle the problems more effectively.*
>
> *Recognise that these problems are such that they call for a relevant knowledge of trade union organization, aims and history, industrial structure and company finance, law, economics, political institutions, and social relationships as well as skills of communication, expression and numeracy.*
>
> *In this way introduce the study of basic concepts and ideas of the Labour Movement, in as non-sectarian a way as is possible; can, by these methods, lead on to more advanced studies.*

Where Industrial Studies emerged, so Fyrth argued, 'training is wedded to the traditions of liberal education and becomes training to make social changes'. It was, to this extent, recognisably in the tradition initiated by the Creech Jones committee. The notion of Industrial Studies was central to the formation of the Society of Industrial Tutors in 1968 and 1969: 'One of the aims of its founders was to bring together the industrial tutors who were experienced in the "liberal" tradition with those who were coming into the

Post-war Methods and Philosophies

field to meet the demand for shop steward and other training in polytechnics and other colleges.' (Fyrth 1980: 151.)

The distinction between Role Education and Industrial Studies is virtually identical to the distinction, made originally by Frank Pickstock of the Oxford extra-mural department in 1966, between an 'industrial relations approach' and an 'industrial community approach' (see McIlroy 1988a: 64-5). As a broad generalisation, the Role Educators held sway in the southern English extra-mural departments, while Industrial Studies took hold in the north. The distinction was primarily one of emphasis, and in part a matter of tutors cutting their educational coats according to the political cloth of the areas in which they functioned. One real factor in this was the nature of trade unionism and of union politics in the area concerned. Both approaches sought initially to base themselves in single industries. For the Oxford role educators, it was mining, the motor industry, and road passenger transport (Pickstock 1963: 56) — later car manufacture was broadened to engineering as a whole; work also developed for other industries, such as printing. (Oxford's mining work eroded as it lost first Staffordshire, and later Kent, from its extra-mural area.) Industrial Studies in the 1960s and 1970s, more securely based in such industries as mining, and iron and steel, especially after nationalisation, tended to reflect the character and strength of the local union and political cultures.[7]

To generalise — there were exceptions — Industrial Studies and Role Education also differed in politics. Neither was driven solely by educational aims. Industrial Studies tended to be associated with the socialist left; Role Educators were more of the centre-left. Key personalities on each side bespeak this difference: Michael Barratt Brown, Ken Coates, Tony Topham, all leading figures in the Institute for Workers' Control, were prominent advocates of Industrial Studies. The Oxford school, with whom Role Education was closely associated, were of course intimately involved in the 1960s Labour project for industrial relations reform, and linked with 'corporatist' union leaders such as George Woodcock. For the first group, the agenda in union education was a labour movement agenda, in which trade unionism and politics were inseparable. For the Role Educators, in contrast, union education was a contribution to good industrial relations. Its agenda was collective bargaining — from a union viewpoint, to be sure, but with no prominent political agenda, and broadly accepting that the framework of collective bargaining was set.

As a general rule, the Role Educators tended to place less emphasis on the length of their courses. This made it somewhat easier for them to co-operate with the WEA — and, in due course, the TUC. They were also keen to extend their approach further:

> *the universities and the WEA cannot hope to meet the enormous extent and variety of demand for courses from trade unionists which is revealing itself. We have a duty to help the trade unions and probably technical colleges too, to educate and train tutors for this work and to give them the assistance they will need by providing appropriate teaching material. (Pickstock 1963: 58-9.)*

This view of co-operation with a wide spectrum of educational institutions, together with their rather different view of the curriculum, meant that the Role Education approach was less encumbered by liberal educational impedimenta than Industrial Studies. For the staff of university extra-mural departments, the question as to whether Role Education was liberal education was a real one. Their answer was typically akin to that given by the Oxford committee (e.g., Ireland 1966). But as the approach began to be practised in the management departments of technical colleges, it was liable to interpretation as a form of vocational education.

Fundamentally, the TUC's response to the thorny questions of liberal or instrumental education — on which the Responsible Bodies expended such vast emotional and intellectual energies — was to regard them as historical curiosities, byways from the main road of enhancing the effectiveness of trade union representatives. *Training Shop Stewards* (TUC 1968a) wasted no time on the matter. Having developed an approach in the late 1960s under the banner of training, the TUC was prepared to accept — especially in the light of lessons learnt during 1970-74 — that training was too narrow and instrumental a concept. But while shifting to the notion of education, it stood away from the liberal embrace. The TUC remained committed to the further education sector as the main mechanism for delivering courses. Indeed, the TUC's shift from 'training' to 'education' can also be seen in the light of the redesignation of technical colleges as further education colleges.

Nevertheless, the TUC could not alter history. A major strand of trade union education had emerged from the liberal tradition. In addition, a great many of the tutors teaching trade union courses, whether in WEA, extra-mural departments, colleges or polytechnics, had come into the subject from WEA or extra-mural courses, or through one of the adult residential colleges. Among the more experienced tutors, and those more actively involved in developing the TUC's courses, such backgrounds were still more common. Such people were unwilling to regard union education as 'mere training', as a purely instrumental pursuit — though they were as a rule wholly committed to the notion that union education should strengthen the effectiveness of union organisation. Moreover, if the liberal tradition was one source of union education, a second was independent working-class education. And whilst this could be criticised, in its later years, for sliding

Post-war Methods and Philosophies

into instrumentalism in the service of 'the Movement', its guiding beliefs — the assumptions which motivated its supporters, tutors, and students — were beliefs about the role of education in the movement for socialism.

This was the background to a debate about content in trade union education which emerged strongly in the early 1980s (in tandem with the debate on method). During the seventies the TUC and its fledgling course development unit had developed three major courses. By 1980 there were printed course materials for the Introductory Course for Union Representatives, the Health and Safety at Work course, and for the 'follow-on' course, Rights at Work — a course on the law and its role at work. Each tried to adopt a student-centred approach, although there were significant variations. But in the early 1980s, with the swing in course development unit thinking, a number of decisions coincided. In the autumn of 1981 it was decided to discontinue the Rights at Work course: this was phased out (or, apparently, in certain TUC regions ceased forthwith) (Spencer 1984: 52). At roughly the same time, the ten day Introductory course was replaced by a twenty day course, made up of two sections, Stages 1 and 2. Printed materials were made available for Stage 1, but not for Stage 2. (In reality, however, the TUC was largely unsuccessful in establishing a twenty-day course, and many — perhaps a majority of — representatives made do with no more than the ten days of Stage 1.)

As we have seen, part of the shift in thinking was a re-evaluation of methods in trade union classes. But these specific decisions on course materials and structure had a further important implication. *De facto*, the Stage 2 course had replaced Rights at Work. It was now to Stage 2 that most shop stewards would proceed when 'following-on' from their first ten-day course.[8] The Rights at Work course pack had been a very substantial piece of documentation: a major learning package on employment and trade union law. There was, indeed, a case that it was too advanced for many representatives after a mere ten days of study. The Stage 2 course took a very different approach, with no printed materials whatever circulated.[9] The 'Briefing Notes' (TUC 1981c: 2-3) envisaged that the 'emphasis will be on skills development':

> *Particular topics for inclusion in the course will depend on the balance of the particular group [of students], so flexibility will be important. To maintain a clear structure, it may be necessary to define a number of core topics ... This is the practice with the health and safety course, in which more materials are provided than can be covered in the course.*

Similarly, the printed Stage 1 books, while far more flexible than the former Introductory pack, were also rather less substantial in terms of the volume of sheer information which they contained. The emphasis was rather on 'activities' (the term which had replaced 'exercise'), and passages which informed or generated discussion. (The Health and Safety at Work course was unaffected by this trend for several years: only in 1985 was the structure of the printed materials altered; and then in part it was a recognition of the need for more material, rather than less.)

A number of articulate tutors, particularly in the university extra-mural sector, took issue with this apparent downgrading of content. McIlroy initially (1982b: 70) took issue with the Stage 2 course for overstressing 'workplace organisation and workplace bargaining'. Spencer (1984) attacked the decision to phase out the Rights at Work materials. Presently they broadened their criticism. The suggestion became, in effect, that the stress on active methods (at the expense of 'content') was associated with the political requirements of the time. There were a number of themes to the argument, which emerged in several articles. The most prolific advocate of this view was (and remains) McIlroy, but a number shared his views (cp, e.g., Campbell 1983; Campbell and McIlroy 1986; Edwards et al. 1983; Fisher 1984a).

The essentials of this case may be summarised thus. The nature of TUC education has always been determined fundamentally by the TUC's overall corporatist strategy, by its economism, and by its bureaucratic needs. This accounts for its preference for training rather than education. In the era of Thatcherism, union education needed to attend even more to politics, economics, history. Instead, the TUC replaced its more political courses by courses which on the one hand were even more centred on immediate workplace issues than formerly, and on the other were student-centred in a very narrow way. The particular version of student-centredness adopted by the TUC had the effect, according to McIlroy, of preventing — or strongly discouraging — study of wider political or economic issues. Probably this was the intention: the TUC was concerned to retain government funding, and saw the elimination of political content as a necessary price for this. The student-centredness was in any case largely bogus, as only a limited range of decisions was in reality left to students. Along with this there had been an administrative assault on tutors who took a different view from the TUC's.

This argument was developed and deployed at various levels and in a variety of adult and union education journals. Its advocates' language was often strong and polemical, even unrestrained.[10] How are we to assess their case? First, its tone was not calculated to encourage a sympathetic hearing. The fault was by no means confined to one side,[11] but several of McIlroy's articles appear unwilling to attribute any but the basest motives to the TUC and its staff. Second, it seems to have been part of a wider critique of the TUC's response to the Thatcher government. This may have been fair comment, but it was grossly unrealistic, in view of the nature of the beast, to expect the TUC to have behaved in any markedly different way. Third, it is frankly a matter of opinion whether it was preferable, or politically or educationally more valuable, for the TUC to have continued to accept public funds (with the formal and informal compromises which were inevitably involved), or to have substantially wound up the TUC education programme in the early 1980s.

Fourth, the decision to suspend the Rights at Work course was an error (implicitly acknowledged in the Review of the TUC's Education Service (TUC 1987a: 14-15, see also 25)). In the light of the Thatcher government's wholesale revision of longstanding views on the nature of law in relation to trade unions and employment, some indecision or error in this area is hardly surprising. Fifth, there was a case for greater provision of material in the TUC packages; but to argue this and simultaneously against central control of the curriculum is frankly to have it both ways.

Sixth, and to turn the last point on its head, it is *prima facie* implausible that a reduction in the volume of centrally-provided content really involved tighter control over the curriculum. Indeed, the reverse would appear more likely. (It was certainly the present author's experience that the bounds on content in TUC courses during the 1980s were in practice wide.) McIlroy maintains that the TUC vigorously 'policed' (1985a: 13) the approved methods and content (cp McIlroy 1985c: 50-51, 57-8; 1988b: 118-20). Certainly the regional education officers were expected to know and oversee the tutors working in the colleges, extra-mural departments and WEA districts within their region. In judging whether a tutor was appropriate for TUC courses, trade union commitment was at a premium: on occasion, TUC staff could conflate their own immediate priorities with the aims and interests of the movement as a whole. During the early 1980s, moreover, the ideological struggle over methods and content was bitter (and combined with fierce competition for resources in a context of decline). But 'policing' is not generally an appropriate term to describe the relations between TUC regional education officers and tutors, who continued to embrace a range of political persuasions and teaching styles.

In sum, the critique of TUC methods and course content developed by McIlroy and his associates contains important and valuable elements. The TUC was by no means free from error. Certainly — during the early- to mid-1980s — it went through a phase of devaluing the importance of expertise among, and the role of, its tutors. But neither was it the anti-educational monolith which they paint. The TUC and its education scheme were far from perfect: but neither were they catspaws of Conservatism.[12]

Let us recall that the fundamental decision of recent times in this area was the decision to accept government funding. The terms of this arrangement, first made in 1975, did not substantially alter until the late 1980s.

activity — safety reps — key functions

aims — to help you state clearly the main functions laid down for safety reps in the SRSC regulations

— to bring out trade union points about the implementation of this part of the SRSC regulations.

Here are some problems which could arise about safety reps' functions. Read the relevant part of the *SRSC Booklet* (mainly pages 12-17) and note down the key references from the Regulations, Codes, and Guidance Notes, and then the main points for your report.

1 A member complains that the guards on her machine are defective, and asks you to take a look. The supervisor says that you did an inspection tour of the shop only two days ago so you will have to wait three months before looking at the machine again.

What would your reply be?

2 You are concerned about slippery floors. You approach the foreman who says that the matter can be discussed at a safety committee in three weeks' time, and that he does not intend to do anything about it in the meantime.

What would you do?

3 You have been having problems with a ventilation system in the machine shop. Management says that the system is adequate and that they intend to call in the HSE inspector to prove it. A few days later you hear that the inspector has come and gone without you being told. The management say that he said that the ventilation system was OK.

What would you do about this?

4 You inspected the stores last week. Today one of the shelves in the stores collapsed and injured a foreman. Management say you may be prosecuted because you failed to notice that the shelf was coming away from the wall.

Is this right?

5 A can of solvent has been spilled in your workplace and the fumes are quite strong. The foreman opens the windows and instructs everyone to keep working. You think this is unacceptable because of the risks of fire, drowsiness and accidents, and possible poisoning. You want to stop the job, but management says you have no right to do this, and should take the matter up through procedure.

What would you do?

Fig. 7.3: Activity. Discussing a problem in small groups (usually three or four people) has been a dominant method in TUC courses. This 1980 example involved applying law (the Safety Representatives and Safety Committees regulations), but emphasised working out union responses. Succeeding pages provided commentary and advice.

Post-war Methods and Philosophies

discovery exercise **handling and lifting**

> aim — this exercise will help you to review any problems in your workplace caused by handling and lifting
>
> 1 Are any groups of workers in your workplace expected to lift heavy weights, occasionally or regularly? If so, please give details.
>
> 2 Do the accident and ill-health figures for your workplace show a high rate of accidents incurred in materials handling, or of complaints about back pain? If the figures are available, please bring them along to the course.
>
> 3 Please write in any examples from your experience of:
>
> - bad workplace design or lack of proper handling equipment, causing strain and awkward working positions, thus leading to back complaints
>
> - improvements in the design of your workplace or purchases of handling equipment aimed at reducing handling and lifting problems
>
> 4 Is any training given at your workplace in lifting techniques?
>
> 5 Are any members of management trained in ergonomics? (This is the study of how workplaces and machinery can be designed to fit human needs and human characteristics). If so, have any workplaces or machines been redesigned with ergonomic factors in mind?

Fig. 7.4: Discovery Exercise. Finding things out at the workplace, through getting access to documents, talking to members, or asking management or other union representatives, helps bridge the gap between classroom and reality. Information gathered forms the basis for work the following week.

They were set down in the Regulations and Codes of Practice which gave entitlement to paid release from work for union representative students. We have, of course, discussed these in Chapter 5: fundamentally, they tied release (and hence public funding) to training in aspects of the functions of a safety representative or shop steward. They did not define very closely what constitutes 'relevant' training: but it was widely accepted that much broader historical, economic or political material would not be treated as 'relevant' in this sense. To this extent, of course — and it is a major one — the content of trade union education was determined by the state.

The Conservative government in fact made two clear attempts to influence the content of courses during these years. First, after 1983/84, a proportion of the total allocation of public funds to the TUC was 'earmarked' for expenditure only on courses specifically endorsed by the representative's employer as 'relevant to [the employer's] workplace and ... likely to be of benefit to good industrial relations or to improved health and safety in that workplace'. Initially, these were offered in the form of courses on 'Change at Work'. Though their content varied, they were to be 'specifically relevant to industrial relations and collective bargaining at local level' (TUC 1984b). This was a method of placing pressure on the TUC, and was widely seen by tutors (and others) as a 'thin edge of a wedge' of closer employer and government control. In practice, however, the government did not increase the proportion of public funds (roughly 12 per cent.) allocated under this category; if anything it declined marginally (see Appendix C). It is also far from clear that the requirement was in practice tighter than the general requirement for union representatives to win their employers' consent to paid release: in theory, this could not be unreasonably withheld, but 'cases' were typically settled in the workplace rather than in court. The TUC also found that many employers (especially Labour-controlled local authorities) were happy to endorse its programmes — for example, on the implications of local management of schools. If, therefore, TUC negotiators' judgement was that the threat to independence contained in employer endorsement could be dissipated administratively, they appear to have been vindicated.

The second government attempt to influence the content of courses is less well-established in documentary terms. The government (in particular, the Secretary of State for Education, Sir Keith Joseph) clearly lay behind the TUC's decision, in 1984, to introduce 'economic awareness' as an issue for study. Materials were first issued in August 1984, and updated and complemented thereafter. However, this case indicates not just that the state can attempt to influence the content of courses: it also shows that such attempts can be resisted. Joseph's assumption, apparently, was that 'economic awareness' would educate shop stewards in the economic realities of the market, the importance of profit, the dependence of the public sector on the private, and so forth. Education for trade unionists should be about 'self-interest, properly understood', Joseph (1992) recalled, quoting de Tocqueville's 'great phrase'. The TUC's resistance to this initiative was determined — but canny. It did not suggest that 'economic awareness' was an inappropriate topic for trade union courses. But how was the topic to be handled educationally? Clearly the development of economic awareness for shop stewards should begin with their immediate concerns: the finances of their enterprise. But for this to be achieved, employers must release financial information. In short, 'economic awareness' implied disclosure of company information: generally perceived by Conservatives as an illegitimate intrusion into managerial prerogatives. (Grant 1992a; Greaves 1992.)[13]

The TUC also consulted tutors around the country about how economic awareness could be handled in courses. As a result, the course development unit had by 1986 identified the issues for consideration as (*inter alia*):

> — *the impact of competition at home and abroad on jobs in productive industry, the role of customers and markets.*
>
> — *the mutual dependence of jobs in the public sector and jobs in the private sector.*
>
> — *the changing balance of production and service sectors in the economy, and between different types of jobs ... (TUC 1986c: 2.)*

Joseph (1992) could not recall why he 'did not make more progress' on union education. The answer may well be that the TUC's education service was no mere 'transmission belt' for his views.

The issues of content were, then, placed firmly on the agenda by Creech Jones, and the solutions available have changed little since. The issue, at root, is the appropriate balance between what is relevant and what is educational. Broadly, the adult education tradition accepted that one should start from the former in order to proceed to the latter. It saw relevance in terms of workplace issues (wage bargaining, negotiating skills, and so forth), and it found educational value chiefly in wider political, historical, economic or literary studies — or, in the case of one important strand, in education for socialism. The Creech Jones solution was — to put it starkly, and to iron out the nuances — to redefine the relevant as of primary educational value. Roughly, in the years since, others have attempted to do likewise. Role Education and Industrial Studies can be seen as ways of encouraging serious study of subjects which relate closely to workplace questions. The TUC education scheme has been a similar exercise in many ways, though it has put the emphasis — but this is a matter of emphasis only — on organisational rather than individual or educational outcomes: more on workplace issues, perhaps, and less on the related subjects.

Union Education and Industrial Relations Research

The intemperance of the early- and mid-1980s debates about method in trade union education, centring so much on the alleged 'depoliticisation' of the curriculum, masked a deeper issue. The need for effective union organisation and action at the workplace was in many respects a sound basis for a trade union studies curriculum. The story of trade union education testifies to the importance of responding to what trade unionists, whether officials or students, perceive as their learning needs. Education primarily designed for trade unionists (as opposed to education designed more generically for active members of a labour political movement) must begin by addressing such immediate workplace questions.

Yet the TUC's trade union education — certainly from the 1970s — conspicuously avoided basing itself on a substantial body of theoretical or empirical research which would enable students to analyse and understand the nature of workplace industrial relations. This is noticeable in, for instance, the Stage 1 course materials of the 1980s. Like its predecessor, the Introductory Course for Union Representatives, Stage 1 was based on a highly institutionalised approach to collective bargaining. Union-management relations, for instance, were seen as based on agreements (which, certainly in the Introductory pack, were taken to be normally written), and negotiated through relatively formalised collective bargaining structures — joint union management committees and the like. Inter-union co-operation (so often a major problem) was conceived in terms of inter-union committee structures.

This weakness of theoretical and empirical underpinning stemmed partly from the nature of the industrial relations research then available, and partly from the TUC's failure to develop alternative research approaches. Industrial relations research in Britain developed in the 1950s and 1960s in a strongly institutional and pluralist mode. The dominant theoretical framework was Dunlop's notion of an industrial relations system composed of various actors — managers, trade unions, government, and so forth. Politically, the ethos of the academic industrial relations community was reformist. The role of unions in society would be institutionalised through developing systems of joint regulation commanding broad support. This reformist trend was also influential in the higher reaches of trade union policy-making, where it was very much in sympathy with the 'corporatist' outlook of such leaders as George Woodcock. The Donovan Commission, of which two prominent Oxford industrial relations academics (Hugh Clegg and Otto Kahn-Freund) were members,[14] can be

case study 3

safety reps and the law

internal transport

aims

- *To examine legal standards relating to internal transport.*
- *To develop a trade union response to a dangerous system of work.*

tasks

- Groups representing internal transport and material handlers meet separately to work out their view of the problem.
- A joint meeting is held to try to arrive at a joint position to put to management.

brief 1 – material handlers

You are the steward for a section of material handlers feeding a production line. Recently there has been some friction between your members and one or two of the fork lift truck drivers. Your members have complained that they have nearly been hit by trucks as they cross gangways collecting components from nearby stillages.

Recently, an incident in which a truck was damaged, although nobody was hurt, led to a driver being suspended for two days for driving dangerously. Now the company are having a big drive to 'bring employees' attention to their responsibilities under Section 7 of the Health and Safety at Work Act'. They have warned drivers that 'any further cases of dangerous driving will be dealt with severely'.

Unfortunately for you, management are also looking into a variety of the material handlers' unofficial working practices, such as 'doubling up' on various jobs, and hinting that some of these could represent unsafe working practices and therefore a breach of Section 7 of the Health and Safety at Work Act.

brief 2 – fork-lift drivers

You are a steward for a group of fork lift truck drivers working in a factory. Material handlers work in the same area feeding a production line. Recently there has been some friction between one or two of your members and the material handlers. They have complained that they have nearly been hit by your trucks as they cross gangways to collect components from nearby stillages.

Recently an incident in which a truck was damaged, although nobody was hurt, led to one of your members being suspended for two days for driving dangerously. Now the company are having a big drive to 'bring employees' attention to their responsibilities under Section 7 of the Health and Safety at Work Act'. They warned the drivers that 'any further cases of dangerous driving will be dealt with severely'.

Management are also looking into some of the material handlers' unofficial working practices, such as doubling up on various jobs, and hinting that some of them represent unsafe working practices and therefore could be a breach of Section 7.

Fig. 7.5: Case Study. Realistic case studies, usually incorporating role play, are intended to develop understanding and skills. Some (such as this) have been circulated by the TUC and adopted or adapted; others are developed by tutors from local experience.

regarded as the outstanding policy statement of this school.

Clearly an approach concentrating on the regulation of collective bargaining was not designed to develop perspectives which would strengthen the activities of workplace union representatives. In recommending amendment to the 'formal' system, the Commission suggested how shop stewards' activities might be better regularised. On the reformist view, this would have strengthened the role of unions in the body politic, and led to a better deal overall for workers. But such improvements would not come through independent workplace bargaining by shop stewards. Collective bargaining structures could be reformed, and this would have a profound impact on the nature of workplace industrial relations (including what shop stewards might achieve). But shop stewards operated within these structures: any 'initiative in changing the structure of bargaining had to be taken by management' (Clegg 1990: 2-3).

Whether this view was correct — to a large extent it was — need not detain us, for it had two important results. On the one hand, for many active trade unionists, academic industrial relations was inextricably bound up with Donovan and the subsequent attempts to legislate for, and control, workplace collective bargaining — the differences between Donovan and *In Place of Strife* counted for little. This bolstered long-standing scepticism about academic research and theory: a scepticism supported for half a century by the labour colleges' assaults on the class nature of academia. Academic industrial relations served the interests of employers — it even denied the possibility of trade unionists' changing profoundly the nature of workplace industrial relations by their own efforts![15]

On the other hand, this approach meant that industrial relations theory and research were not engaging with the needs of the most active and creative section of the union movement, and the group at whom trade union education was now increasingly targetted. Trade union studies tutors found they could make relatively little use of research contributions in industrial relations, beyond the formal, descriptive typologies of agreements, bargaining structures, union structure, and so forth. Even when such tutors engaged in related research themselves, moreover, they tended to investigate in more detail the institutions which existed in the various industries with which their teaching was concerned (e.g., Marsh 1965). They did not develop a distinct theoretical or research perspective relevant to workplace industrial relations: they tended merely to add (or adapt) detail.

The weaknesses of industrial relations research and theory did not go entirely unnoticed at the time (though they were not perceived in the terms discussed here). During the 1970s studies began to be carried out on the activities of shop stewards, and in time these did produce potentially valuable research results for union education (e.g., Armstrong, Goodman and Hyman 1981; Batstone, Boraston and Frenkel 1977). Unfortunately, these emerged too late — just when the possibilities of shop steward action *were* becoming increasingly limited — and they emerged against a background of deep-seated union suspicion of academic inquiry.

The weakness of academic industrial relations research in the 1960s and 1970s — for the purposes of trade union education — can only partly explain why no body of union-oriented research on workplace industrial relations emerged. The union prejudice against theory and research persisted, and intensified through a period when many of the chief academic figures in industrial relations were also strong advocates of incomes policy. Academic industrial relations research normally addressed an academic audience in language inaccessible to most trade unionists. Many academics involved in union education were concerned with aspects of theory and research in areas other than industrial relations as such. Several were prominent in movements for industrial democracy and workers' control; others were primarily historians, sociologists or economists. Some made major contributions to debate on union-related issues, but in fields with little direct bearing on workplace industrial relations and collective bargaining.

Above all, however, there was no attempt — at least, no successful, sustained attempt — by trades unions as such to develop research in industrial relations. This was a failure of vision. For trade unions, research remained primarily a matter of finding evidence to support a position: whether in bargaining, with figures about pay trends, or in the political sphere, with evidence about the plans of governments. This role was allotted by the major unions to their research departments, of course; and it was played independently by such bodies as the Labour Research Department. But the linkage between unions and academic research remained weak. Attempts to develop such links tended to be initiated by academics themselves (for example, by the Trade Union Research Unit at Ruskin College); they met with little enthusiasm among unionists, except when addressing major and pressing issues. The Ruskin Trade Union Research Unit, for instance, reached a wide audience with its support for the Mineworkers in the 1972 dispute (Hughes and Moore 1972); its later work on topics more immediately relevant to the needs of shop stewards (Hull 1978; Gold, Levie and Moore 1979) had far less impact.

The notion of a research and curriculum development unit for union education was a recurring theme. In the 1950s, Creech Jones, and Clegg and Adams had vainly proposed that such a unit should be an important priority for the WEA. To a degree, J.P.M. Millar had seen his postal courses section as a curriculum development and dissemination unit: but for the NCLC as for the WEA, the resources were never available. For both voluntary organisations, too, research and curriculum development could never be conceived on a grand scale. For Creech Jones, the 'bureau' would 'collect and disseminate information about activities and experiments in the field ..., and make available books, pamphlets and other educational material' (WEA 1963: 72). Clegg and Adams (1959: 82) considered this view overly narrow and proposed a 'college' — an 'institution for research and teaching'. But an Association unable to organise a modest bureau was equally ill-suited to making decisive moves to establish a college. Had it done so, history might have been different. But moving decisively to exploit historic opportunities has never been one of the WEA's strengths: the moment passed, and within a few years the TUC had taken centre stage in the union educational world.

As for the TUC, it seems never to have contemplated substantial initiatives in industrial relations research. It did, of course, take over the concept of a curriculum development unit: the unit established at Congress House from the early 1970s had a profound effect on union education. But it was never a research unit: it never had a research focus or function. This failure to imagine any role for itself in stimulating or influencing the direction of industrial relations theory or research was also reflected in the TUC's passive role (in this respect, at least) in the expansion of universities following the Robbins Report. There was no serious attempt to construct union-oriented research centres in industrial relations, or to sponsor or seek funding for research projects. Academics with trade union sympathies did, of course, initiate research. In the 1960s and 1970s the TUC might well have been able to secure public (or even private) funds for substantial research initiatives. The Industrial Relations Research Unit at the University of Warwick, headed by Hugh Clegg, and with strong funding from the Social Science Research Council, became the most prominent institution in the field. But as a rule the TUC, and unions generally, responded — often less than enthusiastically — to research ideas and initiatives from the academic community, rather than *vice versa*. The notion of developing research to set broad agendas for change seems to have been entirely foreign to the TUC and its leaders.

Educating for Change: TUC Course Content 1980-1987

The TUC Education Department lost a good deal of its educational originality after the early 1980s. Leaving aside the debates about government interference over 'Economic Awareness' and 'Change at Work', few major issues of principle blew through trade union education after the debate on content and method, and that storm had substantially blown itself out by 1985 or 1986. Nevertheless, some very positive developments in educational content and methods occurred in the 1980s, particularly in the preparation of courses and topic areas. These arose, or were encouraged, as a product of the opportunities available (after 1984/85) for the TUC to organise short courses for individual unions. They were also developed in areas of TUC policy and priorities. TUC Education, to that extent, was in part a servant of the movement, in part an agency which allowed the TUC to play an important role for its affiliates, in part a mechanism for initiating change. But it was also, in part, a means by which praiseworthy policy priorities could be acted upon without taking politically difficult or impractical options, or without devoting real efforts and resources in other areas.

Some important areas stand out. First, far greater emphasis was placed on equal opportunities. In principle, of course, this was always a matter for consideration on TUC courses; but the 1980s saw a number of important developments. In 1980 the TUC introduced 'bridging' courses for women (from three to five days in length, and timed to fit into the school day). These were designed to encourage more women to become involved in the ten-day courses. The reality at that time was that general courses were often all male in composition; a woman student would not infrequently be one among sixteen or so men. Bridging courses also aimed to help women to develop the skills and confidence required to take on union offices, so that the number and proportion of women union representatives would increase. The courses were taught by women, and an emphasis was placed on providing a relaxed and non-competitive atmosphere. From about 1983 further short courses were promoted specifically for women, on issues such as 'Women and Pensions', 'Women and Sexual Harassment at Work', and 'Equal Pay for Work of Equal Value'. In 1983 *Working Women* (TUC 1983c) was published, designed to support the consideration of equal opportunities issues on all TUC and union courses. Partly as a result of these developments, no doubt (though shifts in occupational and industrial structure also played a role, and the balance between the two factors is hard to assess), the proportion of women attending TUC day release courses rose from 7 per cent (1978) to 24 per cent (1987).[16] However, major weaknesses remained: for instance, there were relatively few women tutors,[17] and childcare was too frequently unavailable to students attending trade union courses.

Race also became a priority, though it is less clear that substantial progress was made. In 1983 the *TUC Workbook on Racism* (TUC 1983b) was published. This was intended for use in general courses, supporting tutors in the very difficult task of encountering and dealing with the racist

Union Education in Britain: A TUC Activity

About Trade Union Education

In this part of the booklet we look at **what** trade union education is for, **who** it is for, and **how** it is provided.

Aims

What is trade union education **for**? It's different in many ways from school and college education. We don't have exams, so there is no fear of "failure". So we have to put a lot of time into finding out whether our materials and methods really **help** people to learn.

There is more emphasis on **cooperation**, a good trade union principle. Everyone has skills and ideas to share on a trade union course. While books and pamphlets are important for many of the courses, experience in the real world is the usual starting point.

Any good trade union course must help the participants to **apply the lessons** of the course in the branch, workplace, and community.

Here are some of the general aims for trade union education:

- encouraging **participation** in unions and strengthening **democracy**
- **strengthening union organisation** by having more **skilled** and **effective** union representatives and officials
- getting a greater **awareness** of issues facing unions, and the **policies** they have developed
- helping union **policy making** through discussion of key issues
- helping union members and officials to be more **confident**.

How do we achieve these aims?

System of courses

First, by planning a system of courses that covers different needs, such as new stewards or full-time negotiators.

The courses cover a wide range, such as:

- **campaign workshops** to get over discussions of policy issues
- special courses for groups that are under-represented in the union movement — like women, and Asian workers
- a series of courses on union organisation and bargaining, and
- **short courses** aimed at keeping active trade unionists up-to-date with developments.

There is easy access to the courses. Most are run locally, and are free to individual participants.

Methods

Second, a great deal of effort is spent on making sure the **methods** on the courses are suitable and effective.

TUC courses are not run like traditional schools. We don't have lectures from experts who sound as if they've swallowed a dictionary. And we don't have tests that people "pass" or "fail".

Involvement

The methods we use are based on **involving everyone** in learning, treating them with **respect**, and using an **active** approach.

Small groups

A lot of the time is spent working in groups of about three or four. Course members pick problems or projects that concern them. They then work out solutions with the help of their colleagues.

Fig. 7.6: Guide to TUC Education. Two pages from a 1984 Guide explain the TUC's approach: note the emphasis on aims and methods, and the range of courses. Later pages gave information about specific programmes and rights to paid release.

Post-war Methods and Philosophies

Members

A key feature of most of the courses is that we involve other trade union members through a system of 'workplace reports'. These ask you to go back to work and discuss problems with your members.

Active trade unionists who want to do more trade union educational work have two special courses designed for them — the *Discussion leaders'* course held in the regions, and the national *Educational methods* courses aimed largely at full-time officers and executive members.

There is also a series of special courses for **trade union tutors.**

Who it is for

Union representatives

TUC courses are for representatives and active members, full-time officers, and the membership generally. The range of courses is listed below and full descriptions are given in the section on Regional courses.

Courses for union representatives are mainly run locally. There are some national courses that are also relevant to representatives.

A lot of time is spent working in small groups.

Here are the main types of programmes:

Starter courses

These are for newly elected stewards or for active union members who want to get more involved. They include special courses for:

* **newly elected stewards** on a union *induction course*

* **young trade union members:** at present a national **Youth School** is run. Local courses are planned for the future.

Some of these courses are aimed at particular groups who are currently under-represented in the union movement:

* **women trade unionists**

* trade unionists from the **Asian community.**

Introductory Stage 1 courses

The essential foundation courses for all union workplace representatives. They cover the key issues involved in union organisation and bargaining; and

Introductory Stage 2 courses

Which extend and broaden the work carried out on Stage 1.

Health and safety courses

These courses are aimed not only at safety representatives, but all union representatives involved in health and safety issues.

Here again there is a basic **Stage 1** course on health and safety, and a **Stage 2** course which is the natural follow-on.

Specialist courses

These are the next step in the course system for union representatives. They cover a wide range of topics including:

* Discussion leaders' courses
* Bargaining information
* New technology and collective bargaining
* Work study, productivity and pay
* Pensions and bargaining

Short courses

New short courses on key issues facing

179

attitudes of many union representatives. But it was also seen as the material basis — as it were — for a specific programme of courses on 'Tackling Racism'.[18] Some TUC courses were advertised (and some materials made available) in ethnic minority languages. However, since no ethnic monitoring of TUC course students was carried out before 1986 (and the monitoring form then introduced was perhaps ill-designed) the effectiveness of the programme is difficult to gauge.

Greater emphasis was also placed on equal opportunities for disabled trade unionists, with certain materials (the Stage 1 course books, for example) available after 1984 on sound cassette. The question of workers with disabilities was also encouraged as an issue for consideration on Health and Safety courses after 1985, with resource materials made available.

These concerns with equal opportunity permeated both the general provision of courses for union representatives, and the short course programme. They should be seen in the light of TUC concern that trade union education must address genuine problems facing the movement itself. One major problem identified, and which intensified in the early 1980s, though it was present rather earlier, was 'de-industrialisation': the more rapid erosion of employment in manufacturing than in service industries. Since trade union membership was disproportionately concentrated in the manufacturing sector, a rapid loss of union membership was feared. It was therefore vital that unions educate themselves about the problems confronting workers in the services, public and private. The shifts in course content mentioned in this chapter should be seen partly in this light. There was also an increasing sense that courses must deal with basics: how to establish organisation, how to sustain members' commitment, how to assert the union's presence with unco-operative management, and so forth. TUC course materials of the 1980s could no longer be based on an image of the shop steward (sic) as a man working in the private manufacturing sector, probably engineering, with well-established procedures agreed between his shop stewards' committee and management. (This caricature of the 1970s TUC course materials contains more than a germ of truth.)

But union education could only contribute to a wider response to eroding organisation and membership. The overall trends are subject to contradictory interpretations: declining membership should be seen in the light of international and historical comparisons; it perhaps masks advances in certain sectors; it appears to mask improvements in, or at least sustaining of, union organisation in a number of sectors (as we have seen in relation to numbers of union representatives in Chapter 6). But it is difficult to interpret the 1980s as other than years of union decline, and it is clear —

though hardly surprising — that union education has not been able to stem this tide.[19]

Associated with this awareness of the need to recruit and represent new categories of membership, the TUC Education Department addressed itself to producing issue-based course materials relevant to the problems which such groups faced. The intention was that where unions must tackle important organisational, bargaining, or strategic issues, trade union education should provide a supporting mechanism. To this end the TUC promoted a number of programmes of short courses for all trade union representatives (for example, on AIDS, or the programmes on sexual harassment at work, equal pay, tackling racism). But there were two other major developments in this area. One, the developing programme of 'campaign workshops' — seen as campaigning or political, and thus not financed from public funds — was discussed in Chapter 6.

The second was the relaxation of the public funding rubric in 1983/84, allowing the TUC to work jointly with unions and groups of unions in developing and mounting short courses on industrial relations matters which affected single unions or groups of unions. A number of contrasting examples illustrate this. When the Inland Revenue in 1986 sought to introduce new methods of financial management, the TUC provided a programme of three-day courses for union representatives on their implications. The course materials were developed in association with the education officer of the Inland Revenue Staff Federation. The TUC adopted this approach particularly in association with relatively small unions, which might alone have been unable to resource, tutor, and arrange the programmes. A similar example was the TUC's support for the small Bakers' Union in relation to changes, proposed in 1985, relaxing the long-established legislation limiting hours of work in the baking industry. TUC Education was also in a position to bring together various unions faced with a common problem. Thus in 1988 it worked with a number of local government unions (the National and Local Government Officers, the National Union of Public Employees, the General, Municipal and Boilermakers, the Transport and General Workers) in a programme of courses on the implications for union organisation and strategy of the Local Government Act 1988, which required local authorities to introduce competitive tendering for a range of services. Previously there were similar examples in programmes of courses on work study in local government and the health service.[20]

Short courses also enabled the TUC education scheme to make fuller use of the network of experienced tutors which had been built up in the colleges and WEA districts. These tutors were encouraged to strengthen and extend their links with unions, at a local level, and to develop short (or indeed ten-day) courses for them. This in itself — where it occurred — nourished union education's roots in the movement. The WEA (1989: 9-10), for instance, outlined some of its initiatives to involve 'new groups of workers in trade union education'. These involved women local government workers in London, Asian workers in the West Midlands, young workers in several regions, printworkers in small workplaces in Kent, the unwaged and unemployed. Some such local initiatives became a basis for wider developments: for example, the WEA Southern District's programme with the South-West Thames Region of the Confederation of Health Service Employees. It was, therefore, no longer the case — if it ever was — that tutors were confined rigidly to 'delivering' courses tightly packaged by the denizens of Congress House (or Hornsey). Quite the contrary.

Schools, Youth and Members

The TUC's educational involvement was not confined to education for union representatives. Three main areas were developed during the 1980s. As with the short course provision, they represented responses to policy or strategic priorities for the movement. The first area was training and support for lay and full-time trade union officers involved, or who wished to become involved, in raising trade union issues in schools. The TUC prepared a book of learning materials, *Learning About Trade Unions* (TUC 1984c), designed for use by teachers and pupils in schools. This contained discussion of methods and approaches which teachers might take, together with a number of case studies and role plays for school use. (For a discussion of some of the issues, see Abell 1982 and Lockyer 1982.) The short courses for trade unionists who wished to become involved in work in schools was linked to a programme known as 'Adopt a School', in which union organisations were encouraged to develop continuing links with a local school. This work also proceeded in liaison with the Schools Curriculum Industry Partnership (SCIP: formerly the Schools Council Industry Project), and some openings were created by the government's Technical and Vocational Educational Initiative — although, it must be added, the resources which unions, as voluntary organisations, could devote to this work was minute in comparison with the interventions of private capital. Too many schools, moreover, continued to regard trade union involvement as political, or at least controversial — whilst warmly embracing the involvement of employers.

The second area of development was linked: the TUC had some success in its attempts to ensure that trade union studies components within the Youth Training Scheme were provided by its own recognised trade union studies tutors through TUC trade union studies centres. Rather more was achieved in the Midlands and North of England, and in Scotland, where — Labour-controlled — local authority 'managing agents' formed a large part of the Scheme. Nonetheless, there was a measure of success throughout the country. Again, the TUC education service developed materials for use in these courses.

Finally, the TUC maintained a commitment to membership education. A major focus of its work in this area during the mid-1980s was the TUC Open School. This initiative, introduced in 1986, was organised through trade union studies centres. It was to provide

> *help in setting up and supporting study circles, training for study circle leaders, drop-in sessions for students, help in devising study plans, and support for individual study. Study circles are a relatively new development designed to provide membership education in a new way ... The circle works to a study plan, and bases its education on study materials provided by unions and the TUC. (TUC 1988: 168-9)*

The study circles typically consisted of seven or eight people and met five or six times. The 1988 TUC Report was approving: 'high quality learning materials, which reflect union priorities, can stimulate and guide study circle work'.

> *The General Council further believe that proper support for discussion leaders and study circles could provide a self-sustaining mode of trade union education worthy of national support. ... The long term benefits of the development of widespread membership education could include improved organisation, the increased ability to get the union message across and increased involvement of union members in union activities. (TUC 1988: 169)*

TUC membership education was not limited to the Open School — nor, on one view, is membership education best achieved by such exercises. Rather, members are most effectively educated by changing the role of union representatives, so that they see their function as partly educational. Membership education, on this view, is best achieved through the education of representatives. It could be argued that this position was always implicit in the representative-education approach, because membership education is far too large a task to tackle without making vastly greater resources available. Union representatives inevitably educate their members, and better-educated representatives will produce better-educated members.

From the late 1970s, however, TUC course materials began to address explicitly the educational nature of the relationship between representative and member. In about 1978 the 'discovery exercise' was introduced into day release courses: this required or encouraged students to find out, research, some aspect of their workplace between sessions of the course, that aspect then being taken up at the following course session (see Gee

1978: 10). In the early 1980s, in the Stage 1 and 2 courses, these were renamed 'workplace reports', and about the same time their essence changed slightly. Now students were encouraged not merely to find out some concrete fact about their workplace, perhaps by raising it with management or consulting some document, but to enter into dialogue with their members — say, to discover what their members regarded as the major failings of the union. The process was thus a way of encouraging representatives to discuss issues with, to teach and learn from — to educate — their members.

To support this, a series of educational methods and discussion leaders' courses were encouraged. They aimed to train union representatives to lead educational discussions with their members. They clearly drew inspiration from the Swedish trade unions' study circle experience (cp Jackson 1981; Karlsson 1985a and 1985b): it cannot, however, be said they were a conspicuous success, at least in terms of numbers. But they represented a clear commitment by the TUC's course development staff (cp Gowan 1981), and there was enough general TUC policy backing for the trend to allow it to continue (TUC 1981b: 13). The Open School, which drew heavily on the Swedish study circles, with small groups (between five and fifteen), study circle leaders, study packs, and a study plan 'worked out at the *first meeting*' (TUC 1986a: 5; emphasis in original), thus formed part of an overall strategy in which TUC education was seen as an exercise in educating not only representatives, but members. The strategy was not entirely successful. Many union representatives remained profoundly unconvinced that their role was an educational one. But it is an important qualification to the view that TUC educational strategy has concentrated solely on union representatives.

The thrust of post-war change in union education was for it to be seen increasingly as a servant of the trade union movement itself, rather than as a semi-independent educational movement more or less closely linked to a more broadly defined labour movement. This shift had a number of very definite, and broadly positive, consequences. The union movement began to think far more coherently about what it wanted from education. It began — vital to the intellectual processes of any organisation — to establish institutions (committees, departments, units and so forth) which could enable it to do this thinking, and to act on the results. Of course, these institutions were created in an ideological and political world, and the approaches adopted reflected (though often in a distorting mirror) both contemporary fashions and the power relationships within the union movement. But the importance of the trade union movement's taking responsibility for its own education cannot be overstressed. To take responsibility was to take risks: but to have left union education to muddle along in the 'haphazard' hands of a terminally ill NCLC, an under-resourced WETUC, a very patchy extra-mural contribution, and the burgeoning activities of individual unions and further education would have been an evasion of duty.

Having assumed a major role, of course, the TUC could only work with the materials to hand. These included the ideological and political baggage of the day: tripartism, good industrial relations, and so forth. They also included a range of educational thinking developed partly by the TUC itself, chiefly since 1945, and partly adopted from contemporary fashion. TUC leaders were wedded to notions of educational standardisation, and this brought tensions with educationalists, especially in the universities, who were then used to a high degree of autonomy. The approaches adopted by the TUC were, however, often innovative and original. The Education Department's success in establishing and maintaining — with limited resources — a varied but coherent and generally high-quality programme of union education for workplace representatives was remarkable.

1   The meaning of this phrase, first enshrined in Section 3 of the Trade Disputes Act 1906, has been materially altered by the employment and trade union legislation of the 1980s: probably it no longer so closely reflects the commonsense distinction between industrial and non-industrial action. But this is, of course, in large part a matter of opinion. For a discussion of the development of this and related notions in the common law, see Kahn-Freund 1954; Saville 1967; Wedderburn 1986: esp. ch. 7.

2   McIlroy (1990b: 212, 217-8), following Corfield (1969: 108), sees the Creech Jones enquiry as an exercise in legitimising a narrow, technical training oriented, view against broader traditions of workers' education. This over-simplifies the Report, which was a genuine attempt to seek a new ground for workers' education — although its analysis and prescription reflected an image of political and industrial reality which proved flawed.

3   The accuracy of this view, in the light of subsequent debate and research on the nature of ability and the effectiveness of selection, seems far from clear. But at the time it was perhaps not unreasonable; and it certainly seems to have been regarded as simple fact by the working party.

4   The tension between the mass aim and the specific, local or individual approach was also a major problem in practice for colonial mass education and community development: see Holford 1988b.

5   The term 'course committee' was widely used among tutors in discussion of this approach (see, e.g., Miller 1985): the term used in TUC documentation was, however, 'course meeting'. It has been suggested to me that

6   Trends in the adult education literature also tended to support these approaches. Adult education literature in the early 1980s was heavily influenced by the approaches of Malcolm Knowles and Paolo Freire. An ideology about adult education teaching method was also developing, partly supported by the growing number of adult education tutor-training courses organised following the Advisory Committee on the Supply and Education of Teachers report on training of part-tutors in adult education. See Jarvis (1983: 193-200) for a description of this scheme.

7   It is also worth noting that within each approach, there were (sometimes important) variations in approach. Within Industrial Studies, for example, the approach at Nottingham was distinctive (see esp. Thornton and Bayliss 1965); London seems to have had a foot in each camp.

8   One qualification is that shop stewards were often taking the Health and Safety at Work course as their second course. Technically, Stage 2 was not considered a 'follow-on' course, but part of the new 20-day Introductory course.

9   A briefing note for tutors was issued, together with various sample activities, case studies, etc., were issued in duplicated format (see Appendix A). It was also envisaged that various other materials which were printed (e.g., some of the materials on New Technology) would be used on these courses. But the emphasis was strongly on what representatives could produce for themselves.

10   Some quotations from McIlroy give a flavour of the argument and its tone. 'TUC Education creates its own sealed world; its overwhelming focus on plant bargaining is like using bows and arrows to combat nuclear technology' (1985a: 4). 'Underneath the hot air of free student choice, it [TUC education] is motivated by the attempts to mould both choice and the student' (1985a: 13). *'The tutor has always been perceived by the TUC Education Department as a potential stumbling block to the success of their bureaucratic desire for a predictable and controllable operation reflecting their interests'* (1985a: 13; emphasis in original). 'The TUC magnify to a megalomaniac degree one pedagogy.' The TUC's 'critics are not talking about using Black and Decker drills to inject preconceived ideas into the heads of students' (1985a: 15). 'In a situation where the TUC's basic impetus is towards a negotiated accommodation with Thatcherism TUC education must not play a role which is dysfunctional.' (1985a: 18.) 'The TUC concern with pedagogy is not a concern with liberating classrooms but with controlling them. Its prompting by considerations not of education but of finance and of the maintenance of institutional power explains the incoherence of the arguments of its proposers...' (1985a: 19).

11   McIlroy would also no doubt argue that the tone of his writing was matched by the character of the TUC's administrative response to his case. See, e.g., McIlroy 1988b: 118-20.

12 McIlroy's comment (1988: 71n2) that 'Authors often fail to transcend the double burden of being both participant and analyst in trade union education' could equally well be addressed to his own writings.

13 The TUC also argued that economic awareness was not an appropriate topic for Stage 1 courses.

14 Other Oxford industrial relations academics were also involved in the Commission's work: Bill McCarthy was Research Director, while George Bain, Alan Fox, John Hughes and Arthur Marsh were commissioned to write research papers (cp Clegg 1990: 3). George Woodcock was also, of course, a Commissioner.

15 There were, of course, academics involved in the field of industrial relations who took different approaches, but they were arguing against a dominant 'school', and they did not develop a distinctive research perspective at this stage. Cp e.g., Allen (1966 and 1971); Hyman (1972). Other academics involved with trade union action at this time, especially those who took the extra-mural Industrial Studies approach, tended to concentrate on different issues: industrial democracy and workers' control, in particular (cp, e.g., Coates and Topham 1970).

16 The trend continued: by 1991/92, the proportion of women on TUC courses stood at 28 per cent (TUC 1992: 51).

17 A survey of colleges and WEA districts providing TUC courses, conducted in April 1990, found that of the 264 full-time tutors teaching on TUC courses in the regions, 42 (16 per cent) were women; of the 118 part-time tutors, 39 (33 per cent) were women (TUC 1990b, Annex 2).

18 It is worth noting that the approach developed in the TUC courses represents a trend distinct from the 'Racism Awareness Training' which had become not uncommon among employers, especially within the public sector. To simplify, whilst the Racism Awareness approach begins from the assumption that everyone is racist, the 'Tackling Racism' approach begins from a standpoint of solidarity: as it were, assuming that course members are not racist, or at least that black and white course members have many matters of common interest. The relative merits of the two have, of course, been matters of intense debate (see, for example, Grayson 1983: 10-11; Gurnah 1987; TUC 1986: esp. 43-5).

19 Kelly (1988) tries hard to provide a more optimistic view of trade union strength in Britain in the 1980s through a critical discussion of the literature, but Marsh's more pessimistic account (1992) is more convincing.

20 An indication of the range of short course materials developed by TUC education in the 1980s can be had found in Appendix A.

Chapter 8

Late Thatcherism and After: the Educational Challenge

By the mid-1980s the British trade union movement had clearly lost its way. The Thatcher government, for whom trade unionism — if not all trade unionists — was 'the enemy within', had seen the destruction of trade union power as central to its political project. Against a background of escalating unemployment, it had out-thought and out-manoeuvred the unions, effectively exploiting a popular suspicion of 'union power'. To the consternation of many committed trade unionists, this suspicion proved widespread among union members as well as the public: the union generals, and indeed the NCOs, found that the troops would not fight.

Those committed to a corporatist approach could, of course, legitimately cry 'foul'. Their entire philosophy had been based on building up a stable relationship, as 'responsible' trade unionists, with the state and employers. Now the government itself declined to behave 'responsibly', and even encouraged employers to flout established standards of behaviour — was busy, in short, redefining the very notion of responsibility in labour relations. The rules of the game were changing, and faster than most union leaders could cope with. The character of the union leadership — of the TUC General Council — was also changing. The figures who had dominated during the seventies, particularly Hugh Scanlon and Jack Jones, had made their names on the union left. They had been reluctant corporatists: striking, as they saw it, a hard bargain for union collaboration. Their successors were of lesser stature. Some lacked their predecessors' authority over their unions, or led lesser unions. Others saw collaboration with employers and government as duty rather than bargain: if the goalposts were moved, the game remained the same. None had authority over the TUC comparable to the duumvirate of the seventies. TUC leadership was more diffuse, less consistent, and less effective.

As the corporatist approach failed, so too did the militant alternative — partly because, when tried (as by the NGA in the early 1980s and by the Mineworkers in their epic if ill-judged strike), it was pursued too indecisively or too late. The problem was that this approach rested on an illusion: the illusion that union strength, union organisation, persisted. It did not. Union workplace strength in the 1960s and early 1970s, founded on two decades of 'full employment', had been buttressed by a network of semi-political organisation: a shop stewards' movement with national structures, the industrial organisation of the Communist Party, the Institute for

Workers' Control, and so forth. During the 1970s, and still more in the 1980s, the threat of unemployment had again become a reality of working class life. This network had been eroded. But it was not simply an organisational erosion. Thatcher's electoral success in 1979 had reflected the 'desertion' from Labour of many skilled manual workers: this stratum had been central to militant trade union organisation since the early years of the century, and its electoral realignment had profound implications.[1]

The TUC leaders' indecision was little helped by the further electoral setback of 1983. The nearest the TUC came to a clear strategy for Thatcherism was the 'new realism', but for many this was too insipid and collaborationist to be pursued with conviction. (There was, of course, the new union right, epitomised by Eric Hammond's aggressive leadership of the Electricians, which gloried in such collaboration.) In any case, the new realism was overtaken by the defeat of the Mineworkers' strike in 1985. After that, the leaders of the TUC had still fewer cards to play: when the new realism re-emerged, it was even more a matter of accommodating to a bleak reality. They had failed to resist the early changes in employment law effectively, and the government by the later 1980s was able to introduce legislation more or less at will. Waves of 'privatisation', and intensifying requirements for local authorities and other public bodies to 'contract out' services previously offered by directly employed union labour, cut away at union strength in the public sector. The TUC found its authority over affiliated unions questioned — especially over competition between unions for members (the so-called 'single union deals' issue), which led to the suspension and expulsion of the Electricians' Union in the summer of 1988, and the establishing of the TUC Special Review Body at the 1987 Congress. And gradually, through the later 1980s and early 1990s, the remaining vestiges of corporatist tripartism — the Manpower Services Commission's short-lived successor, the Training Commission, the National Economic Development Council — were cast aside.

By the late eighties it was more than ever clear that the unions' future would be determined by whether Labour was returned to office. Of course, many — including a number of trade union leaders — felt that the close relations between the Labour Party and the trade union movement were an electoral handicap, and sought to distance the party from the trade unions. There would be no return to corporatism, to a major union role in national economic management, even under a Labour government. To this extent the ground had shifted irredeemably. But under Labour the unions might, at least, find a legitimate role, and a respite from the continued onslaughts of the eighties. And where in the early eighties the issue had been how to defeat and reverse what the Tories had achieved, by the end of the decade the very survival of the movement was at stake. Membership of TUC-affiliated unions had fallen to the level of thirty years earlier: the decline must not continue.

The election of 1987 was a turning point. Despite — unrealistically — high hopes, the result was another overwhelming victory for the Thatcher government. The scale was such that the election of a Labour government even in 1992 appeared difficult. Certainly trade unions should do whatever they could to achieve electoral victory: and from the middle of 1989 it seemed that the impossible might be within Labour's grasp. But they had also to find acceptable strategies for survival — and, if possible, achievement — under a Conservative government. Three main trends emerged. At a political level, there came an acceptance that many of the changes of the 1980s were irreversible: as Ron Todd, General Secretary of the Transport and General Workers, said in 1990, 'We accept the principle of balance in relation to strikes and executive elections ... We accept that there will be some limits on secondary action ... We are asking for no more than exists in other European countries' (quoted Kellner 1990). This resort to 'Europe' was the second plank of the emerging strategy: the commitment of the European Community to civilised standards in labour relations was rather stronger than the British government's.

In addition to accommodating themselves to the new legislative framework, and strengthening their commitment to the European Community (no small departure in view of the TUC's long opposition to British membership), the unions indulged in an orgy of amalgamation. By the early 1990s, British trade unionism was dominated by a few 'mega-unions': large general unions, each with many hundreds of thousands of members. Along with this went a review of the nature of union activity. British trade unions had long seen their workplace bargaining and national political functions as predominant: in the later 1980s, as success in these areas was increasingly denied to them, they began to investigate anew their welfare services for members.[2]

Change at the Top

The TUC's strategic indecision of the mid-1980s had some impact on union education. More prosaic factors also played their part. When Norman Willis succeeded Len Murray as TUC General Secretary, a number of personnel changes followed. Among them, Roy Jackson, Head of the Education Department since 1974, was promoted to be Assistant General Secretary. Jackson had been central to the development of TUC education since he had joined the Training College as Director of Studies in 1958. When he took over as Head of the Education Department in 1974, the change was opportune: where Dennis Winnard's primary interests had been in public education policy, Jackson was a specialist in trade union education. He had, of course, been responsible for the development of the workshops on the Industrial Relations Bill under the Heath government. He masterminded the negotiations with the Labour government on public funding and rights to paid release. He played a major role in identifying the role of the workplace representative as the subject-matter of union education. He saw the need for a course development unit to ensure TUC's centrality in the field, and built it up. He also enjoyed the confidence of the General Secretary, who 'relied very heavily indeed on Roy Jackson in this particular area'. With 'rare exceptions, when he trundled me up as a 25 pounder, I didn't get involved' (Murray 1992).

With Jackson's departure, the opportunity was taken to reorganise. Union education had now become one of the TUC's major activities — indeed, its largest single function. A Trade Union Education Committee replaced the former Education Committee. The Education Department was similarly streamlined into a Trade Union Education Department, shedding its concern with public education policy.[3] The Head of the new Department, and Secretary to the Committee, was Alan Grant. Grant had entered the TUC Education Department — specifically the course development unit — in the late 1970s, having previously been a student in trade union education, and a Father of the Chapel in NATSOPA. He came to prominence in the mid-1970s as presenter of television programmes in the multi-media 'Trade Union Studies' series. Although his appointment, over the heads of more senior staff, caused some ill-feeling, he soon established his authority — indeed, his control of the Department was to become rather greater than his predecessor's. (Jackson, of course, had run a larger and rather more disparate department.)

Following Grant's appointment, the later 1980s saw marked changes in the personnel of TUC Education, especially in course development. Of the members of the course development unit during its most creative and dynamic years (from the mid-1970s into the very early 1980s), only one remained by the early 1990s. Some had, of course, departed earlier: but Doug Gowan, Ruth Elliott, Andy Fairclough, Paul Simpson, Richard Ross, all left during the Conservatives' third term. In part, these were career moves. In the late seventies union education had been at the cutting edge of political and educational innovation. A decade later ideas, opportunities and careers were all stagnating. But Grant's appointment also heralded a period of intense internal disagreement within the Department. He introduced a marked shift in emphasis and approach. He had a strong sense that TUC courses would succeed or fail by their ability to meet the needs of the movement, and saw these in very practical, organisational terms. The ambitions and aspirations of the seventies were no longer relevant. Grant was, in particular, increasingly to distance himself and his Department from some of the more extreme positions of the early 1980s course development unit.

The 1987 Reviews

One of Alan Grant's first moves was to initiate a thorough review of trade union education. This enabled the new head of department to present himself to tutors, and lay and full-time union officers, in the regions. But it also allowed him to establish priorities for his leadership. No radical change in strategy was on the cards, but Grant did set some markers for future development. The review of trade union education was also broadly to coincide with the work of the TUC's Special Review Body established at the 1987 Congress: this was concerned to review the role and function of the TUC, but was to ask some questions which related centrally to trade union education.

The review was conducted in the winter of 1986/87, and the contrast with the previous (1975) review was clear. That had been important in 'shaping the development of education and training ... over the next decade'. But in the 1980s the trade union movement was 'required to respond to circumstances beyond its control and to measures designed to frustrate trade union involvement in the decisions shaping those circumstances'. The review, 'by obtaining the general and specific view of officers and activists on today's education and training needs,' was intended to develop 'a wider acceptance of the importance of trade union education to the development of trade unionism'. (TUC 1987a: 1.)

At the same time, concern was mounting about the financing of union education. This was part of the TUC's wider financial problems, which arose from shrinking union membership and affiliation fees. But finance is the foundation of educational provision and has often been the fulcrum of debate over control. The difficulty in 1987 stemmed from the fact that, while grant-aid from the government had declined in real terms by 20 per cent since 1983/84, course programmes and support services had been maintained. As a result,

> in 1986-87, expenditure on regional course fees would exceed grant-aid by slightly more than £9,000, whereas an allowance was made for additional spending in the region of £20,000; the contributions from TUC resources needed to meet the shortfall in public funds for course development and tutor training were approximately £42,000 and £15,000 respectively (TUC 1987: 97).

the changing role of reps

Reps have a range of different jobs, and some of these have been changing over the last 10-15 years.

national or local agreements?

In many industries where there used to be national agreements to set wages and conditions of employment, these are now negotiated locally. So some reps who were never involved in bargaining for wages in the past, may be today.

In industries or sectors with national agreements, reps may be involved in bargaining on local issues eg bonus payments, overtime premiums, equal opportunities agreements.

developing good communications

Union members face a stream of information from the media and their employers about the economy and the role of trade unions within it.

It's important that union reps talk to members, and produce local literature, to put the union's view. Often publicity is provided by union head offices and this is useful. Locally produced leaflets and posters can be more relevant, so try doing your own.

There is no substitute for talking to members on issues that concern them. Listening to members is also very important.

public or private sector?

As a result of the privatisation of a number of public services and utilities (for instance: gas, water, electricity, some local authority services, some parts of the Civil Service and the NHS) many people that were once employed directly by the government or a publicly controlled organisation now work for private companies or for parts of the public sector which have to cover their costs or make a profit.

This has meant a major change to both the running of these organisations and the way wages are agreed and problems resolved. Reps need to keep up-to-date with these changes so they can continue to:

- provide a full service to members
- recruit new and existing staff
- monitor all collective agreements closely to make sure they are honoured by the new employer.

Fig. 8.1: Facing up to the 1990s. The 1992 Stage 1 course discusses how the tasks facing representatives have changed. The emphasis on involving members grew during the 1980s (see also Fig.7.2).

In the light of this, the General Council felt it 'necessary to provide the additional finance'. In addition, however, it introduced several cost-controlling measures. Regional programmes should be maintained 'at their present level'. Printed 'course materials made available free to all course students would be reduced in range and in production quality', and there would be fewer tutor briefings. The financial position would be reviewed annually. (TUC 1987: 97.) These measures would, over a period, tend to lower the quality of educational provision, and to erode central control.

The 1987 Review attempted — albeit in adverse circumstances — to make some proposals for union education policy and practice. But it began with a brief account of the history of the TUC education service, and then reasserted some 'essential points arising from [TUC] policy development in this area' since 1946. There was nothing new in these points — the significance was in their reassertion. Union education was for union purposes. It 'must be based primarily upon a proper consideration of the representatives' role in furthering the aims and policies of their union'. It should help representatives 'to carry out their functions as responsible officers of their union and to promote trade union competence in the conduct of industrial relations and in improving trade union organisation'. There could 'in educational terms ... be no sensible separation' of representatives' trade union and industrial relations functions — the latter must be 'constantly informed by union organisation, rules, policies and attitudes'. Moreover, 'the objectives and methods of training lay representatives and the control of recruitment and selection of those to be trained' were union responsibilities which 'cannot be shared with employers and other bodies', although 'consultations on course syllabuses and facilities for paid release from work' were possible.

If 'trade union purposes' were to be achieved, training for union workplace representatives 'must be conducted sympathetically and seek to establish confidence and motivation'. Courses should be held in 'an educational setting, free from any undue influence by managements and employers', and should be 'clearly distinguished from courses offered by employers or by organisations acting on their behalf'. The 'education and training of union workplace representatives is adult education in its fullest sense' which should, 'therefore, be supported by ... public funds': indeed, it should 'seek to match the effective training available to managements'. But while union education would 'contribute to a representative's individual development,' its collective dimension was fundamental. It 'must reinforce the collective nature of lay representatives' functions and responsibilities and should bring together representatives from different unions, occupations, industries and establishments.' (TUC 1987a: 3.)

While this summary certainly ironed out a good number of the infelicities, discontinuities and contradictions of history, as a summary of the policies eventually arrived at it was not unfair. The General Council, in considering the Review, reasserted that 'these essential policy themes, developed during periods of both adversity and of growth, are equally valid today' (TUC 1987a: 3).

Having reasserted these groundrules, the Review turned to course development and quality. There were strengths. Central course development, including tutor training and standardised course materials, was seen as 'the TUC's most effective means of ensuring quality and consistency in all TUC courses across the UK'. The TUC was 'the only credible organisation' for promoting multi-union courses on a wide scale. There was a reassertion of long-standing TUC views on judging achievement in trade union courses, and what their content and methods should be. (TUC 1987a: 4.) Success in establishing trade union studies centres in colleges and with the WEA around the country was a cause of pride, as was the fact that many tutors were 'former union representatives and activists who have qualified for the work through diploma and degree studies and part-time teaching with the WEA' (TUC 1987a: 5). A different kind of pleasure was found in the findings of the Workplace Industrial Relations Survey (Millward and Stevens 1986) on the number of representatives who attended training. These were 'broadly confirmed' by information available to the TUC (TUC 1987a: 6): the TUC's own data on the impact of workplace representative education appeared to be correct.

But the survey also indicated, according to the Review, some factors behind the weakness of trade union education.

> *[The] failure to maintain recruitment to trade union education is due to the decline of trade union membership in the traditional, well-organised manufacturing industries; growing reluctance among employers to implement union workplace representatives' right to paid release from work to attend courses; and, possibly, a failure to ensure that representatives in some sectors and in small enterprises are aware of trade union education opportunities and their legal rights to access. ... [I]t was in larger establishments that trade union representatives were most likely to have had a significant level of training. (TUC 1987a: 6.)*

These findings were supported — and elaborated — by tutors, and lay and full-time officers, who attended review conferences around the country in early 1987.[4] These showed there were few written or formal agreements governing release for union education — despite a strong TUC emphasis on achieving such agreements during the late 1970s and early 1980s. The most successful representatives relied on maintaining standards of release through 'custom and practice'. Even where formal agreements did exist (as in the Civil Service), these were victim to widely varying managerial interpretations. Employers were particularly resistant to the TUC Stage 2 course. Many union organisations also reported difficulty in getting members to stand for office. In addition, union courses 'were occasionally regarded by potential representatives with a great deal of apprehension and suspicion' (TUC 1987a: 8). Especially in small workplaces, access to courses was difficult.

It was no surprise when conference participants 'overwhelmingly endorsed' the TUC's policies of 'maintaining trade union education under the direction of the Movement and free from unwarranted influence by employers'. However, this endorsement was not unqualified. Many saw virtues in joint sessions with management on issues such as 'company policy and investment', even though it was clear that employers were frequently 'attempting to use such sessions ... in place of TUC or union provided courses, particularly on such issues as pensions and health and safety'. Some employers were apparently also offering company courses to all union representatives while restricting or refusing access to TUC or union courses, or insisting that all applicants for TUC courses should first attend a company course. It was reported that employers' courses were widely seen as 'intended to foster a corporate identity and ... had sometimes grown out of the use of quality circles and team briefings'. (TUC 1987a: 9.)

The conferences identified a number of other thorny problems of the mid-1980s. Union representatives were increasingly younger, and less influenced by 'the traditional pattern of high-density union organisation in the private sector'. Generating membership interest and commitment were frequent concerns. More attention needed to be given to representatives in the — increasingly common — small or newly-organised workplaces, who were 'often unaware of educational opportunities, or do not expect to be granted release, or who doubt the relevance of trade union education to themselves' (TUC 1987a: 9). In practice there was competition between the TUC's 10-day courses and courses promoted by individual affiliated unions, with 'management often arguing that, by comparison, TUC courses were too long' (TUC 1987a: 10).

Finally, in opposition to a suggestion that the TUC should press for all union members (rather than merely representatives) to be given statutory rights to paid release for trade union education, many argued that employers would then 'never recognise the union voluntarily'. Indeed, some pointed out that existing rights to paid release for representatives were already 'a barrier to obtaining union recognition in new establishments and small units' (TUC 1987a: 10).

Having established policy and explored the problems, the Review made a number of recommendations. In a discussion of legal rights to paid release, it argued that industrial tribunals were often interpreting relevance and reasonableness (in relation to rights to release) too narrowly. In an important statement, the General Council departed from the thrust of practice (if not always precisely policy) over two decades. It was now 'inadequate ... in a modern industrial society' to require that a union course should be relevant to those of a representative's functions 'which are concerned with industrial relations between the employer and any associated employer, and their employees' (TUC 1987a: 12). Further,

> *The General Council consider that today's union workplace representatives require not only sound skills-based training in their function and responsibilities as lay union officials, but also wider education in those issues which affect workers, employment, the operation of industry and the local and national economies (TUC 1987a: 12).*

The aim was, therefore, that the law should be changed — but this could only be a long-term aim, since in 'the present climate' pressing 'a series of recommended changes to the law and legal procedures on paid release for trade union education would be pointless ...' (TUC 1987a: 13).

The Review also proposed a statutory minimum entitlement to paid release for union representatives, and legal status should be given to the General Council's schedule (or programme) of education for newly-appointed union representatives. In essence, this followed the standard pattern developed since the early 1970s, of a short 'induction' course, to be followed by Stage 1, Stage 2, and 'special topic' courses (of 60 hours each or — an innovation, and probably a concession to union educational schemes — 30 residential study hours), and subsequently by short courses and briefings from time to time after the first two years in post. (A similar structure was proposed in relation to health and safety courses.) (TUC 1987a: 12, 15-16.) In addition, the 'status quo on the test of reasonableness' should favour the workplace representative, so that it would be for employers to initiate tribunal proceedings if they did not wish to grant release (TUC 1987a: 12). Finally, there were practical proposals relating to publicity and promotion of courses. One — which emanated from the conferences — was that appointing one representative within a workplace as 'trade union education co-ordinator' was 'an organisational development worthy of wider adoption' (strong words from the General Council!): *inter alia*, such a co-ordinator might ensure that newly-elected representatives secured release to attend their first course.[5]

The overall tenor of the 1987 reviews was 'steady as she goes'. Some nudges on the tiller were called for, but overall the TUC was endorsing its long-standing views on education. They had served the movement well in a difficult period; the foundations were sound; achievement could be built on. There was some justification for this view. A structure which, constructed in a period of unprecedented union strength *vis a vis* government and employers, had yet managed to withstand the rigours of unprecedented post-war weakness, must have been marked by a good number of strengths. In particular, the central strategy — the notion of viewing education as intimately linked with workplace organisation and strategy — had proved a valuable method of ensuring that the effectiveness of provision could be measured against a yardstick, albeit a rough and ready one. Indeed, the 1987 review was in part a method of bringing this 'workplace organisation' criterion to bear on the educational policies and practices of the early eighties.

Educational Strategies: Regional Courses for Workplace Representatives

The dilemmas of TUC Education[6] in the late 1980s were those of an organisation encountering radical change in its environment. The structures and approaches developed in the 1970s and 1980s had made assumptions about the nature of union activity: that it was focussed in the workplace, that it was about negotiation between responsible employers and trade unions, that workers' interests could be advanced through collective bargaining. It had also been assumed that the structures of provision would remain broadly similar: that trade union representatives would be recruited to day release courses held in further education colleges within the public education service and extending over ten or twelve days.[7] Further Education, the role of the DES, its relationship with the local education authorities, the WEA and university extra-mural departments — all these had seemed, in the 1970s, immutable realities of educational life. By the late 1980s, their immutability was no longer certain: by the early 1990s, their future — in anything like their long-established forms — was in many cases in serious doubt.

The bedrock of TUC provision remained the ten-day, day release programme. The scale of the programme continued to decline, but the free-fall of the early eighties had passed. (See Appendix B.) The decline was most rapid in the Stage 1 and 2 courses for workplace representatives: from 762 courses in 1986/87 to 613 in 1990/91. Provision of health and safety at work courses remained more or less stable in the second half of the decade (indeed, there was a slight increase in the number of courses provided from 565 in 1986/87 to 581 in 1990/91). Provision of Follow-on courses was far more variable, fluctuating from year to year, but these were a modest aspect of the total programme. Taken overall, however, the picture is by no means one of crisis: the TUC programme of ten-day day release courses was, at the beginning of the 1990s, still slightly larger than it had been in the mid-1970s — 1,277 courses in 1990/91, compared with 1,149 in 1975/76, although the number of students attending was significantly smaller. The great disappointment, of course, lay in the decline from the high point, and high hopes, of the late seventies and early eighties.

With the ten-day programme as the core of TUC education, the course development unit continued to develop and revise course materials. The chief commitment in this area was to the Stage 1 courses (Health and Safety and Union Representatives). There was no radical revision to the Union Representatives course materials. Revised materials were issued in 1988 and 1991: if the changes had a general thrust, it was to respond to the needs of representatives in less well-organised workplaces, and to representatives who (as the 1987 Review had shown) were now on average younger and less experienced. This continued the trend of the mid-eighties, but took it rather further. It was reflected in the course materials issued in late 1991, when one of the three standard workbooks was retitled: rather than *Organisation, Bargaining* and *Skills*, the titles of the three books in successive editions since 1981, they were now *Union Organisation, Representing Members*, and *Skills 1*.[8] Bargaining was no longer a meaningful description of the activities of many union representatives — or at least, not meaningful to many representatives themselves.

At the beginning of 1992 a more substantial revision — amounting to an entirely new edition — of the Health and Safety Stage 1 materials was issued. In place of the single workbook, supplemented by the general *Skills* book, there were now three: *Health and Safety Organisation, Representing Members on Health and Safety*, and *Skills for Health and Safety Reps*. These continued the shift away from a heavily 'industrial' view of health and safety at work, and also reflected the themes underlying the new Union Representatives materials: that the baseline, the level of union organisation which educational materials could assume to exist in the typical workplace, had declined over the decade, and that far more attention had to be given to fundamental organisational tasks.

The Stage 2 and Follow-on programmes continued to be less well-supported by centrally-developed printed course materials. The 1987 Review had indicated that a greater emphasis should be placed on the law, and on bargaining: but though these were strengthened within the syllabus, little by way of printed materials was offered. The printed materials available were the *Skills 2* booklet (1989), which covered issues from dealing with the local press, membership surveys, and handling meetings, to negotiating with management, and a new edition of *Working with Figures* (1988).[9] The problem was essentially logistical: the programme of

Stage 2 and Follow-on courses was relatively small, and did not justify the resource input required in the development of a printed course package. Of course, this did permit greater flexibility, and it called for greater input by tutors locally. The project approach, which had been so much a hallmark of the Stage 2 courses in the early 1980s, was somewhat downplayed, but there was still an assumption that the Stage 2 and Follow-on courses would be tailored to individual representatives' needs.

Student recruitment to the day-release programme remained difficult. The average number of representatives attending each Stage 1 or Stage 2 course in 1982/83 was 13.65; by the middle of the decade (1986/87) it had declined to 12.53, and by 1990/91 it was a mere 11.08. The Health and Safety courses fared only slightly better; the Follow-on courses recruited even fewer students.[10] In a world increasingly obsessed with quantitative performance indicators and value for money, this was cause for concern. Part of the problem lay in the need to preserve a range of courses (especially Stage 1 and Health and Safety Stage 1) across the country, so that representatives could (as far as possible) enrol at the time most convenient to them. There was a certain point — an irreducible minimum, as it were — beyond which the number of courses could not be reduced (and the average attendance thus raised) without severely damaging the range of provision available. Employer resistance continued to be a factor — and recalcitrant employers were lent support by changes to employment legislation. Among trade unionists too, there was some support for the view that courses were too long. With the changing structure of industry — increasingly services, and smaller workplaces — the problems of negotiating release were likely to grow.[11]

A growing problem during the 1980s was an increasing tendency for students who enrolled for TUC ten-day courses to fail to arrive for the course: to drop out, as it were, before the course had even begun. By the early nineties, about one-fifth of the students who enrolled for a course typically failed to arrive at the college on the first day.[12] Although there seems to have been no rigorous study of this phenomenon, 'anecdotal evidence' suggested that the major factors were employer resistance to granting release and peer pressure. (Grant 1992a.) Attending a course daily each week for over two months could seem a considerable 'perk' of office, especially given generally tighter staffing levels. (The number of representatives did not decline so fast as the number of union members.) Members could be hostile to the prospect of their representative being absent — and representatives, uncertain of how to handle such hostility, might well never get as far as applying to attend a course.

Despite these pressures, the TUC maintained its commitment to the ten-day course. Certain minor experiments were tried: the concession (chiefly a concession to affiliated unions, rather than a matter of practice within TUC education itself) that thirty hours of residential course would be equivalent to sixty non-residential hours, for instance. In 1992 some courses were to be offered on a 'block release' basis: in two groups of five days,[13] rather than daily each week over ten weeks, in the belief that it would be more convenient to employers and many shift workers.[14] (While this change may appear trivial, the ten day courses in the 1980s had been designed around the notion that students would be able to relate their classroom experiences to their workplace activities between each session. There were also logistical problems for tutors' teaching timetables, since they normally taught a different course each day of the week.)

If the ten-day programme continued to decline, the number of short courses, which had escalated so fast in the mid-1980s, remained high. In 1982/83, just 467 short courses had been offered to 5,914 students. By 1986/87, the figures had more than doubled, to 1,183 courses and 14,401 students; in 1990/91 they were still higher (1,340 courses for 15,529 students) — and this represented a slight decline from the previous year. For TUC education short courses remained challenge, opportunity — and threat. They enabled the TUC centrally to act educationally on priorities which did not themselves justify ten-day courses (or where the number of representatives who required training was too great to allow for such in-depth coverage). If these were of a transient nature, the organisational approach was not unlike that of the campaign workshops against the industrial relations legislation of the early 1970s and early 1980s: although the priorities were generally not politically controversial.[15] These might be national priorities across a wide range of industries, such as the programme of courses on the Control of Substances Hazardous to Health regulations in 1989 and 1990, or the workshops on 'Europe 1992' in 1988 and 1989. They might respond to social issues touching the movement generally, as when legislation on local management of schools raised new issues not only for union representatives, but for union school governors (TUC 1990: 67).

Some short course programmes were related to longer-standing concerns for the whole movement. Chief among these were issues related to equal opportunity — by the early 1990s, 'equality bargaining' was of general importance for trade union education, affecting the ten-day programme as well as short courses. A second edition of the *Tackling Racism* workbook was issued in 1988. During 1989 and 1990, the workbook on *Working Women* was revised (the first edition had been published in 1983). However, other topics were tackled, such as pensions and using computers

(TUC 1988: 164-5). The short course programmes continued to enable TUC education to respond to approaches from unions locally, at district or workplace level. (In practice, these would often result from links between tutors, union officers and workplace representatives, built up through the ten-day courses.) For some topics, these local initiatives could make use of centrally-developed materials: for example, on flexibility at work, or equal pay for work of equal value. But very often these materials would be only partially relevant to a particular short course, and would have to be supplemented or revised.

TUC educators long debated whether developing short course strengthened or eroded union involvement in the ten-day programme. This was intrinsically difficult to gauge: in general, however, any attempt to offer a course which appeared to be a shorter substitute for the ten-day courses was resisted. As a rule, the short courses did not conflict, in aims or content, with the ten-day programme: the chief problem area, paradoxically, was with induction courses. In the structure proposed in the seventies (see Fig. 5.3), union representatives would attend an induction course (provided by their union) of between one and three days shortly after taking office. The content of an induction course would naturally seem quite similar to that of a ten-day course, and the risk was that induction courses might 'grow' from three to four or five days. How far this threat could be addressed depended, of course, in large part on the relations between the TUC and the union concerned.

In a potentially important experiment, initiated in 1990, the TUC offered induction courses for the General Municipal and Boilermakers union. The course content was discussed and agreed between the TUC and the GMB: the TUC then wrote the course materials, which were approved by both organisations. The TUC briefed tutors, liaised regionally with the union as to how many courses should be held, provided tutors and a suitable venue (usually through a local educational body), and met course costs. In return, the GMB undertook to ensure a minimum of twelve students attended each course, and that a full-time officer was present at some time. The GMB's regional secretaries were given targets to meet (one-third of their workplace representatives should attend such a course in the first year of the experiment, and two-thirds by the end of the second year: by the end of the third year, all union representatives should have attended one of the courses).[16] In fact, by the end of the second year (1991/92), the target had been met in all GMB regions except one. The arrangement had advantages for both sides: for the TUC it ensured well-attended courses, and — in most regions — GMB involvement in the ten-day programme apparently improved. (Grant 1992a.)

Educational Methods and the Quality Initiative

If in the 1987 Review of trade union education Alan Grant had been attempting to lay the foundations for a shift in emphasis in TUC education, by the end of the decade his regime was well-entrenched at Congress House and Hornsey. The changes to the various ten-day courses were implicitly influenced by this new thinking, but in 1989 a debate was initiated which involved making explicit statements about educational methods strongly at odds with central tenets of the educational approach developed by the course development unit in the early 1980s. This debate was not billed as an assault on former articles of faith. It was articulated around the question of 'maintaining, and where necessary improving,' the quality of TUC courses. There were discussions in late 1989 with the HMI. An 'audit of all teaching centres' which provided TUC courses commenced. In this context, a paper on 'Aims and Methods in Trade Union Education' (TUC 1990b) was issued 'for discussion with tutors and trade union officials' (TUC 1991: 66).[17]

But if the debate started from concern about 'quality' (and the Department of Employment's infatuation with performance indicators and quality control), neither was there any reluctance to take on the shibboleths of the former course development unit. The 'Aims and Methods' paper was a statement by the new master, and for a TUC document the critique of past positions was unusually explicit. Since the mid-1970s, the TUC had

> *established a strong preference for what is called 'active learning' or 'learning by doing'. However, this may no longer mean precisely what it meant in 1975, 1979 or 1983. ... [In fact, there was] a marked difference ... [and] this should not be surprising for if there was no difference we would effectively be saying that we had got it absolutely perfect ten or fifteen years ago, that we had learned nothing since, that there was nothing to learn and that tutors had had no ideas from teaching courses. (TUC 1990a: i.)*

The paper's critique of the former regime was not just explicit. In what seems an allusion to the tone and structure of Gowan's controversial 1982 paper, Grant remarks that while it 'might be interesting ... to chart the nature and extent of changes that have occurred' this would 'hardly be an effective use of resources and would probably generate more dispute than agreement'.[18]

Though representing a significant shift of emphasis, the 'Aims and Methods' paper was no wholehearted rejection of earlier positions. The 'core of standard course materials' was still sacrosanct (indeed, more so than it had been in certain earlier courses, notably the Stage 2 course.) The emphasis on students' experience remained; so did the importance of building on and reviewing this experience 'mainly through working collec-

Union Education in Britain: A TUC Activity

Introduction

Trade union education is not like school. TUC courses aim to be informal and friendly. They give participants the chance to learn by doing, as well as from each others' experience.

Women who attend TUC courses discuss their problems at work. The courses help them to develop the skills and confidence they need to take an active part in their union.

Equal opportunities at work runs through all TUC courses, because it's important that men trade unionists discuss issues that affect women at work. Many women though prefer to start out with a women-only course – and then join a mixed course later on.

Aims

This section will help you to:
know your rights in relation to time off work for trade union education
find out about TUC courses that are available for you
work out which are the most appropriate courses for you

WORKING WOMEN

Fig. 8.2: A Trade Union Class. Union classes normally work in small groups; study of documents and problems is common. The 1980s saw determined efforts to redress the male bias of courses, but women still make up only one-third of TUC students.

tively', and the stress on applying the results of course work in the student's own workplace and union (TUC 1990a: 9). A 'systematic approach' to problem solving was still encouraged. Workplace reports and small group activities remained central — though the 'danger that small group or syndicate work would be seen as an end in itself, rather than a means' was now acknowledged (TUC 1990b: 4). Role-playing was still a valued technique. Good methods developed during the 1980s were endorsed: 'things to find out' and 'jargon' lists to fill gaps in information and demystify. The importance of addressing widely varying levels of literacy and numeracy among course members was emphasised.

The shift in emphasis can be reduced to three key aspects. First, there was a far greater stress on the importance of centrally-established course aims and objectives. To be sure, these had always been present at a general level, but during the early 1980s the emphasis had been on student-determination of course aims and content. The 'course meeting' had been the fundamental mechanism for achieving this. (This approach had been most marked in the Stage 2 course.) Now the stress was on the clear statement of course aims by the TUC, and of relatively specific learning aims and objectives by tutors.

> *By thinking clearly about learning aims we can make sure that any new materials, activities and case studies are successful. Course aims should determine the materials and methods to be used and must be the starting point for course evaluations. (TUC 1990a: 1.)*

With this stress on course aims was a playing-down of the early 1980s emphasis on 'confidence'. 'Confidence,' it was now stressed, 'is strongly rooted in competence' and 'in trade union activity in the real world' (TUC 1990a: 2).

Second, as compared with the early 1980s the status of the tutor was enhanced. Tutors were now 'to organise and teach an effective course' (TUC 1990b: 4), and to ensure that learning aims were achieved. No longer was the tutor merely 'a course member like everyone else' (TUC 1983a: 6). The role of course meetings — one useful technique, no longer a fundamental principle — was delimited:

> *Course meetings do not decide the agenda for the course but they can often indicate to the tutor areas of work which need to be covered. Tutors should ... intervene if course meetings appear to be trying to make decisions which they have no authority to make, or if they become bogged down in formalities to the extent that the planned work of the course is obstructed. (TUC 1990a: 17.)*

The enhanced importance of the tutor was supported by a paper on 'Maintaining Quality in the TUC Education Service' (TUC 1990b), prepared following the meetings with tutors (February-May 1990) at which the 'Aims and Methods' paper had been discussed. This led with a section on 'Tutors and Course Quality' which addressed quality primarily in terms of tutor training and development, but tried to recognise contemporary realities. In the 1970s and early 1980s tutors had been required to attend TUC briefings prior to teaching, and to teach the Stage 1 course first. With the growth of the short course programmes and the increasing use of part-time tutors by colleges and the WEA, this 'traditional pattern ... was no longer valid' (TUC 1990b: 3).

The tutor training courses and support systems were therefore re-thought. New tutors 'should be introduced to a range of education methods appropriate to adult learning.' Regular 'de-briefings' should be built into the tutor training programme, and the training of each individual tutor should be logged. For experienced tutors, networks should be encouraged, with meetings in each region two or three times annually. Subject-specific tutor briefings (formerly regarded as course briefings for follow-on courses) should concentrate on 'knowing the subject', rather than teaching methods. (TUC 1990b: 3-6.)

Thirdly, the importance of the course pack was re-emphasised, and with it the role of 'a model course syllabus including timings'. The 'Red Pack' of the 1970s was explicitly resurrected as a model — 'more "user-friendly" for tutors than current materials' (TUC 1990b: 5). This had two dimensions. It was a further contribution to tutor support, especially for new tutors. At the same time, however, it helped to ensure that a range of common aims were met across the country for each of the major courses. As Grant (1992b) commented, new courses would be accompanied by much fuller tutors' manuals, with explicit guidance on activities, timings and expected learning outcomes. Experienced tutors might change the activities and approaches, but the aims and objectives met for the course should be those of the TUC.

In sum, the 'new' official view on educational method — developing during the later 1980s but formally underscored by the 1990 debate — was a reformulation, in the training language of the 1990s, of the strategy established by the TUC in the 1960s. The main concern was to ensure some uniformity of provision — in character and quality. To this extent, the aberration had been in the early 1980s fetishising of the democratic classroom. However, we should not over-stress the degree of change implied by the 'new line'. In the field, tutors' practices had always varied. Approaches had certainly been influenced by current fashion at Congress House and Hornsey (especially for new tutors). But with little beyond anecdotal evidence available, we may speculate that the impact on the vocabulary by which teaching was described in the early 1980s may have been more marked than any changes in real classroom practice.

Educational Services and the Future of the TUC

While the regional education courses for workplace representatives remained the central feature of TUC education, the Trade Union Education Department continued — though against increasing odds — to support a wider range of educational activities. As with regional short courses, the cruel irony was that for TUC education as a whole, diversification was called for just when resources were most scarce. By the early nineties the TUC's role was openly questioned. Liaison with the Labour Party was no longer a priority. The role in economic policy-making was gone. With the growing trend toward amalgamation, many unions could afford on their own the kinds of service which the TUC offered. In research, the TUC could offer little that a large union could not do for itself. Its role in inter-union disputes was no longer clear: arbiter it could be, but with increasingly fierce competition for members, its adjudications might be ignored. Possibly it had a role as the 'foreign office' of the movement, especially dealing with European institutions. More and more, however, senior TUC staff recognised that union education was an important strength — one of relatively few — on which the TUC could base its institutional future. As the General Council noted in 1992, while the TUC could provide 'a wide range of advice and services' to its affiliates, its 'main service to unions' was education — national courses for full-time officials and regional programmes for union representatives (TUC 1992: 7; see also Weston 1992).

However, this strength was not to be taken for granted. There were, of course, very clear threats to union education's funding, which could undermine the resources and expertise which the service had built up since the 1960s. But there was also a threat from the unions themselves. This was starkly posed by Sarah Howard, Director of Education for Manufacturing, Science, Finance: the union formed in 1989 when the Association of Scientific, Technical and Managerial Staffs merged with TASS, the Technical, Administrative and Supervisory Section of the (never properly) Amalgamated Union of Engineering Workers. In a paper to the Society of Industrial Tutors (Howard 1990), she explained that the National Executive Committee of MSF had quickly established five committees to integrate the work of the two unions. One was dedicated to education. This set down five 'organising principles' for the new union's 'future educational strategy'. The first was that 'as far as possible MSF will provide its own education and training for its own members, representatives, activists and full-time officials'. The new union would 'look inwards in order to meet our educational and training needs'.

'Going in-house' was not *faute de mieux*: MSF, 'like other trade unions', saw 'positive benefits through in-house provision of education'. Chief among the benefits was 'a single-minded emphasis upon MSF's own organisational needs'. It was, for example, 'the immediate and overriding need of our organisation ... to establish a single identity for the union in the eyes of our members'. Other benefits included ensuring that each course was 'specifically structured to the particular organisational circumstances of those attending', particularly through 'single company, or single industry courses', and being able to give priority to residential courses. 'We believe that living and working together over a five day period provides a better platform for the development of ideas and confidence and establishes a clearer identification with the policies of the new union'. Although nationally the capacity of MSF's residential college was 'fixed at 3,000 students per year', Howard (1990: 29) hoped that the union's regional programme would expand to involve similar numbers around the country.

Such an approach raised problems for the TUC. MSF was a large union, with 7.4 per cent of the TUC's affiliated membership in 1989. In that year, its representatives took up 4.7 per cent of places on TUC ten-day courses, and 5.1 per cent on short courses (TUC 1989: 155; this represented about 760-770 students, or the equivalent of roughly 50 courses, in each case). If other major affiliates began to adopt a similar 'in-house' approach (and increasingly their thinking was moving along these lines),[19] the threat would be serious indeed. This was not, however, one of Howard's concerns. 'One of the challenges for MSF,' she said (1990: 29), was 'how we can work with the TUC, local colleges, the WEA and universities to implement the strategy we have determined.' MSF would, however, 'need to be convinced' that such 'outside organisations' — not a term the TUC would wish to see used about itself by an affiliated union — were 'fully committed to the organising principles which the [MSF's] NEC has laid down'.

In the face of such threats, TUC education could not stand idly by. It had, in the National Education Centre, an important centre for residential courses. This was not, however, an unmitigated advantage. By the mid-eighties it had become a considerable burden on TUC finances. In 1986 its operating deficit was £88,000; this was halved the following year through introducing three charge bands for different periods of the year, discounts for advance bookings, and higher cancellation charges. In 1989 it was established as 'an independent cost centre aiming to recover fully its running costs through its own operations'[20] (F&GPC document 4/4, 16 December 1991). But now the National Education Centre had to 'effectively compete' with 'comparable residential facilities in the London area'. A survey of these competitors in 1991 found that the Centre had only 'sparse leisure facilities for residents': improvements required included tea

Late Thatcherism and After

and coffee facilities and televisions in residents' rooms, more syndicate rooms, and an office to provide private telephone, fax and word-processing. With these alterations, utilisation levels (then running at 73 per cent) could be raised, and the Centre 'could achieve a small but consistent surplus' (F&GPC document 4/4, 16 December 1991).

The National Education Centre was important not merely because it was making a loss: it was also crucial to the emerging strategy of developing for the TUC a key role in the training of union full-time officers. The TUC had, of course, been providing training courses for full-time officials for many years — this had been a primary function of the Training College since the 1940s. In the late 1960s, a Working Party had commissioned a study from Warwick University (Brown and Lawson 1973), on the basis of which a report, *Training Full-Time Officers* (TUC 1972a) had been issued. That had recommended the establishment of a residential centre for officer training — achieved, if a decade later. During the 1970s and 1980s, however, the priority had been firmly on building up — and then defending — the programme for lay workplace representatives: courses for union officers had continued, but no clear strategy had emerged or been followed through. In 1990 the General Council, anxious to make the TUC's activities more relevant to its new situation, selected two 'key tasks' for the Trade Union Education Department. One was 'to improve the quality and relevance of training provided for full-time officers employed by unions' (TUC 1992b: 1).

There clearly was a need to develop a better approach to training for full-time officers. However, from the TUC's institutional viewpoint, the prospect was exciting for another reason also: the TUC was supremely well-placed to take a leading role in this field. Even for the largest individual union — with at most a few hundred full-time officers — providing more than a very partial programme of training was impossible.[21] The TUC was already the major provider. Full-time officers needed 'a training framework of the quality and frequency essential to a profession', the Trade Union Education Committee (TUC 1991: 57) asserted: they were 'professionals'. The TUC was determined to develop a structure which would be widely accepted as the national programme of professional training for union officers. There were consultations with the National Council for Vocational Qualifications, with the Department of Employment's Training, Enterprise and Education Directorate (whose Qualifications and Standards branch agreed to provide financial and technical assistance), with the European Commission, the European Trade Union Confederation, and other European trade union confederations. A Project Advisory Group (no mere working party) of senior union officers was appointed. An independent (and private sector) consultancy, Prime Research and Development, was appointed — after a tendering process — as project advisors. The project would then conduct fieldwork (surveys, conferences, and other research), and produce 'a set of national standards which explicitly define the important elements of an officer's work' (TUC 1992b: 2).

The broad strategy envisaged would identify certain common core competencies — or 'standards'. These would have to be 'highly relevant to a full-time officer's job and, most important, have credibility with unions and full-time officers'. They could not be 'rooted in the past or the present — they will need to take on board likely developments in the immediate future'. They would be used in several ways:

> *to define training needs and objectives and to improve training programmes; to evaluate learning programmes and provide clear goals for learners; to enable learners to recognise achievements; and to assist unions in planning commitments to provide personal development and training opportunities for union full-time officers. This latter point would be especially important with induction programmes for new officers. (TUC 1992b: 4).*

The Trade Union Education Department's agenda clearly included establishing National Vocational Qualifications for full-time union officials though there was 'no automatic link between standards and obtaining credits', and this 'would undoubtedly be debated within unions, as it quite rightly should be'. However, if a 'Lead Body' were to be established — it had happened in a 'wide range of sectors and industries', including personnel managers (TUC 1992b: 4) — it could only be under General Council auspices. And it could only add to the authority of the TUC generally, and TUC education in particular.[22] The momentum was maintained. By late 1992, a 'complete set of draft occupational standards' for full-time officials had been drawn up; general secretaries (as the employers) were being consulted (Grant 1992c). By early 1993 the standards were agreed. Phase 1 of the project had been completed.

The explicit plan was then to move on to such issues as assessment, accreditation, NVQs, and the application of the standards in TUC full-time officers' courses. This would involve seeking the support of the TEED[23] ('highly likely' to include funding, as well as technical assistance in establishing standards). This would 'be crucial to a successful application to NCVQ/SCOTVEC'. With support from TEED, a Lead Body could be established.[24] 'This would be an extremely important step according to affiliated unions, through the TUC, specific rights and responsibilities for training, development and national qualifications in the "Trade Union Sector".' (TUC 1993a: 6.) As work on standards and NVQs developed, TUC education staff clearly came to see them as having relevance to voluntary officers also.²⁵

In these straitened times, hard bullets had to be bitten. Professional education and training for full-time officers was a major strategy for 'product diversification' in TUC education. As it was introduced, however, so the decision was made (following the financial review of 1991) to close the Open School and to discontinue the TUC postal courses. The postal courses, taken over from the NCLC, had only 76 students in 1989/90 (TUC 1990: 71); although 'regrettable, ... the level of investment required to re-write the existing postal courses completely and properly to fund a tutorial support system could not be justified in the existing circumstances' (TUC 1991: 56).

The decision to jettison the Open School, lauded only three years earlier as 'membership education which can help build trade unions for the future' (TUC 1988: 169), was in part an admission of the gravity of the financial problems. The School had not been a conspicuous success. It had been extremely demanding of organisers' time — time more profitably employed in other tasks. More important, by the early 1990s its chief architects and advocates had left the TUC. In the eyes of the new regime, the Open School was half-baked attempt to import Scandinavian study circles without proper support, based on an idealised notion of what might be expected of lay (and semi-trained) discussion leaders. In a world of cuts and trimming, such a utopian relic of former, more optimistic, days was doomed.

The Open School had, of course, been the latest in a line of essays at 'membership education'. The desire not to reduce TUC education to provision for officers, lay and full-time, remained. The new view was that this should be achieved through a system of 'structured own-time study'. In effect, the finance which had been devoted to the Open School was redirected to supporting a series of part-time programmes offered by educational bodies and approved by the TUC. These programmes had to be of between 10 and 36 weeks' duration. The key difference between them and the Open School, however, were the requirements that they must involve regular weekly tutorial contact, and that the syllabus (which should cover issues 'wider' than the workplace) must be set and approved in advance.

Tutors and regional education officers were now able to request support for local and regional initiatives: long-cherished ideas could be developed; established programmes could receive new support. The response was encouraging. Quite soon, requests were being received in all regions. Projects supported included diploma and certificate courses in labour and trade union studies offered by colleges and the WEA, often in association with universities and polytechnics. Some of these included an 'Access' (to higher education) dimension, but this was no requirement.[26] Such schemes had several advantages. They tapped the expertise and enthusiasm of experienced TUC tutors, allowing them to diversify and contributing to their professional development. The system validated local initiative, rather than requiring local developments to conform to a national mould. But perhaps most important, it facilitated a renewal of TUC education's links with higher education. With threats to state support growing in the early 1990s, such renewed ties might prove invaluable.

1 That many, especially on the left, were initially reluctant to acknowledge these shifts or seriously to consider their significance is shown in the reaction to Eric Hobsbawm's 1978 Marx Memorial Lecture, 'The Forward March of Labour Halted?': see Hobsbawm (1981) and especially the contribution by Ken Gill.
2 Welfare services had always been a part of union activity, of course, but in the 1960s and 1970s they had seemed a remnant of the days before the welfare state. In the later 1980s, they began again to be seen as important union functions.
3 The wider educational concerns of the Education Committee now came within the aegis of a newly-formed Education and Training Committee, serviced by the Organisation Department.
4 These conferences were something of an innovation: previous TUC reviews of union education had not involved such methods of consultation — partly, no doubt, because the number of trade union studies tutors had been far smaller. Nevertheless, this was a significant exercise in encouraging participation in evaluation and review.
5 Interestingly, this option had been suggested during the 1980-81 review of *The Organisation, Structure and Services of the TUC* (cp TUC 1980a: 16, 1981a: 10), but had eventually been downplayed in the final report to Congress (TUC 1981b: 13).
6 Although the Education Department had been replaced by the Trade Union Education Department, the TUC still referred to its trade union educational provision as 'TUC Education'.
7 By some quirk of history, the 'ten day' courses in Yorkshire and Humberside extended over twelve days.
8 The terminology *Skills 1* was in fact introduced in 1988, and intended to imply a linkage through to a *Skills 2* workbook for use in Stage 2 and Follow-on courses.
9 *Working with Figures* had first been issued in 1979. The new edition was 'entirely revised', in part to take account of the possibilities offered by advances in calculator technology.
10 Corresponding figures for Health and Safety courses (Stage 1 and 2) are: 1982/83: 13.75; 1986/87: 12.34; 1990/91: 11.60. For Follow-on courses they are: 1982/83: 11.60; 1986/87: 10.68; 1990/91: 9.75. The figures are

calculated from TUC 1991: 63. Prior to 1982/83 the courses were categorised rather differently, and the figures are not strictly comparable.

11 This view tended (in Alan Grant's view) to come from white collar unions, where representatives returning to the workplace found their work had not been dealt with during their absence. For union officials, of course, it was always easier to negotiate release for shorter courses.

12 Normally, representatives enrolled for TUC courses with the TUC Regional Education Office direct (by post). They would then be then sent 'joining instructions', giving them full details of the course venue, etc.: a register containing the names, workplace and union of all the students was sent to the college or WEA district for each course, and kept by the tutor.

13 A minor historical curio: this arrangement had long been the practice for TUC courses with unions at ICI in Stockton and Billingham (Grant 1992a).

14 Shift workers often lost out from the ten week pattern of day release. Since employers were often unwilling to release a worker for two shifts in a week, a representative might find himself or herself attending a class all day, having worked all through the previous night (or having to work all through the following night). Occasionally, employers would not give any time off in lieu (on the argument that the course was not actually taking place during working hours). In such cases, students could be excused for 'nodding off' during class!

15 If politically controversial, the courses would be funded by the TUC from its own resources.

16 It is not clear whether turnover of representatives was taken into account in these figures: and in most cases, union records are not sufficient to provide accurate data on such matters.

17 The background to this concern with 'quality' included the shift in responsibility to the DE — always far more concerned than the DES with objectives, targets and indicators of performance, and far less open to doubt as to their value. The shift of funding is discussed below.

18 While the entire paper bears the stamp of Grant's ideas as Head of Department, the Introduction shows every sign of having been penned by Grant himself. Grant also took steps to reduce the distance between the TUC and the Society of Industrial Tutors (in which the TUC's strongest critics were grouped), including speaking in SIT conferences and contributing to *The Industrial Tutor*. His critique of the Gowan position was, however, by no means identical to that of, e.g., McIlroy.

19 As the Engineers put it in a motion to the 1992 TUC (1992d: 4), 'large unions are rightly self-sufficient in matters that affect their organisational or membership needs'.

20 Recovery of running costs was 104 per cent (1988), and 96 per cent (1989 and 1990) (F&GPC document 4/4, 16 December 1991).

21 A TUC document (TUC 1993a: 8) estimated there were roughly 3,750 full-time officers in TUC-affiliated unions. These were categorised as follows: 150 'union "managers"' and 400 'regional officials', both with 'higher management' as their 'key distinguishing function'; 200 national offi-

cials responsible for 'national, trans-national negotiations'; and 3,000 '"field" officers'.

22 In February 1992, the TUEC deferred consideration of an application to TEED for the establishment of a Lead Body for the Trade Union Sector (TUC 1993a: 1-2). However, this seems to have been a political move (it was felt that further consultation with full-time officers and affiliated unions was needed). Certainly within the Trade Union Education Department, there seem to have been few serious doubts about the desirability of establishing a Lead Body with regard to full-time officials.

23 TEED was the latest incarnation of the Manpower Services Commission (alias Training Commission, alias Training Agency), but stripped of any tripartite pretensions and now merely an arm of the Department of Employment.

24 Formally, the TUC would seek 'to establish a body which would be recognised as "having the responsibility for defining, maintaining and improving national standards of performance in the sectors of employment where the competence is based".' For essentially unrelated reasons, recognition of the TUC seemed likely to be as a 'Trade Union Sector Development Body', rather than as a 'Lead Body'. This was a technical matter and, for simplicity, the latter term is used in this and the following chapters.

25 This is discussed further in Chapter 9.

26 By 1992 the TUC was considering developing 'broad guidelines' for an 'own-time certificate', covering course duration, etc. It was axiomatic that any assessment of students must be voluntary. (Grant 1992b.)

Chapter 9

State Challenge, Union Response

Why did a right-wing, fiercely anti-trade union government continue to finance independent union education? If this question puzzled observers during the first two terms of Margaret Thatcher's government, only after 1987 did it gain immediate political (and, for the unions, educational) relevance. Pressure to call an end to the arrangement grew. Union education was always a matter of marginal importance, of course, in the wider scheme of national politics. But correspondingly, by 1987 the unions were diminished industrially and politically: they could no longer so effectively discourage and resist assaults. At the same time, by the late 1980s the Conservatives' offensive on the fabric of British society had cut deep. Institutions and structures long taken for granted — for example, the local education authorities — began to crumble. Some of these attacks, albeit incidentally, also cut away at the foundations of union education.

However, though severely weakened, the trade union movement was neither wholly defeated nor unable to respond. From the mid-1980s, initially at the educational level, it had begun to come to terms with the new reality. While struggling to preserve provision against the odds, new courses and approaches were developed. As the decade turned, the search was for a strategy which could 'reposition' union education in a rapidly changing educational world. This search was closely linked, for the Trades Union Congress, to the need to find a new role for the entire institution in a clearly — and apparently permanently — post-corporatist world.

Defending in Adversity

The 1987 review of TUC education had advocated no major change of strategy, and for the following five years the ten-day and short course programmes were marked by continuity rather than change. But the environment in which trade union education functioned became increasingly adverse, so that by early 1992 the 'preservation of resources' was the 'primary concern' for the Head of TUC education (Grant 1992a). Since the mid-1970s, the TUC education scheme had been founded on three pillars: public funding through the TUC, legal rights to paid release for workplace union representatives, and provision of courses through and in association with public educational bodies (particularly further education colleges and the WEA). Through the late 1980s, each of these pillars was eroded. Some of the assaults on the TUC scheme were mere by-products of social, political and economic trends — but some were matters of clear policy. Both were damaging.

The early and mid-1980s had been marked more by apprehension about what the Conservative government might do to damage union education, than by any real action. Indeed, apart from general attacks on trade unionism, union education policy was left largely alone. The election (in 1987) of the third Thatcher government changed matters. That union education would become the subject of renewed attention was signalled just a few months after the election, when Ann Winterton, Conservative MP for Congleton, put down eight written questions to the Secretary of State for Education (and another to the Employment Secretary). Prior to this, union education had made only rare appearances on the parliamentary stage — often only bland questions providing an opportunity for a junior minister to announce the amount of the annual grant. Occasionally a more antipathetic question would be put; but none showed signs of being based on research, and none was followed up.[1] Some were clearly made in a state of considerable ignorance, as on the only occasion in the eighties when an oral question was raised. Kenneth Lewis, in his follow-up question, outlined his (clearly limited) understanding of the position as follows:

> The TUC distributes the money downwards to the various affiliated unions, including the WEA [sic]. Is my hon. and learned Friend [David Waddington, Under Secretary of State for Employment] satisfied that State support is not going to unions which are acting militantly against the State for example, the Civil Service unions? ... (Hansard 24 March 1981.)[2]

The Winterton questions were of a different — and more threatening — order. They were detailed, well-directed, coherent, and clearly based on evidence. They were given prominence, and added coherence, a fortnight later when Digby Anderson (1987), Director of the Social Affairs Unit — a right-wing 'think tank' — raised the issue in his column in *The Times*. Winterton's questions were no random shots from a backwoodsman, but part of a wider rightist assault on social policy supported by an effective and well-connected research and propaganda organisation.

The Winterton-Anderson case was that public money should not be used for trade union education, because such education was bound to be biased. They believed the TUC was seeking to control the content of courses. Were TUC regional education officers 'being asked to advise upon the selection of ... tutors' or even 'sitting on the interview or section panel for such vacancies'? Was there any requirement for the content of shop steward training courses to be approved first by the TUC? Was there a requirement 'to provide a balanced curriculum and system of visiting speakers'? (Hansard 23 November 1987.) Although they produced no evidence in public,[3] they argued that *courses could be used by ... politically motivated tutors, tutors whose selection and appointment may not be purely academic decisions, to engineer not better but worse industrial relations. There have been cases in which tutors have stirred up trouble in industries from which students were seconded, cases in which colleges, reluctant to run such courses have been pressured to do so by their political masters in the local authorities. (Anderson 1987.)*

The argument was that, given the nature of the subjects covered, many local authorities' alleged 'enthusiasm for politicization in other fields including education', and the unions' 'certain interest' in the subjects taught, 'bias is a real and likely danger'. Further, 'individuals in the colleges who are aware of abuses are frightened to reveal them publicly'. 'In these circumstances, the burden of proof should be not with the critics but with the unions and authorities to show that the courses are *not* biased.' (Anderson 1987; emphasis in original.) It was, however, difficult and expensive to establish whether bias existed.[4] The best solution, therefore, was to 'avoid the whole messy business of proving or disproving bias by ending government funding and government-enforced time off with pay'. 'If the courses are worthwhile to the unions or the employers, let them pay. If they are not, why run them at all?' (Anderson 1987.)

As an HMI remarked when he rang one of the TUC's education officers, 'you're in trouble'. They were. Although the immediate problem was resolved, the exchange was an indication of hard times ahead. As with so much Conservative industrial relations policy, the approach was incremental. Another five years were to pass before the TUC's arrangement with the state was frontally attacked. In that time, the geography was to change substantially. The first change was a raised profile for the Memorandum of Arrangements under which the government made grants for 'trade union education and training by independent trade unions not affiliated to the Trades Union Congress' (Hansard 13 November 1987 c325w). This was, no doubt, mainly a response to broader industrial relations developments, notably the formation of the Union of Democratic Mineworkers and the prospect of the expulsion of the Electricians from the TUC:[5] policy on union education has never been separable from labour relations policy. The following year the government reduced the amount of the TUC's grant by 3.6 per cent 'to take account of the expulsion of the EETPU from TUC affiliated membership' (TUC 1989: 138). (For further information on public funds, see Appendix C.)

The new decisiveness followed a small but important shift in the TUC's educational relations with government. With effect from the financial year 1988/89, the Department of Employment was 'the sole financing Department' (TUC 1989: 138). Formally, this was a purely administrative change:

but reality was different. Previously, with control diffused between two departments, it was not easy to co-ordinate a consistent strategy for what was hardly a matter central to government policy. The two departments had their own interests: the DES was concerned to maintain further education, and had (in the HMI) a body of men and women committed to a relatively strong 'educational' ethos. (HMI reports on trade union education were almost universally very positive.)[6] In the mid-1970s, the TUC had been keen to ensure that the DE was excluded from the funding of union education: fifteen years later, the issues had changed, but the strategy remained sound. Under the DE, union education would be judged by the criteria of industrial relations policy; under the DES, educational factors would also count.

The change did make a difference. The Minister responsible at the DE, Michael Howard, was 'very difficult', taking a far closer interest than his predecessors (whether at DES or DE). At the annual meetings with civil servants, TUC officials found the DE far 'tougher' on the details of expenditure than the DES had been. There were fashionable ideas: for instance a 'quality initiative', whereby regional education officers were to report on a programme of class visiting. But there were also more emphatic moves to tighten the boundaries of publicly funded union education.

The first product of a more co-ordinated government policy on union education, and arguably the most important, came in the Employment Act of 1989 (the Bill was first published in November 1988). This 'ragbag of piecemeal and miscellaneous measures' (McIlroy 1991: 153) introduced amendments to the legislation on paid release for training contained in ss.27 and 28 of the Employment Protection (Consolidation) Act 1978.[7] Under the 1978 Act, representatives were entitled to paid release for training relevant to those duties of theirs 'which are concerned with industrial relations between his employer and any associated employer, and their employees'. Interpretation of this in courts and industrial tribunals had been broad, placing — in the government's view — intolerable strains on business. The position was now redressed.

As amended, union representatives were *entitled* to release for training only when it was relevant to duties of theirs 'concerned with negotiations with the employer', and when it was related to a (quite narrow) list of industrial relations activities. In addition, the training had to be related to an area of negotiation for which the union was recognised by the employer (or to an industrial relations function which the employer had agreed the union could perform, even though it was not a matter recognised for negotiation). The sum total was to limit rights to release to the consideration of matters on which collective bargaining took place, and to matters where the employer agreed to release. The assumption of the 1970s legislation, that extended collective bargaining was to be encouraged, was gone. The topics for which entitlement to paid release remained were now largely to be set by the employer. There was no right to release to study about how to extend negotiation with the employer. And no right to release existed for education relating to associated employers.[8]

It is difficult to gauge the impact of this new legislation. Certainly the enrolment in Stage 1 and Stage 2 union representatives' courses declined rapidly between 1988/89 and 1989/90, while Health and Safety course recruitment remained fairly stable. (Rights to paid release under the Safety Representatives and Safety Committees Regulations remained unchanged.) But Stage 1 and Stage 2 recruitment had been deteriorating rapidly for some time. The TUC put some effort into seeking amendments to the Draft Code of Practice issued by ACAS in April 1990. The Draft Code was considered 'helpful under the circumstances' (TUC 1990: 65), and when the final version was published in 1991, work began on a TUC Guide 'drawing upon appropriate sections of the ACAS code' (TUC 1991: 60). The *TUC Guide to Paid Release for Union Training* (TUC 1992a) outlines the legal position (with excerpts from the ACAS Code), gives guidance on negotiating release, and provides information about TUC courses and how to apply.

The second main assault on union education came over the new edition of the *Working Women* workbook. In 1991 the DE indicated that it wished to see TUC course materials. The subjects to be covered in grant-aided courses were set down in the Memorandum of Arrangements, and TUC course materials had normally been forwarded to the two government departments for information. However, there had been no assumption that materials were subject to approval by civil servants or ministers: indeed, it was on just this kind of issue that HMI would have been called upon to play a role. In early 1991, *Working Women* had recently been completed. Work on the new edition had begun in 1989 with 'review meetings' in all TUC regions; the TUC Women's Committee had been extensively consulted. The intention was that they would be used, by 'all trade unionists', on TUC Stage 1 and Stage 2 courses. At their annual meeting with DE civil servants in March, TUC officials were apparently told of doubts about the 'objectivity' of parts of the book (Rees 1991). Perhaps officials imagined that the objections could be disposed of by some minor amendments; but the DE 'was not prepared to accept one or two, and the TUC refused to make all the changes required' (Rees 1991).

When it was clear that they would not reach agreement, the DE took a strong line.

> *The Secretary of State for Employment took the view that the workbook misrepresented government policies over the past decade, was tendentious and was not objective. [He] further informed the TUC that the Department of Employment would not be prepared to provide grant*

Union Education in Britain: A TUC Activity

Introduction

Millions of people in Britain today live in poverty. Not all of these are unemployed or retired people. 7 million adult workers earn so little that their basic wages fall below what is officially regarded as the poverty line.

Many workers can only make ends meet by working overtime, unsocial hours or by "moonlighting". This affects their health, as well as their personal and social lives. It also helps to keep basic wages low.

The TUC believes that everyone who goes to work should earn enough to meet their needs.

Aims

This section will help you to:
  think about what causes low pay
  work out what unions can do towards eliminating low pay.

Women and low pay

Most of the low paid are women. Many of them are from black and ethnic minority communities.

The government's own definition of low pay is the earnings equivalent to Income Support (previously Supplementary Benefit) – in 1989 this was £128.70 per week gross. In 1988, the Family Credit eligibility limit was £154.29. 80.1% of full-time manual women workers fell below this government poverty level.

The TUC measure of low pay is anything less than two thirds of average male manual workers' gross weekly earnings. In April 1989, this figure was £145.25 per week, or £3.72 per hour.

Yet in that year:

  50% of women working full-time earned less than that amount, while only 15% of men did
  almost 50% of full-time male workers earned more than £200 per week; less than 20% of women did
  the top 10% of men earned £350 per week; only 1% of women did.

Part-time workers and low pay

Most part-time workers earn less than the hourly equivalent of a full-time employee. In 1988, a woman part-time worker only earned 56.6% of what a full-time male employee could expect to get. In 1979, the figure was 59.3% and it has been falling every year since then.

Government policy and low pay

These are some of the actions taken by the government since 1979 which have contributed to holding wages down and which have badly affected women workers:

· Schedule 11 was abolished. This allowed any group of workers to claim parity with a similar group within an industry covered by a national agreement
· the Fair Wages Resolution established in 1891, was abolished in 1983. It ensured that employees of contractors to the public sector could claim pay and conditions in line with the general level in their trade locally
· the powers of Wages Councils are now limited to setting a single minimum rate and overtime rate for adult workers
· casualisation and short term contracts have dramatically increased in areas such as the NHS and the Civil Service
· legal protection for workers has been severely cut back
· Child Benefit has been frozen since 1987
· maternity rights have been reduced and the maternity grant has been abolished.

The Poverty Trap

For many women workers small increases in their take home pay would mean they'd be worse off. Anyone earning below the Lower Earnings Limit (LEL) – from April 1990 £46 per week – does not pay any National Insurance Contributions. So the moment they earn enough to take them over that amount, they will have deductions made.

Low paid workers can claim state benefits such as Family Credit and Housing Benefit. Pay rises could mean these benefits would fall or stop – perhaps meaning a lower income, even though their wages have gone up.

WORKING WOMEN

Fig. 9.1: Offending Passages. Working Women (1991) contained measured and factual accounts of government policy and its effect on women, but the response from the Department of Employment was far from restrained.

> *to those courses where the workbook was used and that this would be a condition of the 1991-92 grant. (TUC 1991: 60.)*

Let us dwell briefly on the enormity of this decision. It is very hard to see *Working Women* as tendentious, or as misrepresenting government policies. Indeed, it says very little about them — and what it does say is no rousing denunciation. *Working Women* is a booklet of 112 'A4 pages'. There are 21 chapters, covering such topics as 'Working Women in History', 'Equal Pay for Work of Equal Value', 'Women and Pensions', 'Women and Trade Unions'. As with most TUC education literature, these contain factual information, activities, checklists, illustrations, model agreements and excerpts from union and TUC policy statements, and 'European News' (examples of helpful standards from the European Community or European countries). Of the 112 pages, a total of rather less than three is devoted to government policies.[9] Among the strongest comments, government actions since 1979, such as the abolition of the Fair Wages Resolution and the freezing of child benefit (five other examples are given), are said to 'have contributed to holding wages down and ... have badly affected women workers' (TUC 1991a: 39). Another is the modest accusation that

> *Cuts in public spending are eating into the meagre provision of local authority nursery places. Government ministers publicly recognise the connection between the availability of childcare and equal opportunities at work for women. They do not accept that it is the state's responsibility to provide this care. It is seen as a 'perk' employers should offer by providing workplace nurseries. (TUC 1991a: 10.)*

In short, *Working Women* was, as the equal opportunities officer of the National Union of Teachers commented, 'good material for promoting women at work ... straightforward, with facts, figures and interesting discussion points' (quoted by Nash 1991).[10]

Hypersensitive the government may have been: but its decision on *Working Women* represented a major shift in the terms of the TUC's educational relations with the state — and one clearly linked to the transfer of responsibilities from DES aegis. The TUC had always trod the boundaries of political acceptability with care. Courses centring on issues of political dispute with the government, for instance, had always been separately funded. The Memorandum of Arrangements with the TUC had always specified the topics to be covered in publicly-funded courses. Before 1987, ministers' references to course content had generally been in broad terms. Replying to a question on 'how education is defined' in respect of public funding of trade union education, a Labour Minister (Harold Walker) had asserted in 1977:

> *the courses provide instruction in (a) the principles of trade unionism and (b) activities concerning the role of trade union members and trade union representatives in industrial relations, including negotiations and consultations; in health, safety and welfare; in the work of unions related to such activities; [and] in the work of statutory bodies ... (Hansard 26 October 1977).*

During the early 1980s, replies were in a similar vein. Like Walker, Rhodes Boyson (Hansard 31 January 1980) had noted the role of HMI, who 'monitor[ed] those courses in the public sector as part of their normal responsibilities' and were 'invited to inspect individual union courses'. They also 'maintain[ed] regular contact' with TUC officials and 'advise[d] the working party of union education officers about the provision of appropriate courses'. In 1981, it was the TUC's proposals 'to introduce certain new *areas* of activity into the grant arrangements' which were subject to further consideration (Hansard 15 April 1981: emphasis added). By 1987, however, in the replies to Ann Winterton, the emphasis had changed. It was the closeness of government control which was stressed:

> *The memorandum of arrangements ... specifies in detail the subject areas which eligible courses must cover. It also requires the Trades Union Congress to seek departmental approval for additions or amendments to the content of courses. ... The Government expect the Trades Union Congress to ensure that the courses funded meet the requirements of the memorandum of arrangements.[11]*

However, while the tone is unmistakeable, it perhaps obscures the precise meaning of the words, which refer only to 'subject areas'. Some subject areas were specified, and differed little from those mentioned by Harold Walker a decade earlier (the only substantial change was the addition of Keith Joseph's 'economic awareness'):

> *democracy at work; the role of members and representatives in industrial relations, including negotiation and consultation; health and safety issues; and the importance of economic realities in the functioning of industry and commerce. (Hansard 23 November 1987).*

Although the 1980s had seen some 'tightening up' — certainly by 1987 the ethos was of close control — government had not policed in detail the educational content of courses, in terms of books to be used. (Indeed, under the educational ethos of the HMI, such policing — political censorship of the content of courses — would have been regarded as quite improper.) The episode is a grim testament to the intellectual immorality of the Thatcher and Major governments.

The TUC now faced the ultimatum: withdraw the *Working Women* books, or face the loss of public funding. The general secretary was consulted, but there seemed little option. A campaign was possible, but was judged unlikely to lead to a reversal of the decision. The threat was immediate—to funding for the 1991/92 financial year, which had already started. And it was general: all courses making use of *Working Women* would lose grant, and these (so the TUC intended) would include the entire Stage 1 and Stage 2 programme. Stan Greaves wrote to regional education officers (a letter later leaked to the press: quoted Nash 1991).

> *I am writing to confirm that the Department of Employment has advised the TUC that they are not prepared to provide grants to courses if a TUC publication,* Working Women, *is used with educational materials. It follows that we will not sanction the use of* Working Women *on grant-aided courses.*

'TUC bans its own booklet' ran the headline in *The Times Educational Supplement* (Nash 1991), which broke the story. This set the tone for other press coverage, which centred not on the grotesque nature of the government's action, but on how the TUC had responded. The surrender certainly appeared pretty abject, and TUC officials felt some embarrassment about the incident. But in the circumstances, their choices were limited. (We should perhaps note that they did not disown the book, nor were they prepared to make changes as required by the DE. *Working Women* would be used on courses which were not grant-aided.) In truth, the incident serves to demonstrate the TUC's weakness after twelve years of Conservative government. Its educational edifice was built on the foundations of post-war consensus and 1970s corporatism. For over a decade it had defended this edifice. Gradually, its ability to resist had been reduced, as the weapons and redoubts at its disposal had been lost. To be defeated over *Working Women* — for defeat it was — was an acknowledgement that the power relationships of the 1970s were not those of the 1990s.[12]

By narrowing the right to paid release, and reducing the scope of the education for which public funding would be available, the new DE regime had successfully attacked two of the three pillars of the TUC educational enterprise. The result was not devastating, but did significantly hinder and limit the educational opportunities available to trade unionists. The third pillar — the provision of education through public educational bodies — was also threatened by the government's education policy. As a result, the TUC had to consider options which, in earlier times, would have been unthinkable.

A major consideration in the TUC's policy, originally made in the 1960s but often reaffirmed, of collaborating with the public education sector was that through this the state subsidised a high-quality education service. Trade unionists, the TUC held, were as entitled to the benefits of this public subsidy as anyone else. In collaborating with public education bodies, union education had to make some compromises: but the result was that it secured the services of (mostly) high-quality tutors, usually in good-quality educational settings, at substantially less than full cost. The drift of government education policy throughout the 1980s was to shift the 'burden' of paying for education from the state to the consumer. This occurred in various forms: the reduction of rate support grant to local education authorities, the reduction of grant-aid to the WEA, pressure on higher education to raise fees. In tandem with this came initiatives to restructure: from the early 1980s, for instance, a changed basis for allocation of grant-aid to Responsible Bodies (the WEA and extra-mural departments). These shifted the 'burden' by requiring educational institutions to charge higher fees to students. Through the 1980s the TUC had responded to this by effective negotiation with local authorities and the WEA — the fees it paid remained remarkably low.

The first intimation of major change to come was in a White Paper and DES consultative document on higher education in 1987. This covered the polytechnics and colleges of higher education, and involved removing them from the control of local education authorities and placing them under restructured governing bodies largely controlled by business interests. Funding for the polytechnics and colleges was to be transferred from local authorities (albeit under guidance from a National Advisory Body) to a new Polytechnics and Colleges Funding Council, and 'dependence on public funding' was to be discouraged. As the General Council remarked, the future of 'many courses that may not appear commercially attractive' might be in doubt (TUC 1987d). Among these were trade union courses, which were sometimes 'fairly heavily subsidised by local authorities'; the loss of this support 'could threaten the continuance of some courses' (NATFHE and SERTUC 1987). The threat was real. In the South East Region, the TUC and NATFHE (the union for polytechnic and college lecturers) organised a seminar to consider the effect of the proposals on TUC course provision. The impact on four higher education providing bodies in the region was examined: Middlesex and South Bank polytechnics, and Slough and South West London colleges. By 1992, the two colleges were no longer offering TUC courses.[13] Indeed, by 1992 only 13 higher education institutions nationally provided TUC courses (TUC 1992c).

Albeit with regret, the TUC could survive the loss of support from higher education. The major concern came four years later, with the Further and Higher Education Act of 1992. In that year, in addition to 14 WEA districts and the remaining polytechnics and universities, TUC education was provided through some 80 further education colleges. Clearly a threat to the colleges put the very existence of TUC education in its post-1975 form at risk. The 1992 Act paralleled in many ways the earlier higher education legislation. Local education authorities were no longer to be responsible for financing further education colleges, which became independent corporations. There would now be a Further Education Funding Council,[14] which would support certain specific categories of provision. Any other courses must cover their full costs through fee income. The categories had no place for union education. Colleges stood to get no funding whatever in respect of their TUC courses — apart from the course fees. Few would bear this heavy burden for long, unless the TUC could increase the fees it paid.

There were several problems. The TUC (through its regional education officers) would now have to negotiate course fees with each college individually. Colleges would increasingly be concerned about their financial viability: uneconomic colleges would face closure. Success in keeping fees low might lead to the erosion of standards on union courses. TUC financial planning would be increasingly difficult.[15] Fees could well escalate. If full ('economic') costs of TUC courses were to be met, the increase in course fees would be immense: a rise 'by a factor of 7 or 8' (TUEC document 2/1, 14 January 1992). But unless the DE grant were similarly increased — and it rightly seemed 'highly unlikely that the DE would consider [this] for one moment' (TUC 1992c) — the programme would be reduced to around one-seventh of its size. 'This would be likely,' an internal TUC paper warned, 'to result in the loss of around 200 full-time and 100 part-time teaching posts in FE, unless other work could be found for those teachers' (TUC 1992c).

Not surprisingly, this prospect caused great concern. Whilst the Bill was being considered, the TUC encouraged Labour amendments which would have allowed the Funding Council to support 'work-related non-vocational education' — but to no avail. Following the passing of the Act, the TUC negotiated with the (now vogueishly retitled) Department for Education to secure support for a memorandum which would tell the Funding Council to count TUC work as fundable, even though it did not fall into one of the approved categories.[16] In the autumn of 1992, the DFE agreed to this, and the main problem was apparently resolved in the short term. Had these discussions failed — and a number of important points still remained to be cleared up[17] — the alternatives were less than palatable: adjusting TUC curricula and course aims so that they could qualify for support in the existing categories of funding. There were two main options here: to redesign the courses as, in some way, 'access' courses preparing students for higher education, or to link them to the award of National Vocational Qualifications. Both approaches seemed to raise difficulties. In the first half of 1992 they were actively considered as 'fall-back' positions. The TUC was beginning to face up to the unthinkable. In the highly uncertain financial environment — support could evaporate more or less at the whim of a junior minister — such planning was only prudent.

Between two unpalatable alternatives, the TUC initially preferred the access to higher education approach. It was, however, extremely hazardous. Agreements would have to be negotiated with universities and polytechnics.[18] The approach would involve accrediting TUC courses as developing students' abilities along certain lines. (These might be accumulated toward a certificate or diploma of a higher education institution.) There would be time-consuming negotiations, and (in all probability) less-than-satisfactory compromises. Very likely, it would introduce a wide measure of diversity, and might signal the end of a national scheme. Given the TUC's long concern to wrest control of union education from the extra-mural departments, there would be irony indeed if the TUC education scheme were to end with control being handed over to the universities.[19]

In addition to raising questions about the unity of the scheme, reliance on the access to higher education route seemed unlikely to deliver arrangements quickly enough. As Alan Grant wrote,

> *it is unlikely that anything practical on a national scale could be completed by Spring, 1993 [when the new Funding Council arrangements were to come into operation]. Many colleges may, at present, be uncertain about the future of the TUC Education Service because of the Bill and may be considering their future commitment of resources if they see doubts about the TUC's ability to maintain a healthy trade union education programme. These resources (people, knowledge, skills and facilities) have been painstakingly established and developed since the early seventies; they would be impossible to replace. (TUC 1992c.)*

So although closer relations with higher education were very much on the agenda, there were a number of drawbacks to the access to higher education route.

It was thus fortuitous that during 1991, 'not inspired by the Government's proposed legislation but, nevertheless, related to it' the Trade Union Education Committee had begun to look at 'the relationship between education and training for lay officials ... and the general movement in further education towards national vocational qualifications'. There had for many years been grumbles from lay representatives that 'they receive[d] no formal acknowledgement (in the form of certificates, for example) of their engagement in courses of trade union training'. (TUC 1991: 56.) HMI thought TUC courses 'of sufficiently high quality' for accreditation (say by NCVQ), and warned the Trade Union Education Committee that changes likely under the Further and Higher Education Act 'would inevitably lead to the TUC having to examine the possibility of accreditation and working in partnership with a validating body' (TUC 1993a: 7). In June 1991, certification was introduced on Stage 1 courses.[20] There were concerns. Some felt that NVQs implied absolute standards and could not permit varying starting points and varying levels of achievement. They were therefore inappropriate for *lay* union representatives. Lay representatives, on this view, appointed by their members, were answerable to and to be judged by their members. High levels of skill were to be encouraged and developed: but given the widely varying skill levels at entry to (and exit from) trade union courses, it would not be realistic to set NVQ-type targets.[21]

By early 1993, such reservations had passed from Trade Union Education Department thinking. The experience of developing occupational standards and NVQs for full-time officers was key. With the Project Advisory Group meeting from late 1991 and through 1992, and a heavy programme of related developmental work, minds were concentrated. 'The movement towards specifying standards and framing occupational qualifications has been taken up in a wide range of occupations'; unions should adopt the advice (for improving training standards) which they gave to employers. Standards for lay representatives could draw 'almost exclusively' on the 'core trade union standards' developed in the work on full-time officers. 'Clearly, standards for voluntary officers would not have the range or depth of those for professional officers but many units of competence would be similar.' There was little evidence that shop stewards opposed assessment and awards — 'in fact, the opposite has been the case'. Tutors had 'valid concerns' that 'fear of "failure" would lower course recruitment', that courses would need to be reorganised, and that the nature of their own jobs would change. But these stemmed chiefly from a misunderstanding of 'the relationship between Standards, Learning, Assessment and Qualifications'. Standards were 'a specification of quality'. Learning was achieved through 'several processes', not only through formal learning in union courses. In assessment both learner and assessor 'work to common assessment guidelines — the standards'; it was not necessarily linked to attendance on particular courses. Qualifications 'are awards made by recognised awarding bodies in recognition of competence achieved', and could be kept quite separate from courses themselves. (TUC 1993a: 7-10.)

More generally, with the prospect of a union Lead Body centred on the TUC, fears of externally-imposed and inappropriate standards of competence were much reduced. There were opportunities as well as threats. A trade union Lead Body could enable the TUC to maintain (and even extend) curriculum standardisation. It would 'ensure that trade unions maintain[ed] nationally-recognised control and authority over standards, assessment and qualifications in their own field'. It would also help 'to build within trade unions effective training and development systems, providing recognition of achievement'. (TUC 1993a: 6.) In any case,

> All the indications are that criteria for FEFC funding will become more stringent over the next few years with the emphasis upon assessed learning outcomes. While standards and NVQs/SVQs will enable the TUC to meet these criteria, their development would not prevent the TUC from pursuing other forms of assessment and accreditation, such as the 'access to HE' route. (TUC 1993a: 9)

For reasons both educational and pragmatic, therefore, by the early months of 1993 NVQs, standards of competence, and the notion of the TUC as a Lead Body for the trade union sector were established as the fulcrum of TUC educational strategy.

Organisation and Resources

With the problems of the late eighties and early nineties — from declining union membership to the 1992 Further and Higher Education Act — organising TUC education was a constant struggle with the unacceptable. Stan Greaves had joined the TUC Education Department in 1968: he had seen the good times as well as the bad. Managing decline, he remarked (1992), was 'very time consuming and emotional' and 'far more difficult that managing growth'. But if the eighties as a whole were a period of managing decline, in the late eighties many of the problems became acute.

The administrative structure of TUC education had been built up in the 1970s and remained little changed through the 1980s. There were four main areas of activity: the administration at Congress House, materials development, the Training College (and, from the early 1980s, the National Education Centre), and the regional education service. The Congress House administration — the Head of the Education or Trade Union Education Department, together with Assistant Secretaries and support staff — was concerned with policy issues, with servicing the Committee, and with leading and overseeing the more directly educational activities. Materials development — the work of the course development unit in its heyday — was always closely integrated with the work of the Training College (and later with the National Education Centre), although in view of the receipt of grant-aid, the activities were kept financially separate. Both were often closely related to the regional education service. The regions were the fulcrum of TUC education. Their ability to cope with the pressures of the eighties and nineties would determine the fate of the service. It is to the organisation in the regions that we now turn.

In each TUC region — there were seven in England,[22] with Scotland and Wales each also counting as regions *de facto* — the TUC maintained a regional education office, consisting of a regional education officer and a small supporting clerical staff.[23] (Initially many REOs were former NCLC organisers, but by the 1980s most had left.) The tasks of the REO were many: to negotiate with colleges and WEA districts to secure the provision of sufficient courses; to advertise courses; to build up relations with union officers to ensure healthy recruitment; to ensure an adequate supply of suitable tutors and to oversee and develop their quality (through tutor briefings and the like); to receive and process all applications for courses; and generally to present a good face for TUC education in the region. For perhaps a majority of union representatives, the REO was the only TUC official — apart from the General Secretary — whose name they knew.

The REOs varied a great deal in temperament and approach. Working from small offices often hundreds of miles from London,[24] they were at the same time isolated and independent. In the eighties, the REOs bore — within the TUC — the brunt of the erosion of courses, losing colleagues and friends in the colleges. Yet despite their high profile and the pressures they faced, REOs enjoyed only a relatively lowly place in the TUC hierarchy. From the beginning, the national leadership sought ways to ensure effective co-ordination among this far-flung band. Roy Jackson instituted a system of monthly national meetings of REOs in 1974: these remained the chief method of maintaining control and overcoming isolation. The meetings normally lasted for one day, but on about three occasions annually for two days. Attendance was more or less compulsory, with the dates set annually for the year ahead. The meetings considered policy, discussed relevant issues, examined new programmes and materials. Here also REOs were informed of their budgets for the year ahead — and some limited negotiation of these might be possible. During the 1980s, the budgets became tighter, and so too did the financial controls: targets and ceilings were set for the various categories of courses in each region. With the spread of computerisation and the eighties mania for cost-accounting, REOs — like their colleagues in the colleges — were judged increasingly by various performance indicators.

Through the eighties, the REOs' work became steadily more demanding. A particular problem was the shift from ten-day to short courses. As a TUC document (TUEC 2/1, 14 January 1992) had it in the early 1990s:

> *The organisational and administrative input to any course is in no way dependent upon whether it is of ten days or two days duration. In fact, the development of the TUC short course provision has placed considerable demands on REOs in responding to specific demands locally. ... While REOs are able to organise and publicise and advance programme of ten/ twelve day courses, large elements of the short course programme are labour-intensive requiring REOs to match demand with local resources and know-how. This inevitably means that while the provision of short courses grows the same level of administrative input is required for a decreasing amount of training time.*

Within each region, the REO worked with a network of colleges and WEA districts, together with a sprinkling of extra-mural departments and polytechnics. The number of trade union studies tutors within these public educational bodies would vary considerably: some might employ only one or two part-time staff, or allocate only a small part of one full-time lecturer's work to the TUC programme. In others there might be as many as four or five (or occasionally more) full-time staff, and perhaps part-time tutors as well. As pressures grew during the 1980s, REOs' skill in establishing and maintaining good resources — dedicated and able tutors — in the colleges (and other educational bodies) became critical. With effective tutors in the colleges, the TUC programme would be likely to remain strong. Effective tutors would not only teach: they would also develop contacts with shop stewards and union officers, identify areas for short courses, plan and develop 'bespoke' courses, develop and circulate local publicity. If such tutors were lost, the programme could only decline.

Of course, many factors influenced REOs' success in this. One was the attitude of the local education authority (and its officials). LEAs funded college activities; often they provided grant-aid to WEA districts too. They could provide more — or less — financial support for trade union studies. It was, of course, increasingly difficult as local authority budgets became tighter. But the amounts of money which a trade union studies centre required (perhaps £100,000 would support a unit of three tutors) were relatively modest, and if the will were present, much could be done. Inevitably, however, the will tended to be greater in Labour-controlled local authorities, and in the Midlands and North the number of strong trade union studies centres was correspondingly greater. There were also more arcane strategies. For instance, the various courses in further and higher education colleges were graded on a scale from one to five. TUC courses were typically grade three. In further education, this was high-grade work, and relatively prestigious; in higher education colleges and polytechnics, it was usually the lowest level. It was therefore normally easier to build up well-resourced centres in further than in higher education;[25] an REO's abilities to develop and carry through such a strategy in association with LEA and college administrators could be vitally important. The record of the various TUC regions during the 1980s was very varied, and suggests they were not uniformly successful in establishing a resilient infrastructure. In the North West and West Midlands, for instance, the programme held up far more successfully than in the East Midlands and East Anglia, or Wales.

Taken as a whole, however, the organisational record of TUC education during the 1980s seems quite good. A paper in early 1992, reviewing the TUC's education, noted that while TUC affiliated membership had declined by 33 per cent between 1978/79 and 1990/91, student enrolments in TUC courses had declined by 32 per cent. The 'penetration' of TUC education remained the same — although, at 0.36 per cent of all trade unionists, it can hardly be regarded as high. (TUC document TUEC 2/1, 14 January 1992.)[26] Despite the vicissitudes of the eighties, the regional education service had managed to recruit similar proportions of trade union members to its courses — albeit that the courses were often shorter and less predictable, and produced less income for the colleges.

However, in 1992 the regional education service — indeed, TUC education as a whole — was threatened by a new problem. Faced with severe financial problems, the TUC proposed large-scale staffing cuts. An investigation of TUC educational costs suggested that for every £1 spent on courses, a further 77 pence went on administration (Grant 1992a). The result was a reduction in the number of TUC regions from nine to six — and consequent loss of three REOs' posts.[27] In the short term, at least, the savings were to be retained in the education budget, to be spent on courses. But clearly there would be a vast increase in the workload of several REOs. Their ability to develop effective links with union officers and lay representatives, college and WEA tutors, college and LEA administrators, would inevitably be diminished. This would occur at just the time when *additional* efforts would be needed to ensure the retention of resources in the WEA and colleges, as the impact of the Further and Higher Education Act began to be felt. The threat was real.

The Clouds Darken

Any relief which Trade Union Education Department officials may have felt when the Secretary of State for Education ordered TUC courses to be recognised for funding by the FEFC was shortlived. On 10 December 1992 Norman Willis received a short letter from the Secretary of State for Employment, Gillian Shephard. 'I have been reviewing the Trade Union Education and Training (TUET) grant and the Trade Union Ballot Funding Scheme (TUBFS)', she wrote. These had been

> *introduced some years ago, when circumstances were quite different from those we now face. Having reviewed both schemes against their original purposes, I have concluded that public subsidies for these purposes can no longer be justified. I have therefore decided that both schemes should be phased out over three years, from April 1993.*[28]

She enclosed a House of Commons written answer to be delivered that same afternoon. Bearing all the signs of special pleading, this set out the formal grounds for the decision. The grant had been

> *intended to provide training for union officials to ensure that they were well qualified to carry out their collective bargaining duties, with a view*

> *to improving industrial relations and reducing strikes. Industrial relations have improved greatly, and strikes are now at their lowest level since records began. At the same time, fewer than 50% of employees now have their pay determined, directly or indirectly, by negotiations between employers and trade unions. More and more employees negotiate their pay directly with their employer on an individual basis taking account of performance and skills. In these circumstances ... there is no justification for continuing to support the training from public funds.*[29]

Shephard's argument is difficult to sustain. She claimed to have reviewed the scheme against its original purpose, but while it was certainly assumed in 1975 that education for trades unionists would improve industrial relations, there had been no mention of reducing strikes as such either in the TUC's Memorandum to the DES, nor in the Ministerial written answer by which approval was indicated (Hansard, 22 July 1976). Indeed, when meeting the Secretary of State in 1975, the TUC had explicitly rejected an approach which would 'emphasise consideration of industrial efficiency to the detriment of trade union education and training serving trade union purposes' (Education Committee document 1/1, 14 October 1975).

The 1975 arrangements had, of course, been based on a view of the role of unions in an industrial democracy: explicitly stated in the TUC Memorandum (TUC 1975: 199-200). When Fred Mulley, as Secretary of State for Education, announced the first grant, it was 'in order to help trade unionists achieve an improved understanding of industrial and public affairs required for the discharge of their role in employment' (Hansard, 22 July 1976). As for the other 'improvements' in industrial relations listed by Shephard, to ministers in the 1970s (as to trade unionists in the 1990s) these would have seemed quite the reverse. While this is, in one sense, to miss the point, it is well to note how far the rules of the game had changed: in no sense were Britain's trade unions of the 1990s 'social partners'.

If the government's argument provides no adequate explanation, how can the decision be explained? That there was little love lost between the Conservatives and the trade unions provides a general background. But this had been a fact of life since 1979. Three main factors seem to have lain behind the change in policy. First, the government no longer felt a real threat from the trade union movement. The Conservatives had been thirteen years in power; they had successfully weathered the leadership transition from Thatcher to Major, and secured a further term in office. Union membership and organisation continued to decline, and with the deepest depression since the 1930s showing no signs of abating, these trends were unlikely to reverse. Politically, union power was a spent force, although the spectre of its return was still perceived as an electoral millstone for the Labour Party (many of whose leaders continued to distance themselves from the unions).

In this political context, a new regime took control at the Department of Employment. In particular, Michael Forsyth, a ambitious young blood of the Thatcherite right-wing, replaced Michael Howard as junior Employment Minister (under Gillian Shephard, the Secretary of State). Forsyth had a taste for attacking icons of the left. He had gained notoriety as Minister at the Scottish Education Department, where he ended half-a-century's government grant-aiding of Newbattle Abbey College (the Scottish equivalent of Ruskin) in 1989. The contest in his highly marginal Stirling constituency at the 1992 general election was bitter, with trade union opposition to the fore. The fires of his anti-union instincts can only have been stoked.

Perhaps the assault would have come in any case: but an opportunity was created by the economic and financial crisis of 1992. Following the government's failure to preserve sterling's parity within the European Monetary System, with public finances stretched and prospects of continuing high levels of unemployment, pressure was on to cut government spending. For many years TUC staff had known that union education had few friends in government. The TUC's strategy for maintaining public funding had always been to prevent its becoming an issue. This had succeeded for over thirteen years: now the odds were stacked too high. With a determined adversary at the helm in the DE, any review of the grant could only mean its termination.

While formally the TUC continued to contest the decision for several months, there was little likelihood of a major policy reversal. The TUC had not been consulted. It had not even been informed that review was in progress. A modest campaign developed: notably the CBI's Director General wrote asking the government to reconsider its decision. Gillian Shephard agreed to meet a General Council delegation. There was some prospect of retaining some public funding for safety representative training, perhaps channelled through the Health and Safety Commission.

For the TUC, however, the real issue was how far it could sustain a viable national system of education in the last days of public funding, and thereafter. Roughly 97 per cent of public funds were spent on meeting college and WEA fees.[30] The TUC would need to raise an additional £300,000 or so in 1994, £700,000 in 1995, and £1,100,000 in 1996 in order to maintain the 1992 level of provision. These figures might be reduced substantially if a significant proportion of funding for health and safety courses could be retained through the HSC: some £450,000, or nearly half of the public funds, was spent annually on health and safety course fees. On the other hand, costs might well rise faster than general inflation. In particular, the figures assumed that college fees would rise by no more than 4 per cent: with uncertainty about the future of college fee levels under the

FEFC regime, there were many less optimistic scenarios.

Without public funds, the regional education service could be supported in two ways. The TUC could charge a course fee, either to students individually or to their union. Such an approach would be a major departure from the traditions of the service, which had long been free to students. It would be administratively complex, and would discourage participation. Alternatively, the TUC could raise the costs of supporting the service through a higher (perhaps 'earmarked') affiliation fee. To raise even £300,000 would, however, imply an additional fee of nearly 4 pence per union member; the 1996 requirement would be an additional 12 pence, representing a 10 per cent increase in TUC affiliation fees.[31] In the early months of 1993, therefore, the future of TUC education — and indeed of British union education generally — lay very much in the balance. At risk was the entire framework of education constructed over the previous quarter century: curricular traditions and approaches, tutors and experts, recruiting and administrative structures.

There were grounds for limited optimism. Progress on standards, and the establishment of a Lead Body for the trade union sector, were advancing well. This promised to maintain some order in the field; there might also be some funding from TEED.[32] Congress in 1992 had established a 'Services Working Group' of senior General Council members.[33] Union leaders were keenly aware that workplace union organisation was less robust, and education was central to perspectives for the future of the TUC. Consulted at a series of seminars in late 1992 about their changing roles, union full-time officers thought there were now fewer shop stewards than formerly, and turnover was greater. Members were less willing to volunteer for election, partly no doubt because 'demoralisation and loss of confidence' were common. The same TUC document quoted a key finding of the latest Workplace Industrial Relations Survey: the proportion of workplaces where unions were recognised but where there was no union representative rose from 18 per cent in 1984 to 29 per cent in 1991. (TUC 1993a: Annex.) Education remained one of the few mechanisms which trade unions had for raising the morale and competence of the lay union representative, and it was a mechanism which the TUC had a record of delivering successfully. The success in education extended to both a general system of provision for all unions, and 'bespoke' services designed to meet individual needs. The case for maintaining central and flexible educational structures for the trade union movement was strong, and the TUC's own financial strategy was designed to prevent trade union education being 'undermined' (TUC 1992: 105).

But against any grounds for optimism several countervailing factors had to be set. The financial pressures on Congress were intense. In its 1992 report, the General Council had devoted considerable attention to this problem. The view was clear:

> *Unions were unlikely to be willing to compensate the TUC for any loss of income as a result of declining affiliated membership; and realistically only modest increases in the [TUC] affiliation fee could be expected in line with changes in union subscription rates (TUC 1992: 105).*

While the specific scenario of losing educational income from public funds was not addressed, the implication was unmistakeable.

From the viewpoint of an affiliated union, moreover, the threat took on a rather different hue. To be sure, TUC education was a valuable service; its loss would be regretted. But most of the large unions now had their own education services, and their own educational staff. They too had lost public funding (the government's decision did not distinguish between the TUC and individual unions). With their own financial pressures, the temptation would be for any additional fee income raised for education to be retained for the union's own educational services. The pressures would be even greater if pessimistic predictions about rising further education course fees came to pass. Very likely unions' views would differ: but some already preferred to 'go in-house'. If a few major unions 'opted out' of financing TUC education, could the commitment of the remainder — even a majority — long survive?

1. Harvey Proctor asked a series of somewhat more searching questions during the 1979/80 parliamentary session, but they were not comparable with Winterton's. Nor were the times so favourable.

2. Any attempt to follow up David Waddington's reply, which stressed that to 'the best of our knowledge, [the money] ... is being spent properly and to the benefit of unions and managements', was destroyed by a very effective, if largely irrelevant, intervention by Labour MP Arthur Lewis: 'How much money has been spent in educating the various Soviet knights, such as Sir Anthony Blunt and Sir Roger Hollis ...?'

3. Anderson (1988) stated that he had a 'file that thick' of cases; they were, however, confidential. According to her Research Assistant (Whitehouse 1988), Mrs Winterton's interest was stimulated by 'an individual involved in education at a local college [who felt] that in some instances the courses were being abused in order to promote union militancy and to disseminate biased information'. Following Anderson's article, she apparently received 'other letters from individuals around the country ... which confirm the earlier allegations'. Mrs Winterton was MP for Congleton, near Manchester: the 'local college' was probably Crewe and Alsager College.

4. The reason for this difficulty was chiefly because existing procedures were considered inadequate. Anderson's view (1988), for instance, was

that 'if there were bias, the HMIs wouldn't find it'. The approach should therefore be to ask whether, on 'structural' grounds, bias was to be anticipated; and if it was, then to assume its existence until proved otherwise (Anderson 1988).

5   The announcement on the Memorandum of Arrangements for non-TUC unions came in response to a question by John Cartwright, Social Democratic Party MP for Woolwich East (Hansard 13 November 1987 c325w).

6   The HMI, as an independent body, could be very helpful also in dissipating political attacks; there is some evidence that they played some such role relation to Ann Winterton's questions, and this may have played a part in the decision to exclude the DES. However, this should also be seen in the context of generally increasing DE control in work-related further education.

7   This was, of course, the legislation first introduced in the Employment Protection Act 1975 (ss. 57 and 58). The sections cover paid time off for union duties as well as union training, and the 1989 amendments also relate to both. The amended legislation was later transferred into the Trade Union and Labour Relations (Consolidation) Act 1992 (ss. 168-9).

8   This paragraph draws on McIlroy 1991: 154-5.

9   These passages are: three paragraphs headed 'What's happening now?' (p. 10); a section headed 'Government policy and low pay' (p. 39); one paragraph in the introduction to 'Maternity rights and benefits' (p. 59), and the sections headed 'Maternity Benefits — then ...', '... And Now', and 'Maternity Rights' (pp. 60-61). The passages on pp. 60-61 are entirely devoted to a factual description of changes to maternity rights and benefits brought by the 1986 Social Security Act.

10 It is worth noting that *Working Women* also contains a significant amount of criticism, in terms of their policies on women, of trade unions and the TUC.

11 It is illustrative of the Conservatives' low opinion of the HMI that, although the reply came from a DES Minister, there was no reference to inspection or of the HMI.

12 The requirement that TUC materials be approved, asserted by this affair, became general. Prior to the approval of grant for 1992/93, the new Stage 1 and Health and Safety materials were submitted to the DE.

13 The Centre for Trade Union Studies at Slough College, under the leadership of Wolf Wayne, had developed in the late 1970s and early 1980s into the one of the two largest providers of TUC courses in the South East Region. By 1984 it had five full-time tutors, and provided an average of 13 ten-day courses per term in Aylesbury, Slough and Reading. (TUC Education Committee document 6/9, 13 March 1984.) South West London College closed in 1991: its TUC courses were transferred out of higher education.

14 In Scotland, the Scottish Education Department.

15 As late as 26 March 1993, the TUC did not know the fee levels which would

be imposed in the following term (commencing three weeks later).
16 Under s.3(3) of the Act, the Funding Council was empowered to 'secure the provision of facilities for education ... where they are not under a duty to do so'.
17 These included the position of TUC courses in higher education and the WEA, the precise range of TUC courses which would qualify for FEFC funding, and what proportion of college costs would be met by the TUC (Grant 1992c).
18 From mid-1992, polytechnics were renamed universities; since this occurred only in the final months covered by this book, and the distinction between the two former categories remained meaningful, the term 'polytechnic' is retained.
19 Because of the much greater diversity of higher education in the 1990s, any renewed relations with higher education need not have been with the extra-mural departments as such.
20 Both Health and Safety Stage 1 and the Stage 1 course for union representatives.
21 While this was certainly the view of a number of TUC staff (including Alan Grant during when interviewed in March 1992) it was not the universal view in trade union education. It is also worth noting that the TUC was at the same time actively investigating the development of NVQs for union full-time officials (see TUC 1992b).
22 More precisely, there was a TUC regional education officer for each of the following regions: Northern; Yorkshire and Humberside; North West; West Midlands; South East; South West. The East Midlands and East Anglia regions shared a single regional education officer, though each had a separate regional education advisory committee.
23 Northern Ireland was also treated as a region *de facto*, but the education service there was provided through the Northern Ireland Committee of the Irish Congress of Trade Unions. In 1992 there were 15 full-time equivalent clerical staff in the nine regional education offices in Great Britain (TUEC document 2/1, 14 January 1992).
24 The REO in the South East was housed at Congress House.
25 Good centres could be built up in higher education, but they were normally more dependent upon the 'political' abilities of trade union studies staff within the institution. When key staff left, therefore, units within higher education were more exposed.
26 These figures cover all TUC regional student enrolments; ten-day and short course enrolments are not distinguished.
27 The South West Region was merged with Wales; the East Midlands with the West Midlands; and the Northern with Yorkshire and Humberside. The REO was, however, retained in the Northern Region, although he would not be replaced if he left the TUC's employment.
28 In 1993/94, the grant would be set at 75 per cent of each 1992/93 'per capita figure'. This level would be reduced to 50 per cent in 1994/95, and 25 per cent in 1995/96; the scheme would cease altogether with effect

from 1 April 1996. (The reference to 'per capita figure' indicates that the grant would also be adjusted *pro rata* to changes in total TUC-affiliated trade union membership.)

29 The Department of Employment simultaneously notified the TUC of the phasing out (over the same period) of the public funding for Trade Union Ballots, introduced in 1980.

30 In the year ending 31 March 1992, the TUC spent £967,845 in meeting fees for regional courses (TUC 1992: 44). The remaining 3 per cent or so was devoted to tutor training. (These percentages exclude public funds received for expenditure on trade union residential courses, for which the TUC acted only as agent.)

31 TUC affiliated membership in 1992 was 7,757,000; the affiliation fee was £1.23 per member (TUC 1992: 1; 106).

32 This would not, however, cover course fees.

33 Chaired by John Edmonds of the GMB.

Chapter 10

The TUC and Trade Union Education: Retrospect and Prospect

Looking back, British trade union education has developed in several phases. Before the Great War, the way forward seemed to lie in the formation of a college of labour: initially at Ruskin in Oxford, where the 1909 strike sowed the seeds of later disputes. During and just after the Great War, with the general advance of the trade union and labour movement, local labour colleges and Workers' Educational Association branches took root around the country. Their advance tailed off from the mid-twenties, in step with the general fortunes of labour. Workers' education between the wars was also harmed by the bitter ideological dispute between the WEA and the National Council of Labour Colleges. Both were firmly lodged in the trade union movement, and the Trades Union Congress was too weak to override the feud. The state, certainly in the 1920s, was concerned to ensure the survival of the WEA and its supposedly moderating role. After a weak period in the later 1920s, both the NCLC and the WEA began to grow again in the early 1930s: this continued through to the war.

When peace came in 1945 Labour was swept to power. Trade union leaders had unprecedented influence. Many former WEA and NCLC tutors and students were themselves in government. The TUC's attitude continued to be influenced by its inter-war skirmishes with workers' education. Initially, it moved into education to fill a gap — in the area of courses strictly related to trade union organisation and bargaining at the workplace. Developments were modest through the 1950s: but it developed a number of perspectives and approaches which were to play their part later. A number of individual unions also began to organise their own training schemes, and together these trends eroded the WEA and NCLC hold on union education.

The educational bodies' self-confidence and sense of purpose were in any case weakened after the war. The NCLC and the WETUC element of the WEA had been committed to education for socialism, or at least for the labour movement: it was by no means clear what this meant in an era when Labour had achieved power. The natural constituency of workers' education — the intelligent worker prevented by the educational and social system from developing his (or her) potential — seemed to be fading as the Butler Act built on inter-war educational reforms. The WEA sought to find a solution to these dilemmas, and secured from the Creech Jones Report a novel and imaginative set of proposals: these, however, were hardly implemented partly for want of resources; partly, no doubt, because the WEA always has trouble making up its mind.

During the 1950s tutors in a number of university extra-mural departments, and some WEA districts, were experimenting with education for trade unionists as trade unionists — to a considerable extent after the model suggested by Creech Jones. These essays in Role Education or Industrial Studies continued through the 1960s, but the extra-mural world was clearly unable or — according to Barratt Brown (1986-87: 9) — unwilling, to devote very substantial resources to the education of trade unionists. The WEA's attitude was essentially similar. The fifties and sixties were years when social purpose was at a discount in the Association: even as late as 1979, well after the discussions on the Russell Report, it was quite unable to make a clear commitment to this field.

By the early 1960s the NCLC was clearly in terminal decline. It was also plain that the ideological gulf between the labour college and WEA traditions was no longer in reality deep; and while bitter competition between ideological enemies was debilitating, competition stripped of real theoretical justification was merely wasteful. The TUC moved to rationalise trade union education. Compared with the 1920s its status and authority were much enhanced. It also had a training college of its own. Still it took no chances. The NCLC and the WETUC were taken over, lock, stock and barrel: subsumed into the TUC's Education Department.

In the following few years, the Education Department evolved a fundamental strategy for union education. This centred on the training of workplace representatives. It sought to establish a comprehensive and standardised structure of provision, so that all union workplace representatives would be able to secure adequate training of good quality. It began to experiment with active educational methods. In the developing world of tripartism, the TUC also made three important assertions. First, union workplace representatives should be entitled to paid release from work for training. Second, training shop stewards was conducive to 'good industrial relations'. Third, courses for workplace representatives should be organised and run in the public sector, and justified the expenditure of public funds as much as any management course. During the 1960s a number of deals were struck with employers along these lines. But when the Heath government began to chip away at the terms of the 1960s settlement, asserting forcefully that training union representatives should be a joint affair between employers and unions, the TUC reacted strongly.

In its response to the Commission on Industrial Relations' proposals, the TUC added a major principle. Educating trade union representatives must be a matter for the unions themselves. The decision in 1975 to seek and accept public funds to pay for courses in colleges and other public

Retrospect and Prospect

educational bodies was made in the light of this attitude. Congress was keen to defend its autonomy as far as possible. The work would be 'education' — links should as far as possible be with the Department of Education and Science (and with the associated educational Inspectorate), rather than with the Department of Employment. Grants were to be made to the TUC, and it was for the TUC to allocate them to courses. Of course, there was a certain amount of fudging in this. The funds were provided for specific purposes. The rights to release with pay were on quite narrow terms. Employers could decide whether or not to release a shop steward in the light of the course syllabus (though in the final resort it was for industrial tribunals, and the courts, to decide). Nevertheless, it promised to provide the foundations of an imposing trade union education edifice.

It did. On them, a considerable fortress was quickly constructed. But after only a few years, a series of unimagined political and economic earthquakes shook the foundations. Despite this, during the first half of the eighties, the architects and masons of trade union education continued to design and build new wings and turrets. The aftershocks would soon subside: a comprehensive structure would be a lasting source of strength to the movement, and speed its recovery. But the tremors did not abate. By the later 1980s the architects and masons had been paid off, or redeployed. Maintenance was the order of the day. As financial problems mounted even this became difficult: some of the additions, opened with fanfare only a few years earlier, found their doors nailed unceremoniously shut. The main building survived, of course, its doors open, and still providing a valuable service. But the vaulting hopes of earlier days were all but forgotten.

Imagery aside, however, the TUC education scheme weathered the eighties rather better than a number of other educational institutions — and arguably rather better than the trade union movement itself. Local education authorities, universities, further education, non-vocational adult education, had all come under more damaging attack — or had defended themselves less effectively. The gravity of the eighties assault on union and TUC education should not be minimised. But it is well to keep it in perspective.

The successful defences of the eighties were grounded in the structures built in the seventies and earlier. The industrial relations institutions had largely succumbed to assault by the mid-1980s; the educational structures survived rather longer. But toward the end of the decade, the traditions of a locally-administered, publicly-funded, national education system were laid siege. By the early 1990s, bastions were crumbling: schools 'opted out', local education authorities lost their authority, further education became 'independent', educational inspection was privatised. The writing was on the wall for the '1975 settlement'. Trade union education in the

241

public sector might survive, but only if the movement could construct arrangements which would fit into the new educational order. In the early 1990s the TUC was struggling to make sense of an educational world in rapid change. Would there be an acceptable niche for union education? What could be done to ensure the best possible arrangements from a union point of view?

In negotiating any new arrangements, it was apparent that the trade union movement would — politically — be in a far weaker position than it had occupied in 1975. Not for Norman Willis, John Monks or Alan Grant the cosy meetings with Ministers at which Len Murray and Roy Jackson had paved the path to '1975'. Over the seventies and eighties the TUC and others in union education built an impressive network of institutional relationships and educational expertise. They would be invaluable assets in establishing a viable new position for union education: whether they would prove sufficient, time alone will tell.

The Politics of Public Funding

Could the tribulations of the eighties and early nineties have been avoided? Of course, the labour colleges were right: accepting state finance compromised union education's independence. They were also, sadly, wrong: British unions proved unable to provide funding for education on a major and continuing scale.[1] British union finances could not have sustained an educational scheme comparable to that built up by the TUC in the public sector in the 1970s and 1980s. And as the labour colleges' own record shows, while rejecting public funds may minimise *state* interference, it does not prevent problems over who controls union education. Neither does it prevent the state from finding other ways of intervening (from the 1920s WEA to the 1970s industrial training boards).

Given the decision to accept public funds, would union education have been better served by different structures? In particular, were the 1975 arrangements fatally flawed? While smacking of hindsight, such questions have rightly been raised, and some (cp TGWU 1983; SIT 1988) are inclined to answer them in the affirmative. The TUC itself argued by the mid-1980s that the 1975 provisions on paid release were proving too narrow. 'Relevant' course content should encompass 'wider education in those issues which affect workers, employment, the operation of industry and the local and national economies'. Some judgemental element was unavoidable in deciding how much paid release was 'reasonable', for the question was 'not capable of prescriptive resolution'. However, two legislative changes would help: a statutory minimum entitlement with 'legal support' for the TUC schedule of union education, and shifting the onus in the test of reasonableness in favour of the union representative. (TUC 1987a: 12.)

Although important, these TUC proposals did not strike at the heart of the 1975 settlement. (They were, of course, soon followed by statutory changes of a quite different order and inspiration.) Indeed, the TUC expressed some concern that, in any general extension of rights to paid educational leave, 'the need for TUC and trade union approved trade union education is not subsumed or relegated by the demands of vocational education and general education' (TUC 1987a: 12). Such concerns, in the political climate of the late 1980s, were not fanciful. Any extension of rights — even with strong European Community pressure — seemed unlikely: but if any were to occur, it would be driven by vocational training concerns and structures.

As representative of the trade union movement, and in its own institutional interests, the TUC had a vested interest in the terms of the 1975 arrangements. It negotiated them; they enshrined an important element of trade union control; they enabled the TUC to take a central role in the field; and they provided an important element of financial support to one of the main services which Congress offers to affiliated unions. It is not difficult to point out their weaknesses. History tests even the best-laid plans. Yet it is hard to see that, in the political and economic context of the mid-1970s, any much superior structure was feasible: still less today.

Three main types of alternative to the 1975 structures have been suggested. First, the unions could have argued for the distribution of additional, and 'earmarked', funds direct to the colleges, extra-mural departments and the WEA. The standard method in the 1970s would have been through additional staffing.[2] The educational institutions (extra-mural departments in particular) with well-established trade union programmes would clearly have liked this option. It would, however, have produced major problems of allocation — which institutions should receive the funds, and on what basis? Who should decide? Although there would, no doubt, have been HMI-inspired (and other) curriculum development events, it could only have led to a highly diverse system — a minimum of 'standardisation', and rather 'haphazard', to use favoured TUC terms. The field would also have been wide open to colonisation by a government agency — the CIR 'industrial relations training' strategy, for instance, might well have succeeded, had it not been for the wider campaign against the Industrial Relations Act.

Second, the unions might have secured direct funding for themselves, excluding the TUC. They could then have used the funds for their own direct provision, or purchased courses in educational institutions. In some respects, of course, the 1975 arrangements allowed for this, in that part of the grant made to the TUC was more or less directly forwarded to individual affiliated unions in support of their programmes. To have excluded the TUC would, however, have left the field without a co-ordinating body, again leaving the problems of diversity unresolved. (It would, to that extent, have been similar to the first option, but giving bargaining strength to the unions rather than the educational bodies.)

Under the third model, the government would have established an independent statutory body, with substantial trade union representation: an approach adopted in Australia at about the same time. Such an Authority (to adopt the Australian term) could provide programmes direct, through educational institutions, or through unions. Yet it is difficult to see how centralisation through a state agency, albeit with a degree of autonomy, would have been preferable to centralisation through a body under trade union control. It was introduced in Australia to solve a set of problems (far more intense multi-unionism, no real history of union education, few union courses, little contact between unions and educational bodies) which did not apply in Britain. Neither was it especially successful in insulating the field from political pressure — indeed, within three years of its formation, a change of government brought an end to union control in the Australian Authority. (Cupper 1980; Mealor 1981; Knox 1992.) A similar structure, established in New Zealand in 1986, survived only until 1991.

Supping with the state is always a risky business. In doing the deal of 1975 the trade union movement built a good number of safeguards. Grants were made to the TUC; the TUC could purchase courses from educational bodies; it was also provided with funds for course development, and this would ensure a strong measure of union input in course design. The subjects covered by public funding left a good deal of room for flexibility (the TUC was already firmly committed to a workplace-oriented approach). Recruitment to courses would be under trade union control. Courses would be within the educational sphere; the HMI would have a role; the Department of Employment was marginalised.[3] Regional education officers would oversee links with colleges, and — as far as possible — ensure that tutors shared trade union aims. Staff development for tutors would be provided by the TUC.

These measures proved remarkably successful in ensuring trade union control. However, placing the TUC firmly at centre-stage had (perhaps unforeseen) disadvantages. When disputes arose over the curriculum, or over resource allocation (and if there was to be a co-ordinated strategy, they were bound to arise in some form), it was the TUC which bore the stigma of making and executing unpopular decisions.

George Woodcock, in the early 1960s, had taken an uncompromising stand against devolution of educational authority from the General Council

Education Committee. Woodcock was an instinctive centraliser. He also (understandably) despised the torrid and crippling debates which had marred WEA-labour college relations. The centralising of authority meant that the Congress could act decisively in the educational sphere. It is hard to see, for instance, how the TUC could have moved so rapidly to seeking public funds in 1974 and 1975, had its educational decision-making been encumbered by having first to consult a network of specialist advisory committees or conferences. The very delicate, and essentially bureaucratic, discussions with government through the eighties, by which public funding and educational independence were defended, would have become far more complex. At the same time, the absence of such structures could rob the TUC of legitimacy when dealing with the educational sector: some disputes, particularly those over resources (and those involving extra-mural departments), became harder to resolve.

Curriculum: Changing Concepts of Relevance

Institutions and politics are, however, only part of the story. Against this unfolding backdrop, tutors and shop stewards taught and studied, in and out of class. In the process, there was a progression of teaching methods and styles, and of course content, orientation, and subject-matter. Between the wars a great deal of labour college and WETUC provision was in what the Russell Committee later referred to as social and political education: politics, social and economic history, trade union history, economics. The chief difference between the educational organisations was the Marxist orientation of the labour colleges. During the later 1920s and the 1930s, to be sure, both traditions began to include more 'practical' subjects in their curricula: debating, public expression, chairmanship, and so forth, oriented to some of the practical tasks which now faced both trade union and political members of the labour movement.

After the Second World War, the educational bodies remained committed to this type of curriculum, though trade union and working class students were increasingly difficult to recruit. At the same time the TUC and various unions were developing courses related to practical questions of bargaining and union organisation. And in the extra-mural and WEA world, tutors were beginning to experiment with what became known as Role Education and Industrial Studies. After the formation of the TUC scheme proper in 1964, the curriculum moved toward courses related to practical tasks confronting workplace union representatives: organisation, bargaining, health and safety, work study, and so forth.

This trend did not abate. In the 1970s it strengthened. In the TUC curriculum, union organisational development and bargaining dominated in the courses for workplace representatives. Wider issues were covered in courses for trade unionists in general (rather than workplace representatives in particular). These were outside the day release ambit, and often failed to recruit many students. Although during the 1980s a more diverse and issue-oriented range of provision was introduced through the short course programme, this was still almost entirely linked back to practical workplace tasks.

As content changed, so did the duration of the courses in which it was covered. Three developments stand out. First, the TUC in 1975 discontinued its programme of week-end schools. These had been valued by tutors and students, and had played a part in sustaining the shop stewards movement of the 1960s and early 1970s. However, in comparison with day-release courses, they were costly and difficult to justify. Second, to adopt a ten-day model for the TUC day-release programme implied not following the model developed by some extra-mural departments, particularly in association with the nationalised industries. These long courses, typically extending over one, two or three years, had much to commend them. The educational possibilities over such periods are clearly greater than in a ten day course. Such an approach would, however, necessarily have meant educating a far smaller number of union representatives. Finally, in the 1980s the shift to short courses, motivated largely by expediency, did at least mean the introduction of a variety of topical programmes.

Turning from content to method, we can make a number of assertions. In inter-war labour college and WETUC classes, the educational methods used were essentially those of the universities: the lecture, generally followed by class discussion. Serious thought was put into how to enhance clarity of exposition; and occasionally experiments seem to have been made in role playing. But it would not be unfair to characterise teaching in this period as tutor-centred. The chief, if important, qualification is the emphasis placed on self-study and reading, with both WEA and NCLC — especially the latter — issuing valuable text-books and guides to reading, and on writing (though this was more common in the WEA than the labour colleges). After 1945, all the traditions moved away from the lecture as the chief method of teaching trade unionists. We find the development of documentary teaching, of widespread use of case studies, of role-playing.

From the late 1970s the TUC programme moved vigorously in the direction not merely of student-centred, but of group-centred, approaches. This, partly a matter of contemporary fashion, seems to have been based on two types of assumption. There was a belief that student-centred approaches were more effective for adult students, and particularly for adult students who returned to study after many years away, and after — very often — an unrewarding experience of school in any case. In addition, there was a realisation that such students had substantial reservoirs of experience and knowledge, which should not be dismissed. On the other hand, the group-centred approaches seem to have involved assumptions about trade union democracy: that it is appropriate for union classes to function — in terms of decision-making and so on — in a manner analogous to how unions themselves should function. This was, at one level, a point of simple principle, associated with the commitment to union control of courses. At another level, however, it rested on assumptions about the educational value of being involved in decision-making processes if real learning about democracy is to take place.

This trend was, however, linked to a downplaying of the subject content of courses. This was strongest in the courses for workplace representatives: in the early 1980s, consideration of standards — collective agreements, the law — was largely dispensed with, on the argument that union strength is founded on workplace organisation. Standards, especially the law, it was said, could be changed by hostile governments (or employers). This bizarre position ignored the critical reality that union workplace organisation stems very largely from the effective use of standards.[4] Fortunately, this view was never applied with full rigour to the Health and Safety courses, and a more balanced approach emerged from the mid-1980s. Fortunately, too, in the 1980s tutors were more and more supplementing their core materials locally. Downplaying subject content did mean, perversely and perhaps accidentally, that the TUC materials were (in the party political sense) extremely uncontroversial, and this may have helped avoid public disputes during the early 1980s.[5]

The TUC and Trade Union Education

A principal theme of this book has been the emergence of the TUC as a national educational institution: now one of very few wholly committed to workers' education. Its educational activities have, however, been either ignored or scorned. To students of industrial relations, union education has been a side-issue, a peripheral activity of institutions which are properly to be judged by their bargaining capacity. Among most of those who study adult education, the TUC's work has seemed outside the main avenues of educational concern.[6] For a few, finally and fortunately, it has been a subject worthy of serious research: too often, however, their approach has been clouded by a strong sense that the TUC's record represents a betrayal of truer, broader forms of workers' education.

That the TUC has presided over a narrowing of the focus of union education is undeniable: this was quite explicitly one of its aims, at least from the mid-1960s. Its case was precisely that the record of workers' education up to that time, heroic and glorious as it was, had also utterly failed to provide the movement with a coherent and rigorous programme which met union aims and objectives. It did not suggest that other forms of workers' education were improper: only that they were not priorities for the trade union movement, and should be conducted largely by other agencies.[7] The assumption was that the 'Movement',[8] acting collectively through its legitimate central body, could identify needs, and plan, design and carry through an educational programme which would meet those needs — and could do so more effectively than if education remained on a 'haphazard' basis.

This was a major programme of modernisation in British workers' education, and it is now hard to imagine that the field would have been stronger without it. But if the TUC sought to modernise, its project was also very much a 'modernist' one. The language used to justify change in the 1960s and 1970s — 'comprehensive', 'standardisation', 'co-ordination' — has little resonance today. The mechanisms by which it pursued its aims were those of a former age (there is a strong air of C.P. Snow about the TUC documents of the period). The TUC was (as in many respects it remains) a product of the era of planning, of centralisation, of belief in the rationality of bureaucracy, of confidence in the conscious judgement of men and women as the best basis for organising human affairs. Contemporary fashion has little time for such views: but human projects are inevitably fashioned from the ideas of their time.

Educational innovation, particularly on a large scale, is never a painless affair, and rarely made without error and injustice. In certain respects the TUC's outlook and character adversely affected the field. Like all human institutions, the 1970s TUC was far from perfect. The TUC Education Department found itself quite suddenly dominant — a reversal of fortunes which seems to have taken TUC educators rather by surprise. As late as 1974 we find Dennis Winnard (in a letter to Frank Pickstock, 22 March 1974: TUC file 817) complaining of the extra-mural departments' 'patronising manner', their 'arrogance', and their 'surprising ignorance of our aims and policies'. For a few years, in the late 1970s and early 1980s, the boot was definitely on the other foot: the TUC could choose its own partners, and did so. Its decisions were sometimes arbitrary. Hard choices had to be made. Collaborators who preferred the old rules might protest that the game had changed: but so it had.

The TUC's educational self-image throughout the post-war period has been as a provider and organiser of trade union education. Its orientation has been toward issues of programme design and management, from writing course materials to resource allocation. In these areas, especially during the seventies and eighties, it record was remarkable. But with the expansion of its education in the 1970s, there was a profound need for deeper research into problems of labour relations: research whose results could be used in the design and development of union educational materials. Regrettably, the TUC never recognised the link between union education and industrial relations research — at least until the late 1980s, when it was too late to secure funds. (Neither has it seen a significant role for itself in promoting social research, even in areas such as labour relations.) Certainly in the 1960s and 1970s the TUC could have established — and secured funding for — strong links with research institutions in higher education. These would also, at least until the 1980s, have enabled it to do rather more by way of setting the labour relations agenda.

But even with this failure, the expansion of trade union studies provision suggested that the extent of union-oriented research in the field would increase. A significant number of academic staff would now be committed to teaching programmes in association with the TUC. This expansion in union-oriented research hardly occurred, and for two main reasons. First, the TUC's fragile relations with extra-mural departments — many of whose staff felt that its approach to union education was excessively narrow, and would damage their own programmes — implied continuing tension between the TUC and its main potential research collaborators in the universities. Some extra-mural departments had groups of trade union studies lecturers, some very able. More could have been made of them, but for the over-riding priority of instituting the new programme, and for the tendency to see disagreement as opposition. Second, as the TUC began more and more to collaborate with further, rather than higher, education (an inevitable decision, given the unco-operative attitude of many extra-mural departments, and the unpredictability of the WEA), it distanced itself from institutions with commitment to research. At the same time, therefore, as creating a field of trade union studies, with (relatively) large numbers of tutors committed to its teaching, it failed to exploit the opportunity to develop trade union studies research.

This has had a profound influence on the field, which has remained theoretically and empirically under-developed. Several years ago, Vulliamy (1985: 26) suggested that the debates 'on the politics of educational methods suggest the beginnings of the development of a theory of trade union education'. In fact, however, significant contributions to debate about politics and method in trade union education are not new: indeed, they are the very stuff of the history of union education. The contributions of Clunie (1920), Casey (1979), Gibbons (1927), and Hodgen (1925) in the 1920s, for instance, were very much concerned with appropriate content and method in workers' education. The Creech Jones Report (WEA 1953), Williams (1954), Clegg and Adams (1959), were concerned with similar questions — though their solutions were rather different. *Training Shop Stewards* was, if nothing else, deeply concerned with educational method. The pages of *The Industrial Tutor* and *Trade Union Studies Journal*[9] are replete with these issues. The problem is that such consideration of method and politics, while contributing to debate, has proved an inadequate base for a field of studies.

No theory of trade union education has emerged. It is truly remarkable that no book-length study has been published (aside from a single edited volume of — rather slight — essays (Schuller 1980)) since Clegg and Adams reported in 1959: there is, in fact, no full-length treatment of British trade union education whatever, apart from official and semi-official reports. The authorities cited by McIlroy (1985a) illustrate this: they are general, and by no means socialist, adult education texts such as Knowles (1970) and Jarvis (1983). Much of the early 1980s debate on methods and politics in trade union education was conducted by reference to research on child-centred learning in schools (cp Brown et al 1983; Gowan 1982; Edwards et al. 1983).

At the same time, the research contributions to academic literature of the early 1980s went largely unnoticed in the trade union studies world. Schuller and Robertson (1983), for example, provided important evidence of the role of existing union organisation in determining what a union representative learns from trade union education. Yet it is difficult to find a single reference to this in the pages of *The Industrial Tutor* or *Trade Union Studies Journal*. Unless union education can develop a body of sustained enquiry, research, and debate — another sign of this would be the emergence of fuller-length studies — it is difficult to be sanguine about the arrival of a theory of trade union education. Needless to say, the less than optimistic prospects for the practice of union education do not suggest a secure foundation. Significant funding for trade union studies research is likely to depend on whether the promotion of 'good industrial relations' again becomes a matter of public policy: this does not appear imminent. The result may well be that the literature on union education will continue to be marked by sporadic interventions of an essentially political nature, rather than by sustained empirical research relevant to practice.

A Road Ahead?

The fortunes of British workers' education have always been inextricably linked to the fortunes of the labour movement. Trade union education — sadly, perhaps the only part of workers' education which retains vitality — is no exception. The notion that trade unions should develop a form of education which primarily addresses the needs of trade unions and trade

Retrospect and Prospect

unionists took root between the wars. From 1945 it was nurtured by the TUC, and by a growing number of unions. Its increasing importance was linked to the unions' new role in post-war welfare state, and to their sense that workplace bargaining was an unavoidable, and highly desirable, element of a healthy democracy. This view extended beyond the trade unions themselves into a range of educational institutions (the WEA, the labour colleges, the extra-mural departments, further education colleges), though each formed its own characteristic approach.

For three decades (roughly the years since 1964), the TUC has dominated this world. The various unions and educational organisations have enjoyed some autonomy and influence, but the TUC has set the rules of the game. It has promoted its approach to union education, reaching a zenith with its negotiations with government in the 1970s. It has defended this approach with skill and determination: primarily against the state (hostile when not unsympathetic), but no less doggedly against alternative approaches to education (particularly when they have seemed to threaten its terms of settlement with the state). During this period its authority has been cemented both by its general authority in the trade union movement (virtually unchallenged until the mid-1980s), and by its ability to secure funding from government.

The prospect of the loss of this funding, albeit on a phased basis, raises many issues. Will it help British industry to become more efficient and productive? Unless motivated solely by ideology and spite, the government presumably believes that it will. Their underlying assumption has, of course, long been that unions have nothing to contribute (other than through being weak) to improving industrial relations. On this rationale, the decision is entirely sensible. Unfortunately for the nation, this approach has been resolutely pursued by both Thatcher and Major governments over fourteen years. It has led neither to economic prosperity nor industrial regeneration; but rather the reverse. Unpalatable as it may be to many, unless British labour is integrated into a national economic strategy and sense of purpose, committed to rebuilding the economy, it is difficult to see how economic decline can be reversed. Such an integration must, in the British context, accept that labour's interests are expressed most effectively through trade unions — which, weakened though they are, represent still some forty per cent of the nation's workforce.

Of course, unions *are* now far weaker than they were in the sixties and seventies, and many employers will no doubt continue to exercise their 'right to manage' (or mismanage) with little regard to the views of workers' elected representatives. Some take the view that high levels of unemployment are now a permanent feature of the British scene, and that unions can continue to be ignored with impunity. The prospects on this scenario are, however, dismal: economic decline, growing poverty, social decay, disaffection. If, on the contrary, governments plan for sustained growth, for renewed high levels of employment — for plenty, not poverty — then a renewed union role is unavoidable. At the level of economic management, therefore, the government's decision is at best shortsighted.

The end of public funding will, in all probability, lead to a reduction of educational opportunity for active trades unionists, for it is difficult to see how the union movement can match the finances of the Department of Employment. (Even if it can, the burden will shift from the taxpayer to the trade unionist: the net effect will be regressive.) At the least, it will alter and narrow the pattern of educational options open to trades unionists. The actual impact remains, of course, to be seen, and will depend greatly on the unity and effectiveness of the movement's response.

Will trade unionism be strengthened? Some old labour collegers may well incline to this belief. Independence of the state is, in principle, desirable. Certainly *if* the unions could collaborate to create, and finance, a national and co-ordinated educational structure comparable in scale to current programmes, the result would be positive. This seems a remote possibility. Most likely, unions will be weaker. Just as staff training (or 'human resource development') is vital to employers for maintaining skill, knowledge and commitment among their employees, so education is unions' main mechanism for organisational development at the workplace. Indeed, it is probably more important now than in the past. Full-time officers were never able to make more than a token contribution to workplace organisation; their time is today in ever shorter supply. Erosion of union organisation means newly-elected shop stewards are typically less experienced than in the 1970s. They have fewer supportive and experienced colleagues from whom to learn 'on the job'. More, union representatives have in almost every respect a more difficult role than when employers act responsibly, when procedures are followed, when routine rules.

How will the loss of funding affect the future of the TUC, and the politics of the trade union movement? Here we are in less predictable waters. In the later 1980s, senior TUC officials began to realise how important its educational activities were. Long perceived as a minor 'extra', peripheral to the main activities of Congress as political representative of the movement and arbiter in inter-union disputes, education is now seen to be a major service to affiliates. With much of the TUC's political authority gone, such services matter. Yet amalgamation is the order of the day; the 'mega-unions' can provide more and more services 'in-house'. The TUC therefore faces the risk of declining, as the General Federation of Trade Unions before it, into providing services for a dwindling band of small unions. While the TUC is likely to survive — if it did not exist, unions would have to invent some other mechanism for co-operation — its authority in the movement will depend on how far it is able to sustain major roles in a range of areas.

In education, clearly, the TUC has played a central and invaluable role, at least since 1964. It has dealt with government; it has secured funding for its affiliates' programmes as for its own. Can it maintain its position in years ahead? The omens are mixed. Without public funds to dispense, its position as a purchaser of college resources will be difficult to maintain. This will be compounded if fees rise steeply. A large-scale loss of college tutors would be extremely harmful, for they form much of the TUC's fund of educational expertise. With fewer regional education officers, nurturing and defending this network will be more difficult. A great deal of careful diplomacy and strategic planning is called for to persuade affiliated unions to make good a significant proportion of the lost funding. And there is always the risk that government will attack on other fronts, perhaps by reducing further (or eliminating) the legal right to paid release.

On the other hand, the TUC has a strong position in the field. Since the late 1980s it has moved adroitly to ensure that its role is based not simply on provision of low-cost resources, but on central features of the curriculum. This began with the recognition that full-time officer training could be a major TUC strength, and has continued through the development of standards of competence for lay representatives. There are, of course, important arguments to be made against formal assessment of adult education in general, and union education in particular. Equally, we should retain a healthy scepticism about the notion of 'competence' and its applicability in the education of (particularly lay) trade unionists.[10] Outcomes in union education must always retain some unpredictability. But curriculum is about power as well as educational ideal.

The trade union movement now faces two critical problems. How can the movement maintain (and extend) the strongest possible programme of union education? How can union control of the curriculum best be maintained? It is, of course, easy to maintain control of a programme which is wholly union-financed. The difficulty is that it would be triflingly small. The TUC has always sought to maximise union control, and thus relevance to union needs, but within the public sector with its much greater resources. There is, however, a further dimension. If the programme under union control is small, the field is likely to be colonised by employer-sponsored 'joint' training, so prevalent in the years before 1975. Already some hard-pressed colleges and WEA districts have been tempted by the 'high' fees which many employers can offer. Trade union control would soon be a dead letter. The movement must, therefore, seek a mechanism to ensure that union courses follow a union curriculum.

In these circumstances, establishing a Lead Body for trade union education, under trade union auspices, may prove an effective option. It could form the cornerstone of a viable strategy for maintaining a substantial programme of education relevant to union aims. It would integrate union courses more into the structures of adult and further education: this may be thought a mixed blessing, but will be advantageous to many students. It would provide routes along which students can progress to further study and qualification. It offers another potential advantage. It would call on the movement to conduct a clearly-focussed review of its training aims (a process already under way), for centrally-developed standards will set parameters for all union education. To date, while very much in command of its own courses, the TUC has enjoyed little influence (and no control) over the curricula developed by its individual affiliates. In the 1970s it proposed a structure for training, but unions paid little heed. A Lead Body would not control unions' curricula as such, but its influence would be profound. The result could well be a more closely integrated curriculum for trade union education, with more effective structural linkages between (still diverse) programmes offered by the TUC, individual unions, colleges, WEA districts and universities.

None of this is inevitable. The resource problems will not disappear: though limited external finance may be secured, the movement must expect its members to bear a larger share of the costs of union education. Agreed standards may help, to the extent of reducing competition between unions and other providers based on cost alone (without reference to effectiveness or quality). Major dangers will remain. Concentration on 'competence' may reduce the scope for free inquiry in the curriculum. For unions, colleges and tutors, there will be a financially-inspired temptation to identify a 'core' of irredeemably union-related material (to be delivered or approved by unions themselves), with other competencies to be developed in joint courses. This would be 'industrial relations training' by the back door.

Most of all, however, the trade union movement must ensure that a Lead Body has strong legitimacy. The criteria and procedures for establishment of standards, for recognition or approval of courses, must be seen to be appropriate and fair. Such legitimacy could hardly be achieved other than through the Trades Union Congress, but there is a strong case for new advisory structures, involving expertise from the education sector. If this can be achieved, the TUC may establish a new, and central, role in union education, adding to its authority in the movement and the nation.

This will, however, represent a change of direction, with administrative implications for the TUC. The Trade Union Education Department (and the Education Department before it) has long been primarily concerned with course development and provision. With skill and luck, these functions will continue on an important scale. Even so, the activities associated with taking on a Lead Body role will be significantly different, and will call for reorganisation of the Department's work. (One particular concern, for example, will be to ensure that approval procedures are seen to be independent of the TUC's own interests in course provision.) At the same time, the Lead Body role must not dominate the thinking of the Department. This may be difficult to avoid. (The politics of provision dominated the Education Department in the early 1980s.) But the Department must preserve its independence of judgement, and its structural ability to act decisively in the interests of the trade union movement.

Until the process of review which began when the General Council identified full-time officer training as a priority in 1990, TUC thinking had advanced little beyond tactical defence of the status quo (complemented by important, if diversionary, internal struggles). Standards, competencies, and the Lead Body role by no means solve the problems which now threaten union education. They do, however, provide some basis for a strategy. Whether the TUC can build from this foundation, construct a plan of action and marshal its forces effectively to carry it through, remains to be seen. The TUC has a good record of political achievement in education, but success is far from certain. Better plans have foundered on the movement's contradictions and jealousies.

The stakes are high. Union education's traditions and achievements stretch back over a century. In its various forms, workers' education has played no small part in the formation and periodic restructuring of the British labour movement. For some forty years, trade union education has been a central feature of workers' education; the TUC and its Education Department have been fundamental to its growth. Largely unsung, education has become a major area of union and TUC activity. Trades unions' organisation rests very largely on their lay officials at the workplace: education is now a vital method for developing the abilities, attitudes and morale of these men and women. Few unions — still less the TUC — would now mount a campaign without an educational component; some campaigns consist of little else. The movement's ability to support its voluntary organisers, to organise campaigns, to shift opinion at the workplace, to improve (or resist the erosion of) working conditions, will be severely impaired unless its educational work can be sustained. TUC education — its expertise in course design and development, its networks of tutors and organisers, its workplace contacts, its political skills — is an invaluable resource. On its future, the prospects of trade union education as a whole rest.

1. Not only British unions: few trade union movements have successfully raised funding from their members for substantial programmes of trade union and workers' education. In Britain, the NCLC experience comes nearest to contradicting this assertion, and while their record was a proud one, as we have seen, it was also flawed.
2. This would have carried through, on a far more ambitious scale, the approach suggested in the 1950s by the Creech Jones (WEA 1953) and Clegg-Adams (1959) reports. It was also implicit in the Gold report (DES 1972).
3. To begin with. The DE's ability to re-establish a central role for itself, which suggests a firm determination to do so, is an issue which needs further exploration.
4. This point was well shown in some of the industrial relations literature, then beginning to emerge, on how shop stewards mobilise opinion in the workplace. See, e.g., Armstrong, Goodman and Hyman (1981); Batstone, Boraston, and Frenkel (1977).
5. Political, economic or historical material had never been a major part of TUC course materials (although certain more specialist courses, such as Rights at Work, had rather more such content). But TUC courses in this period also played down legal and industrial relations standards, and how to use them.
6. In the fields of both industrial relations and education, there was a brief period in the late 1970s and very early 1980s when workers' education seemed to merit research and publication. Thus in industrial relations journals, Coyne and Wright (1982), Cupper (1980), and Schuller and Henderson (1980), all result from research initiated in the late 1970s. In the education literature, apart from the mainly historical articles by McIlroy, only Burkitt (1982), Fieldhouse (1981), Fisher (1984), Mackie (1983, 1986), and Schuller and Robertson (1983) appeared in scholarly journals. Outside this period, little has been published in mainstream academic journals (apart, again, from the work of McIlroy and his co-authors). Banks (1966), Brown and Lawson (1973), Robinson (1968), and the classic Senturia (1930) are the chief exceptions.
7. Especially the WEA and extra-mural departments. The TUC was, however, at times concerned about the 'persistent tendency' of the WEA 'to include some element of "liberal" workers' education' in TUC courses. This was 'resisted' by the Education Department as 'it introduced a confusion of purpose into the facilities in question, diminished the value of facilities from the point of view of trade union education, and tended to introduce into course syllabuses subjects which could not be effectively studied within the available time' (Education Committee document 5/2, 6 April 1971).
8. In TUC documents, the 'trade union Movement' is almost invariably spelt with a very definite initial capital 'M'.
9. *The Industrial Tutor*, the journal of the Society of Industrial Tutors,

commenced publication in 1969. *Trade Union Studies Journal*, first issued by the WEA in 1980, was discontinued in 1990.

10 This notion of competence is critically discussed by Field (1991). Field and Weller (1992) survey trade union attitudes to National Vocational Qualifications.

Appendix A: Course Materials Issued by the TUC Education Service 1977–1992

Below are listed trade union educational course materials issued by the Trades Union Congress education service during the period 1977-1992. The list is designed to give some impression of the range of issues dealt with in TUC programmes, and how these have developed. Whilst it attempts to be as full a listing as possible, it makes no claim to be complete. Materials issued after January 1992 are not included. Note that the titles given are of duplicated or printed course *materials*: titles of courses taught were not always identical.

No attempt has been made to distinguish materials issued for courses financed from public funds from those developed for 'campaign workshops' and other courses financed directly from TUC funds. Course materials listed range from printed packages or booklets to duplicated sets of 'activities'; in length they vary from a few pages to several hundred. No attempt has been made to distinguish between these. Tutors' notes issued by the TUC are included on the same basis, and marked 'T'.

Where a month of publication is given, this is included in brackets. Undated materials are listed under the year in which the present author believes them to have been issued, but are marked 'n.d.' Reprints which incorporate no revisions are not included.

Certain materials issued in recent years have been given a 'number' by the TUC: this is included, where available, in square brackets.

1977

Introductory Course for Union Representatives ['Red Pack'] — 10 sections (Your Job as a Shop Steward; Trade Union Organisation; Terms and Conditions; Disputes and Grievances; Discipline at Work; Job Security; Rights at Work — Employment Law; Organising for Safer Work; Industrial Democracy; Skills for Shop Stewards).
Introductory Course for Union Representatives in the National Health Service ['Blue Pack'] — 10 sections, essentially as above.
Basic Introductory Course for Union Representatives in Local Government ['Green Pack'] 10 sections, essentially as above.
Basic Trade Unionism. A Short TUC Postal Course
Basic Trade Unionism. Postal Course Workbook (n.d.)
Health and Safety at Work — A short course for union safety reps

Appendices

1978

Health and Safety Materials for Distribution to Course Students, Revised Pack, September [?]
Work Study, Productivity and Pay — Management and Productivity (n.d.)
Work Study, Productivity and Pay — Method Study (n.d.)
Work Study, Productivity and Pay — Time Study (n.d.)
Work Study, Productivity and Pay — Standard Times and Incentive Schemes (n.d.)
Work Study, Productivity and Pay — Predetermined Motion Time Systems (PMTS) (n.d.)
Rights at Work [Duplicated pack] (n.d.)
Rights at Work — Objectives, Structures, Methods (n.d.) (T)

1979

Working with Figures — A trade unionist's guide to calculations for bargaining (January; reprinted with amendments May)
Health and Safety at Work: A Course for Union Representatives — 7 booklets. 1: *The Safety Rep and Union Organisation*; 2: *Health and Safety and the Law*; 3: *Information for Safety Reps*; 4: *Skills for Safety Reps*; 5: *Work Hazards: Fire/Lighting/Lifting/VDUs*; 6: *Noise at Work*; 7: *Chemical Hazards at Work* (August)
Rights at Work [printed pack] — 12 sections: Disclosure of Information; The Legal Framework; The Contract of Employment; Equal Opportunities and Race Relations; Collective Bargaining and the Law; Wages and Conditions; Discipline and Dismissal; Union Organisation; Women's Rights; Job Security; Social Security; Skills. (August)
Rights at Work — Sample Case Studies (August)
TUC Day Release Course Outlines (February) (T)
Rights at Work — Notes for Tutors (T)
Health and Safety at Work — Tutors' Notes (T)

1980

TUC Introductory Course — Supplement for Union Representatives in Local Government
Workshops on the Conservative Government's Employment Bill — Resource Materials
Workshops on the Conservative Government's Employment Bill — Case Studies, Tasks, Activities
Workshops on the Conservative Government's Employment Bill — Additional Resource Materials

Union Education in Britain: A TUC Activity

The TUC Case Against the Employment Bill (March)
The New Technology — Materials for TUC Short Course on the New Technology (n.d.)
The New Technology — Agreements, Samples, Models (n.d.)
New Technology — Case Studies (August)
Health and Safety at Work, second edition — 7 books, titles as for first edition (August)
Case Studies — Basic Course for Union Reps (August)
Educational Methods — Case Studies Produced by Union Officers (n.d.)
New Technology — Tutor's Notes (n.d.) (T)
Health and Safety at Work Day Release Course — Tutor's Notes, Second Edition (T)
Revised Tutors' Notes — Basic Course for Union Reps (August)

1981

Unemployment: the fight for TUC alternatives, first edition (January)
Unemployment: the fight for TUC alternatives, second edition (February)
Beat the Act [Employment Act 1980] (March)
New Technology and Collective Bargaining — a workbook for union reps (March)
The Chip at Work — a discussion book on new technology
New Technology Resource File (n.d.)
Stage 1 — Bargaining Workbook (August)
Stage 1 — Organisation Workbook (August)
Stage 1 — Skills Workbook (August)
Social Security Benefits: Representing Members Before National Insurance Local Tribunals and Supplementary Benefit Appeal Tribunals (n.d.)
Social Security Benefits: Part Two — Preparing a Case to a Supplementary Benefits Appeal Tribunal (n.d.)
Stage 1 Course for Union Reps: Tutors' Notes — Day by Day Guide and Book Commentary (T)
Stage 1 Course for Union Reps: Tutors' Notes — Aims (T)
Stage 1 Course for Union Reps: Tutors' Notes — Methods (T)
Stage 1 Course for Union Reps: Tutors' Notes — Main Themes (T)
Stage 2 Course for Union Reps: Briefing Notes (May) (T)

1982

Defend Your Unions — The New Legal Attack — Selected Activities (n.d.)
Defend Your Unions — The New Legal Attack — Activities (n.d.)
Defend Your Unions — A TUC Workbook (May)
Stage 2 Course for Union Reps — Briefing Notes (February)
Stage 2 Course for Union Reps — Case Studies (n.d.)
Stage 2 Course for Union Reps — Projects: Examples (n.d.)

Stage 2 Course for Union Reps — Tutor Reports Jan.–April 1982, Sample Activities, Leaflets and Bulletins
Stage 2 Course for Union Reps — Bulletins, Leaflets, Reports Produced by Union Reps
Stage 2 Course for Union Reps — Sample Materials
Sick Pay: Employers Sick Pay Schemes; Self-Certification; Statutory Sick Pay. TUC Course for Union Reps (August)
Health and Safety at Work: Case Studies (by Peter Caldwell)
Sick Pay: Tutor's Notes (September) (T)

1983

Update Workshop on Pesticides (n.d.)
Youth Training Scheme: Workshops for Union Negotiators (n.d.)
MSC's Youth Training Scheme: TUC Handbook (draft, March)
New Technology for NGA (n.d.)
TUC Workbook on Racism
Stage 1 — Organisation Workbook, first revision (March)
Stage 1 — Bargaining Workbook, first revision (April)
Privatisation in the NHS — TUC Workshops (November)
Course for Trade Union Discussion Leaders (December)
Working Women — A TUC Discussion Book for all trade unionists
Bargaining Information [10-day] Course for Union Representatives (December)
Methods in Trade Union Education (November) (T)

1984

Union Strategies and Sexual Harassment (January)
Learning About Trade Unions — Activities and Case Studies (January)
Using 'Working Women' on General TUC Courses —Tutors Notes and Case Studies (February) (T)
Young Workers and Unions (February)
Communication Skills: A TUC Short Course (July)
Equal Pay for Work of Equal Value (August)
Health and Safety at Work — Hazards File: Temperature (December)
Health and Safety at Work — Hazards File: First Aid at Work (December)
Health and Safety at Work — Hazards File: Lighting at Work (December)
Health and Safety at Work — Hazards File: Young Workers (December)
Health and Safety at Work — Hazards File: Workers with Disabilities (December)

Health and Safety at Work — Hazards File: Smoking at Work (December)
Health and Safety at Work — Hazards File: Alcohol and Work (December)
Health and Safety at Work — Hazards File: Noise (December)
Stage 1 — Bargaining Workbook, second revision (December)
Stage 1 — Skills Workbook, first revision (December)
Working Women — How to use the book in discussions (January) (T)
Technology at Work — Guidance Notes (February) (T)
Learning About Trade Unions — How to Use the Book (February) (T)
Developments in TUC Health and Safety Courses (January) (T)
Tutor's Notes: New Materials for TUC Health and Safety Courses (n.d.) (T)

1985

Health and Safety at Work, completely revised [i.e., third edition] (January)
Health and Safety at Work — Hazards File: Asbestos
Health and Safety at Work — Hazards File: Stress
Health and Safety at Work — Hazards File: Advising Members — Benefits and Damages
Health and Safety at Work — Hazards File: Machinery
Health and Safety at Work — Hazards File: Reproductive Hazards
Women and Pensions (August)
Our Right to a Voice — Trade Unions and the Political Levy: Briefings for Union Officers and Tutors (January)
Our Right to a Voice — Trade Unions and the Political Levy: Union Examples (January)
Our Right to a Voice — Trade Unions and the Political Fund: Fire Brigades Union (November). [Note: packs such as this were produced for many unions in relation to the ballots on maintaining political funds required by the Trade Union Act 1984.]
Trade Unions and the Economy: Activities, Workplace Reports, Sources of Information (November)
Understanding Your Local Council — Services and Jobs in Local Government [developed by TUC Education and the Local Government Information Unit] (December)
Health and Safety at Work: Reporting of Injuries, Diseases and Dangerous Occurrences Regulations 1985 (December)
Tutors' Notes: Introductory Course for Union Reps: Stage 1 Developments 1984-85 (T)
The Study of Economics on TUC Courses: Background, Tutors' Comments, Sample Materials (March) (T)
TUC Workbook on Racism: Guidance Notes for Tutors (July) (T)

1986

Attacks on State Benefits — Activities (January)
Attacks on State Benefits — The System Now; Government Plans; Campaign Points (January)
Our Right to a Voice — National Communications Union Clerical Group Campaign for a Political Fund: Workbook and Fact Sheets
Women's Health — at the Workplace (April) [28]
Computers and TUC Education. Aims, Methods, Outline (October)
Stage 1 — Organisation Workbook, third revision (March)
Flexibility at Work — A Workbook for Trade Union Studies Courses (April) [66]
Tackling Racism: A Course for Union Activists (April) [37]
Youth Training Schemes — Fact Sheets (June) [22]
Baking Industry Hours of Work, third edition (June) [24]
Understanding Your Local Council — Campaigning and Local Government Structure: How Councils are Structured and How they Operate; How Councils can be Influenced; How to Build Alliances to influence the Council [TUC Education & LGIU] (June) [23]
Understanding Your Local Council — Services and Jobs in Local Government, TUC Education & LGIU, second edition (October) [33]
Understanding Your Local Council — Local Government Finance: Where the Money Comes From; Where the Money Goes to; Who Makes Decisions, [TUC Education & LGIU]
Work Study in the NHS (August)
Stage 1 — Bargaining Workbook, third revision (September)
Trade Unions and Young People (October)
TUC Open School — A Guide (October)
TUC Introductory Courses Stage 1: Notes for Tutors — Changes in the Organisation Book (April) (T)
Trade Unions and the Economy — Notes for Tutors (January) (T)

1987

Beating Apartheid — Resource Pack: Campaign Skills (January)
Beating Apartheid — Campaign Briefings (January)
Beating Apartheid — Resource Pack: Issues (January)
Beating Apartheid — Resource Pack: Activities (January)
Trade Unions and Young Workers: YTS: Work in Progress — Tutors Pack (January) [58] (T)
Trade Unions and Young Workers: YTS: Work in Progress — Notes on Outlines of trade union studies modules for trainees (January) [62]
Paying Your Wages: The Government's Wages Bill; Cashless Pay; Deductions and Fines — Activities and Resources (February)
Women and New Technology (February)
Data Protection (February)

Financial Management Initiative — Short Course (March)
Financial Management Initiative — Resource Pack (March)
Financial Management Initiative — HMI Brookside — A Case Study (n.d.)
Understanding Local Government — A Guide for Trade Unionists, [TUC Education and LGIU] (April)
Maternity: Changes in Maternity Benefits, Improving Maternity Agreements, Advising Members of their Rights (April)
Understanding the TUC: Resource Materials for TUC and Union Courses (August)
Say Yes to a Voice: NALGO's Campaign for a Political Fund — Workshop Activities and Briefing Notes (October)
Union Policies in Action [linked to Open School] (n.d.)
Aids. A TUC Course (November) [69]
Aids. A TUC Course, second edition (November) [69]
Understanding Pensions Schemes — A TUC Workbook, first edition (November) [75]

1988

What's Happening to Your Local Council — A TUC Course (January) [79]
What's Happening to Your Local Council — the Local Government Bill and Privatisation: Factsheets (January)
What's Happening to your Local Council? A course for discussion leaders (April) [79]
Pensions: What is Happening? A TUC Workbook, third edition (May) [82]
Using Computers for Negotiating, Organising, Communicating (May) [94]
TUC Workbook for Union Reps: Skills 1, new edition; (May)
TUC Workbook for Union Reps: Organisation (fourth revision, July)
Working with Figures. A Workbook for TUC Stage 2 Courses, revised edition (August)
Local Government Act Compulsory Competitive Tending — Employment and Industrial Relations Implications Specification Workshop (October) [94]
Using Computers for Negotiating, Organising, Communicating. Getting Started (December) [99]
Using Computers for Negotiating, Organising, Communicating. Handling Figures (December) [100]
Health and Safety at Work. A TUC Coursebook for Union Reps, fifth edition (December)

1989

Using Computers for Negotiating, Organising, Communicating. Putting the record straight (January) [102]
Using Computers for Negotiating, Organising, Communicating. Paperwork (January) [103]

Tackling Racism. A TUC Workbook (February) [reprint]
Trade Unions and Europe: Towards 1992 (May) [109]
Union File on Europe. A TUC Workbook for Trade Unionists (May)
Tackling Health Risks. A Briefing on the New Control of Substances Hazardous to Health [COSHH] Regulations (June)
Skills 2. TUC Workbook for Union Reps (August)
TUC/GMB Induction Course for Union Reps (November)

1990

Noise at Work. TUC Education Workbook on the Noise at Work Regulations 1989 (January)
Local Management of Schools. A Workshop for Trade Unionists (March) [111]
Tackling Health Risks COSHH Part 2. A TUC Course (April) [162]
Equal Pay for Work of Equal Value: Workbook (5 October) [125]
Europe 1992: Catching up on Europe. Health and Safety in Europe. A Two-day Course for Health and Safety Representatives (17 September) [130]
The NHS Act 1990. Activities. Factsheet 1, 2, 3 (n.d.)

1991

Working Women, new edition (January)
Health Service Bargaining. A TUC Short Course. Activities, second edition (August) [206]
Violence at Work. A TUC Short Course for Health and Safety Reps (30 August) [213]
Health Service Bargaining. A TUC Short Course. Resources, second edition (5 September) [211]
Representing Members. TUC Stage 1 Course for Union Representatives. A TUC Workbook (December)

1992

Union Organisation. TUC Stage 1 Course for Union Representatives. A TUC Workbook (January)
Health and Safety Skills. A TUC Course Book for the Stage 1 Health and Safety Course (January)
Representing Members on Health and Safety. A TUC Course Book for the Stage 1 Health and Safety Course (January)
Health and Safety Organisation. A TUC Course Book for the Stage 1 Health and Safety Course (January)

Appendix B: TUC *Ten Day and Short Course Programmes 1975–1992*

Statistical data on day release programmes have been published each year in TUC Annual Reports. This Appendix reproduces and collates some of these published figures.

Some general observations should be made. 'Ten day' courses listed were occasionally of twelve days' duration. 'Short courses' typically varied between one and five days. The data were collected for administrative purposes, and the categorisation of courses has changed from time to time. Some of this is relatively trivial. Until 1989 the term 'union workplace representatives' was used to describe those courses which were not Health and Safety courses (the latter in some years being referred to as courses for 'safety representatives'); from 1990, the term 'workplace representatives' has been used to describe all courses, with the distinction made within this heading between courses for 'union officials' and 'health and safety' courses. Neither approach is strictly accurate. Health and Safety courses have never been restricted to safety representatives, who are in any case both workplace representatives and union officials; as such, they have not been excluded from Introductory, Stage 1, Stage 2, and Follow-on courses. In the tables which follow, the term 'workplace representative' is used in the former sense: i.e., to describe courses (principally the Introductory, Stage 1 and Stage 2 courses) which are not Health and Safety courses.

Two other issues of classification are more significant: *(a)* the separate listing of short courses, and *(b)* the introduction of the Stage 1 Union Representatives course (to replace the former Introductory course). Linked to the latter was the reclassification of the Stage 2 course as an 'Introductory' (rather than 'Follow-on') course.

(a) Short Courses. Separate figures for the number of short courses held were introduced with effect from 1984/85. Prior to that date, the figures for short courses were included in a 'Follow-on and Short courses' category. However, in 1989 the figures for 1982/83 and 1983/84 were retrospectively reclassified, distinguishing for those two years the number of short courses from the number of follow-on courses. Although there is no comment in the tables as to the basis for this, Alan Grant, Head of the TUC's Trade Union Education Department, asserted unambiguously in a letter (27 April 1993) to the present author that the statistics published in 1989 'are correct'. 'I am afraid that the statistics in the 1982-1984 reports were originally confused between short courses, follow-on and Stage 2. We completely "overhauled" them in 1989 ....' The 'overhauled' figures

Appendices

appear consistent (in that the revision represents only a redistribution within the same overall total number of courses).

In Table B1, the figures for 1982-1984 issued since 1989 have therefore been preferred. The alteration in the stated number of Introductory courses is in any case relatively minor.

(b) Stage 1 and Stage 2 Courses. The retrospective reclassification in 1989 also saw an altering of the figures (for 1982/83 and 1983/84) for Stage 1 and Stage 2 courses. The only explanation is that offered by Grant (quoted above).

In the regional listings of Ten Day Courses (Tables B2 and B3), Follow-on courses have been excluded chiefly because of the uncertain status of the figures prior to 1984. (This problem is particularly acute in respect of the regional figures, since these have been issued only annually, and no revision has been published. The totals in these tables for 1982/83 and 1983/84 are not, therefore, the same as the figures in Table B1, and there must be doubt as to their accuracy for those two years.) These regional tables are therefore reflective of trends, rather than the total volumes of work in each region; however, in most years, the number of Follow-on courses was relatively modest in comparison with the Introductory and Health and Safety programmes. The regional Tables for Short Courses commence in 1984 because it is only from 1984/85 that these are separated from Follow-on ten-day courses in regional listings.

The indices and mean figures are calculated from the published figures. The remaining figures are as published, with the single exception that (in Table B1) two published 'total' figures are incorrect (in that they add up the relevant columns incorrectly). The error is very small in each case, but the published figures for courses in 1988/89 (2,665) and for students in 1986/87 (31,750) have been replaced by the correct sum of the relevant columns.

Table B1: TUC Day Release and Short Courses:

	Workplace Representatives			Health & Safety		
Year	Courses	Students	Mean	Courses	Students	Mean
1975-76	684	10,640	15.56	361	5,370	14.88
1976-77	752	10,917	14.52	578	7,803	13.50
1977-78	1,023	14,047	13.73	741	10,398	14.03
1978-79	1,105	13,421	12.15	1,744	27,361	15.69
1979-80	1,208	15,701	13.00	1,441	18,738	13.00
1980-81	1,049	14,910	14.21	879	12,067	13.73
1981-82	1,008	12,917	12.81	714	8,934	12.51

	Workplace Representatives Stage 1 & 2			Health & Safety Stage 1 & 2		
Year	Courses	Students	Mean	Courses	Students	Mean
1982-83	962	13,131	13.65	672	9,243	13.75
1983-84	943	11,984	12.71	636	8,362	13.15
1984-85	925	11,600	12.54	587	7,870	13.41
1985-86	859	10,599	12.34	599	7,307	12.20
1986-87	762	9,546	12.53	565	6,973	12.34
1987-88	792	9,475	11.96	568	6,944	12.23
1988-89	708	8,408	11.88	560	6,539	11.68
1989-90	637	7,296	11.45	584	7,065	12.10
1990-91	613	6,794	11.08	581	6,741	11.60
1991-92	546	6,454	11.82	543	6,635	12.22

Provision, Student Numbers and Mean Student Attendances 1975-1992

Follow-on, Stage 2 and Short Courses						Totals		
Courses	*Students*	*Mean*				*Courses*	*Students*	*Mean*
104	1,441	13.86				1,149	17,451	15.19
230	2,652	11.53				1,560	21,372	13.70
244	3,034	12.43				2,008	27,479	13.68
251	3,074	12.25				3,100	43,856	14.15
383	4,542	11.86				3,032	38,981	12.86
545	6,940	12.73				2,473	33,917	13.71
675	8,234	12.20				2,397	30,085	12.55
Follow-on Courses			Short Courses			Totals		
Courses	*Students*	*Mean*	*Courses*	*Students*	*Mean*	*Courses*	*Students*	*Mean*
231	2,680	11.60	467	5,914	12.66	2,332	30,968	13.28
190	1,520	8.00	640	6,341	9.91	2,409	28,207	11.71
155	1,067	6.88	730	10,161	13.92	2,397	30,698	12.81
83	846	10.19	1,139	13,558	11.90	2,680	32,310	12.06
76	812	10.68	1,183	14,401	12.17	2,586	31,732	12.27
106	1,134	10.70	1,097	13,083	11.93	2,563	30,636	11.95
132	1,305	9.89	1,261	15,142	12.01	2,661	31,394	11.80
92	885	9.62	1,552	19,594	12.63	2,865	34,840	12.16
83	809	9.75	1,340	15,529	11.59	2,617	29,873	11.41
95	1,014	10.67	1,329	16,402	12.34	2,513	30,505	12.14
						41,342	524,304	

Table B2: TUC Ten-Day Workplace Representatives Courses Provided,

	1979-80	1980-81	1981-82	1982-83	1983-84	1984-85
Northern	91	78	68	64	69	67
		85.7	74.4	70.3	75.8	73.6
E.Midlands & E.Anglia	111	86	77	63	70	63
		77.5	69.4	56.8	63.1	56.8
Yorks & Humberside	139	115	112	103	125	133
		82.7	80.6	74.1	89.9	95.7
North West	177	166	192	174	168	159
		93.8	108.5	98.3	94.9	89.8
Midlands	144	117	122	94	94	131
		81.3	84.7	65.3	65.3	91.0
South West	88	76	73	63	72	50
		86.4	83.0	71.6	81.8	56.8
South East	221	205	188	163	174	156
		92.8	85.1	73.8	78.7	70.6
Wales	60	68	45	41	39	42
		113.3	75.0	68.3	65.0	70.0
Scotland	148	113	109	104	83	94
		76.4	73.6	70.3	56.1	63.5
N.Ireland	29	25	22	27	21	30
		86.2	75.9	93.1	72.4	103.4

Index: 1979-80=100
Source: TUC Annual Reports, each year

by Region 1979-1992

1985-86	1986-87	1987-88	1988-89	1989-90	1990-91	1991-92
60	53	49	54	46	40	35
65.9	*58.2*	*53.8*	*59.3*	*50.5*	*44.0*	*38.5*
54	48	57	44	41	43	41
48.6	*43.2*	*51.4*	*39.6*	*36.9*	*38.7*	*36.9*
108	105	110	74	72	68	56
77.7	*75.5*	*79.1*	*53.2*	*51.8*	*48.9*	*40.3*
158	160	168	156	141	188	138
89.3	*90.4*	*94.9*	*88.1*	*79.7*	*106.2*	*78.0*
122	117	107	96	93	89	88
84.7	*81.3*	*74.3*	*66.7*	*64.6*	*61.8*	*61.1*
52	48	41	34	35	29	27
59.1	*54.5*	*46.6*	*38.6*	*39.8*	*33.0*	*30.7*
148	119	122	120	116	110	75
67.0	*53.8*	*55.2*	*54.3*	*52.5*	*49.8*	*33.9*
42	42	50	39	32	26	27
70.0	*70.0*	*83.3*	*65.0*	*53.3*	*43.3*	*45.0*
82	50	68	66	47	46	43
55.4	*33.8*	*45.9*	*44.6*	*31.8*	*31.1*	*29.1*
33	20	20	25	14	19	16
113.8	*69.0*	*69.0*	*86.2*	*48.3*	*65.5*	*55.2*

Table B3: TUC Ten-Day Health and Safety Courses Provided,

	1979-80	1980-81	1981-82	1982-83	1983-84	1984-85
Northern	116	76	63	36	52	49
		65.5	54.3	31.0	44.8	42.2
E.Midlands & E.Anglia	135	75	59	42	49	44
		55.6	43.7	31.1	36.3	32.6
Yorks & Humberside	167	85	75	52	69	61
		50.9	44.9	31.1	41.3	36.5
North West	220	137	116	88	112	108
		62.3	52.7	40.0	50.9	49.1
Midlands	196	112	82	63	76	67
		57.1	41.8	32.1	38.8	34.2
South West	92	54	49	43	56	55
		58.7	53.3	46.7	60.9	59.8
South East	257	171	144	114	120	116
		66.5	56.0	44.4	46.7	45.1
Wales	85	45	35	23	31	30
		52.9	41.2	27.1	36.5	35.3
Scotland	139	85	61	50	50	36
		61.2	43.9	36.0	36.0	25.9
N.Ireland	37	39	30	15	16	21
		105.4	81.1	40.5	43.2	56.8

Index: 1979-80=100
Source: TUC Annual Reports, each year

by Region 1979-1992

1985-86	1986-87	1987-88	1988-89	1989-90	1990-91	1991-92
46	40	37	40	52	33	46
39.7	*34.5*	*31.9*	*34.5*	*44.8*	*28.4*	*39.7*
39	33	32	43	45	47	42
28.9	*24.4*	*23.7*	*31.9*	*33.3*	*34.8*	*31.1*
65	65	58	59	61	57	53
38.9	*38.9*	*34.7*	*35.3*	*36.5*	*34.1*	*31.7*
112	110	122	114	121	140	115
50.9	*50.0*	*55.5*	*51.8*	*55.0*	*63.6*	*52.3*
63	71	73	71	64	63	64
32.1	*36.2*	*37.2*	*36.2*	*32.7*	*32.1*	*32.7*
43	41	36	34	40	40	41
46.7	*44.6*	*39.1*	*37.0*	*43.5*	*43.5*	*44.6*
130	113	121	119	127	121	97
50.6	*44.0*	*47.1*	*46.3*	*49.4*	*47.1*	*37.7*
37	33	35	33	28	27	24
43.5	*38.8*	*41.2*	*38.8*	*32.9*	*31.8*	*28.2*
48	48	44	38	35	41	48
34.5	*34.5*	*31.7*	*27.3*	*25.2*	*29.5*	*34.5*
16	11	10	9	11	12	13
43.2	*29.7*	*27.0*	*24.3*	*29.7*	*32.4*	*35.1*

Table B4: TUC Short Courses Provided,

	1984-85	1985-86	1986-87
Northern	57	67	92
		117.5	*161.4*
E.Midlands & E.Anglia	10	17	43
		170.0	*430.0*
Yorks & Humberside	100	155	100
		155.0	*100.0*
North West	128	210	238
		164.1	*185.9*
Midlands	70	199	158
		284.3	*225.7*
South West	89	103	113
		115.7	*127.0*
South East	131	260	278
		198.5	*212.2*
Wales	28	22	32
		78.6	*114.3*
Scotland	108	96	105
		88.9	*97.2*
N.Ireland	9	10	24
		111.1	*266.7*

Index: 1984-85=100
Source: TUC Annual Reports, each year

by Region 1984-1992

1987-88	1988-89	1989-90	1990-91	1991-92
101	86	78	68	70
177.2	*150.9*	*136.8*	*119.3*	*122.8*
41	39	42	47	44
410.0	*390.0*	*420.0*	*470.0*	*440.0*
67	113	126	122	160
67.0	*113.0*	*126.0*	*122.0*	*160.0*
203	283	364	393	351
158.6	*221.1*	*284.4*	*307.0*	*274.2*
208	207	204	176	229
297.1	*295.7*	*291.4*	*251.4*	*327.1*
106	105	173	112	117
119.1	*118.0*	*194.4*	*125.8*	*131.5*
241	237	284	260	221
184.0	*180.9*	*216.8*	*198.5*	*168.7*
15	28	37	32	39
53.6	*100.0*	*132.1*	*114.3*	*139.3*
95	144	214	97	63
88.0	*133.3*	*198.1*	*89.8*	*58.3*
20	19	30	33	35
222.2	*211.1*	*333.3*	*366.7*	*388.9*

Appendix C: Public Funds for Trade Union Education

Public funds were made available for trade union education with effect from 1976, when amendments were made to the Further Education Regulations 1975. In a Parliamentary Written Answer (5 August 1976), the Secretary of State for Education and Science, Fred Mulley, outlined the 'categories of expenditure' which would be 'eligible for reimbursement':

> *(a) fees paid by the TUC to local education authorities and responsible bodies in respect of employees who attend courses of trade union studies;*
> *(b) course development in trade union studies and necessary research by the TUC Training College;*
> *(c) the provision of courses in trade union studies, including courses for teachers in these studies, at the TUC Training College and, under the auspices of the TUC Education Service, elsewhere;*
> *(d) the provision by independent unions of residential courses in trade union studies.*

Definitions of the subject matter to be covered in these courses are discussed in Chapter 9. Public funds made available to the TUC in each year under this scheme are listed below. Until the financial year 1987/88, the grant was paid in equal shares by the Department of Education and Science and the Department of Employment; since 1988/89, the Department of Employment has been the sole financing Department.

On two occasions (29 June 1982 and 23 November 1987) government Ministers have provided figures on the actual grant paid to the TUC in various years in Parliamentary Written Answers. These figures are also listed below. The sums paid in 1979/80 'included grant held over from the previous years as a result of a Civil Service industrial dispute'.

Table C1: Public Funds Allocated and Paid to the TUC for Trade Union Education 1976-1993

Year ending 31 March:	Allocated	Paid
1977	400,000	399,852
1978	650,000	640,942
1979	1,000,000	355,632
1980	1,455,000	2,099,368

1981	1,674,000	1,674,000
1982	1,840,000	1,837,641
1983	1,600,000	1,598,570
1984	1,700,000	1,545,725
1985	1,704,000	1,542,239
1986	1,704,000	1,695,510
1987	1,704,000	1,704,000
1988	1,749,000	
1989	1,686,000	
1990	1,728,000	
1991	1,785,000	
1992	1,734,351	
1993	1,690,488	

Source: TUC Annual Reports, each year (1993 figure from 1992 Report).

In the years 1984-1988 inclusive, £200,000 of the sum allocated to the TUC was recorded by the TUC as 'earmarked by the DES/DE for courses specifically endorsed by employers'. The reduction in grant-aid in 1988/89 by £63,000 (3.6 per cent) was to take account of the expulsion of the EETPU from the TUC. The 2.9 per cent reduction in 1991/92 reflected the fall in TUC-affiliated membership: the grant continued thereafter to be tied by the DE pro rata to TUC affiliated membership.

In the Parliamentary Written Answer (10 December 1992) announcing the end of the Trade Union Education and Training grant scheme, the Secretary of State indicated that in 1993/94 the 'grant will be set at 75% of the 1992/93 per capita figure'. The levels of support would be reduced to 50 per cent (1994/95) and 25 percent (1995/96). The scheme would 'cease to operate from 1 April 1996'.

In addition to the DES/DE grant, a sum of £500,000 was made available in July 1979 by the Department of Industry 'towards financing a trade union educational programme on new technology' (TUC 1980: 156); these funds were to be available during the period 1 August 1979 to 31 March 1981 (subsequently extended to 31 December 1981).

A Parliamentary Written Answer (29 June 1982) stated that government grants for trade union education and training had 'since 1978-79 ... included grants to unions not affiliated to the TUC'. These sums paid were: £1,309 (1978/79); £38,789 (1979/80); £27,120 (1980/81); £34,739 (1981/82). A Written Answer (29 June 1988) stated that grants of £38,439.71 had been paid to unions not affiliated to the TUC in the financial year 1987/88, and claims totalling a further £61,016.82 were still under consideration. Some 19 such unions had claimed grant in that year.

Appendix D: TUC *Tutor Briefings 1977-1992*

Tutor briefings are courses for TUC tutors, normally taught by course development staff of the TUC (but on occasion by trusted tutors with particular experience or knowledge). From the late 1970s they fell into two main categories (unfortunately not distinguished in the statistics). Some were courses designed to provide an essential foundation for teaching a particular TUC course. Thus there were briefings for tutors beginning to teach the Stage 1 Course for Union Representatives, the Health and Safety Stage 1 course, the Rights at Work course, and so forth. (The Introductory or Stage 1 Union Representatives briefing also stood as the initial induction for tutors into TUC educational approaches.) In principle, and for many years in practice, a regional education officer was not supposed to approve a tutor for a course unless he or she had attended the appropriate briefing.

The second type of briefing was related to a particular issue or topic: thus there might be briefings on equal opportunities, pensions or tackling racism. They were often formally linked to some programme of short courses, but served in practice an up-dating and general support function.

Attendance at tutor briefings was by nomination by the TUC REO, normally following a proposal from the senior trade union studies tutor in the relevant educational body. Sometimes demand for places on certain course briefings was very high, and tutors might have to wait some considerable time before being accepted.

From 1978 to 1980, the formal definition (which relates to the figures given below) was: 'Courses of between 2-5 days provided ... to brief trade union studies tutors employed by the public educational bodies and engaged in teaching trade union students.

Since 1981 the definition has been slightly wider, including courses of just one day. In 1987 the rubric was amended to 'Tutor briefings of between 1 and 5 days duration provided ... to update trade union studies tutors teaching TUC-provided courses'.

Table D1: TUC Tutor Briefings 1977—1992

Provided	Regionally:		Nationally:		Total:	
	Courses	Participants	Courses	Participants	Courses	Participants
1977/78(b)	15	216	10	144	25	360
1978/79	18	350	17	238	35	588
1979/80	23	451	14	245	37	696
1981/82	21	428	14	324	35	752
1982/83	23	334	9	144	32	478
1983/84	9	101	17	230	26	331
1984/85	12	192	7	101	19	293
1985/86	13	153	13	215	26	368
1986/87	16	219	12	178	28	397
1987/88	9	131	10	140	19	271
1988/89	21	303	13	218	34	521
1989/90	40	508	8	125	48	633
1990/91	24	267	12	117	36	384
1991/92	23	248	6	115	29	363

Note: The figures for 1977/78 are taken from the 1978/79 Annual Report. The 1978 Report gives different figures in respect of nationally-provided (and consequent changes to the annual total of) briefings, *viz*, Courses: 4 (19), Participants: 64 (280).

Source: TUC Annual Reports, each year.

Appendix E: TUC Campaign Workshops

Campaign Workshops were short courses originally defined in 1981 as 'One day workshops for full-time trade union officers and senior workplace representatives'. By 1988 the description had broadened slightly: they were 'usually of 1 day's duration, organised for Union Full-time Officers, Workplace Representatives and Members'.

Their origins can be traced back to the campaign against the Industrial Relations Bill in the early 1970s. However, the Campaign Workshops which were a feature of the 1980s grew out the 1979/80 'Campaign against the Employment Bill'. In connection with this, 82 two-day workshops (with 1,149 students) were provided around the country for briefing full-time officers and senior union workplace representatives. These were listed in the TUC Annual Report (1980) as 'Courses for Full-time Union Officers'. The 'Campaign Workshop' was included in Annual Reports as a category of course in its own right only from 1980/81. No Campaign Workshops have been recorded since 1988.

The Campaign Workshop was essentially a short course closely linked to a contentious political issue in which the TUC was campaigning against some aspect of government policy. It was judged important that in such circumstances, the costs of courses should be met from TUC (as opposed to public) funds. Campaign Workshops held during the 1980s are listed below.

	Courses	*Students*
1980/81		
Economic and Social Advance	119	2,022
Against the Employment Act	49	560
1981/82		
Industrial Relations Legislation	547	8,600
1982/83		
Industrial Relations Legislation	198	2,810
1983/84		
Against Privatisation	34	631

	Courses	Students
1984/85		
Political Fund Campaign:		
— Full-Time Officers	30	450
— Senior Workplace Reps	152	2,111
1985/86		
Social Security Review	66	753
Political Funds	119	1,908
Public Services Pay	10	152
1986/87		
Social Security Review	2	13
Political Funds	32	288
Economic Policy	8	256
Beating Apartheid	24	348
1987/88		
Political Funds	142	1,457
Economic Policy	8	256
Beating Apartheid	15	157

Source: TUC *Annual Reports, each year.*

BIBLIOGRAPHY

Undated items have been ascribed a date for reference purposes, but are marked : [n.d.]

Abell, P. (1982), 'Developing an Educational Approach to Teaching about Trade Unions in Schools', *Trade Union Studies Journal* 6 (Winter), 11-13.

Aird, E. and S. Henderson (1985), 'Adult Education and Political Change: Experience, Awareness, Action', *Trade Union Studies Journal* 11 (Summer), 5-8.

Aldred, C. (1981), 'Men and the Unions — Just a Side Issue?', *Trade Union Studies Journal* 4 (Autumn), 9-10.

Allaway, A.J. (1964), 'Human Relations Training', *Adult Education* 37(1) (May), 17-23.

Allen, V.L. (1960), 'The Reorganisation of the TUC 1918-1927', *British Journal of Sociology* 11(1) (March), 24-43.

—— (1966), *Militant Trade Unionism. A Re-Analysis of Industrial Action in an Inflationary Situation*, London, Merlin Press.

—— (1971), *The Sociology of Industrial Relations*, London, Longman.

Allum, C. (1982), 'Students in Trade Union Education: Trends', *Trade Union Studies Journal* 6 (Winter), 25-26.

Anderson, D. (1987), 'Academies of Union Unrest?', *The Times*, 9 December.

—— (1988), Telephone interview with present author, 11 January.

Armstrong, P.J., J.F.B. Goodman, and J.D. Hyman (1981), *Ideology and Shop-floor Industrial Relations*, London, Croom Helm.

Atkins, J. (1979), 'The TUC and Trade Union Education, 1909-1964', *WEA Trade Union and Industrial Studies Newsletter* 3 (March), 1-21.

—— (ed.) (1981), *Neither Crumbs nor Condescension. The Central Labour College 1909-1915*, Aberdeen and London, Aberdeen People's Press and WEA.

—— (1985), 'Course Meetings: A Comment', *Trade Union Studies Journal* 12 (Winter), 9-10.

—— and J. Stageman (1981), 'Living on the Breadline: Part-Time Tutors in Trade Union Education', *Trade Union Studies Journal* 3 (Spring), 12-13.

Attfield, J. (1981), *With Light of Knowledge. A Hundred Years of Education in the Royal Arsenal Co-operative Society, 1877-1977*, London, RACS/Journeyman Press.

Bacon, R. and W. Eltis (1976), *Britain's Economic Problem: Too Few Producers*, London, Macmillan.

Bagwell, P.S. (1963), *The Railwaymen. The History of the National Union of Railwaymen*, London, Allen and Unwin.

Baker, C. (1984), 'Health and Safety: an Agenda for Change', *Trade Union Studies Journal* 10 (Summer), 4-6.

Baker, H.L. (1931), 'Adult Education in Kent', unpublished thesis for M.A. (Education), Section B, King's College, London. [A carbon copy of this thesis is in the possession of the WEA South Eastern District; King's College has no copy, nor any record of its being submitted.]

Banks, R.F. (1966), 'Labor Education's New Role in Britain', *Industrial Relations* 5(2), 67-82.

Barker, A., O. O'Brien, M. Fox, and P. Lewis (1979), 'Problems encountered when Running Research Groups for Trade Unionists', *The Industrial Tutor* 2(10) (March), 20-26.

Barratt Brown, M. (1969), *Adult Education for Industrial Workers. The Contribution of Sheffield University Extramural Department*, London, National Institute of Adult Education and the Society of Industrial Tutors.

—— (1976), 'Aide Memoire. Paid Educational Leave', *The Industrial Tutor* 2(4) (March), 3-7.

—— (1978), 'Northern College', *The Industrial Tutor* 2(8) (March), 3-4.

—— (1986-87), 'What has Really Changed in the Educational Needs of Workers?', *The Industrial Tutor* 4(4-5), 7-14.

—— (1991), 'The Demands of New Technology: the Sheffield University Programme of Day Release Courses in the 1960s', *The Industrial Tutor* 3(5) (Autumn), 9-15.

—— and K. Coates (eds.) (1973), *Trade Union Register: 3*, Nottingham, Spokesman.

Batstone, E. (1984), *Working Order. Workplace Industrial Relations over Two Decades*, Oxford, Blackwell.

—— (1988), *The Reform of Workplace Industrial Relations. Theory, Myth and Evidence*, Oxford, Clarendon Press.

——, I. Boraston, and S. Frenkel (1977), *Shop Stewards in Action*, Oxford, Blackwell.

Baxter, V.J. (1976), 'The Training Services Agency and Industry Training Boards', *The Industrial Tutor* 2(5) (September), 53-78.

Bayliss, F.J. (1964), 'The Response to Adult Education in Industry', *Adult Education* 37(2) (July), 55-67.

—— (1970), 'Adult Education for Industrial Workers: a review', *The Industrial Tutor* 1(2) (March), 29-32.

—— (1991), 'Day Release Courses at Nottingham', *The Industrial Tutor* 3(5) (Autumn), 16-18.

—— and J.T. Rhodes (1962), 'Courses in Factories', *Adult Education* 35(3) (September), 102-9.

Beale, J. (1982), 'What Can we Learn from Women's Courses?', *Trade Union Studies Journal* 6 (Winter), 20-21

Bell, J.D.M. (1954), 'Trade Unions', in Flanders and Clegg (1954), 128-96.

Beynon, H. (1974), *Working for Ford*, Harmondsworth, Penguin.

Black, J. and K. Locke, (1982), 'Trade Union Education against Racism: a grass roots approach', *Trade Union Studies Journal* 5 (Summer), 13-15.

Bowen, G. and S. Ledwith (1975), 'Printing — Relations at Work', *The Industrial Tutor* 2(2) (March), 23-29.

Bowen Thomas, G. (1960), 'The British Worker', *Adult Education* 33(1) May, 35-6.

Briggs, A. and J. Saville (1967), *Essays in Labour History*, London, Macmillan.

Bright, D., and T. MacDermott (1984), 'Trade Union Tutors and Their Work', *The Industrial Tutor* 3(9) (Spring), 58-71.

British Broadcasting Corporation (1975), *Trade Union Studies. A Course for Active Trade Unionists*, London, BBC.

—— (1976), *Trade Union Studies. A Course for Active Trade Unionists. Book Two: Trade Unions and the Economy*, London, BBC.

—— (1977), *Democracy at Work. A Book for Active Trade Unionists*, [Trade Union Studies Book Three], London, BBC.

Brodie, M.B. (1963), 'Management and Adult Education', *Adult Education* 36(3) (September), 102-7.

Brown. D. (1975), 'Adult Tutors and ASTMS', *The Industrial Tutor* 2(2) (March), 17-19.

Brown, G. (1977), 'Working Class Adult Education', in Thornton and Stephens (1977), 52-64.

—— (1980), 'Independence and Incorporation: the Labour College Movement and the Workers' Educational Association before the Second World War', in J. Thompson (ed.) (1980), 109-25.

Brown, J., J. McIlroy, and B. Spencer (1983), 'Fundamental Questions about Student-centred Learning', *Trade Union Studies Journal* 7 (Summer), 4-6.

—— (1984), 'Student-centred Learning: A Note', *Trade Union Studies Journal* 9 (Summer), 27.

Brown, W. and M. Lawson (1972), *The Training of Trade Union Officers: The Training Experience and Requirements of Full-time Trade Union Officers*, Coventry, University of Warwick Industrial Relations Research Unit Discussion Paper.

—— (1973), 'The Training of Trade Union Officers: the Training Experience and Requirements of Full-time Trade Union Officers', *British Journal of Industrial Relations* 11(3) (November), 431-48.

Buick, A. (1975), 'Joseph Dietzgen', *Radical Philosophy* 10 (Spring), 3-7.

Burchill, F. (1974), 'The Teaching of Industrial Relations', *The Industrial Tutor* 1(10) (March), 22-25.

—— (1976), 'The Teaching of Industrial Relations', *The Industrial Tutor* 2(5) (September), 87-94.

Burkitt, A. (1982), 'Trade Union Education and its Relationship to Adult Education in England and Wales', *International Journal of Lifelong Education* 1(1), 63-76.

Cadbury, J.G. (1979), 'Statement on the Principal of Fircroft College', *The Industrial Tutor* 2(10) (March), 9-10.

Caldwell, P. (1979), 'The WEA's Work in Trade Union Studies', *The Industrial Tutor* 3(1) (September), 3-10.

—— (1981), 'State Funding of Trade Union Education', *Trade Union Studies Journal* 3 (Spring), 3-6.

—— (1982), 'Membership Education', *Trade Union Studies Journal* 5 (Summer), 12.

—— (1983), 'Educational Work with Unemployed People: Would MSC Funding take us Forward?', *Trade Union Studies Journal* 7 (Summer), 11-14.
—— (1985), 'Just Ten Days ... Methods and Curriculum in Trade Union Education', *Trade Union Studies Journal* 12 (Winter), 3-6.
Campbell, A. (1983), Letter in *New Statesman*, 30 September.
—— (1985), Letter in *The Times Higher Education Supplement*, 14 June.
—— and L. Toale (1981), 'TUC Courses: Problems of Recruitment', *The Industrial Tutor* 3(5) (September), 77-79.
Campbell, A., E. Healey, J. McIlroy, and B. Spencer (1986), 'Beyond Industrial Relations Training', *Trade Union Studies Journal* 13 (Summer), 3-6.
Campbell, A. and J. McIlroy (1986), 'Trade Union Studies in British Universities: Changing Patterns, Changing Problems', *International Journal of Lifelong Education* 5(3), 207-40.
Carlisle, M. (Lord Carlisle) (1992), Letter to the present author, 10 February.
Carr, P. (1970), 'Shop Steward Courses in Technical Colleges', *The Industrial Tutor* 1(2) (March), 16-19.
Casey, F. (1979), 'Beginning with the Beginner', *Capital and Class* 7 (Spring), 117-21; first published in *Plebs*, 1920.
Chemical and Allied Products Industry Training Board (1970), *The Training Implications of Manpower Productivity Agreements*, Staines, CAPITB.
Civil Service Union (1984), 'Project Work on Trade Union Courses', *Trade Union Studies Journal* 10 (Summer), 7-10.
Clegg, H.A. (1972), *The System of Industrial Relations in Great Britain*, 2nd edition, Oxford, Blackwell.
—— (1976), *The System of Industrial Relations in Great Britain*, 3rd edition, Oxford, Blackwell.
—— (1990), *The Oxford School of Industrial Relations*, Warwick Papers in Industrial Relations No 31, Coventry, University of Warwick Industrial Relations Research Unit.
—— and R. Adams (1959), *Trade Union Education with Special Reference to the Pilot Areas. A Report for the Workers' Educational Association*, London, WEA.
Clegg, H.A., A.J. Killick, and R. Adams (1961), *Trade Union Officers*, Oxford, Blackwell.
Clinton, A. (1977), *The Trade Union Rank and File. Trades Councils in Britain 1900-40*, Manchester, Manchester University Press.
Clunie, J. (1920), *First Principles of Working-Class Education*, Glasgow, Socialist Labour Press.
Coates, K. and T. Topham (eds.), *Workers' Control. A Book of Readings and Witnesses for Workers' Control*, London, Panther Books.
—— (1980), *Trade Unions in Britain*, Nottingham, Spokesman.
Coates, K., T. Topham, and M. Barratt Brown (eds.) (1969), *Trade Union Register*, London, Merlin Press.
Cohen, M. (1990a), 'The Labour College Movement between the Wars: National and North-West Developments', in Simon (1990a), 105-136.

—— (1990b), 'Revolutionary Education Revived: the Communist Challenge to the Labour Colleges, 1933-1945', in Simon (1990a), 137-52.
Coker, E. (1973), 'Survey of Members', *The Industrial Tutor* 1(8) (March), 49-50.
—— (1976), 'Education and Training for Industrial Democracy', *The Industrial Tutor* 2(5) (September), 27-33.
—— and G. Stuttard (eds.) (1976), *Industrial Studies 2: The Bargaining Context*, London, Arrow and Society of Industrial Tutors.
—— (eds.) (1980), *Industrial Studies 3: Understanding Industrial Society*, London, Arrow and Society of Industrial Tutors.
Cmd. 321 (1919), *Ministry of Reconstruction: Adult Education Committee. Final Report*, London, HMSO.
Cmnd. 3623 (1968), *Report of the Royal Commission on Trade Unions and Employers' Associations 1965-1968* (Chairman: Lord Donovan), London, HMSO.
Cm. 95 (1987), *Trade Unions and their Members*, London, HMSO.
Commission on Industrial Relations (CIR) (1972a), *Industrial Relations Training* (CIR Report No. 33), London, HMSO.
—— (1972b), *Industrial Relations Training: a Practical Guide for Unions and Employers*, London, HMSO.
—— (1972c), *Industrial Relations Training* [summary of 1972a], London, HMSO.
Connell, J. (1990), 'In Memoriam: Jim Millar', *The Industrial Tutor* 5(1), (Spring), 6-8.
Conservative Central Office (1976), *The Right Approach*, London, Conservative Central Office.
Corfield, A.J. (1969), *Epoch in Workers' Education. A History of the Workers' Educational Trade Union Committee*, London, Workers' Educational Association.
—— (1979), 'Fircroft College', *The Industrial Tutor* 2(10) (March), 3-8.
Cosgrove, F. (1980), 'Education within the Transport and General Workers' Union', *Trade Union Studies Journal* 1 (Spring), 15.
Count, R. (1976), 'Trade Union Studies. A Joint BBC/TUC/WEA Multi-media Scheme for Studies for Active Trade Unionists. Reactions to the BBC's Contribution to Year 1', [BBC] Further Education, Television [n.d.].
—— (1980), *The WEA and the Trade Union Studies Project*, London, WEA [n.d.]
—— and R. Turner (1978), 'The Effects of the Trade Union Studies Project. A Multi-media Venture between the BBC, TUC and WEA (1975-8), Final Report to the Social Science Research Council (Grantholder: M. Barratt Brown)' [n.d.].
Cowper, H. (1981), 'Some Aspects of Working Class Education and Imperialism', *Scottish Labour History Society Journal* 16, 12-18.
Coyne, C. and M. Wright (1982), 'The Changing Needs in Company-Based Shop Steward Training', *Industrial Relations Journal* 13(2), 62-74.
Craik, W.W. (1964), *The Central Labour College 1909-29*, London, Lawrence and Wishart.

Croucher, R. (1985), 'Second Chance to Learn and Trade Union Studies', *Trade Union Studies Journal* 12 (Winter), 7-9.
—— and J. Halstead (1990), 'The Origin of "Liberal" Adult Education for Miners at Sheffield in the Post-war Period: a Study in Adult Education and the Working Class', *Trade Union Studies Journal* 21 (Summer), 3-14.
Cupper, L. (1980), 'Public Funded Trade Union Education in Australia', *Industrial Relations Journal* 11(1), 57-68.
Cuthbert, N.H. (1963), 'Approaches to Subjects: Industrial Relations', *Adult Education* 36(3))September), 134-7.
Daniel, W.W. and N. Millward (1983), *Workplace Industrial Relations in Great Britain. The DE/PSI/SSRC Survey*, London, Heinemann.
Davies, P. and M. Freedland (1984), *Labour Law: Text and Materials*, Second Edition, London, Weidenfeld and Nicolson.
Dawson, M. and K. Grainger (1984), 'Women's Workplace Education Project', *Trade Union Studies Journal* 9 (Summer), 5-6.
Department of Education and Science (1972), 'Report of a Working Party on Shop Steward Education and Training' [the Gold Report], Circular FECL 9/72 T2003/08 (dated 5 July 1972).
—— (1973a), 'Circular re CIR Report on Industrial Relations Training', *The Industrial Tutor* 1(9) (September).
—— (1973b), *Adult Education: A Plan for Development* [the Russell Report], London, HMSO.
Disney, R. et al. (1982), *Unemployment*, special issue of *Studies for Trade Unionists* 8(30) (July), London, Workers' Educational Association.
Donaldson, P. and J. Farquhar (1988), *Understanding the British Economy*, Harmondsworth, Penguin.
Dorfman, G.A. (1983), *British Trade Unionism against the Trades Union Congress*, London, Macmillan.
Douglas, F. (1955), 'Commotion in the Capital', series of 17 articles in *Edinburgh Evening Dispatch*, 8-29 August.
Doyle, M. (1982), 'Cuts in Funding', *Trade Union Studies Journal* 5 (Summer), 4-5.
—— (1983), 'The Voluntary Projects Programme and the WEA', *Trade Union Studies Journal* 7 (Summer), 8-10.
Duncan, R. (1992), 'Independent Working-class Education and the Formation of the Labour College Movement in Glasgow and the West of Scotland, 1915-1922', in Duncan and McIvor (eds.) (1992), 106-28.
Duncan, R. and A. McIvor (1992), *Militant Workers. Labour and Class Conflict on the Clyde 1900-1950*, Edinburgh, John Donald.
Easton, L.D. (1958), 'Empiricism and Ethics in Dietzgen', *Journal of the History of Ideas* 19(1) (January), 77-90.
Edinburgh and District Trades Council, Minutes, Manuscript, at the Council's Offices.
Edinburgh and District Trades and Labour Council (1938/39), *Annual Report*, Edinburgh, The Council.

Editor, The (1971), 'Teaching Industrial Relations: Some Questions by the Editor', *The Industrial Tutor* 1(4) (March), 4-5.
'Editorial' (1984), *Trade Union Studies Journal* 9 (Summer), 3-5.
'Editorial' (1987), *Trade Union Studies Journal* 15 (Summer), 3-4.
'Editorial Comment' (1980), *Trade Union Studies Journal* 2 (Autumn), 2.
Edwards, C., J. McIlroy, T. Mooney, and B. Spencer (1983), 'Student Centred Learning and Trade Union Education: A Preliminary Examination', *The Industrial Tutor* 3(8) (Autumn), 45-54.
Elliot, R. (1980), 'Women in Unions: The Contribution of Trade Union Education', *Trade Union Studies Journal* 2 (Autumn), 3-6.
—— (1981), 'Update on Women's Courses', *Trade Union Studies Journal* 3 (Spring), 17.
Emmett, D. (1928), 'Joseph Dietzgen, the Philosopher of Proletarian Logic', *Journal of Adult Education* 3(1) (October), 26-35.
Eva, D. (1982), 'Development Work and Potential Membership Education on Merseyside', *Trade Union Studies Journal* 6 (Winter), 7-8.
Evans, S. (1983), 'The Employment Acts, Management Practice, and Trade Union Education', *Trade Union Studies Journal* 7 (Summer), 19-21.
Evans, T.F. (1974), 'The Industrial Relations Act and the WEA', *The Industrial Tutor* 1(10) (March), 12-21.
Farley, M. (1982), 'Youth Training Scheme: An Opportunity for Advance', *Trade Union Studies Journal* 6 (Winter), 13-17.
Fatchett, D. (1982), 'What Happens to Trade Union Day Release Students?', *Adult Education* 55(1) (June), 39-42.
Faulkner, S. (1982), 'Unemployment and Trade Union Education: Time to go on the Offensive', *Trade Union Studies Journal* 5 (Summer), 6-8.
Fellner, W. et al. (1964), *The Problem of Rising Prices*, Paris, Organisation for Economic Co-operation and Development (first published 1961 by Organisation for European Economic Co-operation).
Feickert, D., K. Forrester, and C. Thorne (1981), 'A Workers' Investigation into Stress at Work', *Trade Union Studies Journal* 3 (Spring),15-16.
Field, J. (1985), 'From Trade Union Education to Work with the Unemployed', *Trade Union Studies Journal* 11 (Summer), 3-5.
—— (1991), 'Competency and the Pedagogy of Labour', *Studies in the Education of Adults* 23(1) (April), 41-52.
—— and P. Weller (1992), 'Trade Unions and Human Resource Development: the Case of the National Vocational Qualifications System', *The Industrial Tutor* 5(6) (Autumn), 41-8.
Fieldhouse, R. (1977), *The Workers' Educational Association: Aims and Achievements 1903-1977*, Syracuse, Syracuse University Publications in Continuing Education.
—— (1981), 'Voluntaryism and the State in Adult Education: the WEA and the 1925 TUC Education Scheme', *History of Education* 10(1), 45-63.
—— (1985a), 'Conformity and Contradiction in English Responsible Body Adult Education 1925-1950', *Studies in the Education of Adults* 17(2) (October), 121-34.

—— (1985b), *Adult Education and the Cold War. Liberal Values under Seige 1946-1951*, Leeds, Leeds Studies in Adult and Continuing Education.

—— (1990), 'Bouts of Suspicion: Political Controversies in Adult Education, 1925-1944' in Simon (1990a), 153-72.

—— and K. Forrester (1984), 'The WEA and Trade Union Education', *The Industrial Tutor* 3(9) (Spring), 5-15.

Fisher, J. (1984a), 'Some Recent Developments in Trade Union Education in the United Kingdom', *International Journal of Lifelong Education* 3(3), 211-22.

—— (1984b), 'Report to TGWU on the University of Surrey/TGWU Distance-Learning Course 1983-1984', unpublished report, London, Transport and General Workers' Union No. 1 Region.

—— (1989), 'Industrial Studies: An Example of University/Union Co-operation', *The Industrial Tutor* 4(9) (Spring), 57-66.

—— and B. Camfield (1986-87), 'Missing Link in Trade Union Education? The TGWU-University of Surrey Distance-Learning Course', *The Industrial Tutor* 4(4/5) (Autumn/Spring), 30-36.

Flanders, A. and H.A. Clegg (eds.) (1954), *The System of Industrial Relations in Great Britain. Its History, Law and Institutions*, Oxford, Blackwell.

Food, Drink and Tobacco Industry Training Board (1971), *Industrial Relations Training: A Systematic Approach*, Gloucester, FDTITB.

Forrest, H. (1980), 'The Politics of Pension Funds: a Neglected Educational Opportunity', *Trade Union Studies Journal* 2 (Autumn), 9-10.

Forrester, K., A. Morgan, B. Spencer and M. Stinson (1988), 'Industrial Studies in a University Adult Education Department' *The Industrial Tutor* 4(8) (Autumn), 57-65.

Foster, J. (1976), 'British Imperialism and the Labour Aristocracy' in J. Skelley (ed.), *The General Strike 1926*, London, Lawrence and Wishart.

Foster, J. and T. Ellison (1976), 'The North East Trade Union Studies Information Unit', *The Industrial Tutor* 2(4) (March), 23-35.

Fryer, B. (1984), 'Trade Union Studies at Northern College', *Trade Union Studies Journal* 9 (Summer), 6-8.

Fryer, P. (1983), 'Education from Below: The Oxford Industrial Branch and the WEA', *Trade Union Studies Journal* 7 (Summer), 6-8.

Fyrth, J. (1980), 'Industrial Studies and the Labour Movement', in Coker and Stuttard (1980), 133-60.

Gee, D. (1982), 'Getting Things Done ...? Impressions of the TUC Courses for Safety Representatives 1974-81', *The Industrial Tutor* 3(6), 7-14.

Gennard, J. (1972), 'The LSE Trade Union Studies Course', *The Industrial Tutor* 1(6) (March), 8-14.

Gibbons, C. (1926-27), 'Education for Emancipation', *The Labour Standard*, 18 and 25 December, 1 and 8 January.

Gold, D. (1972), 'Further Education for Shop Stewards', *The Industrial Tutor* 1(6) (March), 4-7.

Gold, M., H. Levie and R. Moore (1979), *The Shop Stewards' Guide to the Use of Company Information*, Nottingham, Spokesman.

Goldstein, J. (1952), *The Government of British Trade Unions. A Study of Apathy and the Democratic Process in the Transport and General Workers Union*, London, George Allen and Unwin.

Goode, H. (1982), 'Youth Opportunities and Trade Union Organisation and Education', *Trade Union Studies Journal* 5 (Summer), 9-11.

Gowan, D. (1980), 'TUC Course Development — the Tasks Ahead', *Trade Union Studies Journal* 1 (Spring), 13-14.

—— (1981), 'Membership Education', *Trade Union Studies Journal* 4 (Autumn), 3-5.

—— (1982), 'Student-Centred Approaches Revisited', *Trade Union Studies Journal* 6 (Winter), 4-7.

Gramsci, A. (1971), *Selections from the Prison Notebooks*, ed. Q. Hoare and G. Nowell-Smith, London, Lawrence and Wishart.

Grant, A. (1990), 'Trade Union Education: A TUC Perspective', *The Industrial Tutor* 5(1) (Spring), 9-21.

—— (1992a), Interview with the present author, 13 March.

—— (1992b), Interview with the present author, 28 August.

Gravell, C. (1983), 'Trade Union Education: Will State Funding lead to State Control?', *Trade Union Studies Journal* 8 (Winter), 11-12.

Gray, R.Q. (1981), *The Aristocracy of Labour in Nineteenth Century Britain c.1850-1900*, London, Macmillan.

Grayson, J. (1983), 'The Challenge of Short Courses', *Trade Union Studies Journal* 8 (Winter), 9-11.

—— (1985), 'Power, Sex and the Unions: a New Look at Strategies for Anti-Sexist Teaching', *Trade Union Studies Journal* 11 (Summer), 8-12.

Greaves, S. (1979), Notes taken by the present author of a speech made on 11 July to the TUC Education summer school, Sheffield.

—— (1992), Interview with the present author, 11 March.

Gregory, W.C.E. (1958), 'Three Aspects of the WETUC', *Adult Education* 31(3), Winter, 210-15.

Griggs, C. (1983), *The Trades Union Congress and the Struggle for Education 1868-1925*, Lewes, The Falmer Press.

Grinter, S. (1980), 'Notes on Education and Training in the T&GWU', *The Industrial Tutor* 3(2) (March), 16-18.

Halstead, J. (1973), 'Industrial Day-Release, University of Sheffield Extra-Mural Department', *The Industrial Tutor* 1(8) (March), 19-21.

—— (1984), 'Workers' Education, the Universities and the Funding Crisis', *The Industrial Tutor* 3(9) (Spring), 23-29.

Handley, D. (1981), 'The APEX Education Programme', *Trade Union Studies Journal* 4 (Autumn), 21-22.

Harper, K. (1980), 'School for the likes of Kite', *The Guardian*, 2 August.

—— (1991), 'Government in Row over TUC Booklet "Gag"', *The Guardian*, 15 June.

Harris, J. 'Consultative Document: Safety Representatives and Safety Committees', *The Industrial Tutor* 2(4) (March), 36-40.

Harrison, J.F.C. (1959), 'The WEA in the Welfare State', in Raybould (1959a), 1-29.
—— (1961), *Learning and Living 1790-1960*, London, Routledge and Kegan Paul.
Hayward, G. (1983), 'Education in the NGA', *Trade Union Studies Journal* 7 (Summer), 22-23.
Henderson, S. (1977), 'Trade Union Education in Scotland: Recent Developments', *The Industrial Tutor* 2(7) (September), 14-19.
HMI (1980), *TUC Courses in Further Education Colleges in Scotland. A Report by HMI*, Edinburgh, Scottish Education Department.
Hobsbawm, E. (ed.) (1981), *The Forward March of Labour Halted?*, London, Verso.
Hock, A. (1981), 'Trade Union Education for Agricultural Workers', *Trade Union Studies Journal* 3 (Spring), 22.
Hodgen, M.T. (1925), *Workers' Education in England and the United States*, London, Kegan Paul, Trench, Trubner & Co.
Hodgson, K. (1978), 'The Establishment of the North East Trade Union Studies Information Unit', *The Industrial Tutor* 2(9) (September), 51-54.
Holford, J. (1988a), *Reshaping Labour*, London, Croom Helm.
—— (1988b), 'Mass Education and Community Development in the British Colonies 1940-1960: a Study in the Politics of Community Education', *International Journal of Lifelong Education* 7(3), 163-83.
—— (1988c), 'Continuing Education in the Trade Union Movement', in Jarvis (1988), 45-54.
Holton, R. (1976), *British Syndicalism 1900-1914. Myths and Realities*, London, Pluto.
—— (1980), 'Syndicalist Theories of the State', *Sociological Review* 28, 5-21.
Horner, A. (1960), *Incorrigible Rebel*, London, MacGibbon and Kee.
Houlton, B. (1971), 'Supply and Demand Relationships in Industrial Adult Education', *The Industrial Tutor* 1(5) (September), 4-9.
—— (1976), 'Industrial Studies Research', *The Industrial Tutor* 2(4) (March), 7-12.
—— (ed.) (1978), *Residential Adult Education — Values, Policies and Problems*, Society of Industrial Tutors.
—— (1991) 'Day Release: "It's Worse than Working"', *The Industrial Tutor* 3(5) (Autumn), 21-24.
Howard, S. (1990), 'Which Way Forward? A View from MSF', *The Industrial Tutor* 5(1) (Spring), 22-29.
Howarth, T. (1977), 'The Use of a Library on Shop Steward Courses', *The Industrial Tutor* 2(7) (September), 30-32.
Howell, D. (1983), *British Workers and the Independent Labour Party, 1888-1906*, Manchester, Manchester University Press.
Hughes, J. and R. Moore (eds.), *A Special Case? Social Justice and the Miners*, Harmondsworth, Penguin Books.
Hull, D. (1978), *The Shop Stewards Guide to Work Organisation*, Nottingham, Spokesman.

Hutchinson, E. (1965), 'Commentary', *Adult Education* 38(4) (November), 181.
H[utchinson], E.M. (1959), 'NCLC Golden Jubilee Dinner', *Adult Education* 31(4) (Spring), 309-10.
Hyman, R. (1975), *Industrial Relations. A Marxist Introduction*, London, Macmillan.
—— (1977), *Strikes*, London, Fontana.
Income Data Services (1988), *Retraining*, Study No. 405, March.
Ireland, J. (1966), 'Industrial Relations: Thoughts on Teaching', *Adult Education* 38(5) (January), 283-5.
Jackson, P. (1981), 'Membership Education and Study Circles in Sweden', *Trade Union Studies Journal* 4 (Autumn), 6-8.
Jacobson, S. and W. Connor, with G. Kaufman (1956), *The Daily Mirror Spotlight on the Trade Unions*, London, The Daily Mirror.
Jarvis, P. (1983), *Adult and Continuing Education. Theory and Practice*, London, Croom Helm.
—— (1988), *Britain: Policy and Practice in Continuing Education*, New Directions for Continuing Education, 40, San Francisco, Jossey-Bass.
Jenkins, W.E. (1960), 'Intermediate Courses for Trade Unionists: Some Problems of Organisation', *Adult Education* 32(4) (Spring), 293-6.
Jennings, B. (1973), *Albert Mansbridge*, Leeds, Leeds University Press.
—— (1976), *Albert Mansbridge and English Adult Education*, Hull, Hull University Department of Adult Education.
Jerrome, K. (1972), 'An Experiment in Hospital Trade Union Education', *The Industrial Tutor* 1(7) (September), 31-3
Jones, B. (1977), 'Teaching Industrial Relations and Communications: A Possible Framework', *The Industrial Tutor* 2(7) (September), 32-40.
Jones, J. (1973), 'The Russell Report: a Comment', *The Industrial Tutor* 1(9) (September).
Jones, J. (1984), 'A Liverpool Socialist Education', *History Workshop Journal* 18, Autumn, 92-101.
Joseph, K. (Lord Joseph) (1992), Letter to the present author, 28 January.
Jowitt, J. and R. Taylor (eds.) (1985), *The Politics of Adult Education*, Bradford, University of Leeds Department of Adult and Continuing Education, Bradford Centre Occasional Paper No. 5.
Kadish, A. (1987), 'University Extension and the Working Class: the case of the Northumberland Miners', *Historical Research* 60(142), 188-207.
Kahn-Freund, O. (1954), 'Legal Framework' in Flanders and Clegg (1954), 42-127.
Karlsson, L. (1985a), 'The Study Circle in Sweden: Methods and Ideology', *Trade Union Studies Journal* 11 (Summer), 18-19.
—— (1985b), 'The Study Circle in Sweden: Learning for Democracy', *Trade Union Studies Journal* 12 (Winter), 17-18.
Keegan, W. (1984), *Mrs Thatcher's Economic Experiment*, London, Allen Lane.
Kellner, P. (1990), 'A quiet revolution in British trade unions', *The Independent*, 27 July.

Kelly, J. (1987), *Labour and the Unions*, London, Verso.
—— (1988), 'The Decline of Trade Unionism?', *The Industrial Tutor* 4(7), 5-17.
Kelly, J. and C. Grooms (1986), 'TUC Basic Course: Participants' Views', *The Industrial Tutor* 4(3) (Spring), 49-56.
Kelly, T. (1962), *A History of Adult Education in Great Britain*, Liverpool, Liverpool University Press.
Killeen, J. and M. Bird (1981), *Education and Work. A Study of Paid Educational Leave in England and Wales (1976/77)*, Leicester, National Institute of Adult Education.
King, T.J. and A. Chambers (1973), 'Teaching Industrial Relations at South West London College', *The Industrial Tutor* 1(8) (March), 17-19.
Kisby, M. (1977), 'The University and College Labor Education Association', *The Industrial Tutor* 2(7) (September), 20-22.
Knowles, M. (1970), *The Modern Practice of Adult Education. From Pedagogy to Andragogy*, Chicago, Cambridge Book Co.
Knox, E. (1992), 'G'Day! Trade Union Education and Training in Australia', *The Industrial Tutor* 5(6) (Autumn), 25-40.
Labour Standard, The, Edinburgh.
Lenin, V.I. (1970), *Selected Works*, Volume I, Moscow, Progress Publishers.
Leopold, J. (1981), 'Participative Teaching Methods: A Survey from Scotland', *Trade Union Studies Journal* 4 (Autumn), 14-16.
Levy, C. (ed.) (1987a), *Socialism and the Intelligentsia 1880-1914*, London, Routledge and Kegan Paul.
—— (1987b), 'Education and Self-Education: Staffing the Early ILP' in Levy (1987a), 135-210.
Lewis, G.I. (1960), 'Dai's on Shift!', *Adult Education* 32(4) (Spring), 296-8.
Lockyer, C. (1982), 'What Do Schoolchildren Think of Trade Unions?', *Trade Union Studies Journal* 6, 9-10.
McCarthy, W.E.J. and S.R. Parker (1969), *Shop Stewards and Workshop Relations*, Royal Commission on Trade Unions and Employers' Associations, Research Paper No. 10, London, HMSO.
MacDermott, T. (1978), 'Education for the Participators', *The Industrial Tutor* 2(8) (March), 33-42.
MacDermott, T. and D. Bright (1976), 'Survey of Shop Steward Education on Tyneside', *The Industrial Tutor* 2(5) (September), 37-45.
McIlroy, J. (1979a), 'Recent Developments in Trade Union Studies Courses', *The Industrial Tutor* 2(10) (March), 11-16.
—— (1979b), 'Teaching Law to Trade Unionists', *The Industrial Tutor* 2(10) (March), 31-44.
—— (1980), 'Day Release for Trade Unionists — Some Problems and Issues', *The Industrial Tutor* 3(2) (March), 3-9.
—— (1981), 'Trade Union Courses: Future Prospects', *The Industrial Tutor* 3(5) (September), 88-90.
—— (1982a), 'Sexism and Trade Union Education', *Trade Union Studies Journal* 5 (Summer), 16-17.

—— (1982b), 'TUC Stage 2 — An Opportunity to Change Course?', *The Industrial Tutor* 3(6) (Spring), 67-71.
—— (1983), 'Lessons in Conformity', *New Statesman*, 23 September.
—— (1985a), 'Goodbye Mr. Chips?', *The Industrial Tutor* 4(2) (Autumn), 3-23.
—— (1985b), 'Pedagogy and Politics in Trade Union Education', *Adult Education* 58(2) (September), 169-74.
—— (1985c), 'Adult Education and the Role of the Client — The TUC Education Scheme 1929-80', *Studies in the Education of Adults* 17(1) (April), 33-58.
—— (1988a), 'Storm and Stress: The Trades Union Congress and University Adult Education 1964-1974', *Studies in the Education of Adults* 20(1) (April), 60-73.
—— (1988b), 'Unions and Universities: a Troubled Marriage', *Studies in the Education of Adults* 20(2) (October), 109-23.
—— (1990a), 'The Demise of the National Council of Labour Colleges', in Simon (1990a), 173-207.
—— (1990b), 'The Triumph of Technical Training?', in Simon (1990a), 208-43.
—— (1990c), 'Trade Union Education for a Change', in Simon (1990a), 244-75.
—— (1990d), 'Paid Educational Leave: Have we Missed the Next Train?' *The Industrial Tutor* 5(1) (Spring), 30-56.
—— (1991), *The Permanent Revolution? Conservative Law and the Trade Unions*, Nottingham, Spokesman.
McIlroy, J. and J. Brown (1980), 'Giving the Workers What they Want: the WEA and Industrial Education', *Adult Education* 53(2) (July), 91-5.
McIlroy, J. and B. Spencer (1984), 'Methods and Policies in Trade Union Education — A Rejoinder', *The Industrial Tutor* 3(10) (Autumn), 49-58.
—— (1989), 'Waves in British Workers Education', *Convergence* 22(2/3), 33-45.
—— (1992), 'Despatches from a Foreign Front: The Decline of Workers' Education in UK Universities', *Labor Studies Journal* 17(3) (Fall), 53-77.
Macintyre, S. (1974), 'Joseph Dietzgen and British Working-Class Education', *Bulletin of the Society for the study of Labour History* 29, 50-54.
—— (1980a), *A Proletarian Science. Marxism in Britain 1917-1933*, Cambridge, Cambridge University Press.
—— (1980b), *Little Moscows. Communism and Working-Class Militancy in Inter-War Britain*, London, Croom Helm.
Mackie, K. (1983), 'The Significance of the Workplace for Adult Education', *International Journal of Lifelong Education* 2(2), 179-88.
—— (1986), 'Trade Union Education in the United Kingdom: the Background to the Current System of Provision', *Studies in the Education of Adults* 18(2) (October), 91-109.
Maclean, J. (1978), *In the Rapids of Revolution. Essays, Articles and Letters 1902-23*, ed. N. Milton, London, Allison and Busby.

MacLeod, D. (1991), 'TUC Booklet on Women Withdrawn', *The Independent*, 15 June.
Marsh, A.I. (1958), 'The New Workers' Education', *Adult Education* 31(2) (Autumn), 126-30.
—— (1959), 'Conference on Trade Union Education', *Adult Education* 32(1) (Summer), 62-62-5.
—— (1965), *Industrial Relations in Engineering*, Oxford, Pergamon Press.
—— (1991), 'The Oxford Area', *The Industrial Tutor* 3(5) (Autumn), 19-20.
—— and E.E. Coker (1963), 'Shop Steward Organisation in the Engineering Industry', *British Journal of Industrial Relations* 1(2) (June), 170-90.
Marsh, D. (1991), *The New Politics of British Trade Unionism: Union Power and the Thatcher Legacy*, London, Macmillan.
Martin, R.M. (1980), *TUC: The Growth of a Pressure Group 1868-1976*, Oxford, Clarendon Press.
Marwick, W.H. (1974), 'Workers' Education in Early Twentieth Century Scotland', *Scottish Labour History Society Journal* 8, 34-8.
Massie, P. (1985), 'SCPS Education Programme', *Trade Union Studies Journal* 11 (Summer), 22-23.
Mealor, G. (1981), 'Trade Union Education and Training "Down Under"', *The Industrial Tutor* 3(4), March, 36-45.
Mee, G. (1984), *Miners, Adult Education and Community Service 1920-1984*, Nottingham Working Papers in the Education of Adults 6, Nottingham, Nottingham University Department of Adult Education.
Middlemas, R.K. (1979), *Politics in Industrial Society*, London, Deutsch.
Miles, A. (1984), 'Workers' Education: the Communist Party and the Plebs League in the 1920s', *History Workshop Journal* 18 (Autumn), 102-114.
Millar, J.P.M. (1965), 'The Value of Postal Courses', Letter in *Adult Education* 37(5), 284-5.
—— (1979), *The Labour College Movement*, London, NCLC Publishing Society [n.d.]
Miller, D. (1982), 'Men and Trade Unions: A Case for Positive Action', *Trade Union Studies Journal* 6 (Winter), 18-19.
—— (1983), 'Student-Centred Learning in Trade Union Education: Some Further Considerations', *Trade Union Studies Journal* 8 (Winter), 6-9.
—— (1985), 'A Note on Course Committees', *Trade Union Studies Journal* 11 (Summer), 20-21.
Millward, N. and M. Stevens (1986), *British Workplace Industrial Relations 1980-1984. The DE/ESRC/PSI/ACAS Surveys*, Aldershot, Gower.
Ministry of Education (1954), *The Organisation and Finance of Adult Education in England and Wales* (the Ashby Report), London, HMSO.
—— (1958), *Report by HM Inspectors on the Contribution of Responsible Bodies to the Education of Trade Unionists in the West Midlands: Inspected During 1956-1957*, London, Ministry of Education (Misc. 6/58).
Mooney, T. (1979), *J.M. Mactavish, General Secretary of the WEA 1916-1927. The Man and his Ideas*, Liverpool, WEA Liverpool Branch.

Moore, R. (1981), 'Political Education in Practice', *The Industrial Tutor* 3(5) (September), 53-61.

Morgan, K.O. (1984), *Labour in Power 1945-51*, Oxford, Clarendon Press.

Moxley, F. (1963), 'Railwaymen and Working Class Education', Appendix A in Bagwell (1963), 671-95.

Munday, J. (1977), 'Reflections on Trade Union Training in Northern Ireland', *The Industrial Tutor* 2(7) (September), 8-14.

Murray, L. (Lord Murray) (1992), Letter to the present author, 4 March.

Nash, I. (1991), 'TUC Bans its own Booklet', *The Times Educational Supplement*, 14 June.

NATFHE and SERTUC (1987), 'White Paper on Higher Education: Effect on TUC Course Provision', unpublished report on joint seminar, 23 October.

Nesbit, T. and S. Henderson (1983) 'Methods and Politics in Trade Union Education', *Trade Union Studies Journal* 8 (Winter), 4-6.

O'Brien, O. (1974), 'Key Issues in the Teaching of Industrial Relations', *The Industrial Tutor* 2(1) (September).

'Open University Industrial Relations Course' (1974), *The Industrial Tutor* 1(10) (March), 33-45.

Oswald, R., Eva, D., and Spencer, B. (1980), 'The Growth of Trade Union Education — the Liverpool Experience', *Trade Union Studies Journal* 1 (Spring), 3-6.

Paine, N. (1980), 'The Problem of Alcohol Abuse in the West of Scotland: A Trade Union Response', *Trade Union Studies Journal* 2 (Autumn), 11-13.

Panitch, L. (1976), *Social Democracy and Industrial Militancy*, Cambridge, Cambridge University Press.

Paper and Paper Products Industry Training Board (1971), *The Board's Approach to the Training of Trades Union Representatives*, Potter's Bar, PPPITB.

Park, T. (1969), 'Trade Union Education', in Coates, Topham and Barratt Brown (1969), 96-100.

Paul, W. (1920), *The State. Its Origin and Function*, Glasgow, Socialist Labour Press.

Pedler, M. (1974) 'The Teaching/Learning of Industrial Relations', *The Industrial Tutor* 1(10) (March), 25-33.

—— (1976), 'Teaching the Teachers?', *The Industrial Tutor* 2(5) (September), 94-7

—— (1978), 'Extending Industrial Democracy: Implications for Management Teaching and Management Teachers', *The Industrial Tutor* 2(8) (March), 23-32.

Peers, R. (1926), *Adult Education in the East Midlands 1920-1926*, Nottingham, University College Nottingham Department of Adult Education.

—— (1972), *Adult Education. A Comparative Study*, London, Routledge and Kegan Paul.

Phillips, A. and Putnam, T. (1980), 'Education for Emancipation: the Movement

for Independent Working Class Education 1908-1928', *Capital and Class* 10, 18-49.
Philo, P. (1984), 'Short Courses: Backing a Winner?', *Trade Union Studies Journal* 9 (Summer), 9-10.
—— (1989), 'Study Circles in Britain: Past, Present and Future', *The Industrial Tutor* 4(10) (Autumn), 5-20.
Pickstock, F.V. (1963), 'Teaching Trade Unionists', *Adult Education* 36(2) (July), 54-60.
Pierce, S. (1981), 'Women's Issues on Trade Union Courses', *Trade Union Studies Journal* 3 (Spring), 9-11.
Plebs League (1923), *What to Read. A Guide for Worker Students*, London, Plebs League.
Pole, T. (1816), *A History of the Origin and Purpose of Adult Schools*, second edition, Bristol, C. McDowall.
Pollins, H. (1977), 'Recent Developments at Ruskin College', *The Industrial Tutor* 2(6) (March), 65-73.
—— (1984), *The History of Ruskin College*, Oxford, Ruskin College Library Occasional Publications No. 3.
Pollock, H.M. (1979), 'The Irish Association for Industrial Relations', *The Industrial Tutor* 2(10) (March), 17-19.
Ponting, C. (1989), *Breach of Promise. Labour in Power 1964-1970*, London, Hamish Hamilton.
Prentice, (Sir) R. (1992), Letter to the present author, 30 January.
Price, R. (1986), *Labour in British Society. An Interpretative History*, London, Croom Helm.
Prior, J. (Lord Prior) (1992), Letter to the present author, 27 January.
Raybould, S.G. (ed.) (1959a), *Trends in English Adult Education*, London, Heinemann.
—— (1959b), 'Changes in Trade Union Education', in Raybould (1959a), 30-51.
Ree, J. (1984), *Proletarian Philosophers. Problems in Socialist Culture in Britain, 1900-1940*, Oxford, Clarendon Press.
Rees, C. (1991), 'Block on TUC handbook is "blatant censorship"', *Tribune*, 21 June.
Reid, F. (1966), 'Socialist Sunday Schools in Britain,1892-1939', *International Review of Social History* 11, 18-47.
Richards, M. (1985), 'TUC and Tutors Clash', *The Times Higher Education Supplement*, 7 June.
Richardson, A. (1980), 'Industrial Studies —The Changing Scene', *The Industrial Tutor* 3(2) (March), 10-15.
Richardson, F.A. (1974), 'Why the Colleges are failing in Trade Union Education', *The Technical Journal* (April-May), 12-13.
Roberts, B.C. (1956), *Trade Union Government and Administration in Great Britain*, London, G. Bell & Sons.
Roberts, J.H. (1970), 'The National Council of Labour Colleges — An Experi-

ment in Workers' Education. A Study of the Growth of the Labour Colleges with Particular Reference to Independent Working Class Adult Education in Scotland', M.Sc. Thesis, University of Edinburgh.

Robinson, J.W. (1968), 'British and American Workers' Education', *Journal of Industrial Relations* 10(1), 64-70.

Rosenfeld, P. and G. Broad (1982), 'Trade Union Training and Education: A Review and Future Prospects', *Employee Relations* 4(3), 17-20.

Rossell, P.E. (1963), 'Courses in Factories', *Adult Education* 36(2), July, 60-68.

Rowntree, J.W. and H.B. Binns (1903), *A History of the Adult School Movement*, London, Headley Bros.

Rushton, L. (1985), 'WEA Discriminates Against T.U. Tutor', *Outwrite* 37, June.

Salmon, J. (1983), 'Trade Union Education and Training: A Critique of Public Policy', *Employee Relations* 5(5), 29-32.

Saville, J. (1967), 'Trade Unions and Free Labour: the Background to the Taff Vale Decision', in Briggs and Saville (1967).

Sawbridge, D. (1973), 'The Teaching of Industrial Relations in a Polytechnic with Special Reference to Sunderland Polytechnic', *The Industrial Tutor* 1(8) (March), 9-13.

Schmoller, S. (1980), 'Sheffield Trade Union Safety Committee', *Trade Union Studies Journal* 2 (Autumn), 17-18.

Schuller, T. (ed.) (1980), *Is Knowledge Power? Problems and Practice in Trade Union Education*, Aberdeen, Aberdeen People's Press [n.d.]

—— (1988), 'Paid Educational Leave: Idee Passee or Future Benefit?', *The Industrial Tutor* 4(8) (Autumn), 5-16.

—— and S. Henderson (1980), 'Worker Representation and the Articulation of Training Needs', *Industrial Relations Journal* 11(2), 49-57.

Schuller T. and D. Robertson (1983), 'Convenors as Parents, Branches as Homes: Influences on Adult Learning', *British Journal of the Sociology of Education* 4(2), 141-53.

Scipes, K. (1986), 'Trade Union Education in the Philippines: its role in the Struggle for National Liberation', *Trade Union Studies Journal* 13 (Summer), 18-19.

Seifert, R. (1984), 'Shop Steward Courses: A Comment on Methods of Assessment', *The Industrial Tutor* 3(9) (Spring), 72-78.

—— (1985a), 'Do Shop Steward Courses Work?: Tests of the NUT School Reps Training Scheme — Part 1', *The Industrial Tutor* 4(1) (Spring), 30-37.

—— (1985b), 'Tests of the NUT School Reps Training Scheme — Part 2', *The Industrial Tutor* 4(2) (Autumn), 24-30.

Senturia, J.J. (1930), 'The Trades Union Congress and Workers' Education', *American Economic Review* 20(4), 673-84.

Shaw, R. (1965), 'Popular Culture', *Adult Education* 37(6) March), 303-09.

Sheehan, B. (1978), 'The Associate Diploma in Industrial Relations at Preston — A Report', *The Industrial Tutor* 2(9) (September), 55-60.

Simon, B. (ed.) (1990a), *The Search for Enlightenment. The Working Class and Adult Education in the Twentieth Century*, London, Lawrence and Wishart.

—— (1990b), 'The Struggle for Hegemony, 1920-1926', in Simon (1990a), 15-70.
Smith, A.E. (1984), 'Trade Union Education: its Past and Future, *Industrial Relations Journal* 15(2), 72-90.
—— (1986), 'Historical Development and Future Direction of Trade Union Education', *The Industrial Tutor* 4(3) (Spring), 37-48.
Smith, J. (1982), 'Trade Union Education in NALGO', *Trade Union Studies Journal* 5 (Summer), 22-23.
Smith, R. (1984), 'Taking on the Multinationals: GLC Initiatives', *Trade Union Studies Journal* 10 (Summer), 12-13.
Smith, S. (1985), 'Teaching Social Security', *Trade Union Studies Journal* 13 (Summer), 6-8.
Society of Industrial Tutors (1970), 'Evidence to the Russell Committee on Adult Education', *The Industrial Tutor* 1(2) (March), 4-15.
—— (1971), 'Evidence to the Alexander Committee on Scottish Adult Education', *The Industrial Tutor* 1(4) (March), 33-35.
—— (1971), 'Evidence to the Commission on Industrial Relations' Reference on Industrial Relations Training', *The Industrial Tutor* 1(5) (September), 14-17.
—— (1974), 'Conference on Student Participation — Report', *The Industrial Tutor* 2(1) (September), 38-40.
—— (1975a), 'Submission to the Committee on the Future of Broadcasting', *The Industrial Tutor* 2(2) (March), 4-16.
—— (1975b), 'Research Conference Papers', *The Industrial Tutor* 2(3) (September), 1-21.
—— (1975c), 'The Grading of Shop Stewards', *The Industrial Tutor* 2(3) (September), 22-33.
—— (1977), 'Preparing for Industrial Democracy - SIT Evidence to the Bullock Committee', *The Industrial Tutor* 2(6) (March).
—— (1978), 'Higher Education into the 1990s: The Response of the SIT', *The Industrial Tutor* 2(9) (September), 3-6.
—— (1988), *The Impossible Dream? The Future of Paid Educational Leave in Britain*, SIT and TGWU.
Speck, Alan (1975), 'Vital Need for Trade Union Education', *Morning Star*, 20 May.
Spencer, B. (1984), 'Collective Bargaining and the Rights at Work Courses', *The Industrial Tutor* 3(9), 52-7.
—— (1985), 'Health and Safety: A Second Opinion', *Trade Union Studies Journal* 11 (Summer), 16-18.
—— (1989), 'Making the Difference: the Two-year TGWU Distance Learning Course', *The Industrial Tutor* 4(10) (Autumn), 68-74.
—— (1991), 'Developments in British Adult Education' *The Industrial Tutor* 3(5) (Autumn), 33-37.
—— (1992), 'Student-centred Courses and Social Awareness: Contrary Evidence from British Workers' Education', *Canadian Journal for the Study of Adult Education* 6(1) (May), 67-80.

Spooner, D. (1984), 'Trade Union Education and Internationalism', *Trade Union Studies Journal* 10 (Summer), 10-11.

Steele, R. (1986), 'Trade Union Education in Northern Ireland', *Trade Union Studies Journal* 12 (Winter), 20-22.

Stinson, M. (1989), 'Labour's Policy Review: Labour Law and Equal Rights', *The Industrial Tutor* 4(10) (Autumn), 75-82.

Stirling, J. (1991), 'The North East Experience', *The Industrial Tutor* 3(5) (Autumn), 25-32.

Stocks, M. (1953), *The Workers' Educational Association: the First Fifty Years*, London, Allen and Unwin.

'Students in Trade Union Education — Is there Really a Decline', *Trade Union Studies Journal* 3 (Spring), 23.

Stuttard, C.G. (1964), 'Industrial Visits International', *Adult Education* 37(4) (November), 208-10.

—— (1966), 'Industrial Relations: Thoughts on Teaching', *Adult Education* 38(5) (January), 285-6.

—— (1973), 'Teaching Industrial Relations: Some of the Problems', *The Industrial Tutor* 1(9) (September), 47-50.

—— (1974), 'The Tyranny of Words', *The Industrial Tutor* 2(1) (September), 41-4.

—— (1975), 'Paid Educational Leave', *The Industrial Tutor* 2(2) (March), 57-9.

—— (1976), 'Bullock Committee of Inquiry on Industrial Democracy in Private Industry: the Implications for Education and Training', *The Industrial Tutor* 2(5) (September), 33-37.

—— (1980), 'Case Studies of the Development of AEL and PEL in the London Area: "Bargaining for Release"', in PEL Project *Report* Volume II, *PEL Source Book*, unpublished.

—— (1987), 'Reminiscences', *Extra: The Newsletter of the Department of Extra-mural Studies, University of London*, July.

—— (1988), '"Trade Union Industrial Studies" Paperback Series: the Inside Job', *The Industrial Tutor* 4(8) (Autumn), 41-50.

—— (1991), 'Day Release: Yesterday and Today', *The Industrial Tutor* 5(4) (Autumn), 5-8.

'Supply and Demand: an Example of Growth in London' (1971), *The Industrial Tutor* 1(5) (September), 10-13.

Sutherland, J. (1982), 'What is to be Done? Another Look at TUC Provision', *The Industrial Tutor* 3(6) (Spring), 72-75.

—— (1985) 'The Political Fund Ballot and Trade Union Education', *Trade Union Studies Journal* 12 (Winter), 9-10.

Sweeney, J. (1973), 'Trade Union Education in the Workers' Educational Association, West Midlands District', *The Industrial Tutor* 1(8) (March), 13-16.

—— (1974), 'Adult Tutors and the ASTMS', *The Industrial Tutor* 2(1) (September), 33-35.

Bibliography

'Syllabuses' (1973), *The Industrial Tutor* 1(8) (March), 35-49.

Taylor, Robert (1975), 'Schooling the Unions', *New Society*, 4 September.

Tebbit, N. (Lord Tebbit) (1989), *Upwardly Mobile*, London, Futura Publications.

Thompson, E.P. (1977), *William Morris: Romantic to Revolutionary*, London, Merlin Press.

Thompson, J. (ed.) (1980), *Adult Education for a Change*, London, Hutchinson.

Thorne, C. (1983), 'Education in USDAW', *Trade Union Studies Journal* 8 (Winter), 21-22.

Thornton, A.H. (1960), 'Liberal Education for Factory Workers', *Adult Education* 33(1) (May), 13-30.

—— and F. Bayliss (1965), *Adult Education and the Industrial Community*, London, National Institute of Adult Education.

Thornton, A.H. and M.D. Stephens (eds.) (1977), *The University in its Region. The Extra-Mural Contribution*, Nottingham, Nottingham University Department of Adult Education.

Toombs, F. and S. Creigh (1983), 'Developments in Joint Industrial Relations Training', *Employment Gazette*, December, 510-516.

Topham, T. (1969), 'Prospects for Industrial Education', *The Industrial Tutor* 1(1)) (September).

—— (1970), 'Hull Portworkers Day-Release Course', *The Industrial Tutor* 1(2) (March), 20-28.

—— (1973), 'Trade Union Lay-Tutors on Humberside', *The Industrial Tutor* 1(8) (March), 22-24.

—— (1981), 'The Need for Political Education', *The Industrial Tutor* 3(5) (September), 47-52.

Trades Union Congress (1940-1992), *Annual Reports*, London, TUC.

—— (1936a), *Trade Unionism: A General Survey in 12 Lessons. History, Structure, Functions, Policy. TUC Study Guide for Classes and Students*, London, TUC [n.d.].

—— (1946a), *What the T.U.C. is Doing*, London, TUC [n.d.].

—— (1968a), *Training Shop Stewards*, London, TUC.

—— (1973a), 'Statement on the CIR Report on Industrial Relations Training', *The Industrial Tutor* 1(9) (September).

—— (1978a), *Public Funds for Trade Union Courses*, London, TUC [n.d.]

—— (1978b), *Time Off for Union Activities. A TUC Guide*, London, TUC.

—— (1978c), *Facilities for Shop Stewards. A Statement of Policy*, [first published 1971; reprinted with amendments,] London, TUC.

—— (1978d), 'The Future of the TUC Teaching Materials for 10-Day Health and Safety Courses', unpublished discussion paper, TUC Education Service, [n.d.].

—— (1979a), 'TUC Day Release Course Outlines', unpublished paper, TUC Education Service, February.

—— (1980a), *The Organisation, Structure and Services of the TUC. A TUC Consultative Document*, London, TUC.

—— (1981a), *The Organisation, Structure and Services of the TUC. Second TUC Consultative Document*, London, TUC.
—— (1981b), *TUC Development Programme. A Special Report ... following a review of the TUC's organisation, structure and services*, London, TUC.
—— (1981c), 'Stage 2 Course for Union Reps: Briefing Notes', TUC Education, May.
—— (1983a), 'Methods in Trade Union Education', unpublished paper, TUC Education, November.
—— (1983b), *TUC Workbook on Racism*, London, TUC Education.
—— (1983c), *Working Women. A TUC Discussion Book for All Trade Unionists*, London, TUC Education.
—— (1984a), *Guide to TUC Education*, London, TUC Education.
—— (1984b), 'Change at Work: Industrial Relations and Collective Bargaining', briefing note circulated by TUC Education Department.
—— (1984c), *Learning about Trade Unions*, London, TUC Education.
—— (1986a), 'Open School: A Guide', TUC Education.
—— (1986b), 'Tackling Racism - A Course for Union Activists', TUC Education.
—— (1986c), 'Trade Unions and the Economy: Notes for Tutors', TUC Education Department, January.
—— (1987a), *Review of the TUC's Education Service*, London, TUC.
—— (1987b), 'Review of TUC Education Service — Background Note', unpublished paper, Trade Union Education Department.
—— (1987c), 'TUC Education Review Conference 1987, South East Region: Workshop 1 — Review', unpublished background paper for conference held 2 February 1987.
—— (1987d), 'DES Consultative Paper: Polytechnics and Colleges Sector. Comments of the TUC General Council', unpublished paper [n.d.]
—— (1990a), 'Aims and Methods in Trade Union Education. Discussion Note for Tutor Meetings', unpublished Trade Union Education Department paper, February.
—— (1990b), 'Maintaining Quality in the Trade Union Education Service', unpublished Trade Union Education Department paper, May.
—— (1991a), *Working Women. A TUC Handbook for All Trade Unionists*, London, TUC.
—— (1992a), *TUC Guide to Paid Release for Trade Union Training*, London, TUC.
—— (1992b), *Training and Development for Trade Union Officers: Progress Report 1* (26 February).
—— (1992c), 'The TUC's Education Service and the F and HE Bill', unpublished internal paper, 13 February.
—— (1993a), 'Occupational Standards and Vocational Qualifications for the Trade Union Sector. A Report on the completion of Phase 1 of the General Council's Priority Task on Trade Union Training and Recommendations for Further Development', attachment to TUEC document 3/1, 3 March 1993.

'Trade Union Education: a draft leaflet' (1971), *The Industrial Tutor* 1(5) (September).
Transport and General Workers' Union (1983), 'Reshaping Trade Union Education: TGWU Proposals for Government Support', *The Industrial Tutor* 3(8) (Autumn), 62-67.
Treasury, H.M., *Economic Progress Report*.
Trotsky, L. (1970), *Where is Britain Going?*, London [first edition 1925].
Tsuzuki, C. (1983), 'Anglo-Marxism and Working-Class Education' in Winter (1983), 187-99.
Turnbull, M. (1986), 'Broadening the Horizon: Second Chance and Workers' Education', *Trade Union Studies Journal* 13 (Summer), 10-12.
University of Oxford (1970), *Report of the Committee on Extra-mural Studies*, Supplement No. 3 to the *Oxford University Gazette 100*, March.
Vulliamy, D. (1981), 'Safety and the NUS', *Trade Union Studies Journal* 4 (Autumn), 13-14.
—— (1985), 'The Politics of Trade Union Education', in Jowitt and Taylor (1985), 5-27.
Wallis, E. (1973), 'The Russell Report: a comment', *The Industrial Tutor* 1(9) (September).
Webb, S. and B. (1911), *Industrial Democracy*, London, Longman, Green and Co.
Wedderburn, K.W. (1986), *The Worker and the Law*, 3rd edition, Harmondsworth, Penguin.
Westbrook, R. and J. Whitehouse (1978a), 'TUC Workplace Representative Training — A National Survey: Part 1', *The Industrial Tutor* 2(8) (March), 5-22.
—— (1978b), 'TUC Workplace Representative Training — A National Survey: Part 2', *The Industrial Tutor* 2(9) (September), 15-34.
Weston, C. (1992), 'Merger Vote may Herald Super Unions', *The Guardian*, 3 February.
Whitston, K. (1982), 'Breaking Fresh Ground? The New TUC Introductory Course', *The Industrial Tutor* 3(6) (Spring), 63-66.
Whyte, J. (1980), 'College-based Provision for Trade Unionists', in Schuller (ed.) (1980), 59-72.
Wigham, E. (1961), *What's Wrong with the Unions?*, Harmondsworth, Penguin.
Williams, J.E. (1954), 'An Experiment in Trade Union Education', *Adult Education* 27(2) (Autumn), 113-24.
Williams, P. (1985), 'Trade Union Education in Brazil', *Trade Union Studies Journal* 12 (Winter), 14-16.
Williams, R. (1961), 'The Common Good', *Adult Education* 34(4) (November), 192-99.
—— (1979), *Politics and Letters*, London, New Left Books.
Williams, S. and R. Nicola (1982), 'Education in NUPE', *Trade Union Studies Journal* 6 (Winter), 23-24.
Wilson, P. (1981), 'Work in Progress — Language Training for Trade Union Representatives', *Trade Union Studies Journal* 4 (Autumn), 10-12.

Winkler, J.T. (1976), 'Corporatism', *Arch. europ. sociol.* 17, 100-136.
Winter, J. (ed.) (1983), *The Working Class in Modern British History. Essays in Honour of Henry Pelling*, Cambridge, University Press.
Workers' Educational Association (1953), *Trade Union Education: A Report from a Working Party set up by the WEA* [and chaired by A. Creech Jones], London, WEA.
—— (1970), *Shop Stewards' and Representatives' Training. Teaching Manual* ['based on teaching undertaken for the TUC's Training College'], London, WEA Service Centre for Social Studies.
—— (1981), Trade Union Studies Advisory Committee: 'Survey of WEA/TUC Provision 1979/80; 1980/81', unpublished paper.
—— (1985), *Report of the National Executive Committee for 1983/85*, London, WEA.
—— (1987), Biennial Conference Minutes, London, WEA.
—— (1988), 'Trade Union Education in the WEA. Report to the 1989 WEA BDC', Draft Report of Working Party, July.
—— (1989), *Trade Union Education and the Future of the WEA. A WEA Policy Statement*, London, WEA.
Workers' Educational Association, East Midlands District (1960), 'Special Work for Trade Unionists', *Adult Education* 32(4) (Spring), 302-03.

INDEX

Abell, P, 182
Adams, Rex, 57, 61, 63, 77, 84n, 150-151, 160, 175, 176, 256
Adopt a School Scheme, 182
Advisory Committee on the Supply and Education of Teachers, 186n
Advisory, Conciliation and Arbitration Service, 106, 116n, 219
Aims and Methods in TU Education Paper, 203, 206
Alexander Report, 108, 110
Allen, V L, 28, 187n
Amalgamated Engineering Union, 61, 77, 107
Amalgamated Union of Engineering Workers, 128, 207
amalgamation of unions, 190, 207
anarchism, 25
Anderson, Digby, 216, 217, 235-236n
Armstrong, P J, 175, 256
Ashby Report 1954, 63
Association of Education Committees, 31
Association of Scientific, Technical and Managerial Staffs, 96, 207
Association of Tutors in Adult Education, 73
Atkins, J, 22, 58, 59, 60, 132
Attfield, J, 35, 36
Australia, 244
Aylesbury, 236n

Bailey, W J, 96
Bain, George, 187n
Baker, H L, 49, 52
Bakers' Union, 181
Banks, R F, 256
Bargaining, 159, 199
Batstone, E, 122, 175, 256
Bayliss, F J, 186n
Belfast WEA, 23
Bell, J D M, 13n, 77, 78
Benn, Tony, 87, 89
Bevin, Ernest, 145

Beynon, H, 154
Billingham, 213n
Binns, H B, 15
Birmingham College of Technology, 148
Birmingham University Extra-Mural Department, 78
Blackpool WEA, 23
Blatchford, Robert, 35
'Blue Pack', 153
Board of Education, 31
Bolshevism, 17
Boraston, I, 175, 256
Boyden, Jim, 73, 85n
Boyson, Rhodes, 222
bridging courses for women, 177
Bristol University Extra-Mural Department, 73
British Employers' Confederation, 78, 79
British Institute of Adult Education, 145
British Motor Corporation, 78
Brown, G, 51, 52, 56n
Brown, J, 158, 250
Brown, Michael Barratt, 163, 240
Brown, W, 209, 256
Bruce, Maurice, 73, 74
building trade workers' union, 29
Burkitt, A, 256
Butler Act, 239

Callaghan, James, 89
Camberwell Trades Council, 84n
campaign workshops, 136, 280-281
Campbell, A, 57, 117n, 141n, 142n, 166
Cannon, Les, 85n
Carlisle, Mark, 127
Carr, J J, 128
Cartwright, John, 236n
Casey, Fred, 38, 39-40, 43, 44, 249
Castle, Barbara, 86, 90
Central Labour College, 18-19, 21,

305

22, 23, 25, 29, 30, 31-2, 33n, 43, 54
Centre for Trade Union Studies, Slough, 236n
Cheshire WEA District, 141n
Churchill, Winston, 145
Citrine, Walter, 28, 32
Civil Service, 196
Civil Service Clerical Association, 50
Clarke, John, 26
Clegg, Hugh A, 13n, 57, 61, 63, 77, 84n, 150-151, 160, 161, 172-4, 175, 176, 249-250, 256
Clinton, A, 23
Clunie, James, 38, 40-41, 44, 249
Clydeside, 17
Coates, Ken, 13n, 163, 187n
Cohen, M, 28, 37, 40, 43, 44, 46
Coker, E, 77, 162
Cole, G D H, 31, 32, 51, 52
Coleg Harlech, 61
collective bargaining, 119-123 passim, 143, 163, 172, 174, 218-219
colleges of further education, 108, 134, 224, 225, 251
Colonial Office Advisory Committee on Education, 146
Commission on Industrial Relations, 84n, 87, 94-5, 102, 105, 108, 116n, 124-5, 240, 243
Commonwealth countries, distance learning in, 44
Commonwealth TUC courses, 138n
Communist Party, 36, 43, 46, 188
competitive tendering, 181
Confederation of British Industries, 78, 83, 90, 93, 106, 110, 125, 233
Confederation of Health Service Employees, 182
Congleton, 216, 235n
Congress House, 14n, 60, 113, 141, 228
Connor, W, 76
Conservative governments
  and incomes policy, 76
  Manifesto, 125
  under Heath, 3, 87, 94, 96, 97, 103-104, 104-105, 107-108, 120, 191, 240
  under Major, 222, 223, 232, 233, 251
  under Thatcher, 10, 118, 119, 137-8, 166, 167, 170, 215, 216, 222, 223, 232, 251
  working with TUC, 77
Control of Substances Hazardous to Health, 201
Co-operative movement, 15, 35, 36
Corfield, A J, 24, 29, 31, 47-8, 49, 50, 52, 62, 64, 75, 78, 185n
correspondence courses, 44, 50
course development unit, 134, 154-6, 165, 191, 199, 206
courses
  access to, 196
  content, 24, 39, 41, 44, 45, 59, 170-171, 177-182
  decline in, 128-131
  development of, 195, 154-5
  fees for, 1-2, 49 see also funding
  materials for, 153-5, 181, 183-4, 199, 206
  organisation and methods, 103, 156, 164
  publicity and promotion, 197
  standardisation, 151-2
  see also individual types of courses
Coventry, 17
Coyne, C, 256
Craik, W W, 19, 26, 31, 33n, 56n
Creech Jones, Arthur, 62, 84n, 145-7, 160, 171, 175, 176
Creech Jones Report 1953, 63, 145-150, 160, 161, 162, 185n, 239-240, 249-250, 256
Croucher, R, 61, 162
Cunliffe, G, 73
Cupper, L, 244, 256
curriculum
  content, 5-6, 29-30, 38, 39, 45, 48, 49-50, 60, 73, 117n, 167, 176-7
  development, 245-7
  method of teaching, 117n, 167, 176-7

Index

specific subjects, 137
student influence over, 24
uniformity, 1, 10, 43, 113-114, 227, 243
union control over, 73, 74, 103, 244, 253-4
curriculum development unit, 10, 176

Dalton, Hugh, 51
Darwin, Charles, 36-7, 46
Davies, John, 86
day release courses, 2, 61, 71, 78, 80, 81, 98, 110, 114, 115, 128-131, 133, 154, 183, 198-9, 200, 213n, 246
day schools, 50, 62, 70, 98-9, 104
Department for Education, 225
Department of Education and Science, 10, 84n, 93, 96, 99, 105, 108, 110, 127, 137, 198, 218, 236n, 241
Department of Employment (and Productivity), 10, 90, 93, 104-106 passim, 127, 203, 217-218, 219, 223, 225, 233, 236n, 237n, 241, 244, 252, 256
Department of Employment's Training, Enterprise and Education Directorate, 209
Derby WEA, 23
Derbyshire, 61
Dietzgen, 33n, 36-7
Dietzgen System of Philosophy, 40
disabled students, 180
Disney, R, 125
distance learning, 44, 53, 140
Donaldson, P, 120
Donovan Commission, 80, 84n, 86, 90, 91, 92, 94, 104, 108, 123, 124, 172-4
Dorfman, G A, 13n, 77, 90
Douglas, Fred, 38-9
Douglass, Harry, 62
Dunn, Jack, 80
Durham
  courses, 61
  miners, 25
East Anglia TUC Region, 230, 237n

East Midlands TUC Region, 230, 237n
economic awareness courses, 170-171
Edinburgh, 26, 31, 38-9, 44
Edinburgh and District Labour College, 45, 144
Edinburgh Trades Council, 33n
Edwardian Britain, workers in, 34-5
Edwards, C, 158, 159, 166, 250
Edwards, John, 238n
Electrical, Electronic, Telecommunications and Plumbing Union, 217
Electrical Trades Union, 85n
Electricians' Union, 189
Elliott, Ruth, 191
Employment Act 1980, 127, 141n
Employment Act 1982, 141n
Employment Act 1989, 218
Employment Protection Act 1975, 106, 107, 112, 117n, 236n
Employment Protection Bill, 105, 106
Employment Protection (Consolidation) Act 1978, 218
Engels, F, 11
engineering industries, 25
engineering unions, 29
Engineers and Managers Association, 128
equal opportunities policy, 180
equality bargaining, 201
European Commission, 209, 243
European Community, 190
European Monetary System, 233
European TU Confederation, 209
extension classes, 25
extra-mural departments, 7, 8, 10, 15, 37, 73-4, 78, 82, 92, 96, 108, 113, 134, 141n, 160-161, 162, 164, 226, 240, 243, 248, 249, 251

Fabian Colonial Bureau, 146
Fairclough, Andy, 191
Farquhar, J, 120
fees for courses, 1-2, 8, 38, 99 *see also* funding
Fellner, W, 76
Field, J, 257
Fieldhouse, Roger, 6, 15, 30, 31, 53,

307

145, 256
Fircroft College, 22
Fisher, J, 166, 256
Foot, Michael, 87, 89, 106
Fords, Dagenham, 78
Forsyth, Michael, 233
Foster, J, 17
Fox, Alan, 187n
Freire, Paolo, 186n
Frenkel, S, 175, 256
funding
  by the Department of Education and Science, 108
  by the Department of Employment, 217-218
  costs of course fees, 225
  distribution of funds, 112, 243
  for officers and tutors, 43
  for research, 250
  for Ruskin college, 22
  for TUC National Education Centre, 138, 140
  from government, 107, 114, 118, 125, 136, 167-170
  loss and effects of loss, 192, 223, 225, 231-4, 252
  public funding, 8, 9, 10, 13n, 81-5, 90, 91-2, 99, 134, 231-4, 240-242, 251
  transfer of funding, 224
Further and Higher Education Act 1992, 224-5, 226, 228, 231
further education colleges, 224
Further Education Council, 231, 233-4
Further Education Funding Council, 225
Fyrth, J, 162, 163

GCHQ Cheltenham, 141n
Gee, D, 155, 183-4
General and Municipal Workers' Union, 61
General Federation of the Trade Unions, 252-3
General, Municipal and Boilermakers' Union, 181, 202, 237n
General Strike, 18, 31

Gibbons, C, 38, 46, 249
Gill, Ken, 212n
Glasgow WEA, 23
Gold Committee, 93, 115n
Gold, D J, 116n
Gold Report, 84n, 94, 96, 108, 110-111, 112, 113, 175, 256
Gold Working Party, 95
Goldstein, J, 77
Goodman, J F B, 77, 175, 256
Gowan, Doug, 155-6, 158, 184, 191, 203, 213n, 250
Graham, K, 97
Grant, Alan, 171, 191-2, 200, 203, 206, 213n, 214n, 215, 226, 237n, 242, 266-7
Gray, R Q, 34
Grayson, J, 187n
Greater Manchester day release courses, 133
Greaves, Stan, 114, 118, 171, 223, 228
Green, Ernest, 52
green movement, 11
'Green Pack', 153
Griggs, C, 13n, 19, 29, 30, 31

Halstead, J, 61, 162
Hammond, Eric, 189
Harper, K, 127
Harrison, J F C, 15, 16, 74, 149
Health and Safety at Work Act 1974, 107, 112
Health and Safety Commission, 233
Health and Safety Commission Code of Practice, 117n
health and safety courses, 115, 129, 131, 155, 165, 166, 180, 186n, 198, 200, 212n-213n, 219, 247
Health and Safety Organisations, 199
Heath, Edward *see* Conservative governments
Hedges, R Y, 84n
Henderson, S, 256
Her Majesty's Inspector(ate) (of Education), HMI, 108, 203, 222, 226, 236n, 243, 244
Hird, Dennis, 19, 21

Index

Hobsbawn, E, 212n
Hodgen, Margaret, 4, 6-7, 16, 249
Holford, J, 18, 25, 26, 35, 145, 146, 185n
Holton, R, 25
Hornsey College of Art, 138
Houlton, B, 22
Howard, Michael, 218, 233
Howard, Sarah, 207-208
Howe, Sir Geoffrey, 119
Howell, D, 16
Hughes, John, 175, 187n
Hull, D, 175
Hyman, J D, 175, 187n, 256

ICI, 231n
In Place of Strife, 86, 90, 91, 92, 93-4, 95, 108, 116n, 123-4, 174
Independent Labour Party, 16, 25, 35, 36
induction courses, 136-7, 197
industrial relations
  academic, 175
  research and theory, 172-4
  training, 124, 125, 132, 247
  workplace, 175
Industrial Relations Act 1971, 86-7, 94, 104, 124, 127, 135, 243
Industrial Relations Act 1980, 135
Industrial Relations Bill, 95, 96-7, 104, 115, 191
Industrial Relations Research Unit, 176
Industrial Relations Training, 94, 95, 124
Industrial Society, 106, 116n
Industrial Studies, 162, 163, 164, 171, 186n, 240, 245
Industrial Training Act 1964, 82
industrial training boards, 82, 83, 91-2, 95, 103, 104, 105, 117n, 242
Industrial Unionism, 17, 25
Inland Revenue, 181
Institute for Workers' Control, 163, 188-9
international courses, 138, 140
International Labour Organisation, 141n
International Monetary Fund, 89
Introductory Course for Shop Stewards, 153
Introductory Course for Union Representatives, 153, 165, 172
Irish Confederation of Trade Unions, 75
Iron and Steel Trades Confederation, 23, 29, 47, 62

Jackson, Roy, 105, 116n, 156, 184, 190-191, 229, 240
Jacobson, S, 76
Jarvis, P, 186n, 250
Jennings, B, 23
Joint Trade Union Education Committee, 65-6
Jones, Arthur Creech *see* Creech Jones, Arthur
Jones, J, 44, 56n
Jones, Jack, 78, 188
Joseph, Sir Keith, 127, 170-171, 222

Kadish, A, 16
Kahn-Freund, Otto, 172-4, 185n
Karlsson, L, 184
Kellner, P, 190
Kelly, Tom, 73, 187n
Kent, 49, 51-2, 80, 163
Killick, A J, 77
Knowles, Malcolm, 186n, 250
Knox, E, 244
Labour college movement, 18, 25-8, 35, 37-47, 68, 92, 103, 149, 239, 245, 251
  funding for, 82, 242
Labour governments, 2, 3, 8, 55, 58, 77, 80, 87, 97, 104, 114, 124, 137, 144, 145, 239
labour movements, 2, 11-12, 17, 21, 35-6, 55
Labour Party, 6, 17, 25, 36, 76-7, 96, 99, 189, 232
Labour Party Liaison Committee, 96-7
Labour Research Department, 175

309

Labour Socialism, 25, 36
Lancashire, 28
Lancashire College of Technology, 78
Laski, Harold, 51, 52
Lawson, M, 209, 256
Learning about Trade Unions, 182
Leeds University Extra-Mural Department, 61, 62
Lees-Smith, H B, 19
legal changes for Trade Unions, 119, 125
Leicester WEA, 23
Leith, 26
Lenin, V I, 143
Levie, H, 175
Levy, C, 16
Lewis, Arthur, 235n
Lewis, Kenneth, 216
Liberal Party, 89
Liberalism, 17, 149
Lindsay, A D, 31
Liverpool University Extra-Mural Studies Department, 73
local education authorities, 108, 230
Local Government Act 1988, 181
Local Government Training Board, 105
Local Government union representatives, 153
Lockyer, C, 182
London, co-operative movement in, 36
London School of Economics, 59
London University Extra-Mural Department, 78, 162
Lowthian, George, 79-80
Lyons, John, 128

McCarthy, Bill, 77, 187n
McCullough, Ellen, 66, 73
MacDonald, Ramsay, 46
McIlroy, John, passim
Macintyre, Stuart, 25, 33n, 34, 35, 36, 37, 40, 46, 51, 56n
Mackie, K, 57, 256
Maclean, John, 5, 44
Mactavish, 22-4, 33n

Major, John *see* Conservative governments
Manchester University Extra-Mural Department, 142n
Manpower Services Commission, 189, 214n
Mansbridge, Albert, 23, 34
Manufacturing, Science, Finance, 207-208
Maritime House, 60
Marsh, Arthur, 13n, 77, 78, 93, 123, 141n, 142n, 161, 174, 187n
Martin, R M, 13n
Marx, Karl, 11, 36-7, 40
Marxism, 17, 21, 25, 26, 36, 40-41, 43, 46, 245
Mealor, G, 244
mechanics' institutes, 15
Mee, G, 162
Methods in Trade Union Education, 158
Middlemas, R K, 17
Middlesex Polytechnic, 224
Miles, A, 37, 56n
Millar, Christine, 45
Millar, J P M, 20-21, 26, 31, 33n, 37-8, 41, 43, 44, 45, 54, 56n, 62, 63, 64, 65-6, 68, 144, 175-6
Miller, D, 56n, 185n
Millward, N, 122, 195
Milton Keynes Development Corporation, 137-8
mineworkers, 25
  dispute 1972, 175, 188
  strike 1973-4, 87
  strike 1984-5, 122, 188, 189
Mineworkers' Union, 33n, 58, 61, 217
Ministry of Labour, 78
Ministry of Reconstruction Adult Education Committee, final report 1919, 14n
Monks, John, 242
Mooney, T, 23
Moore, 175
Morgan, K O, 145
motor industry, 163
Moxley, F, 61

Mulley, Fred, 232
Murray, Len, 99, 103, 105, 106, 190, 191, 240

Nash, I, 221, 223
National Advisory Board in Supervisory Studies, 92-3
National Advisory Council on Trade Union Education, 75, 78-9
National and Local Government Officers, 181
National Association of Teachers in Further and Higher Education, 224
National Council for Vocational Qualifications, 209, 210-211, 225, 226-7, 228, 237, 257
National Council of Labour colleges, 63, 64-5, 82
  between wars, 58
  courses for mineworkers, 61
  courses provided by, 45
  decline, 240
  development of workers' education, 54, 57
  dispute with WEA, 5-7, 30-32, 239
  distance learning, 44
  divisional organisation, 68-9
  establishment, 4, 26, 37
  materials produced by, 246
  post war developments, 144, 149, 185
  postal courses, 211
  resources, 176
  takeover, 3, 8, 89, 140, 240
National Economic Development Council, 76, 189
National Graphical Association, 122, 188
National Health Insurance, 48
National Health Service union representatives, 153
National Incomes Commission, 76
National Industrial Relations Court, 87
National Society of Operative Printers and Assistants, 29, 50, 191
National Union of Furniture Trade Operatives, 72
National Union of Public Employees, 181
National Union of Seamen, 60
New Zealand, 244
Newbattle Abbey College, 233
North West TUC Region, 230, 237n
Northampton WEA, 23
Northern Ireland Committee of the Irish Congress of Trade Unions, 237n
Northern Ireland TUC Region, 237n
Northern TUC Region, 237n
Nottingham University College Extra-Mural Department, 162
Nottingham University Extra-Mural Department, 61, 112, 186n

Organisation, 159, 199
Organisation for European Economic Co-operation, 76
Oxford, role educators, 163
Oxford School of Industrial Relations, 161
Oxford University, 20, 22, 78, 93, 145
Oxford University Committee on Extra-Mural Studies, 161-2, 164
Oxford University Extra-Mural Delegacy, 111, 112, 161-2

Panitch, L, 13n, 58, 77, 80, 85n, 90, 94
Paper and Paper Products Industry Training Board, 105
Parker, S R, 77
Paul, W, 25
Peers, Robert, 52, 53, 162
Percy, Lord Eustace, 18
Phillips, A, 56n
Pickstock, Frank, 113, 161, 163, 164, 248
Plebs League, 20-21, 25, 26, 38
Pole, T, 15
Pollins, H, 19, 20, 21
polytechnics, 10, 108, 134, 224, 230, 237n
Polytechnics and Colleges Funding Council, 224

311

Ponting, C, 90
Post Office engineers, 50, 72
Post Office workers, 50
postal courses, 44-6, 62, 70, 140, 141, 175-6, 211
Prentice, Reg, 99, 103, 116n
Preston, Maurice, 99
Preuss, B K, 73
Prices and Incomes Board, 90
printing industry, 163
printing unions, 29, 122
printworkers, 182
Prior, Jim, 127
Proctor, Harvey, 235n
Project Advisory Group, 227
Pugh, Arthur, 23-4, 29
Putnam, T, 56n

Queen's University, Belfast, 23

racism, 177-180
Racism Awareness Training, 187n
railway clerks union, 29
railwaymen, 25, 61
Rayboud, S G, 62
Reading, ten day courses in, 236n
Reading WEA, 23
'Red Pack', 153, 159, 206
Ree, J, 56n
Rees, C, 219
regional initiatives, 211-212
Reid, F, 35
Representing Members on Health and Safety, 199
residential courses, 61, 138, 201
review of the TUC's education service
  1975, 97-9
  1987, 192-7, 199, 203, 215
Richards, M, 142n
Rights at Work course, 165, 166, 167
Robbins Report, 176
Roberts, B C, 13n, 14n, 61
Roberts J H, 26, 28, 31
Robertson, D, 250, 256
Robinson, J W, 256
Role Education, 161, 163, 164, 171, 240, 245

Ross, Richard, 191
Rowntree, J W, 15
Royal Arsenal Co-operative, 36
Royal Commission on Trade Unions and Employers' Associations, 80
Ruskin college, 4-5, 18-22, 29, 30, 31, 50, 54, 111, 112, 113, 145, 175, 239
Russell, C, 96
Russell Committee, 84n, 112, 245
Russell Report, 108-109, 240

safety representatives, 107, 112, 129
Safety Representatives and Safety Committees Regulations, 117n, 129
Saville, J, 185n
Scanlon, Hugh, 188
Schools Council Industry Project, 182
Schools Curriculum Industry Partnership, 182
schools, trade union issues in, 182
Schuller, T, 250, 256
Scotland
  courses in, 26-8, 50, 61, 129-131
  miners, 25
  YTS, 182-3
Scottish Education Department, 117n, 233, 236n
Scottish TUC, 75
Scottish Vocational Education Council, 210
secondary schools, 36
Senturia, J J, 32, 43, 256
Shanley, Jock, 72
Sheffield, 17
  summer school at, 118
Sheffield Society for Constitutional Information, 15
Sheffield University Extra-Mural Department, 61, 73, 74-5, 112, 162
Shephard, Gillian, 231-2, 233
Shetlands, distance learning in, 44
Shipley, 84n
Shonfield, Andrew, 94
shop stewards
  activities of, 174-5

Index

increasing numbers, 77
inexperienced, 252
terminology, 13n-14n
training, 79, 80, 81, 83-4, 87, 89, 92-3, 95, 100, 104, 108, 110, 115n, 123, 125, 129, 240
shopworkers, 61-2
short courses, 135-6, 137, 160, 177, 181, 201, 202, 208, 215, 246, 266-7, 280-281
Simon, Brian, 5, 26, 56n
Simpson, Paul, 191
Skills, 159, 199
Skills 1, 199, 212n
Skills 2, 199, 212n
Skills for Health and Safety Representatives, 199
Slough College, 224, 236n
Smiles, Samual, 35
Smith, C, 72, 97
Social Affairs Unit, 216
Social Contract, 87-8, 97, 99, 100, 107, 124
Social Democratic Federation, 16, 19
Social Science Research Council, 176
Social Security Act 1986, 236
socialism, 35
Socialist Labour Party, 26
Socialist League, 16
Socialist Sunday Schools, 35
Society of Industrial Tutors, 162-3, 207
South Bank Polytechnic, 224
South East TUC Region, 131, 224, 237n
South Wales
  courses in, 50, 61
  miners, 25
South West London College, 224
South West TUC Region, 237n
Spencer, B, 57, 158, 165, 166
Staffordshire, 163
Stage 1 courses and materials, 165, 172, 180, 184, 187n, 197, 199, 200, 219, 223, 226, 236n, 237n, 266-7
Stage 2 courses, 165, 166, 184, 186n, 196, 197, 199-200, 203, 219, 223, 266-7
Stageman, J, 132
Starr, Mark, 30
Steelworkers Union, 29
Stevas, Norman St John, 95, 96
Stevens, M, 122, 195
Stocks, J L, 51-2, 56n
Stocks, Mary, 23, 28
Stockton, 213n
Stuttard, C G, 78, 162
summer schools, 3, 49, 56n, 61, 62, 118
Sweden, 184
syndicalism, 17, 25

Tackling Racism, 201
Tawney, R H, 51
Taylor, Robert, 104
Technical, Administrative and Supervisory Section of AUEW, 207
Technical and Vocational Educational Initiative, 182
technical colleges, 8, 78, 92, 148
TEED, 210, 214n, 234
ten day courses, 128-131, 134, 136-7, 165, 196, 198-9, 200-201, 202, 203, 208, 212, 215, 246, 266-7
Thatcher, Margaret *see* Conservative governments
Thatcherism, 166, 188-190, 232
Thompson, E P, 16
Thornton, A H, 186
Tillicoultry, 141
Todd, Ron, 128, 190
Topham, Tony, 13n, 163, 187n
Trade Disputes Act 1906, 185n
Trade Union Act 1984, 127, 136, 141n
Trade Union and Labour Relations (Consolidation) Act 1992, 236n
Trade Union and Training Committee, 212n
Trade Union Ballot Funding Scheme, 231-2, 238n
Trade Union Congress *see* TUC
Trade Union Development Fund, 116n
Trade Union Education and Training

Grant, 231-2
Trade Union Education Bureau, 62
Trade Union Education Committee, 191, 212n, 214n, 226
Trade Union Education Department, 191-2, 207, 209, 210, 212n, 214n, 227, 228, 231, 254-5
Trade Union Research Unit, 175
Trade Unions' Educational Inquiry Committee, 29-30, 47
Training Agency, 214n
Training Commission, 189, 214n
Training Full-Time Officers, 209
Training Shop Stewards, 80-81, 85n, 86, 90-91, 94, 110, 111, 112, 114, 151, 154, 164, 250
Transport and General Workers Union, 14n, 61, 66, 78, 84n, 128, 145, 181, 190, 242
Tsuzuki, C, 46
TUC Education Advisory Committee, 58-9
TUC Education Committee, 66, 85n, 104, 116n, 209, 244-5
TUC Education Department, 3, 58, 66, 68, 69, 82, 85, 92, 93, 97, 104, 111, 112, 113, 118, 134, 151, 154-6, 181, 185, 190, 212n, 228, 240, 248, 254, 256n
TUC Education Scheme, 30, 57-85 passim
TUC Education Service Consultative Group, 75, 115n, 153
TUC General Council, 29, 30, 32-3, 59, 60, 64, 65, 66, 75-6, 85n, 90, 91, 97, 140, 188, 194, 195, 197, 207, 209, 210, 224, 233, 235
TUC Guide to Paid Release for Union Training, 219
TUC Memorandum 1975, 100-103, 105, 110, 232
TUC National Education Centre, 137-140, 208-209, 228
TUC Open School, 140-141, 183, 184, 211
TUC Parliamentary Committee, 19, 23

TUC Regional Education Officers, 118, 167, 216, 218, 225, 228, 231, 237n, 253
TUC Regional Education Offices, 213n, 228-231, 237n
TUC Services Working Group, 234
TUC Special Review Body, 189, 192
TUC Training College, 3, 69-70, 102, 104, 113, 116n, 134, 144, 209, 228
TUC/WEA/BBC Trade Union Studies Project, 140
TUC Women's Committee, 219
TUC Workbook on Racism, 177, 180
tutors
 briefings for, 134-5, 278
 enhanced status of, 205-206
 extending links with unions, 181-2
 part-time, 132
 payment for, 43
 quality of, 224
 relations with REOs, 167, 230
 role of, 102, 158, 240
 training and support for, 104, 111, 113-114, 135, 151-5, 158, 160, 202, 237n

unemployed, courses for, 182
unemployment, 120, 189, 251-2
Unemployment Acts, 48
Union of Democratic Mineworkers, 217
Union of Shop, Distributive and Allied Workers, 64
Union Organisation, 199
Universities Council for Adult Education, 73
university extra-mural departments *see* extra-mural departments

Victorian Britain, workers in, 34-5
Vulliamy, D, 57, 110, 113, 123, 249

Waddington, David, 235n
Wakefield, 84n
Wales TUC Region, 230
Walker, Harold, 221-2

Warwick, Countess of, 31
Warwick University, 176, 209
Wayne, Wolf, 236n
WEA
  and formation of NCLC, 37
  as providers of union education, 82, 92, 144-6, 251
  branches and districts, 23, 24, 141n, 224, 239, 240
  classes, 28, 108
  collaborative courses, 8, 10
  conflict with NCLC, 6, 239
  co-operation with TU Education Committee, 65
  courses for shop stewards, 78
  development, 47, 49, 57
  funding for staffing, 141n
  history of, 4-5, 23, 239
  policy statement, 7
  reducation of grant aid to, 224
  relations with TUC, 29
  reports, 62
  resources, 176
  students, 53-5
  teaching methods, 53, 113
  tutors, 51, 73, 111, 113, 132, 134-5, 160, 164, 181-2
WEA Service Centre for Social Studies, 112,
WEA Trade Union Studies Advisory Committee, 132-3
Webb, S and B, 143
Wedderburn, K W, 185n
weekend schools, 49, 50, 62, 70-71, 98, 246
welfare services, 212
Weller, P, 257
West Lancashire WEA District, 141n
West Midlands TUC Region, 237n
West Midlands WEA District, 141n
Westbrook, R, 155
Weston, C, 207
WETUC
  education provision, 18, 49, 50, 51-3, 62, 69, 103, 144, 185, 239, 245, 246
  formation, 23-4
  links with TUC and NCLC, 29, 30, 32, 43, 47, 58, 61-2
  Report, 47-8, 49
  takeover, 3, 8, 57, 65, 89, 140, 161, 240
  tutors, 76
Whitehouse, J, 155
Whyte, J, 141n
Wigham, E, 76
Williams, J E, 61, 162, 249-250
Willis, Norman, 190, 231, 242
Wilson, Harold, 86, 89, 104
Winkler, J T, 58
Winnard, Dennis, 66, 68, 69, 73, 74, 85n, 97, 113, 191, 248
Winterbottom, Alan, 84n
Winterton, Ann, 216, 222, 235n, 236n
women
  courses for, 177, 182, 187n
  movements, 11
Woodcock, George, 66, 68, 72-3, 77, 80, 84n-85n, 90, 92, 163, 172, 187n, 244-5
Woodcraft Folk, 35
Wootton, Barbara, 51
Workers' Educational Association *see* WEA
Workers' Educational TU Committee *see* WETUC
Workers' Travel Association, 84n
working men's colleges, 15
Working with Figures, 199, 212n
Working Women, 177, 201, 219, 221, 222-3, 236n
Workplace Industrial Relations Survey, 122, 195, 234
workplace representatives, 129, 198, 234, 240, 247
workshops, 135-6, 137
Wright, M, 256

Yorkshire, 61, 212n
Yorkshire and Humberside TUC Region, 237n
Youth Training Scheme, 182-3